THE BATTELLE MEMORIAL INSTITUTE

Battelle is the world's largest independent research organization, with headquarters in Columbus, Ohio, and research centers in various parts of the United States and Europe. In form, a not-for-profit charitable trust, the Institute's chief activity is problem solving and research under contract for business firms, governments, and other organizations. Battelle dedicates an important part of its earnings to the free quest for knowledge in the public service. This volume, Uniting the Democracies, was written by a Fellow of the Institute, James R. Huntley, as a Battelle contribution to the exploration of new and interesting channels in the development of public policy and international organization. Battelle is happy to assist in making such responsible works public; all statements of fact and opinion, however, are solely the responsibility of the author.

FIGURE 1

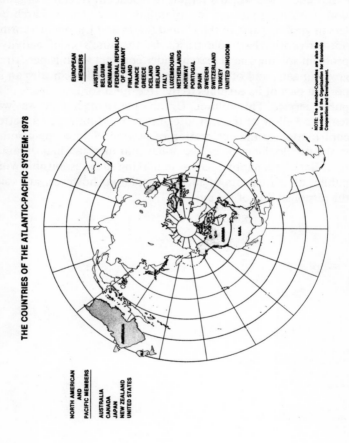

The Countries of the Atlantic-Pacific System: 1978

Uniting the Democracies

Institutions of the Emerging Atlantic–Pacific System

James Robert Huntley
Fellow of the
Battelle Memorial Institute

New York University Press
New York and London

Copyright © 1980 by New York University

Library of Congress Cataloging in Publication Data

Huntley, James Robert.
    Uniting the democracies.

    Bibliography: p.
    Includes index.
    1.   International agencies.   2.   Alliances.
3.   European cooperation.   4.   International
    organization.
I.   Title.
JX1995.H86   341.2   78-20565
ISBN 0-8147-3396-4

Manufactured in the United States of America

PERMISSIONS

To Colleen; and to my
children and grandchildren, for
whose better future it was
done.

Preface

One of the main threads in the story of man's progress over the ages has been the gradual advance in scope, complexity, and effectiveness of his arrangements for organizing communities. These arrangements have developed from the most rudimentary clan and tribal ties of antiquity to the modern nation state, and now, in the twentieth century, to intergovernmental and, in a few cases, supranational structures which attempt to meet the needs of an increasingly interdependent world. Recognition of the need for such structures today seems commonplace, but the means whereby it can or should be given practical effect by creating new structures of government which transcend the nation states is not at all clear.

The United Nations and other universal institutions (such as the World Health Organization or UNESCO); highly specialized bodies, such as the North Pacific Fisheries Commission; and institutions of regional cooperation, represented by the European Economic Community, the COMECON of Eastern Europe, or ASEAN (the Association of South East Asian Nations) are all examples of modern attempts to manage the contemporary interlocking of nations and peoples in a better way.

Although still inadequate to the enormous challenge, some of the best available answers are to be found in the evolution and day-to-day work over the past three decades of the intergovernmental and supranational institutions of western Europe and the Atlantic community. For a variety of reasons, having to do in large part with the degree of relative modernization of the countries involved and with the extent to which their common historical backgrounds make for ease of communication and international teamwork, these efforts are the most advanced yet on record.

Why is this so? What is the scope and significance of these developments among the western countries (and, more recently, Japan)? What can be learned from their experience that might be useful to others, as well as to themselves, in the future? What are the defects and shortcomings of the institutions and patterns of regularized cooperation which together make up an untidy and complicated international system, but one which nevertheless surpasses all others, past or present, in effectiveness? How did this system come about? What does it do for its members? How does it "fit" (or not fit) with other international systems? These questions constitute the general matter of this volume.

Collectively, the complex of intergovernmental and supranational institutions (comprising about 15 major examples) which has developed among the industrialized democracies in the post-1945 period constitutes *a functioning international system*. This system (which, in its present transitional stage, I characterize as the "extended Atlantic System") is neither a state nor an empire, but rather *a voluntary association of states*, formed to defend and promote a variety of common interests. This nascent *international community* comprises a looser set of bodies than a federation; yet, it is a good deal more cohesive than other international bodies, including the more broadly based United Nations or such regional institutions as the Latin American Free Trade Area or the Organization of African Unity. It is useful, if one is searching for better ways of managing interdependence, not merely to examine each individual body in the extended Atlantic System (such as the European Communities or NATO) but to try to see *all of them, collectively, as a whole*.

Together, the countries and intergovernmental organizations (IGOs) in the extended Atlantic System *have contributed substantially and in highly innovative ways* to a contemporary world store of structures and methods which conceivably might be used as models for more advanced or more generalized ventures in international cooperation. This system, with all its shortcomings, on balance is not only of great value to its members, but also to the rest of the world. It forms a likely precursor for a much closer, more dynamic future union, *a truly international community*, of its members and, by the progressive accretion of still other states, a potentially effective parallel or alternative way, on a gradual, realistic, pragmatic, and generally sound basis, to the universal method (i.e., the UN system) of organizing a viable world community. It also offers a clear alternative to the Communist method (typified by such regional institutions as COMECON or the Warsaw Pact), which would more likely consolidate a global empire rather than a community, as it is defined here.

Wise and informed observers may of course differ with my interpretation. It is certainly true, for example, that much of what has grown up within the Atlantic System has done so accidentally. Some developments have remained quite unformed, abortive, and often unrelated to all the rest. But a great deal of what has happened has been intentional, the direct result of farsighted, enlightened leaders who acted out of common conviction and a common perception of the failures of the past and the requirements of the future. These are the theses which this volume will attempt to sustain.

Using the tools of historiography and political science, the book sets forth in Chapter 1 a record of the development of certain ideas and institutions in the field of international cooperation; in Chapters 2, 3, and 4, a structural analysis of the particular set of twentieth-century intergovernmental arrangements which comprise the extended Atlantic System; in Chapter 5, an examination of the dynamics of these institutions as a political system; in Chapter 6, a comparison of the System with other regional arrangements and the United Nations system and an examination of the links between the Atlantic System and the others; and finally in Chapter 7, a look at the likely future of the System, including its possible evolution into an international community.

The reader is encouraged to pay virtually as much attention to the appendices of this book as to its main text. The first three, in particular, can be referred to with profit in conjunction with nearly every chapter. Appendix E gives the reader further guidance in the form of a specialized bibliography.

It is hoped that this work will interest several audiences: diplomats and other practitioners of international relations who need a comprehensive reference to the IGOs of the Atlantic-Pacific System and who perhaps will appreciate an analysis with a new perspective; journalists with a need for a "guide book" to the System; and teachers of the social sciences in schools and universities, as background for their instruction on international relations, international politics, international law, international organization, or international economics. Professors may find the book useful as a text or supplementary text for either undergraduates or graduates. In particular, it is meant to supplement the standard works on the European Communities and other individual IGOs of Europe and the Atlantic, on the one hand; and, on the other, to augment the copious literature surrounding the UN "family" of IGOs. Finally, it is my hope that concerned citizens of any nationality who seek both a practical and a theoretical alternative to the dichotomy of either the nation-state system or some unattainable one-world government as patterns for a hopeful future will find something of value in these pages.

* * *

A few basic concepts, set forth in more detail in Appendix A, are central to this work. Briefly, these are:

An *international system* is defined as a group of nations closely connected with one another, interacting on a sustained basis, subject collectively to processes which sustain or change the system, and related according to some recognizable and coherent scheme.

The *intergovernmental organization* (IGO) is defined as an organization comprised of more than two states. The governing body of an IGO meets regularly; the IGO possesses a permanent joint secretariat or headquarters capable of implementing collective decisions. Within the concept of this book, IGOs are major building blocks for any international system.

Sovereignty is the supreme power in a state, or (rarely) in certain kinds of intergovernmental bodies. It is generally considered in democracies to reside "in the people."

Supranationality is a political quality of certain IGOs, involving some transfer of sovereignty from member states to a collective mechanism. That mechanism enjoys a degree of independence from the constituent states, but it provides for some majority voting of an electorate or a constitutionally empowered representative body. It also allows fairly extensive functions, powers, and jurisdiction for the IGO itself.

A *federation* is formed from a union of states in which individuals as well as member states have rights and in which federal decisions in matters reserved to the federation are binding on states and individuals. Majority decisions are made by representatives of "society as a whole," not by component governments. All individuals enjoy common citizenship; the collective structure is permanent; and the central government, within its allotted scope, exercises sovereignty.

In a *confederation*, the member states retain sovereignty and are the controlling element, even though the union may be strong and virtually permanent. War among members of a confederation is rare.

Functionalism is a theory which describes a gradual progression from conventional forms of international cooperation to supranationalism, by means of a process which "overlays political divisions with a spreading web of international activities and agencies, in which and through which the interests and life of . . . nations would be gradually integrated."[1]

Integration, for the purpose of this work, can be used to refer to the social processes, either within a nation or a smaller community, "of forming into a more complete, harmonious, or coordinated entity," or among a group of nations, of "coming together . . . into a larger unity or group."[2]

Cooperation is a lesser order of interaction, implying that the entities working together retain their separateness. Beginning in the 1960s, cooperation became more important than integration in the working of the Euratlantic System, because—at least for the time being—it was more attainable.

Community, like integration, is also used in two ways, to mean "a body of people organized into a political, municipal, or social unity"[3] or a close association of like-minded states and peoples which carries with it the promise of significant integration. Walter Lippmann defined the second type as: "A body of persons or nations united by historical consciousness or by common social, economic, and political interests," adding that "participation is completely willing and not forced or coerced and without loss of individuality."[4]

Of these concepts, my chief concern in this book is with *integration* and *community*: Integration, because it seems to be the chief process by means of which community growth takes place; community, because it has proven a less rigid, and therefore more publicly acceptable, idea than those of federation or confederation, and because it implies the indispensible element of a *voluntary* coming together which Lippmann stresses. Of course, it is hard to see how a federation could be formed, or at any rate how it could last, unless it also represented a community of the peoples involved. (One is reminded here of the short-lived British attempt at a federation of the Rhodesian states in the 1960s.) Yet the idea that, if peoples are to combine, they must do so of their own free will is consonant with modern concepts of democracy and representative government. Strangely, the same principles today are applied in the case of minorities or even individuals within nation states, some of whom increasingly appear to feel that strong central governments tend to abridge their rights to make decisions in matters which concern them. One therefore has the spectacle of a two-pronged movement that at the same time loosens the bonds of central government and creates new bonds of government over and beyond those of the nation states. Paradoxically, even though they seem to move in opposite directions, both prongs can be seen as integral parts of modern man's striving to gain control—but *democratic* control—over his manmade environment by political means, in order to make his rulers properly accountable to him. The movement for Scottish independence, or at any rate self-rule, is thus seen as fully consonant with and even related, spiritually and intellectually, to the participation of the United Kingdom in the supranational European Communities. In both instances, the aim is a more vital, better functioning, more responsive human community.[5]

This book concentrates on the second branch of the movement for democratic control, the process of integration which is gradually combining nation states into larger groupings, with some corresponding amalgamation of governmental functions. Although my emphasis is on the development of intergovernmental mechanisms, the reader would be wise also to bear in mind that international community building, if it is to be both democratic and effective, must also involve interaction between individuals and nongovernmental institutions across the national borders in question, and especially between them and the new central institutions. The more the central institutions interact with individuals and nongovernmental groups (such as multinational corporations, philanthropies, labor unions, consumers' associations, and the like), the more integrated and the more "supranational" the international polity can become. There can also be a great deal of interaction between nongovernmental groups and individuals across borders and among themselves without the process necessarily leading to integration of the states and peoples involved. Canadian-American relations, for example, have historically been characterized by a vast amount of intercourse of every conceivable kind. Yet, with the exception of "mini-common markets" in automobiles and arms production, a joint-defense command to monitor the North American airspace, and some highly sophisticated arrangements for the mediation and arbitration of disputes between the two countries, the institutional mechanisms of community are only rudimentary. The Commonwealth is another association of peoples which similarly rests mainly on common interests, symbols, and historical ties, but which has little if any institutional substance.

The principal focus of this book is on the question of institutionalizing the links of international community at the intergovernmental level because, in my opinion, that is ultimately the heart of the matter politically. Strong institutions cannot exist unless they reflect the values and feelings of the constituent community. Yet, without the institutions, the community of interests and feeling will, in the long run, prove ephemeral. To argue that one or the other is more important is, in my opinion, a nondebate.

* * *

Why is this a good time for such a book?

For nearly a decade, Vietnam virtually immobilized U.S. diplomacy, effectively stopping up the wellsprings of American political creativity insofar as Europe was concerned. Relations with

Japan and other friendly Asian powers suffered as well. The attempt to improve relations with the USSR and China, not only on the part of the United States but also (to the extent that these efforts have been separate and piecemeal) on the part of its allies, has often had a negative effect on the Atlantic Alliance. In addition, the recent obtrusion of the Middle East into the affairs of the Atlantic System, and most specifically the damaging effects of the 1973 oil boycott, greatly exacerbated strains which were already developing in the western economic and financial system and opened up new fissures in the bulwarks of allied unity. Such problems posed urgent new issues which seemed capable of resolution only within a much more effective, common political framework. Questions of energy, population, food, underdevelopment, mineral and other resources, and environment—all of worldwide scale—also pressed heavily on the richest and most politically capable nations, those which comprise the extended Atlantic System. The Carter administration, reflecting these developments, declared initially that it would put even greater stress on U.S. relations with its closest allies.

It seems thus as opportune a time as ever to take stock of the "state of the System." One cannot, of course, in one relatively short book, do complete justice to such a vast topic, the important ramifications of which seem endless. But perhaps the particular perspectives, as well as the shortcomings, of this work will stimulate scholars, practitioners of international affairs, and serious students of any age to challenge, amend, amplify, and extend my findings.

* * *

There is a philosophical problem connected with this work. Some readers may well ask, Why does this book have an Atlantic focus, and not a strictly European one? I hope that the answer will become apparent in full, ere one has finished the book, but I shall try at this point to give a short initial reply. To begin with, the culture of the United States, and above all its political culture, is predominantly—indeed overwhelmingly—European. We too are a European nation, a "united Europe" in the profound sense of the term; our European heritàge underlies the deepest levels of our values. Most of the urgent problems with which the European unification movement had been expected to deal have not been resolved, partly because Europe did not move fast enough, partly because most of the problems themselves have now moved onto a larger, wider stage and can no longer be resolved within a European frame.

In using the term "extended Atlantic System," or occasionally "Atlantic-Pacific System," I mean to signify that even the North Atlantic community of the fifties and sixties is on its way to obsolescence as a practical political concept (although it may still contain the heart and core of the fundamental values and most of the vital energies essential to significant forward movement in any combination or direction). For many vital questions, not even the Atlantic community is now a sufficient framework. Japan, especially, is today an indispensable actor in the nascent community of developed democracies.

Even though the postwar construction of community institutions in Europe has been quintessentially European in conception, style, and motivation, the United States was from the outset intimately, inextricably, and profoundly involved in the entire process, no matter whether the institutions abuilding were strictly "European" in purpose and membership or more broadly cast (as in NATO). Moreover, in the eye of history, I believe it will be difficult to say that the idea and forms of a united Europe could ever have taken shape without the active participation, encouragement, or protection of the United States.

Finally, while literally hundreds of books have been written over the last two decades about "European unification" or "the new Europe" or the "European challenge," relatively few works have devoted themselves to the broadest "Atlantic" questions.[6] This is yet another reason why I have chosen to train what the French might call an "optique Atlantique" (and sometimes "Pacifique") on this particular set of international relationships and issues.

* * *

Some readers will accuse me of having an "Atlantic" bias, and they will be correct. I make no excuses for it. I believe the

Atlantic System, now in the process of extension to new geographic areas and peoples, on balance is a precious—indeed indispensable—building block for any viable future world order based on acceptable concepts of freedom. It is truly mankind's best hope.

Some nonwestern nations may now and then with reason criticize the countries of the Atlantic System, complaining that the countries of the Atlantic System have done things in their own interest, at the expense of the nonwestern nations. This is unfortunately sometimes the case in an imperfect world order which depends mainly on the outmoded, but still essential, nation state to accomplish its political business and which consists of a congeries of distinct cultures reflecting widely differing and increasingly vocal (thanks to modern communications) views as to what is good or true or right. Yet, this cannot hide my conviction that, for all its imperfections and shortcomings, the extended Atlantic System is so far the most hopeful, constructive, and concrete international reality on the scene, not only in terms of its members' interests, but, over the long run, in terms of the world at large. It remains, of course, for those of use who are part of the Atlantic System, or who might become part of it, to prove by our collective actions that this can be, and can remain, so.

Also, I cannot hide, nor do I wish to do so, my "Pacific" biases. I was born on the Pacific coast of North America and, after living many years in Europe and on the Atlantic fringes of the United States, I am now writing again from the Asians' threshold to America. I see neither an exclusive Atlantic nor Pacific community developing, but one vast community embracing the shores of both oceans. Recent trends in trade, moving towards Asia, tend to reinforce this position.

My "Atlantic-Pacific" convictions, however, should not mislead the reader into believing that I shall not try to examine these phenomena with as much objectivity and impartiality as I can muster. I shall do my best to separate fact from opinion, and to identify the latter. The essence of serious inquiry is to seek the truth in spite of one's biases.

James Robert Huntley

Seattle, Washington

FOOTNOTES

1. David Mitrany, *A Working Peace System*, 4th ed. (London: National Peace Council, 1946), p. 14.

2. Webster's *Third New International Dictionary,* p. 1174.

3. *Oxford English Dictionary*, Vol. 1, p. 486.

4. As quoted in Webster (op. cit.), p. 460.

5. The author is indebted to Jordan Elliot Goodman, who (in an unpublished thesis, *Beyond and Beneath the Nation-State: The Search for New Forms of Political Legitimacy*) has penetratingly explored this distinction and the paradox.

6. The reader is referred to the Bibliography (Appendix E) for a selected list of works on the Atlantic community.

Contents

TABLES AND CHARTS

Acknowledgements

To the Battelle Memorial Institute, my thanks for making possible this study, which I trust is in keeping with the Institute's mission of putting scientific inquiry to work in the active service of mankind; to the Institute's president, Dr. Sherwood L. Fawcett, for constant encouragement coupled with highly stimulating dissension which, coming from a natural scientist, greatly sharpened my perspectives; to my wife, Colleen Grounds Huntley, for monumental patience and encouragement to move the project on; to my secretaries, Christine Jayne, Ann Massie, and Mary Cowger and other Battelle Seattle staff who worked hard to meet impossible deadlines; to Julia Niebuhr Schairer, for her highly skillful efforts in the final editing of the manuscript; and to many colleagues, near and far, who read my manuscript in whole or in part and offered valuable criticisms, insights, and knowledge which made this a far better book than it would otherwise have been. Special thanks is due the following, but this by no means exhausts the list: Homer Angelo, Robert Brand, Theodore C. Achilles, Martha Darling, Brewster C. Denny, Raymond D. Gastil, Elliot R. Goodman, Arthur S. Hoffman, Leslie Lipson, James M. McDonald, Jr., Frank Munk, Toshio Nishi, Charles E. Odegaard, Otto Pick, Peter Rohn, Istvan Szent-Miklosy, and George E. Taylor.

I should also like to thank Forrest Davis, a man whom I never met and about whom I can discover little, for providing me with the germ of a concept for this book. In 1941, he wrote and published a book entitled *The Atlantic System,*[1] lifting the words from Henry Adams' famous autobiography.[2] The latter (alas!) had tantalizingly little to say on the subject, but Davis took Adams' phrase and constructed an entire volume to show how the idea of Anglo-Saxon comity and responsibility for world peace had grown from the time of Jefferson down to the signing of the Atlantic charter on August 14, 1941. Shortly thereafter, just prior to Pearl Harbor, Davis' book went to press. He could not foresee Allied victory in World War II, or the regeneration of Europe in the forties and fifties, or the founding of NATO, or the Cold War, or the Energy Crisis, or the nascent Atlantic-Pacific community. But he did display a sound grasp of the importance of both sea power and democratic ideals in the establishment of a workable, acceptable, peaceful world order. To the work and thought of Forrest Davis, this book owes a very great deal.

FOOTNOTES

1. *The Atlantic System: The Story of Anglo-American Control of the Seas* (New York: Reynal and Hitchcock, 1941).
2. *The Education of Henry Adams, An Autobiography* (London: Constable and Co., Ltd., 1928). (Also published by Houghton-Mifflin, Boston, 1905 and 1918.) For references to the "Atlantic System," see pp. 363, 423–424, 437, and 503 of the 1928 edition.

FOREWORD

What will future historians cite as the most significant political and economic development of this century? A powerful case
can be made for the post-1945 coalescence of the community of
Atlantic democracies, expanded since 1960 gradually to incorporate Japan, Australia and New Zealand. From the initial decisions in 1947 to contain the expansion of Communism and
underwrite the economic recovery of Europe, the development
of the present complex and ramified system of multinational cooperation in the political, economic, military, social and other
fields, which now spans both Pacific and Atlantic, is a story of
remarkable accomplishment.

The inescapable fact of growing "interdependence" has
forced the search for new means of dealing effectively with a
host of problems which respect no national frontiers. That
search has been one of groping, of initiative, of conceiving and
building new institutions of international cooperation. Naturally
the industrialized democracies of Western Europe, North
America and, more recently Japan, with their common heritage
of political thought and organized intellectual effort, have taken
the lead.

The democracies have succeeded in healing the wounds of
World War II and creating a financial and economic system
which has avoided repeating the doleful errors of the interwar
period and deterring Soviet aggression. During more recent
years, there has been the additional challenge of incorporating
into the world community more than one hundred new nations.

Why couldn't the United Nations, established with such noble hopes in 1945, do the job?

Unfortunately, the gap between the Soviet Union and the Western powers with respect to the most fundamental questions of world order has proved an unbridgeable gulf. Furthermore, the interests, perspectives, and capabilities of the newer members of the world community were revealed in practice as vastly disparate. The "one-nation, one-vote" United Nations system, which jealously guards the sovereignty of the members, is unworkable on such a vast scale. Hopes for some kind of world-wide framework of law which would guarantee security for the smallest as well as the largest nations faded rapidly. The United Nations and its affiliated agencies have played a useful global role in improving health, educational standards, and economic development, but, with the exception of a few specific cases in troubled regions, the United Nations has not been able to function as the world's prime peacekeeping instrument. By default, that role—of preventing World War III—fell to the Atlantic powers.

Nor could the United Nations adequately discharge the task of managing the world economy. Again, the Western powers and Japan took on the job. Their industrial machines provided the engine of that economy. They developed a dynamic new trading system, a set of tools for harmonizing economic policies, and an intricate but effective method for the delicate task of guiding financial operations. The United States, Western Europe and Canada were able to do this because they perceived the issues and the common interests, they shared common historical roots, and they had the social capacity to act together. Above all, they knew how to institutionalize their cooperation, with great effect. Because the global community was not yet ready or able to function as a community, the West filled the gap—and continues today to do so.

The history of each individual institution within the Western community, consisting of NATO, the Organization for Economic Cooperation and Development, the European Communities, and Council of Europe, the International Energy Agency,

Western European Union, and others, is heartening for students of world history and international relations. But if one looks at the *joint* record of these bodies, of their accomplishments *as an integrated whole,* one sees the genesis of a practical international system, a whole greater than the sum of its parts. In the pages which follow, James Huntley has, for the first time, told the story of this institutionalized "Atlantic-Pacific System" as a totality. To read in detail how this largely unsung string of achievements came about, how the West for the first time was able to construct such things as international working parliaments, international supreme courts to protect human rights, multinational military commands of unprecedented scope, a system of "fair shares" to allocate oil supplies supranationally, and many other highly innovative creations of the postwar Atlantic-Pacific System, is to realize the tremendous significance for mankind of Western community-building over the past three decades. For the work that has been done is not just for Europe, the United States, and a few other developed democracies; it has profound implications for the entire global order. By the incorporation of Japan, the Atlantic community showed it was not a closed corporation in a racial, ethnic, geographic, or historic sense. There is active discussion today about including in this community of advanced nations still other non-Western countries, nations not long ago considered as "underdeveloped," such as Mexico, Singapore, Brazil, or South Korea, but now, as "newly industrializing countries," moving towards economic maturity and international responsibility.

We have accomplished much in 30 years, but we still have very far to go in establishing effective management of interdependence.

We cannot know what the future will bring, but the Atlantic-Pacific System as described by Mr. Huntley provides a basis—a much sounder framework, in the minds of many, than the United Nations and certainly than the Soviet-led alternative system—for a true international community, one which over decades to come might well provide the best hope for organizing a prosperous, free, stable, and secure world order.

The Atlantic Council of the United States, of which I currently have the honor to be Chairman, has as its mission the promotion of closer, mutually advantageous ties between Western Europe, North America, Japan, Australia, and New Zealand. We believe that the varied and complex relationships between these countries, in the community which Mr. Huntley calls the "Atlantic-Pacific System" have been and will continue to be central to the major economic and political developments which affect the international integrity and national well-being of the United States. The Council has not sponsored Mr. Huntley's book, nor participated in its writing. We believe however that it is a significant contribution to public understanding and to serious scholarship in the field of international relations. May Mr. Huntley's pioneer efforts lead to even deeper penetration by other scholars of the phenomena he describes and to a much greater concentration of public attention on what I believe to be *the* burning international issue of our time: How can the community of developed democracies streamline and modernize itself to face the still greater challenges of the near future and over the long term?

The stakes indeed are great: One is tempted to recall the Belgian national motto, "In union there is strength," as well as Benjamin Franklin's admonition: "We must all hang together— or assuredly we shall all hang separately." On the one hand, the free peoples have made much greater progress towards an operative international community than the vast majority of our citizens today comprehend. But on the other hand, we must keep moving forward if we are to assure a decent, safe future for our descendants and for the world as a whole.

Kenneth Rush

INTERNATIONAL ABC

ASEAN—Association of South East Asian Nations

Benelux—Belgium Netherlands Luxembourg Economic Union

BIS—Bank for International Settlements

BLEU—Belgium Luxembourg Economic Union

CofE—Council of Europe

COMECON (CMEA)—Council for Mutual Economic Assistance

EC—European Communities

ECE—(UN) Economic Commission for Europe

ANZUS—Tripartite Security Treaty (Australia-New Zealand-United States)

ECSC—European Coal and Steel Community

EEC—European Economic Community

EFTA—European Free Trade Association

EURATOM—European Atomic Energy Community

GATT—General Agreement on Tariffs and Trade

Group of Ten—informal consultative body on monetary affairs

IBRD—International Bank for Reconstruction and Development (World Bank)

IEA—International Energy Agency

IMF—International Monetary Fund

NAA—North Atlantic Assembly

NATO—North Atlantic Treaty Organization

NEA—Nuclear Energy Agency

Nordic Council

OEEC—Organization for European Economic Cooperation (defunct)

OECD—Organization for Economic Cooperation and Development

WEU—Western European Union

UN—United Nations

* * *

IGOS—intergovernmental organizations

LDCs—less developed countries

MNCs—multinational corporations

NGOs—nongovernmental organizations

NICs—newly-industrializing countries

NTBs—nontariff barriers

TNEs—transnational enterprises

Books by James Robert Huntley

The NATO Story (1965, 1969).
Europe and America: The Next Ten Years (1970, with W.R. Burgess).
Man's Environment and the Atlantic Alliance (1972).
Uniting the Democracies: Institutions of the Emerging Atlantic-Pacific System (1980).

CHAPTER 1

The Historical Origins of the Modern Atlantic System

Until the most recent times in western history, both international anarchy and imperium far overshadowed efforts at voluntary combination by states or peoples. In Greek civilization, until the advent of the Macedonian and Roman empires, the city states feuded constantly among themselves, much as did the nation states of Europe until 1945. The Delphian League was a notable attempt to combine the Greek states for defense against the Persians. Athenian dominance, however, turned it into a short-lived empire which was replaced briefly by heavy-handed Spartan hegemony until the League died. Provisions for a common defense, treasury, and governing council of the Delphian League in its heyday bear a certain ancestral resemblance to the present-day North Atlantic Treaty Organization.

The Achaean League was an even earlier alliance of Greek cities which combined for defense in the fourth century B.C.; and, for a time, it possessed the earliest known federal constitution. The members retained internal independence, but in war and foreign politics accepted the restrictions of the League. Both the Delphian and Achaean leagues, it is necessary to point out, were not formed for peaceful purposes, but to wage war more effectively. This motive, as well as the desire for peace, has been an important, if somewhat negative, aspect of the history of international cooperation, including that of the modern Atlantic System.

[1]

One can see the beginnings of interstate law and institutions in the Amphictyony, another association of Greek states, this time formed for the protection of common religious shrines and practices. The Amphictyony had a joint treasury and exercised judicial duties of a broad nature in a very limited sphere not too unlike the present-day European Coal and Steel Community.

The first recorded European plan for voluntary international organization was put forward around 1305 by Pierre Dubois, a lawyer and adviser to the king of France. He advocated a federation of Christian sovereign states with France as the dominant member, an international court of arbitration, and even a system of international schools.[1]

In subsequent centuries, some famous men and others less well-known proposed various schemes for world states, all of which have their modern counterparts: world trade organizations, permanent councils of ambassadors, international peace forces, and confederations. Dante, Erasmus, Henri IV of France, Leibniz, William Penn, and Rousseau are among those whose tracts have survived. Hugo Grotius, who lived in the seventeenth century and is considered to be the father of international law, was perhaps the most influential over the long term.

In the aftermath of the Napoleonic wars, peace plans proliferated. Kant, Saint-Simon, and Jeremy Bentham were among those to put forward serious ideas. Permanent guarantees of borders, world courts, disarmament, and the international regulation of commerce all were proposed. At the Congress of Vienna, Czar Alexander I brought about the creation of the Holy Alliance; this was linked with the Quadruple (later Quintuple) Alliance, which dominated Europe for some years after 1815. The Czar's intentions included the aim of a united Europe, but both alliances became associated with policies of reaction and suppression.[2] When the Quintuple Alliance broke up, the "Concert of Europe," a loose system of treaties and association of nations, took its place. Nations, such as Turkey in 1856, were "admitted" to the Concert, which in 1878 was updated at the Congress of Berlin. Structurally, the Concert of Europe was weak, but it was able to establish a sense of common interests among the European nations and to give a new sanction to international law. However, it was a pallid precursor of the later League of Nations and the UN, and of post-1945 regional developments in Europe. It owed its success and longevity to British seapower and Bismarck's diplomacy. When the first was challenged and the second ceased, the system collapsed; 1914 followed.

Until 1815, schemes for international organization had remained untried, limited to plans and projects on paper. But a significant step in the direction of permanent, institutionalized international cooperation was taken at the Congress of Vienna. There, the Central Commission for the Navigation of the Rhine was set up by the great powers, under Articles 108 and 109 of the *Final Act of the Congress of Vienna*, which declared:

> The Powers whose States are separated or crossed by a navigable river undertake to settle by common agreement all matters relating to the navigation of the river.

Although it was intended that these provisions would apply to a number of rivers, international executive machinery (the first in history) was initially set up only for the Rhine. There is provision in the treaty for a governing body, representation by the member states, rules of voting, appointment of an international staff, and even provision for pensions for the first international civil servants and their widows and orphans.[3] The Rhine Commission has continued its work, unbroken except by war, until the present day, with extensive revisions and amendments to the original treaty in 1831, 1868, 1919, 1945, and 1963. A similar regime for the Danube was instituted in 1856 and in recent years for the Moselle.

In the nineteenth century, the Universal Postal Union (1874) and Office Central des Transports Internationaux par Chemin de Fer (1890) were also established. The intergovernmental organization, albeit limited to highly specialized fields of concern and endowed with the weakest sort of powers, had nevertheless come into being. Judged by the limitations of the times, the achievement was remarkable.

In the twentieth century, the development of institutionalized international cooperation bifurcated. One broad track followed the path of universal institutions, or those intending to be universal, from the Permanent Court of Arbitration (1899) on through the League of Nations to the present-day United Nations and its numerous subsidiary bodies with upwards of 150 member states. The other track picked up the thread of European unity, for which some thinkers and statesmen pleaded in the nineteenth century (Victor Hugo, for example, had called on his deathbed for a "United States of Europe"). This second path, while clearly distinguishable and of gathering importance down to the present day, often became entwined after 1918 with another closely related effort, that of transatlantic cooperation and unity.

The story of why and how the increasingly influential movement for European unification came about is a fascinating one, but mine here to tell only insofar as the "European" development has intellectually and practically influenced and affected "Atlantic" and "Atlantic-Pacific" institutional development (and vice versa).[4]

The intellectual origins of the Atlantic System can be discerned in the writings of a few statesmen and thinkers around the turn of the twentieth century. John Hay, Balfour, British Ambassador to Washington Lord Bryce, American Ambassador to London Walter Hines Page, Admiral Alfred T. Mahan (USN), and Henry Adams were among those who grasped the exceeding significance of Anglo-American comity and whose thoughts turned to ways of formulating closer transatlantic ties.

When the United States entered the First World War, Americans differed as to why. The immediate issue had been Germany's unrestricted submarine warfare. Wilson declared that "the world must be made safe for democracy," an idea to which most Americans could subscribe. But Walter Lippmann, writing in the *New Republic* in February 1917, two months before United States entry, saw the issues more clearly and subtly:

> The safety of the Atlantic highway is something for which America should fight. Why? Because on the two shores of the Atlantic Ocean there has grown up a profound web of interest which joins together the Western world . . .

[4]

if that community were destroyed we should then know what we had lost.

Years later, in the midst of the Second World War, Lippmann was to complete his formulation:

The Atlantic Ocean is not the frontier between Europe and the Americas. It is the inland sea of a community of nations allied with one another by geography, history, and vital necessity.[5]

In the same book, Lippmann was to use' the term "Atlantic Community," apparently its first appearance in print.

To win the First World War, the Allies finally had to pool their resources in a system of combined military and political mobilization which far surpassed the efforts of any previous alliance. There were by 1917 combined allied boards for shipping, for munitions, for wheat and other supplies, indeed for every aspect of the war effort. Late in the war, French Marshal Ferdinand Foch was appointed Commander-in-Chief of all the allied armies. Although this did not entirely end allied wrangling, it is thought to have been decisive in the winning of the war. Foch's command was a precursor of the World War II Supreme Headquarters Allied Expeditionary Forces of General Eisenhower, and a lineal ancestor of Supreme Headquarters Allied Powers Europe (SHAPE), which is today the NATO "General Staff."

In 1919 the world's eyes were on Wilson, his Fourteen Points, and his plans for a "League of Nations." Georges Clemenceau, Premier of France, had more modest, but perhaps more realistic, aims. He knew that France alone could not guarantee the peace of Europe, and he perceived the relationship between the nature of governments and the degree to which they might cooperate in peace or war. (For this reason, he had opposed the 1894 alliance between France and Czarist Russia, stating: "There could be no real sympathy between the Republic and an autocrat.") In 1919, he proposed to Wilson and Lloyd George an alliance in which France, Great Britain, and the United States would promise to come to one another's defense in case of a new

German attack. The alliance would have embraced only those which Clemenceau called "constitutional" countries. Wilson's more sweeping plan (which he had taken over from Lord Bryce, Grey, Robert Cecil, and others) for a League of Nations was adopted instead. The League developed the first independent international civil service; pioneered in transferring open parliamentary methods to the hitherto secret and formal counsels of diplomacy; and performed on the whole well in certain functional fields, such as finance, health, and refugees. But, in the end, in terms of its central function, the preservation of peace, the League proved a great failure.[6] Along with the Versailles treaty and the Covenant of the League, the United States and Britain signed a separate pact with France, guaranteeing the latter against unprovoked German aggression. But the United States Senate refused to ratify any of the agreements. The stage was set for World War II, and the chances for a strong Atlantic System were temporarily arrested.

Although the 20 years between the two wars were characterized more by friction and narrow nationalism than by transatlantic cooperation, with the United States' aloofness poisoning the whole, discrete and seemingly (at the time) insignificant actions continued to lay the foundations quietly for a permanent, institutionalized Atlantic System. The Gold Delegation of 1920 was important in guiding whatever monetary stability the west enjoyed in the first postwar decade; this arrangement continued until after World War II. Cooperation between central banks grew in the interwar period, as European reliance on the U.S. Federal Reserve banks and New York's international bankers increased. With U.S. leadership, the first international banking institution, the Bank for International Settlements (BIS), was created in 1930. The occasion was the revision of German war reparations payments, but the goal of the U.S. progenitors was to "stimulate world trade and economic development . . . by perfecting the machinery of international finance."[7] The bank functioned as "the central banker's central bank" and although the world depression greatly restricted its intended influence, it nevertheless can be considered a progenitor of the International Monetary Fund and the World Bank created after 1945, in which institutions the original purposes of the BIS were reborn. The BIS continues today as an active institution, serving as agent for OECD and ECSC in certain financial matters and (during the 1960s) as the catalyst in so-called "currency swap" arrangements on which the United States and other powers have relied greatly to finance their balance-of-payments deficits. Its periodic and dispassionate reviews of the world economic scene are closely read by central bankers and national treasury officials.

Still another international institution that was developed at the time, no doubt considered then as of the merest importance, was the Belgium-Luxembourg Economic Union (BLEU), which came into force in 1922. This involved a complete customs union between the two countries, with the Luxembourg franc tied to the Belgian. More than 20 years later, the BLEU experiment (minus the currency union) was broadened into Benelux, including the Netherlands, and in the 1950s it was expanded still further, when the European Communities were created.

With the rise of Hitler, the deepening of the Depression, and the approach of World War II, rivalries, jealousies, and suspicion overcame the tendencies towards cooperation (which had not been strong in any case) among western Europeans and North Americans. Except in the organization of postwar relief, in the case of international finance (noted above), and uncertainly in the areas of lofty concepts for world peace (as envisaged in the Kellogg-Briand Pact of 1928, which called for international conciliation and arbitration of disputes, but provided neither sanctions nor the means to impose them), the United States failed utterly to exercise leadership in international cooperation. By backing out of the 1933 London Gold Conference, the United States reached the depths of interwar "go-it-alone-ism," rejecting timid European attempts to rescue the west's collective finances.

Europe itself experienced a brief period of increasing amity, with nascent arrangements for continental security and the settlement of disputes reflected in the Locarno treaties of 1925, but this movement died too with the onset of the Great Depression and the rise of Nazism in Germany. The League of Nations played a major, but in the end unsuccessful, role in European affairs during this period. The League's failure, however, inspired Clarence K. Streit to write a book which marked both an end and a beginning in the effort to create an effective Atlantic System.

* * *

Streit, the Geneva correspondent of *The New York Times* from 1929 to 1939, in 1938 published his book, *Union Now: The Proposal for Inter-democracy Federal Union.*[8] Streit was a visionary. Viewing at first hand the rise of Fascism, Nazism, and Japanese militarism, he was concerned with the pressures on the western democracies. He watched the League of Nations crumble as World War II became inevitable. In *Union Now*, he proposed a simple solution, but one that would be exceedingly difficult to implement: a federal union of the democracies situated around the North Atlantic Ocean, a "union of these few peoples in a great federal republic built on and for the thing they share most, their common democratic principle of government for the sake of individual freedom."[9] His book excited considerable public controversy in the United State and Europe. During 1940 and 1941, for example, Streit's revised proposal for a federal union between the United States and Britain was the debate topic nationwide in American high schools.

Streit agreed with small bands of idealists that in the long run some kind of "world government," with powers of enforcement over its universal membership, was needed. But Streit wished to begin with a nucleus of countries he considered "workable." The main purpose of such an Atlantic union, as he saw it, would be to safeguard freedom and democratic institutions; therefore, he logically proposed beginning with the group of nations which, in his view, embodied freedom and democracy in their manners and institutions. Once the Atlantic democracies were united into a combination of overwhelming power, the other nations of the world could be added gradually and as they expressed the desire. Streit's plans were, and still are today, based almost entirely on the American historical experience; that is, as the United States in 1787 had created the first federation, which had lasted and worked demonstrably well, it should be the model for the new union.

With the onset of war in the summer of 1939, Streit's ideas were perforce overshadowed by the momentous events in Europe. But the concept remained remarkably alive, particularly in the United States and Britain. Citizens' groups were organized and gradually a number of prominent thinkers and civic leaders were enlisted in an effort to promote the acceptance by governments and peoples of the goal of an Atlantic federal union.[10] Wendell Willkie, Roosevelt's opponent in the election of 1940, proposed "an economic and social union of the United States and the British Commonwealth."[11]

The "Atlantic Union movement" probably reached its highwater mark in 1949, with the formation in the United States of the Atlantic Union Committee, whose Chairman was Owen J. Roberts, Justice of the U.S. Supreme Court, and whose officers included Will Clayton, former Under Secretary of State, and Robert P. Patterson, former Secretary of War. Senator Estes Kefauver was the most active of many members of Congress who backed the idea of an international federal union at the time. In 1962, the Atlantic Union Committee actually achieved its principal tactical aim: the calling of an "exploratory convention" of delegates from NATO countries, named by their parliaments. Ninety eminent citizens met in Paris for two weeks and subsequently issued a "Declaration of Paris." The declaration set forth lofty principles of unity, but was unable to resolve the political dilemma facing the governments: how to achieve some closer form of unity without exciting popular and political passions by suggesting the "sacrifice of sovereignty."[12] With little time and little apparent ground for agreement on essentials, the Convention wavered and finally recommended that the NATO governments appoint a "Special Governmental Commission to draw up plans for the creation of a true Atlantic Community, suitably organized to meet the . . . challenges of this era."[13]

The governments proved remarkably immune to this suggestion, perhaps principally because United States policy and that of the six Common Market governments put first priority on European, not Atlantic, integration and regarded the Paris proposals as untimely, if not actually obstructive. Later in the year, on the 4th of July, President John F. Kennedy stated in Philadelphia that U.S. policy recognized "Atlantic interdependence," but that it would be implemented by means of an "Atlantic Partnership" between the United States and a to-be-united, presumably "equal," Europe. For the better part of the ensuing decade, this policy of promoting European integration and deferring a broad approach to Atlantic unity until Europe had organized itself to "speak with one voice" remained the cornerstone of U.S. relations with Europe. President Nixon, who seemed personally well-disposed toward the "Atlantic Union" idea,[14] and Secretary of State Henry Kissinger, whose views on both European integration and Atlantic unity were less categorical and more *nuancé* than those of his predecessors or of the civil servants who had guided American policy in this field in the past, appeared desirous of giving the Atlantic concept a somewhat new lease on life. The Administration proclaimed 1973 to be the "Year of Europe." On April 23, 1973, Dr. Kissinger invited the Europeans to join the United States in drafting a "new Atlantic Charter." On June 19, 1974, a declaration was finally approved by the NATO governments at Ottawa, but it had been so watered down in months of wrangling and public criticism that its psychological and political value proved minimal.[15] Among other things, the Middle East War, the oil boycott of Autumn 1973 and Watergate had effectively intervened to turn the spotlight away from "domestic" Atlantic affairs once again.

In April 1973, the U.S. Congress nearly passed a new version of the "Atlantic Convention" resolution, but effectively laid it to rest for the session by a close procedural vote in the House of Representatives after unanimous adoption in the Senate. In 1975, still another version of the resolution was put forward by its Congressional backers. Mr. Streit, along with many other private supporters of the initiative to create a temporary institution not unlike the U.S. Constitutional Convention of 1787, once more was active in presenting his views, which in essence had changed very little since 1938. The measure, however, was once again defeated in the House of Representatives; elections for Congressmen were never more than 24 months away, and espousal of such novel ideas could easily turn volatile electors "sour."

In 1977, the new Carter administration pledged redoubled efforts to strengthen arrangements with America's principal allies. Increased emphasis on beefing up NATO militarily and the de facto institutionalization of annual economic "summits" were features of this policy, but little was said of a sweeping or visionary nature. Concepts such as Atlantic partnership or Atlantic community lay dormant, at least publicly.

* * *

Mindful of Streit's brilliant (but also brittle) crystallization of the conceptual development of the Atlantic System, we must return to 1939 and follow the development of the idea during the Second World War. At the instigation of the Frenchman Jean Monnet (who later was to become the "father of European integration"), the British and French again set up a joint supply system, based on the embryonic allied combined boards of 1917.[16] In the dark days of June 1940, Monnet was the bearer of an idea embraced by Churchill, which he subsequently proposed to the French Cabinet: an indissoluble, complete union of France and the United Kingdom. This idea had been put to Monnet by Emmanuel Monick, then financial attaché at the French Embassy in London. Monick had been struck by Clarence Streit's proposals for an Atlantic union; he advanced the Franco-British proposal as a first step in that direction.[17] However, the idea came too late to be of practical use. France was overrun, its government split in two, and half of the country occupied by the enemy.

In March 1941, the British and American general staffs had begun conversations looking toward a combined system of planning, supply, and operations in the event U.S. forces became engaged in the war. "Atlantic principles" were advanced again, this time publicly and with considerable effect, at the historic meeting between President Roosevelt and Prime Minister Churchill in August 1941. An "Atlantic Charter" was adopted, stating in eight points certain common principles of British and U.S. policy on which the two leaders based their hopes for a better international order after World War II.

By January 1942, the United States had entered the war, and a Combined Chiefs of Staff, formed of the British Chiefs of Staff and their U.S. counterparts, was set up with subsidiary commands for the various theaters of war and a wealth of other combined committees, boards, and agencies which were remarkably efficient and ultimately indispensable to the winning of the war. The highest degree of allied military integration was achieved in June 1944, when the invasion of France was launched under the direction of General Eisenhower and his Supreme Headquarters Allied Expeditionary Forces.[18] Even though these arrangements were formally dismantled at the end of the war, the substance of Anglo-American cooperation (which came to be called the "special relationship") continued for at least two decades more and provided a core around which other forms of postwar allied cooperation could develop.

At various conferences of allied leaders during World War II, the outlines of a joint occupation and administration of a defeated Germany were gradually agreed upon. The four occupying powers (Britain, the United States, the USSR, and France) were each assigned zones of occupation and joint responsibility for governing Berlin. These arrangements were greatly elaborated at the Potsdam Conference (August 1945). Emergency aspects of the restoration of the European economy were undertaken by such temporary bodies as the Emergency Economic Committee for Europe, the European Coal Organization, and the European Central Inland Transport; the USSR participated in some, but not all of these bodies.

Allied plans for a common policy in Germany proved abortive; the Russians (and, to a lesser extent and for different reasons, the French) had different aims and pursued different policies in their zones of occupation. In January 1947, the British and U.S. zones were combined economically. Repeated efforts of the "Big Four" foreign ministers to agree on the future of Germany ended in December 1947, with angry words between the USSR and the western powers. Thereafter, the western powers discussed the future of Germany without Russia.[19] Then, on March 20, 1948, the Russians withdrew their representative from the Allied Control Council in Berlin, declaring that it no longer existed. By June 1948, the U.S., British, and French zones were being run according to an agreed-upon three-power plan. A year later, the Federal Republic of Germany was born, receiving full sovereignty in 1955.[20] Meanwhile, there were increasing signs that neither the United Nations nor the restoration of Europe would work as Britain and the United States had envisaged, because their views and aims were obviously divergent from those of the USSR in virtually all important respects. Under the United Nations, regional economic commissions were set up, but the commission for Europe was virtually moribund from the start because of disagreement between the USSR and the other allies.

In 1946, the USSR sponsored an "indigenous" secession movement in the northern provinces of Iran, promoted a civil war in Greece, and demanded territorial and other concessions from Turkey. When negotiations began in the summer of 1947 for the Marshall Plan, the USSR decided not to participate and effectively prevented its client states in eastern Europe (including Czechoslovakia, which at that point still had a western-model democratic regime) from doing so. In February 1948, the Czech Communist party took over that country's government, with Russian backing. In the summer of 1948, Russia blockaded the allied garrisons in Berlin and the 2½ million German residents of West Berlin, with the obvious intention of driving out the western powers. By 1949, Soviet vetoes in the UN Security Council had amounted to 30.

All these events brought responses from the United States, including the Truman Doctrine (May 1947), the offer of the Marshall Plan (June 1947), the airlift to Berlin (1948), the Vandenberg Resolution in the Senate (June 1948), and the signing of the North Atlantic Treaty (April 1949). The Cold War had begun; it proved to be a major catalyst for the combining of nations on a scale, at a level, and with a duration never before seen in history. From 1947 on, the most significant chapter in western man's history has been the knitting together of the European-

Atlantic (and more recently the "Atlantic-Pacific") System, for it has undoubtedly prevented World War III and a repetition of the Great Depression.

* * *

Before closing this account of the Atlantic System up to 1948, when the story I have to tell begins in a modern sense, a last thread remains to be traced, that of the European unity movement. After World War I the European states had insisted on retaining all prerogatives of national sovereignty; their efforts to achieve unity were more successful after World War II. The European Economic Community (EEC) is especially important in the history of these efforts.

Harking back to Greek, Renaissance, and Enlightenment ideas discussed earlier, the interwar period spawned a "pan-Europe" movement. From the twenties until after the Second World War, this movement was dominated by Count Richard Coudenhove Kalergi, an Austrian who in 1923 published an influential book, *Paneuropa*, and founded the "Pan-European Union." The French Premier, Briand, later advocated such a union before the Assembly of the League of Nations, on September 5, 1929:

> I think that among peoples constituting geographic groups, like the peoples of Europe, there should be some kind of federal bond; it should be possible for them to get into touch at any time, to confer about their interests, to agree on joint resolutions and to establish among themselves a bond of solidarity which will enable them, if need be, to meet any grave emergency that may arise. . . . Obviously, this association will be primarily economic, for that is the most urgent aspect of the question. . . .[21]

During the Second World War, the resistance movements in Italy, France, the Low Countries, and elsewhere took up the theme of European unification. In May 1943, some Italian federalists succeeded in publishing a clandestine newspaper, *Unità europea*. In 1944, a French Committee for European Federation, citing the failure of loose unions such as the League of Nations, proposed that the "nation-states federate and hand over to a federal European state control of the economic and commercial organization of Europe, the sole right to have an army and to intervene against any attempt to re-establish authoritarian regimes, the administration of foreign relations, the administration of colonial territories that are not yet ready for independence, and the creation of a European citizenship alongside national citizenship."[22] During the war, Churchill called for the creation of a "Council of Europe" and (at Zurich on September 19, 1946) for a "United States of Europe."

From 1946 on, private groups favoring European federation and other forms of union began to organize. In 1948, a great "Congress of Europe" was held in The Hague under private auspices, but bringing together many of Europe's leading statesmen. The meeting yielded proposals for a Council of Europe, the intended vehicle for achieving a political union; a European Charter of the Rights of Man; a Supreme Court for Europe; and lesser bodies, all of which would promote European unification. Following The Hague Congress, all the various citizens' groups formed themselves into one "European Movement." These can be credited with much of the subsequent progress towards an actual political union of Europe.

The movement for the unification of Europe formed an integral part of the postwar efforts to create an effectively functioning Atlantic System, even though the "Europeans" and the "Atlanticists" often found themselves over the years in at least three separate camps. The first included those who believed that Europe must unite itself as a "third force" (the USSR being the "second force") to moderate and mediate the Cold War; the united Europe was to function independently of the United States, even though it might be linked loosely with the United States by ties which some later called "partnership." Others believed that efforts to create a united Europe should be dropped in favor of an "Atlantic Federal Union" or a "true Atlantic Community." A third group saw the two ideas as complementary, with European unification taking place (if it did) as a nucleus within the broader Atlantic grouping. This group favored

[15]

making progress toward integration pragmatically, as conditions and events afforded opportunities on either front. The passage of time has rendered these debates increasingly sterile, in part because the stage for a "European" or "Atlantic" type of integration has now widened to include at least three other powers, Australia, Japan, and New Zealand, which are far removed geographically (and, in the Japanese case, culturally) from the others.

* * *

In 1947, several new global institutions, including the United Nations, the International Monetary Fund, the World Bank, UNESCO, and others, dominated the international organization scene. The postwar victors had assumed that most international cooperation could be managed through structures which had universal aspirations.

Yet, the events of 1946 and 1947 (that is, Soviet pressure in the Balkans and Middle East and failure to agree on the Baruch Plan for controlling nuclear energy under the UN) proved to western leaders that the UN structure unfortunately could not be relied on for the most critical aspects of keeping "the big peace," and avoiding yet another world war. This realization, plus the perilous economic and social condition of Europe in the immediate postwar era, called forth a profoundly creative surge of western political innovation, based on fertile ideas and experiments (detailed earlier in these pages) which reached back decades and, in some cases, even centuries. They were concepts whose time had finally come. They included new international courts of appeal before which individuals who believed their human rights had been violated could bring their own governments to the bar of justice; a "sliding escalator" of constantly more binding institutional arrangements by which the new Common Market could gradually turn itself from a classic intergovernmental organization into a supranational political body; and a number of unprecedented international public corporations to build European railway cars, manufacture new fighter planes for NATO, or process nuclear-irradiated fuels for several countries.

[16]

The European-Atlantic System proved surprisingly successful, eventually far surpassing the UN in effectiveness and importance. Indeed, the emergence of a network of interlocking intergovernmental organizations by means of which the advanced democracies have developed and institutionalized this highly integrated system of managed interdependence rivals the creation of the nation state itself in the annals of social invention. In large measure, because of and by means of this system, Franco-German enmity was effectively ended, Britain was brought close to the rest of Europe for the first time in centuries, the encroachment of the USSR into western Europe (and perhaps the advent of World War III) was effectively prevented, the economy of the Atlantic world was transformed and protected against the recurrence of another Great Depression, and a policy of American world leadership replaced traditional policies of isolation.

Why did this "explosion" of regionalism take place in the North Atlantic world, and not somewhere else? This and related questions are dealt with in the pages which follow.

FOOTNOTES

1. Sylvester John Hemleben, *Plans for World Peace Through Six Centuries* (Chicago: University of Chicago Press, 1943), p. 1. Hemleben's book contains a comprehensive survey of such plans up to the formation of the League of Nations in 1919. I have drawn much of the material in the early part of this chapter from Hemleben.

2. When Nicholas II, in 1899, called the first international peace conference in The Hague, there is evidence that he harked back to his ancestor's project. (Elizabeth York, *Leagues of Nations: Ancient, Medieval, and Modern*, London, 1919, p. 315.)

3. A.H. Robertson, *The Council of Europe* (2nd ed.), (New York: Frederick A. Praeger, 1961), pp. 266–267.

4. Others have traced this development thoroughly and well. See, for example: A.H. Robertson, ibid.; Ernst B. Haas, *The Uniting of Europe: Political, Social, and Economic Forces, 1950–57* (Palo Alto, CA: Stanford University Press, 1958); Henri Brugmans, *L'Idée Européene 1918–65* (Bruges: de Tempel, 1965); and René Albrecht-Carrié, *One Europe: The Historical Background of European Unity* (Garden City, New York: Doubleday, 1965).

5. *U.S. Foreign Policy*, (London: Hamish-Hamilton, 1943), p. 83.

6. The struggle for the shape of the peace of 1919 is well described by Solomon F. Bloom in *Europe and America: The Western World in Modern Times* (New York: Harcourt, Brace and World, 1961) pp. 531–545. The French historian J. Néré sheds important light on Clemenceau's ideas, reinforced by those of Marshal Foch, which to a remarkable extent foreshadowed the NATO of three decades hence. At Versailles, Wilson and Lloyd-George gave guarantees to France against unprovoked German aggresion; Foch urged that Allied armies be stationed in the Rhineland permanently, because if "the line of the Rhine (were) abandoned, Anglo-American aid would arrive too late." But to this practical proposal the British and American governments were firmly opposed. French proposals for the League of Nations Security System had teeth: they "foresaw in particular the formation of an international army, equipped with a general staff . . . with extensive powers." But this too the Anglo-Americans rejected, preferring instead the text finally adopted, which "made the League of Nations into an international debating society which was quite incapable of guaranteeing itself the disarmed security which was its official objective." *The Foreign Policy of France from 1914 to 1945* (London and Boston: Routledge and Kegan Paul, 1975), pp. 15–16 and 24; *La Troisiéme République (1914–1940)* (Paris: Librairies Armand Colin, 1965), pp. 35–37. France tried again in 1922 to restore the British-U.S.-French alliance. Clemenceau, without political office, but with the support of the French government and his great moral prestige, gave a speech at the Metropolitan Opera House (November 22, 1922), in which he suggested "a mutual guarantee of the Rhine frontier which was, all things considered, a foreshadowing of Locarno, but a Locarno whose effectiveness would have been far greater because the United States would have been the guarantors." (Op. cit., *The Foreign Policy of France from 1914 to 1945*, p. 29.)

7. Frank Costigliola, "The Other Side of Isolationism: The Establishment of the First World Bank, 1929–1930," *The Journal of American History*, Vol. LIX (December 1972), p. 609.

8. Published by Harper and Brothers, New York, 1939, and in numerous subsequent versions in the United States and abroad. The most recent edition (1961) was entitled *Freedom's Frontier—Atlantic Union Now* (Washington, D.C.: Freedom and Union Press).

9. *Union Now* (New York: Harper and Brothers, 1939), p. 4.

10. It is interesting that Trygve Lie, the wartime Foreign Minister of Norway (and later first Secretary General of the United Nations) seemed to echo Streit's ideas when he wrote, for the Times of London,

an article entitled "A Community of Nations" (November 14, 1941), p. 5, which called for "strong organized collaboration between the two great Atlantic Powers: the British Empire and the United States"; for permanent military and economic cooperation after the war; for the Atlantic peoples "to give up part of their sovereignty"; and for "effective union between Great Britain and the allied countries in certain regional tasks." At the very least, Lie's proposals can be considered precursors of NATO, of the Marshall Plan, and of OECD.

11. Jacques Freymond, *Western Europe Since the War, A Short Political History* (New York: Praeger, 1964), p. 25.

12. For a balanced, comprehensive account of the Atlantic Convention of 1962 and the evolution of Streit's ideas and the related ideas of others, plus a study of their practical applications and relative influence from 1939–64, see Istvan Szent-Miklosy, *The Atlantic Union Movement: Its Significance in World Politics* (New York: Fountainhead, 1965).

13. The Declaration is summarized in Szent-Miklosy, ibid., pp. 67–69. The full text can be found in House of Representatives Doc. No. 433, *87th Congress, 2d Session* (Washington, D.C. U.S. Government Printing Office, 1962).

14. On March 10, 1973, the President wrote Congressman Paul Findley, commenting on a resolution before the Congress which called for a new "Atlantic Convention." "As a goal and a concept I have favored Atlantic Union for many years, dating back to my service in the Congress. As President I have made it a policy not to give specific endorsement to resolutions of this kind, but I want you to know that my longstanding position on the concept and the goal which you are seeking to achieve through this resolution has not changed." (Quoted in a memorandum of April 25, 1973, to members of the International Movement for Atlantic Union, from Walden Moore, New York [unpublished].)

15. The text of Secretary Kissinger's April 23, 1973 speech can be found in the *Department of State Bulletin*, vol. LXVIII, no. 1768 (May 14, 1973), pp. 593–598, and of the Ottawa Declaration of June 19, 1974, in vol. LXXI, no. 1828 (July 8, 1974), pp. 37–44.

16. Merry and Serge Bromberger, *Jean Monnet and the United States of Europe*, (trans. Elaine P. Halperin) (New York: Coward-McCann, 1969), p. 26ff. The general story of allied cooperation in World War I, in which Monnet also played an important role, is told in Frank P. Chambers, *The War Behind the War, 1914–1918* (New York, 1939) and in Monnet's *Memoirs* (Garden City, New York: Doubleday and Co., 1978).

17. Freymond, op. cit., pp. 8, 26.

18. For details of the integrated commands and combined boards in World War II, see especially: Arthur Bryant, *The Turn of the Tide: A History of the War Years Based on the Diaries of Field-Marshal Lord Alanbrooke, Chief of the Imperial General Staff* (Garden City, New York: Doubleday, 1957); John Dalgleish, *We Planned the Second Front* (London, 1945); and Sir Frederick Morgan, *Overture to Overlord* (Garden City, New York: Doubleday, 1950).

19. Louis J. Halle, *The Cold War as History* (London: Chatto and Windus, 1971), p. 163.

20. Two useful accounts of this early postwar period are to be found in Jacques Freymond, op. cit., pp. 29–49, and Ernst H. van der Beugel, *From Marshall Aid to Atlantic Partnership* (Amsterdam: Elsevier, 1966), pp. 18–52.

21 René Albrecht-Carrié, op. cit., p. 223.

22. Freymond, op. cit., pp. 9–10.

CHAPTER 2

The Membership

Beginning in 1948, the Atlantic powers engaged in an unprecedented effort of regional institution building, partly confined to western Europe, partly transatlantic in scope. Between 1947 and 1961, eight major structures and a number of minor ones were established. (A ninth major body, the International Energy Agency, was formed in 1974, and a tenth, the annual "Economic Summits," inaugurated in 1975, will probably become a permanent institution.) A great deal of attention has been given by the press and by scholars to some of the better known organizations, such as the Common Market or NATO. But the entire group of institutions, to my knowledge, has rarely, if ever, been considered as a whole, *as a single international system*. This chapter examines the varied patterns of membership in the extended Atlantic System, sets forth the common interests which have brought the countries together, and discusses common characteristics. It is these interests and these characteristics which have made close cooperation possible and so surprisingly durable. Chapter III discusses the institutions themselves and how they have "worked," or not.

At this point, to understand well the method of this chapter, the reader is advised to turn to Appendix B and consult, successively, the six historical charts which are meant to show the institutional growth from 1947 to 1978 of this system which has recently been extended from the Atlantic to include some Pacific countries. Accompanying each chart in Appendix B is a historical description of the institution-building process which went on during that particular period. Appendix C contains a summary of the essential facts concerning each of the nine major institutions still functioning in 1978 and indicates briefly the purpose and function of each, dates of origin, and membership. In Appendix D, additional intergovernmental organizations of lesser importance or specialized character are listed. These too, along with a few bilateral treaties which antedated World War II and remained in force following it, may be considered part of the structure of the present community of developed democracies.

A "circular matrix" has been chosen for the charts in Appendix B because it seemed a suitable way to portray growth, more or less like rings in a tree. It is possible, using the charts, to answer quickly the question, "Which countries belong to Organization X?" Alternatively, one can ask, "To which organizations does Country Y belong?" In addition, the circular matrix is intended to suggest:

1. The tendency towards cooperation and unity among the member countries.
2. The interrelated character of the economic, political, military, social, and cultural interests and activities represented by the various structures. (For example, juxtaposing the European Communities, NATO, and OECD may seem strange, but my purpose is to signify a certain synergism among the three institutions).
3. The relative wholeness and integrity of the system.
4. The interrelatedness of "European," "Atlantic," and "Atlantic-Pacific" institutions.

Furthermore, by comparing Chart 6, which shows the institutional pattern in 1978, with Chart 1, which shows the pattern in 1947, the reader can readily comprehend one of the most important conclusions of this book. *The Atlantic World has progressed from virtually no intergovernmental or supranational institutions to a highly complex and many faceted structural ensemble in three short decades.*

The reader may wonder why the 24 members of the System are arranged in these charts as they are; this has been done so that all the participants in the more important organizations will appear contiguous. The most important (by criteria which will be developed later in this chapter) áre NATO, the European Communities, and the OECD.

It will be seen that a few countries belong to more organizations than do others. The Netherlands, for example, is a member of six institutions, as are most other members of the EC. Norway, not a member of the EC, is nevertheless also a "heavy joiner." The non-European participants are "light joiners." Japan, for example, belongs to only two Atlantic IGOs and Canada to three.[1] Generally speaking, the more such structures in which a state participates, the more its freedom of action becomes circumscribed, which might by some be considered a negative outcome. But there are other, positive outcomes which tend to correct any imbalances. A "heavy joiner," for example will find its bureaucratic and political thought processes set in new and stimulating channels. Also, it will probably find its security and prosperity relatively greater. (If this were not so, it would hardly continue to accept the burdens and constraints of membership.) This weighing of costs and benefits is a matter to which we shall recur frequently in subsequent chapters.

It would of course be possible to show institutional and membership patterns in other forms. The conventional method has been by means of a two-dimensional matrix: countries down the side of a page, organizations across the top, with appropriate boxes filled in (Appendix D, Table 4 is an example). It might also have been possible to show these patterns in a manner which suggested a dichotomy between Europe and the United States or between strictly European organizations and Atlantic ones. Such a design might portray rather well the "dumbbell" or "two-pillar" model of transatlantic relations, which was a main theme ("Atlantic Partnership") in U.S. policy for some years. But because this book is concentrated on the Atlantic and Atlantic-Pacific, rather than the European, in geographic scope and focus, I have chosen to use the circular matrix, which shows the European institutions closely linked with those of the Atlantic and Atlantic-Pacific. This suggests that a main function of the European bodies is to form a tighter, more integrated nucleus for a looser net of wider associations. It acknowledges implicitly the powerful U.S. role in the conception and development of most of the European institutions. It also demonstrates the "pace-maker" role of Europe and implies the essential wholeness and "systemicity" of all the relationships depicted.

It can be argued that the dichotomous view of transatlantic ties is entirely valid too, at least in terms of some powerful U.S. and European aspirations. That view has certainly prevailed for the past two decades; but as there is no clear place in such a "two-pillar" arrangement for Japan, Canada, and the other members of the broader System, a more encompassing view may have advantages in helping to clarify both current and historical realities. It may also suggest fresh perspectives and approaches in the pursuit of a better, more durable international system generally.

* * *

What countries might be considered as "belonging" to this incipient community of developed democracies? There can be no easy answers, especially as the criteria for membership seem to be constantly evolving. "Membership" itself is derived in a variety of ways. Sometimes a country is simply "there" when a new organizational pattern is decided upon and is thus automatically incorporated into the pattern. For instance such countries as Britain or Belgium have always been part of the System, even before institutionalization began to occur; they would thus be considered "members" from the start. In other cases, some outside countries campaign actively to get in. Spain long sought membership in such "core" bodies of the System as EC and NATO, but was refused; nevertheless, she remained a partial, or peripheral, member by virtue of her participation in OECD; eventually, more formal doors began to open. In still other instances, a country clearly "outside" (such as Japan) may become increasingly important to the whole System for overpowering reasons (in Japan's case, economic) and be invited to join because the System cannot be managed without that country on the inside.

This suggests that, at present, there are two types of members of this incipient community: those which can be considered "core" members (the majority), and those whose commitments and characteristics make their involvement peripheral, if nonetheless important. And, of course, members can and do move from one category to the other.

There are several important attributes which I believe the "core" countries (roughly 19 or 20 out of the 24), and to a lesser extent, the "peripheral" countries share. They are all, or nearly all:

1. Modern, pluralistic civic cultures, characterized by such features as representative parliamentary institutions, strictly construed constitutions, sovereignty directly or indirectly residing in the people, free elections, multi-party systems, majority decisions, an unfettered press, widespread enjoyment of basic rights and freedoms, well-established protection for minorities, and socially widespread democratic habits of thought and behavior.

2. Noncommunist regimes, in the sense that Communist parties do not play a leading role in government (even though in a few countries they may constitute significant parliamentary minorities).

3. Sufficiently integrated domestically (economically, politically, socially) to be capable of projecting themselves actively and constructively onto the world scene, radiating influence, power, and culture.

4. Interdependent with and dependent on the other members, to a greater or lesser degree, for their external security.

5. Highly unlikely to go to war with other members of the system.

6. Maritime powers.

7. Highly industrialized.

8. Free market or mixed economies of an advanced type.

9. Active in trading abroad.

10. Active in investing abroad.

11. Culturally western or "parawestern,"[2] such as Turkey or Japan.

12. Part of a general social pattern which is increasingly typical of highly industrialized cultures.

13. Educationally well-developed, with numerous universities and other centers of learning and research which attract large numbers of students and scholars from other countries, including the nonwestern world.
14. Developed countries which rely extensively on science and technological innovation and engage in large research and development efforts.
15. In close and frequent communication with other members, in all elements of their societies, but most particularly among the politically relevant strata.
16. Easily accessible to other members for businesses, other nongovernmental institutions, and individuals.
17. Observant of minimum standards of civilized intercourse in all their relations with other members.

These criteria fall naturally into five classifications: government, security, economics, social patterns, and communication.

GOVERNMENT

Evidently, not all members of the System meet fully the first criterion. That is, they do not possess a modern, pluralistic civic culture.[3] In fact, probably no citizens of any member country would avow that they meet all of the exacting standards which those who have striven for this particular kind of political system, associated in modern historical terms with the Enlightenment and the liberal Atlantic west, have traditionally set for themselves. Yet most would probably agree with Churchill that "Democracy is the worst form of government—except for all the others!" Even citizens of countries acknowledged to be among the most politically advanced in the System, such as the Scandinavians or the Anglo-Saxons, have recently experienced serious self-doubts. That some of the "peripheral" members of the System, such as modern Greece or Portugal or Spain, have had recent difficulty in meeting the criteria of a civic culture is evident. Such peripheral countries were "chosen" to enter the System, not because of their political cultures, but for other reasons: historical, strategic, geographical, commercial, or even sentimental. Their involvement is a continuing challenge to those core members of the System whose political cultures are more stable and clearly democratic. Yet, it is likely that Spain, for example, will have a better chance of developing a durable modern representative democracy as an associate of the community of developed democracies, than it would were it ostracized by them.

Although the practical motives which lay behind most of the treaties and intergovernmental institutions of the extended Atlantic System appeared to have little to do with the question of a common civic culture, the framers of several of them felt it essential at the outset at least to recall this fundamental attribute of the common civilization; and subsequently some of the Europeans IGOs have actually done something concrete about it. In the preamble to the North Atlantic Treaty, for example, the signatories stated their determination

> to safeguard the freedom, common heritage and civilization of their peoples, founded on the principles of democracy, individual liberty and the rule of law.

Article II of the treaty then committed the parties to

> contribute toward the further development of peaceful and friendly international relations by strengthening their free institutions, by bringing about a better understanding of the principles upon which these institutions are founded, and by promoting conditions of stability and well-being.

The Statute of the Council of Europe, signed just 30 days later in 1949, included a similar statement in its preamble (Chapter 1), reaffirming the signatories'

> devotion to the spiritual and moral values which are the common heritage of their peoples and the true source of individual freedom, political liberty and the rule of law, principles which form the basis of all genuine democracy. . . .

The Statute of the Council included explicit requirements for membership, among which Article 3 seems particularly relevant:

> Every Member of the Council of Europe must accept the principles of the rule of law and of the enjoyment of all persons within its jurisdiction of human rights and fundamental freedoms, and collaborate sincerely and effectively in the realization of the aim of the Council as specified in Chapter 1.

The NATO treaty contained no such membership requirement. However, it was apparently assumed (and correctly, as it turned out) that such countries as Portugal, which at the time would not pass democratic muster, but which for strategic reasons and for their own safety were included in the Atlantic Alliance, nevertheless would be willing to support a collective security organization whose ultimate aim was to safeguard the very liberties which they could not or would not provide for their own peoples.

When the Greek Colonels overthrew parliamentary democracy in their country in 1967, the other member states of the Council of Europe began proceedings to expel Greece. In 1969, the Colonels withdrew from the Council, just before expulsion was to become mandatory. The Council had no other sanctions, yet the moral opprobrium expressed by the de facto expulsion probably contributed at least in small ways to the pressures, internal and external, which eventually restored constitutional government to Greece.

The Brussels treaty (1948), which antedated the Atlantic Alliance and the Council of Europe by more than a year, also contained a pledge

> to fortify and preserve the principles of democracy, personal freedom and political liberty, the constitutional traditions and the rule of law, which are their common heritage. . . .

These words remained unchanged when, in 1954, Italy and the German Federal Republic acceded to the treaty (transformed substantially and renamed "Western European Union").

And when the Treaty of Rome, establishing the European Economic Community, was signed in 1957, its preamble also referred to the civic culture:

> Resolved by thus pooling their resources to preserve and strengthen peace and liberty. . . .

Except for the Council of Europe none of these new postwar IGOs appears to have done anything direct, concrete, or explicit to further such affirmations of support for the common political culture. The cynic might go further and suggest that, at least in some cases, such provisions appeared in the treaties only as a propaganda gloss for the benefit of political constituencies back home, of peoples behind the Iron Curtain, or of those in still other parts of the world.[4] Yet the words stand, and they remind the casual reader as well as those now responsible for executing the various treaties of similar wording in the several national constitutions of the framers and in such documents as the 1941 Atlantic Charter. Such references are, at the very least, an explicit acknowledgement of the most fundamental, implicit criterion of membership in what is now the extended Atlantic System: that the applicant be a *democracy*.

In all the diversity which characterizes civic culture, one searches for a central thread with difficulty; yet, it is present, in the form of *pluralism*. In sociological terms, Ernst Haas has described well this aspect of modern western civic culture:

> With the exception of Greece, Turkey, Portugal, parts of Spain and southern Italy, the Western European social scene is dominated by pluralism. Articulate voluntary groups, led by bureaucratized but accessible elites, compete with each other more or less rationally for political power and social status. The population is mobilized and participates in this process through affiliation with mass organizations. In the countries mentioned, however, affective and functionally diffuse social relations prevail.[5]

Everything Haas says of course applies to certain countries outside of Europe: the United States, Canada, Australia, and New Zealand, which share the same civic culture; and increasingly (and today quite generally) to modern Japan, most recently assimilated to the "extended Atlantic System." Pluralism today is also growing abundantly in the "exceptional" countries cited by Haas.

* * *

Off and on for 20 years, there have been Communist ministers in the coalition governments of Finland, for special reasons, domestic and external. From 1945 to 1947, although not at the cabinet level since then, governments in both Italy and France included Communists. From 1971 to 1974 and again beginning in 1978, a Communist-dominated party participated in an Icelandic coalition cabinet. Some of Portugal's post-Caetano "revolutionary" governments contained Communists as minority members. It is entirely possible that in the governments of at least two or three more members of the extended Atlantic System, a domestic Communist party may be brought into a coalition government in the next few years. Although at the time these words are written, the second criterion for membership in the System ("regimes in which Communist parties do not play a leading role in government") still stands for all members of OECD (except Finland and Iceland), in fact this may not always continue to be the case. Some critical observers maintain that even if coalitions involving Communists are formed in Italy or France, for example, this need not necessarily mean the end of western-style parliamentary democracy in those countries. However, the experience in such countries as Czechoslovakia, or more recently Portugal (1976), where Communist participation in government could not be reconciled with Atlantic-style democracy, suggests at best a wait-and-see attitude. It is obvious, however, that popular attitudes towards Communist parties in some western countries have changed substantially since the early years of the Cold War; at the very least, it is demonstrably no longer sufficient for governments to justify the European and

[30]

Atlantic institutions solely or even mainly on the grounds of anticommunism.

* * *

It is extremely difficult, if not impossible, for a nation to play a significant part in the integrated life of an international system as complicated and sophisticated as that of the advanced democracies unless its domestic life is also reasonably well integrated.[6] Nations whose economies hover at the subsistence level, whose political life is riven with open strife and violent change, whose peoples have little respect for law,[7] whose decision-making mechanisms are inadequate,[8] or whose social backwardness drains their budgets and their national vitality do not have the strength necessary to project themselves internationally within cooperative systems such as OECD, NATO, or the Common Market. In such underdeveloped states, able, well-trained civil servants are scarce; whatever technical experts exist are needed at home, and politicians have all they can do to cope with continuing domestic economic crises and the uncertainties endemic to underdeveloped political cultures. An individual whose own house is not in tolerable order can hardly expect to play a significant and constructive role in the active life of his community. So it is with nations on the international scene. To be sure, in the counsels of the United Nations, many less-developed nations are highly vocal. However, they rarely exercise the kind of moderating influence or display the capacity for compromise and joint action for which the more sophisticated, positive forms of international life call.

To some extent, of course, a dictatorship can produce another kind of domestic integration that is different from that of liberal democracy. Integration that is imposed by a dictator, however, tends to be precarious as well as negative and unreliable in its international dealings. Seldom is it, or can it be, a constructive force in international life. This criterion of integration explains, for example, why such states as Greece, Turkey, and Portugal so far have remained on the periphery of the extended Atlantic

System. It also explains why the great majority of nations in Asia, Africa, or Latin America, at this stage in their development, could not undertake the responsibilities of membership in such a System, even if they were to perceive their interests as making it desirable.

SECURITY

The next two criteria for membership (defense interdependence and no war with other members) have to do with *collective security*, or perhaps, more precisely, collective self-defense. All 24 members, core and peripheral alike, are dependent on one another and on the formal alliances (NATO, WEU, the U.S.-Japanese Treaty of Mutual Cooperation and Security, Canadian-U.S. defense treaties, and the ANZUS Pact[9]) for their external security, whether they are actually signatories of the treaties or not. Thus, Sweden, Switzerland, Austria, Ireland, Spain, and Finland, although not members of NATO, nevertheless benefit practically and substantially from the existence of the NATO defense system. With geography, commercial and monetary interests, cultural ties, and political affinities as they are, the situation in Europe could hardly suggest a different conclusion. Again, Chart 6 (Appendix B), which displays the contemporary pattern of alliances, economic organizations, "Communities," and so on, graphically suggests this pragmatic security interdependence, over and above the formal commitments enshrined in specific treaties.

While the de facto dependence of the European neutrals on NATO may not be too difficult to accept, particularly if one does not talk much about it, it requires a somewhat greater stretch of the strategic imagination to comprehend NATO's relevance to security in the Far East. The Japanese might not like to admit their substantial dependence on NATO; yet, if NATO is a key element in U.S. strength and if U.S. strength is important to Japan, the connection is unmistakable. Australia and New Zealand find the concept a little less foreign, and China, even less so, for her own peculiar reasons, at least at the end of the 1970s.

That the Atlantic security community has de facto been extended to cover the Pacific is convincingly argued by the provisions of the U.S. Arms Control Act (Public Law 90-629, October 22, 1968, amended by Public Law 91-672, January 12, 1971, Chapter 3, Section 38):

> No license may be issued under this Act for the export of any major defense equipment . . . to any foreign country which is not a member of the North Atlantic Treaty Organization. . . . The prohibition . . . shall not apply . . . to Australia, Japan, or New Zealand. . . .

Not only are the mutual security commitments of the extended Atlantic System important in terms of defense against potential outside enemies; these and most, if not all, of the other institutional commitments, including the economic, political, and cultural, appear to play a fundamental (and sometimes determining) role in promoting internal peace within the System. To take the most obvious case, it is clear that the possibility of war between France and Germany, perennial enemies for centuries, has now been reduced virtually to nil. There are many complex reasons for this, some of them psychological or sociological in character and thus extremely difficult to isolate; yet, all but the most biased observers would have to admit that, beginning with the European Coal and Steel Community treaty of 1951, every European and Atlantic institutional and treaty link between the new Federal Republic of Germany and her former western enemies (the foremost of which was France) became part of an increasingly solid, long-term structure of peace in western Europe.

Specialists in politics, institutions, and social structures can of course debate credibly on both sides of the question: Do institutions influence behavior or do they merely reflect or ratify sociological reality? There is evidence for both points of view. If large parts of the French and German publics, and more particularly their political elites, had not in 1945 decided that future recourse to war between the two would be utterly futile, the "no-war" status could not have been reached, nor would common institutions have been of any avail. Building on this common recognition of the futility of war, however, Konrad Adenauer, Robert Schuman, and the other architects of European unity constructed institutions which would more or less "lock in" the French and German governments and peoples and give them mutual assurances which in turn would build more confidence, provide no other practical route between them but cooperation and integration, and insure that the 1945 recognition of the futility of war would eventually evolve into the "unthinkability" of war. Institutions, if established with a sincere desire on all sides to make them work, can have an important reinforcing effect. They can also have a stabilizing effect when, as has sometimes occurred in the postwar period, one nation or another thinks momentarily of "going it alone." Without the institutions, this becomes rather simple in many cases; with the institutions and all that they stand for in practical terms, the usual inclination is to "remain in the fold," or at least to mute one's actions and return as soon as possible to full and faithful participation.

The U.S.-Canadian "no-war" border is another example of how the System can work. In this case, the "no-war" relationship was established in the second half of the nineteenth century, long before Atlantic interdependence was generally recognized or institutionalized. But institutions, beginning with the International Joint Commission (1909), have made a considerable difference and continue to do so, even in the case of Canada and United States, between which there are such strong bonds of common culture and mutual trust.

Among some peripheral members of the Atlantic System, this "no-war" state of affairs does not yet fully obtain. More prominently, Greece and Turkey have teetered on the brink of war several times in the past three decades. Although war was not actually threatened between Austria and Italy, at various times since 1945 their relations have been greatly strained as a result of controversy over the Austrian minorities in the south Tirol. Iceland's relations with Britain and, to a lesser extent, with West Germany, have been anything but cordial as a result of recurring disputes over fishing rights. Yet, it is a fact that none of the 24 members of the extended Atlantic System, neither in the Atlantic area nor the Pacific, has gone to war with another member since 1945. While war is, of course, not impossible at some future point, this kind of war within the west is no longer at all likely. One can, on the contrary, maintain with reason that the existence of the institutional and other ties of the System, reflecting a broad congruence of interests, usually well perceived by its members, has on occasion prevented hostilities. Again, Greece and Turkey offer the most obvious case: in 1921, the two countries went to war; after 1945, the existence of the Atlantic System prevented war between them. This state of affairs may not last forever, but if it does not, they will in any case have "left" the System.[10]

SEA POWER: GEOGRAPHY, STRATEGY, AND COMMERCE

The sixth criterion for membership was *maritime power*. Like many of the criteria, this one can hardly be applied rigidly; neither Switzerland, Austria, nor Luxembourg, for example, borders on the sea. But it is striking that all the other countries of the System are sea powers, in either a naval or a commercial sense or both, and most particularly in an almost spiritual sense.

The mental image which comes to mind ordinarily when one mentions "maritime" is that of naval or commercial exploitation of the seas or of lands bordering on the seas. Yet, if one looks at the matter historically, a good deal more is implied. The ancient Greeks, whose open, questing, venturesome spirit contrasted sharply with that of contemporary Asian despotism, lived by and on the sea. This ocean-going tradition carried on into Atlantic Europe, where it was reinforced by that of the Vikings. In the Age of Discovery, European ships carried commerce, power, and ideas to all corners of the earth.

The United States and Canada carried on the European maritime tradition, with Admiral Mahan in the 1890s reminding Americans that they were in effect an "island" which had depended after 1783 on the British fleet for its protection. Japan, an active maritime power, may be contrasted with China, which has traditionally never looked to the sea for commerce, cultural contacts, or strategic gain. It is only in the past decade or two, for example, that the USSR has attempted determinedly to become a maritime power. Her likely motives, however, which seem to be overwhelmingly strategic, fly in the face of her traditions, no matter how impressive her naval build-up may seem.

One can of course cite bold, nonwestern seafaring peoples of renown, such as the medieval Arabs or the ancient Polynesians, but in the modern era, since the fifteenth century, western man has been preeminently oceanic in implanting his civilization virtually everywhere by means of maritime power. The tradition has been carried on in the twentieth century in the exploitation of the air. Whatever cultural values remain as a residue of this questing spirit in modern western man appear to be a significant part of his heritage and yet another attribute linking together the members of the modern Atlantic System.

ECONOMICS

Economically, all but five or six of the 24 members are *highly industrialized*, and all of them possess so-called *free market or "mixed" economies*. In some of these countries, the state's role in economic planning is more important than in others. However, in none of the countries of the extended Atlantic System is business and industrial life completely dominated by government as it is in the Communist countries or, for example, as it was in Hitler's Germany. I have carefully avoided the word "capitalism" in characterizing these industrial economies of the west because it is today an emotion-laden and, in any case, inaccurate, term. Marx thrust the word into the lexicon of every modern man, yet the economic system of the modern west and Japan is remote from the capitalism of the nineteenth or early twentieth centuries. The burgeoning of technology, the increasing role of the state, the influence of modern economic thinkers (Keynes in particular), and the growing accession to demands for social benefits and social equity have all combined to produce the modern free-enterprise or mixed system, which is far different from old-style capitalism, and yet correspondingly remote from Russian-style Communism, considered by some to be a form of "state capitalism."

Some countries of the extended Atlantic System are more advanced economically than others, and in some the state exercises a more interventionist role than in others. There is great variety as well as considerable anomaly. The concept of "pluralism," so important to understanding the modern west's political culture, is also a good descriptive term for its economy. Evolution, change, experimentation, adaptation, variety, pragmatism, and innovation are the key words.

The similarities in external economics among the System's members are just as important as the common attributes of their domestic economic systems.

All of the 24 members of OECD are active in trading abroad and depend, in most cases, on the maintenance of strong commercial ties with their OECD partners above all others. They rely as well on the preservation of an international trading system which is as free and open as possible, with generally convertible currencies and in most cases minimal tariffs.

The most advanced OECD countries are not only heavily involved in international trading, but have invested abroad (and especially in the other member countries) to such an extent that they could today hardly disentangle themselves without severe economic consequences. From the fringes of the Atlantic System to its inner core, the Common Market, the System is characterized by economic interpenetration and interdependence on an unprecedented scale. It has become profitable and fashionable for firms (and not always large ones by any means) to invest directly in manufacturing, banking, or other types of business abroad, and above all in any of the other countries of the extended Atlantic System where markets and trained manpower (and often capital) can be found.

The "typical" or "full" member of the extended Atlantic System thus depends heavily on foreign trade and increasingly on the placement and active management of extensive economic investments in other countries. Indeed, economic frontiers have been broken much more than have political ones, and the more advanced Atlantic-Pacific countries are in the forefront of the worldwide development of "interdependence." The members of the System interact with one another in the marketplace. They

[37]

also borrow ideas and coordinate planning at the intellectual and intergovernmental levels in OECD, in and around the European Communities, in the Group of Ten (see Appendix D), and in other organs of Atlantic or Atlantic-Pacific cooperation. As a result, the members of the System tend to reinforce the common characteristics of their economies. Consequently, for example, the free-market industrialized world has developed its own set of economic and social measurements: productivity, per capita income, economic growth, pollution indices, the evaluation of management performance, and so on. The rest of the world may become interested in the concepts and may employ them, but it is the Atlantic System which sets these fashions and which is indeed the heart and core of the world economic system.

SOCIAL AND CULTURAL PATTERNS

With the exception of Japan and Turkey, all the peoples of the extended Atlantic System are clearly *western*, historically and culturally. This demarcates them from those who are "eastern" in the old sense (of or derived from Asian civilizations, as, for example, are the nations of modern North Africa).

There are, of course, countries which lie outside the extended Atlantic System, as it is defined here, but which nevertheless have cultures stemming from western civilization; all of Latin America or eastern Europe would fall under this heading. Because most of the other "membership" criteria do not apply to them, however, they must be considered as belonging to "non-Atlantic" branches of the west at the present time. Perhaps the clearest line of demarcation is that which separates the nations possessing a civic culture typical of the modern "Atlantic" west from those which do not. In this sense, Iberia has been set off until recently from the "core" members of the extended Atlantic System, belonging culturally more with its former colonies in Latin America. If it were not for the geographical proximity, commercial linkages such as the tourist trade, and the strategic importance of Spain and Portugal to Europe and the United States, it is unlikely that they would have become members before the mid-1970s.[11]

Turkey and Japan are both clearly nonwestern in historic and cultural origin, yet today they are so intimately tied to the Atlantic world in virtually every aspect of their political, economic, security, and social life that we may be justified in terming them "parawestern." That is, they are on the way to incorporation in western civilization itself. There is, of course, nothing inexorable about such a course. Turkey's westernization, begun seriously with Atatürk in the 1920s, reached a peak when it became a member of NATO in 1952 and an associate member of the European Economic Community in 1956. At best, however, Turkey has experienced considerable difficulty in assimilating itself domestically to the political culture of the Atlantic west, even though the tenacity of its military leadership in clinging to the concepts of democracy—and insisting that the civilian leaders respect them—is both fascinating and touching. After Cyprus gained its independence from Britain in 1960, Greek-Turkish and (more recently) NATO-Turkish and American-Turkish relations deteriorated steadily. In 1978, the EC agreed to a timetable for full Greek membership; a parallel development for Turkey seemed more distant than ever. Add to this the perceptible waning of the Cold War and a lag in the western economic boom which carried Turkey along for the first two postwar decades, and it is entirely possible that this essentially eastern, Moslem country may at some point simply "opt out" of its present "associate membership" in the community of developed democracies.

Japan's case is quite different. One of the most discrete and isolated of the world's cultures until the middle of the last century and possessing cultural and social forms of unique character, Japan assimilated itself with amazing speed, industrially and technologically, into the civilization of the modern west. Its political assimilation however was, at best, highly problematical until after 1945, even though at various times (as in the 1920s) it seemed that the main attributes of the west's civic culture, including political parties, constitutional cabinet government, the free interplay of ideas and interests, and a growing respect for civil rights, were flowering in Japan. By fiat of the conquering United States, Japan received a modern Atlantic-type constitution in 1946. Japan was, in effect, ordered to "westernize" in virtually every conceivable aspect of her national life. To discuss this fascinating process of "instant social innovation," without precedent in history (even if one includes the equally fascinating post-1945 German renovation), is beyond the scope of this book. It is important to note however that, both because of these consequences of World War II and because the national leadership and people themselves sought eagerly to resume the process of westernization begun in the 1850s, Japan today seems in most respects a thoroughly westernized country. Yet the careful observer balks at such a categorical judgment, for it is evident that the many centuries of development in relative, and sometimes complete, isolation from other countries and especially from the west created value patterns, social structures, and ways of thinking and acting which are today as remote from the typically western in their character as are those of the Eskimos or the modern Mongols (both of whom share common roots in antiquity with the Japanese). Furthermore, the shift of domestic forces and external policy in China after Mao's death in 1976, culminating in the friendship treaty between Japan and China in 1978 and American recognition of China, may well cause the Japanese cultural pendulum to swing once more, as it has several times in the past two millenia, towards China.

It might seem to the casual observer that neither Turkey nor Japan "belongs" in this clearly western Atlantic camp, yet, if one takes a very long historical view, there is nothing strange or unprecedented about their possible assimilation into the west. The Gauls, the Belgae, the Britons, and the various Germanic tribes, for example, were clearly nonwestern before the Roman conquests; today these countries and peoples are western through and through, if indeed any peoples deserve the name. The Vikings of Scandinavia may be an even better example, for they have assimilated themselves into the west of their own volition, even though in the ninth century, they (like the Japanese from 1600 to the 1860s) were hostile to the west. The process of assimilation to the old Roman nucleus was virtually complete for the "barbaric" tribes of western Europe within a millennium. It may be of interest that the East Germans, whose political culture today remains distinctly non-Atlantic, are those who today still live beyond the Roman *Limes*, in the never-Romanized parts of Germany.

Assimilation to Rome of course was never a one-way process; the ancient cultural heritage of the barbaric peoples influenced the Romans and their inheritors substantially, and by the time of the Renaissance the geographic center of western power and cultural influence had moved from Rome to northern Europe. This suggests that westernization is a relative concept, depending upon one's time frame. Under modern conditions, if the Atlantic System continues to thrive and Japanese or Turkish aspirations continue to be directed westward, there is no particular reason why western civilization could not assimilate unto itself many cultural traits and patterns from these new members. Indeed, by the time westernization of Japan in particular and Turkey as well is more or less complete, western civilization itself will also almost surely have been substantially changed.

* * *

The twelfth criterion for membership concerned the extent to which the participant countries were part of *a developing social and cultural pattern which seemed to be characteristic of highly industrialized societies*. Daniel Bell has termed this the "post-industrial society,"[12] although one must avow that not even the United States seems yet able to assign manufacturing completely to others and move into an economy and society based entirely on computers and the knowledge industry. Leaving aside the question of whether or not the United States is already post-industrial, it is nevertheless clear that the societies of northwestern Europe (including Scandinavia), Italy, North America, and— even if superficially, nonetheless, in a very important sense—Japan are more and more taking on a broad range of common social characteristics.

The development of an "Atlantic society" requires *a high volume of communication between members of the System*. In particular, the advent of radio and television, plus the ease of air travel, have reduced the spatial barriers among the peoples of the earth and to a much greater extent among the peoples of the extended Atlantic System. Thanks largely to TV, the "youth revolution" of the late sixties burgeoned and spread, sometimes virtually overnight, from Berkeley to Berlin to Paris and thence to London and back again to the United States, as well as to Tokyo and Melbourne. The growth of a distinctive youth culture or counterculture common to the highly industrialized west and Japan (and to some extent beyond) was obviously made possible by the ease of travel and communication between them.

In similar fashion, nearly all parts of society in the most-developed countries have been brought much closer to one another and are experiencing (albeit often in somewhat different ways) the effects of social movements, fads, and mundane changes in lifestyle as they develop in one place or another and then spread with astonishing rapidity and pervasiveness. Even in Japan, long the citadel of female submissiveness, there is increasing talk today of "Woman-Rib." In art, architecture, music, and drama, at a very obvious, if still superficial level, national and subnational distinctions throughout the vast Atlantic-Pacific area are fast disappearing. One need only cite rock-and-roll music, the sameness of skyscrapers, or the thoroughly polyglot character of modern painting to make this point. Unpleasant as this may seem to many people, there is today in the most advanced countries a superficial sameness about ordinary life which justifies talking about a virtually common "industrial society." Because social moods, patterns, and aspirations tend more and more to spill over national boundaries throughout the extended Atlantic System, governments find themselves confronted with increasingly similar social needs and demands. A good example is the growing emphasis on "worker participation" in the direction and management of industrial firms which began as an idea advanced by trade unions and the Social Democratic party in early postwar West Germany and is today the object of experimentation and intense discussion in most of western Europe. U.S. and Japanese industrial cultures are somewhat different from the European industrial culture; yet, by virtue of their industrial holdings in Europe as well as the flow of intellectual traffic across both the Atlantic and the Pacific, many U.S. and Japanese firms today cannot escape the question. U.S. industrial practices, of course, have greatly influenced Europe, and very recently Japanese ideas about worker-management relations have begun to receive serious attention in both Europe and North America.

The increasing congruity of social characteristics among these countries, however, goes deeper than the phenomena of social trends and fashions, whether frivolous or more serious. In the advanced societies of the Atlantic System, there is a distinct openness to new ideas. There also is a general possibility for upward mobility at virtually all social levels. Because elites and intellectuals can meet easily, the possibility for constant reinvigoration of leadership exists in all fields. Thus, geographical as well as vertical mobility are much easier in comparison with other societies.[13] There are, of course, differences among the core countries of the extended Atlantic System, but the common openness is undeniable and appears to be growing "more common." There is, moreover, evidence of a developing "multinational leadership group," transatlantic in composition, among the higher echelons of academia, government, business, and the labor unions. More recently, members of the Japanese elite have also begun to participate in this development.

Another feature of "industrial society" in the advanced democracies is the *tremendous growth in and emphasis on education* (Criterion 13), which has especially characterized them since 1945. This is an additional aspect of Bell's "post-industrial society": increasing social emphasis on learning, research, scholarship, and higher education. Universities have burgeoned, and, although there are important differences in the quality, rate, and direction of this growth throughout the Atlantic and Pacific world, a much greater percentage of young people (and more recently in some countries, older people) are attending post-secondary institutions of learning. The universities of the chief western nations, as a result, have constituted a huge magnet to the aspiring professionals of the less-developed countries, whose displacement, sometimes permanent, has added both to the burdens and the opportunities on each side.

There is, finally, a considerable flow of students and professors back and forth among the countries of the extended Atlantic System, adding to intellectual stimulus and cultural cosmopolitanism, but paradoxically perhaps also lending a degree of superficial sameness to today's advanced industrial societies.

The heavy emphasis on higher learning is coupled in turn with Criterion 14, *the extensive reliance on science and technological innovation* which is a distinctive feature of modern industrial societies. On the assumption that much of the success of U.S. industry has been due to massive governmental and private expenditures on scientific research, the OEEC and its successor (OECD) undertook extensive studies of science policy, research and development, and, later, virtually every aspect of higher education in their member countries, in order to find out how science could be made to stimulate economic growth and to control its adverse affects. NATO, quite unobtrusively, has also provided an important focus for its members' scientific and technological concerns and by no means has confined its efforts to strictly military applications.[14]

While some countries outside the extended Atlantic System—and one thinks mainly here of the Soviet bloc—are also adding to the "knowledge component" of their societies and are striving to develop and apply scientific knowledge for practical purposes, it is still to the advanced democracies that others invariably look for their model in these fields.

COMMUNICATION

The *extent of communication* among the member nations, especially between nongovernmental agencies, is important. Nations may be friendly to one another, but if their relations are essentially quiescent there is little occasion for developing sophisticated systems of official cooperation between them. Moreover, it would be extremely difficult, with the best will on both sides, to organize such a system unless there were already a highly developed, significant volume of communication and transaction among their citizens.[15] The relations between most of the countries of the extended Atlantic System are of this character: close, active, and pervasive at all levels. Of course, the communications ties between the 24 members are not uniformly strong or active. Until very recently, for example, unofficial communication between Europe and Japan was highly restricted. Beginning in the late 1960s, however, great numbers of Japanese tourists have appeared in Europe, commercial transactions are increasing rapidly, there is an increase in media interest in both Europe and Japan, and Japanese and European businessmen and governmental elites have recently begun to meet to discuss matters of mutual concern, usually at the instigation of prominent Americans.[16]

Ease of access for communication and transaction between the citizens of the extended Atlantic System is also important. Among the most advanced and democratic members, the flow is so great and the access so easy that one can hardly distinguish, for example, between patterns of intra- and intersociety interaction. This is especially true in the worlds of business, banking, art, publishing, science, and various other professional and intellectual pursuits. Relations on the unofficial level between these countries are characterized by great openness, which in turn is an important component of their democractic makeup. This is in distinct contrast obviously with the Communist countries (although Yugoslavia's relations with the west are a good deal more open than those of its Communist neighbors) and indeed formed a principal bone of contention in the Helsinki and Belgrade talks in 1974 and 1977.

In considering further the character of communication links among the members of the System, it is finally important to note that *transactions between members are generally characterized by an adherence to minimum standards of civilized discourse.* There are of course exceptions, and particularly at some private levels, where the modifier "relatively" would have to be inserted before "civilized" to safeguard one's accuracy. But once again, the essential point is the contrast between the character of communications within the System and those outside it, or communications emanating from outside but directed to points within. Perhaps the most convenient illustration would be the increasingly strident, propagandistic quality of debates in the UN General Assembly. In the early days of the Cold War, such hyperbole and vitriol emanated primarily from the Soviet Union and its satellites. In the 1970s, they became a steady feature of a great deal of the communication from nations all around the world. They can be strikingly contrasted with the tone of meet-

[45]

ings in the parliamentary assemblies of (e.g.) EC, WEU, the Council of Europe, the Nordic Council, or NATO.

To be sure, contemporary communication within the community of developed democracies displays wide variations in quality. If, as Lord Clark suggested, decorum is an important aspect of civilization, then quality of communication in the present Atlantic System may be greatly wanting.[17] Yet, compared with other contemporary human communities, and with those of our own western past, most of the communication today is more humanized, more enlightened, more civil. These may or may not be the most important human qualities, but they nevertheless rank with at least modest importance in determining whether an individual or a whole society is "civilized."[18]

MEMBERSHIP IN THE SYSTEM: CORE COUNTRIES AND PERIPHERAL COUNTRIES

With considerable trepidation, I have endeavored in Table 1 to characterize the degree to which the 24 individual members of the present extended Atlantic System appear to embrace the various criteria of "commonness" outlined above. While of course one might debate endlessly over such an exercise as applied to the individual nations, one central fact nevertheless does seem to emerge: there are at present two types of members in the System. There are those which might be called "core" members (the clear majority) and others whose commitments and characteristics make their involvement peripheral, if nonetheless important to them and to at least some others.

By applying the 17 criteria, I have derived a "core membership" of 20 nations as follows:

Australia	Austria
Belgium	Finland
Canada	Iceland
Denmark	Ireland
Federal Republic of Germany	Italy
France	Japan

Table 1

Application of Criteria for Membership in the Community of Developed Democracies.

Legend:

- ■ Applies fully
- ◨ Applies only in part
- □ Does not apply

Countries (columns, left to right):
BELGIUM, NETHERLANDS, GERMAN FED. REP., UNITED KINGDOM, NORWAY, DENMARK, CANADA, FRANCE, USA, AUSTRALIA, SWEDEN, ITALY, JAPAN, NEW ZEALAND, LUXEMBOURG, SWITZERLAND, FINLAND, AUSTRIA, IRELAND, ICELAND, GREECE, PORTUGAL, SPAIN, TURKEY

Criteria (rows):

1. Modern civic culture.
2. No leading Communist role in government.
3. Well-integrated domestically.
4. External security interdependence with other members.
5. "No-war" status vis-à-vis other members.
6. Maritime power.
7. Highly industrialized.
8. Free market or mixed economy.
9. Active in trading abroad.
10. Active in investing abroad.
11. Western culture.
12. Advanced industrial society.
13. Highly-developed university and research institutions.
14. Extensive reliance on science and technological innovation.
15. High volume of communication with other members.
16. Ease of access for communication.
17. Minimum standards of civilized discourse with other members.

Netherlands	Luxembourg
Norway	New Zealand
United Kingdom	Sweden
United States	Switzerland

Even within this group of 20 core members, there are distinctions and gradations. The ten countries in the left-hand column (above) are even more "solid core" than those in the right-hand column; each meets the 17 criteria fully.

As Table 1 suggests, because Sweden, Switzerland, Austria, Ireland, and Finland are all neutrals, they are therefore not quite as explicitly interdependent for their security as are the others. Nor are the economies of Ireland, Iceland, New Zealand, and Italy as highly developed, or as reliant on modern industry, as are those of the most advanced western countries. Japan does not share the western heritage to the same extent as the others, nor does she share equally in the high-volume-of-communication characteristic of the community because of linguistic differences. Finland has a delicate status because of her ties with the Soviet Union, both as a major trading partner and by virtue of their mutual security treaty and other links. This status is reflected both in the "security interdependence" column and in the composition of Finland's governments since 1956, most of which have contained Communist ministers. These factors move Finland inevitably in the direction of the periphery.

For briefer periods, Iceland's cabinet also has had Communist membership. Italy, socially and industrially, is really two countries, but inasmuch as it is the industrial north which sets the constitutional and overall economic patterns, Italy is more "core" than "peripheral." Luxembourg, while sharing all major characteristics fully, is too small to develop its own university and related research establishment. This factor has only minimal importance, given Luxembourg's solid integration with other members of the EC. Despite such minor anomalies, all 20 core countries are experienced, practicing democracies and share generally in all the other criteria.

There is a further group of countries, however, which fits the

17 criteria less evenly. In Portugal, Turkey, Spain, and Greece, the Atlantic west's civic culture has still only a shaky hold. Even though, as of 1980, all were constitutional democracies, their political future is problematical. All four of these peripheral countries are backward economically, although both Spain and Greece are moving forward fairly rapidly. The societies of all four are also relatively underdeveloped by comparison with the core countries, sharing much less in the broad advances in living standards, education, science and technology, and the general welfare. If it were not for the strategic requirements of NATO, the geographic proximity of these countries to Europe, and their economic dependence on western Europe, it is unlikely that any of them would presently be members of the Atlantic System. Only the future can tell if they will eventually "join" the System in every sense, philosophically as well as institutionally and industrially. Such marginal memberships have posed obvious "public relations" problems. NATO, for example, chartered to protect democracy, for long periods included some members whose democratic credentials were at best inadequate. Portugal, for example, was a dictatorship until 1973. Yet, if the extended Atlantic System is to be seen as an interlocking whole, based on sets of compatible, but not always identical needs, interests, and goals, and as a "club" with appropriately varying degrees of "membership" and commitment to fit individual cases, then the presence of a few anomalies need not necessarily harm the political coherence or philosophical validity of the whole. On the contrary, the existence of such a complex international system, functioning within a considerable choice of policies and mechanisms, may sometimes turn out to be an important—even a crucial—factor in the domestic political or economic metamorphosis of some of its members.

* * *

Which countries might be candidates to join the "club" of advanced democracies in the near future? Two very small countries, Malta and Cyprus, are already connected with the System, inasmuch as both are members of the Council of Europe.[19] There are of course commercial, cultural, and other ties between

[49]

the two countries and some other members of the System, but because the overall effect seems slight in either direction, their status should probably be considered as "aspirant" at this stage. Events in North Africa and the Middle East will undoubtedly play a major part in determining which way Cyprus and Malta are likely to turn.

Yugoslavia also has a foot—or perhaps a toe—inside the System, by virtue of its "special status" in OECD. Yugoslavia participates in some of OECD's activities, such as studies of economic policy, scientific and technical matters, and agricultural and fisheries questions. She is not however a member, or even an associate member. Her ideological and geographic position suggests that it would be some years, if ever, before Yugoslavia could take such an unequivocal step. Potentially, however, Yugoslavia, as a full member of OECD, would thus be at least a peripheral member of the extended Atlantic System, and if so, the first Communist country to "join."

In many informal ways, both South Africa and Israel might already be considered members, even though none of the major Atlantic-Pacific institutions include them. (Israel is in ECAC, and South Africa belongs to BIS; see Appendix D.) Formal association however is, for the time being at least, out of the question for either of them for obvious political reasons. Each, in a different way, is a political liability for the extended Atlantic System. In the case of South Africa especially, this political isolation is reinforced by geography, although this may be balanced by the country's strategic importance to the System.

If one looks around the world at developing countries which seem to be near political or economic "take-off," a short list of candidates for membership in the System comes to mind: Brazil, Mexico, Singapore, and Venezuela. Because of the sheer magnitude of their new-found oil riches and the potential extent to which these might be used to bring about more rapid industrialization, one might add Saudi Arabia and a few other oil sheikdoms to this list, but with even greater uncertainty. There may be still others such as South Korea, Taiwan, Lebanon, or Tunisia, but for various reasons their candidacy would appear to be some time off. For, in addition to the 17 criteria suggested earlier, there is yet another requirement; that is, the motivation and desire to belong, implying a special kind of perception of a country's interests. If the motivation and desire were not present in every case, no current member of the extended Atlantic System would have accepted or continued the various institutional arrangements which give the System its form, structure, and meaning.

If membership in the extended Atlantic System were to come about for any of these "candidate" countries, or for others, in the future, how would it happen? Since the 1950s, when the original "mix" of core members was firmly established, two traditional ways of joining the System were to join the Council of Europe or the OECD. Both organizations conduct many activities of a technical nature (those of the OECD largely in the economic sphere, those of the Council in virtually every field outside of defense and economics). If, for example, a nonmember of the Council wished to participate in its nature conservation or cultural activities, it could do so without becoming a full member. Spain and Portugal, which until the late seventies were considered unqualified for full membership because of the nondemocratic nature of their regimes, long participated in these kinds of programs. For other reasons, Switzerland began its membership with an "observer" status in the Council and later became a full member. The pattern has been similar for OECD membership. Thus, Finland for many years was an "observer" on certain OECD committees (maritime transport, timber, industry, and machinery among them) and only gradually became a full member. Japan began its association with OECD in 1960 as a member of the Development Assistance Committee and gradually broadened her participation until she was granted full membership in 1964. Australia and New Zealand, a decade later, also began their relationship with OECD in this fashion.

This same mechanism seems a logical way for membership to develop in the extended Atlantic System. Israel has already taken part in some OECD technical activities. If her conflict with the Arab countries were to subside sufficiently, there is every argument in favor of full OECD (and therefore System) membership for Israel. If Finland's delicate relationship with the Soviet Union were to evolve further in the direction of foreign

[51]

policy independence, it is possible that Finland might be able to become a full member of the Council of Europe and thereby increase its participation in the System generally. As Brazil becomes further integrated domestically, both in a political and an economic sense, it may find participation in certain OECD activities essential; eventually, such an association could lead to full membership; Brazil's size and growing weight in world affairs would reinforce such a tendency. And so on.

The pattern of development in other organizations makes dramatic changes in the composition of the emerging community of developed democracies unlikely. The gradual, evolutionary change which has been taking place for three decades is almost certain to continue. It is, of course, possible that certain countries might drop their membership in the evolving community. Were this to happen with one or two of the peripheral members, (such as Turkey or Iceland), the harm to the System would not be irreparable (although in the case of Turkey, it could cause considerable damage to NATO); if, however, it appeared to signal a general exodus, the System would be in trouble. (The questions arising from changes in the membership of the System are ones to which I shall return in Chapter 7.)

FOOTNOTES

1. Of course the sheer number of memberships on the part of one country can be misleading. Even though the United States is formally a member of only three Atlantic IGOs, it has been—and remains—deeply involved in the affairs of some of which it is not a member, notably the EC.

2. By "parawestern," I mean originally nonwestern cultures and civilizations which have imbibed so deeply of western philosophy, technology, and mores—indeed of the entire western way of life—that they now seem to be approaching incorporation in western civilization itself. "Para-" is defined by Webster's *Third New International Dictionary*, p. 1634, as "associated in a subsidiary or accessory capacity" and "closely resembling the true form."

3. The phrase, "the civic culture," is borrowed from Gabriel A. Almond and Sidney Verba, *The Civic Culture: Political Attitudes and Democracy in Five Nations* (Princeton, N.J.: Princeton University Press,

1963), who used it to describe the political culture of democracy, embracing not only formal institutions, but belief systems and codes of personal relations.

4. Article II of the North Atlantic Treaty, for example, would probably never have been included had it not been for the insistence of the Canadians. See N.J. Padelford, "Political Cooperation in NATO," *International Organization* (August 1955), p. 357. In fact, Congressional hearings on the treaty indicate clearly that the Senate Foreign Relations Committee had grave reservations about Article II; it was only accepted after Secretary of State Acheson bent over backwards to convince the committee that it would impose no obligations whatsoever upon the United States, but contained merely "the ethical essence of the treaty." See United States Congress, Senate Foreign Relations Committee, 81st Congress, 1st session on Executive L, *North Atlantic Treaty* (Washington, D.C., 1949), Part I, pp. 32–33, 269–271.

5. Ernst B. Haas, "International Integration: the European and the Universal Process," in B. Landheer (ed.), *Limits and Problems of European Integration* (The Hague: Martinus Nijhoff, 1963), p. 14. For authoritative assessments of the state of the civic culture worldwide, the reader is referred to the yearbook *Freedom in the World,* published annually since 1978 by Freedom House of New York.

6. Karl W. Deutsch, R.W. Van Wagenen, et al., *Political Community and the North Atlantic Area* (Princeton, N.J.: Princeton University Press, 1957), p. 50. This pioneer work is highly relevant to any consideration of the problems of international integration among states. See also my definition of integration, Appendix A.

7. W. Andrew Axline observes: "The authority of a European supranational institution is effective authority only because the subjects are members of advanced integrated societies and can transfer their habitual obedience to laws emanating from national authority to the new authority." See *European Community Law and Organizational Development* (Dobbs Ferry, N.Y.: Oceana Publications, Inc., 1968), p. 9.

8. R. Cooper, K. Kaiser, and M. Kosaka make a good case that "cooperation in a functioning world order presupposes national structures of decision-making capable of assembling information and implementing agreed decisions. Many states lack this requisite political and administrative infrastructure for cooperation." See *Towards a Renovated International System*, The Triangle Papers: 14 (New York: Trilateral Commission, 1977), p. 13.

9. ANZUS is a treaty binding Australia, New Zealand, and the United States for mutual defense. (See Appendix D.)

10. Karl Deutsch has developed an interesting concept, the "security

community," to describe "no-war" relationships between two or more powers. See his article in James N. Rosenau (ed.), *International Politics and Foreign Policy* (Glencoe, Ill.: Free Press, 1961), pp. 98–105.

11. The late Hans Kohn, in discussing this question, pointed out the way in which this "civic culture" boundary of Atlantic civilization had shifted: In 1825, during the Decembrist uprising in Russia, it included that country (and again briefly in 1917). In June 1940, this boundary was on the English Channel.

12. Daniel Bell, *The Coming of Post-Industrial Society; A Venture in Social Forecasting* (New York: Basic Books, 1973).

13. Again, the case of Japan is a separate one. Not having shared in any important respect in the currents of western civilization until the mid-nineteenth century (the sixteenth- and early seventeenth-century contacts with the west having been essentially ephemeral), and having been almost totally shut off from any foreign influences for the preceding 250 years, Japan developed its own unique society. Today, many Japanese social trends are in the direction of modern western development, especially in superficial matters; yet, society there remains considerably different and distinctive in essentials. See Chie Nakane, *Japanese Society* (Berkeley: University of California Press, 1972).

14. See Andreas Rannestad, *NATO and Science* (Brussels: North Atlantic Treaty Organization, 1973); and James R. Huntley, *Man's Environment and the Atlantic Alliance*, 2nd ed. (Brussels: NATO Information Service, 1972).

15. Deutsch, et al., op. cit., pp. 54–55.

16. The activities of both the Atlantic Institute for International Affairs (Paris) and the more recently formed Trilateral Commission (New York) are noteworthy in this respect.

17. Kenneth Clark, *Civilisation: A Personal View* (London: John Murray, 1969), pp. iii, 253.

18. Webster's *Third New International Dictionary* (p. 413) defines "civilization" in part as "beyond the purely animal level."

19. Although Cyprus participates fully in the intergovernmental work of the Council, the Consultative Assembly of the Council will not accept a delegation of Cypriot parliamentarians. By its rules, each parliamentary delegation should represent in miniature the strength of the political parties in its national parliament. The Cypriot delegation should be composed of two Greek Cypriots and one Turkish Cypriot. Since the Cyprus Parliament has not met for some years, it cannot elect a delegation made up in this way, and the Council of Europe's Assembly will not accept an exclusively Greek-Cypriot delegation, when Turks effectively control two-fifths of the country.

CHAPTER 3

The Institutions

This short volume does not attempt a complete portrayal of each of the institutions which tie the advanced democracies together. A number of excellent works deal in critical detail with the European Community or NATO, for example, and a lesser (but nevertheless in most cases adequate) number of books treat the others. (See Bibliography, Appendix E.) The purpose of this work is to examine briefly the records of the important IGOs in order to determine their present strengths and weaknesses, their probable durability, their chief problems, their most significant accomplishments, their important failures, and their present and future places in the larger System.

Six principal institutions of the System are examined in detail in this chapter. They are:

- NATO (the North Atlantic Treaty Organization), the operative arm of the alliance which binds North America to western Europe.
- OECD (the Organization for Economic Cooperation and Development), a 24-nation body for economic, technical, and social interchange and planning.
- EC (the European Communities), the chief instrument for unifying Europe economically and, eventually, politically.
- The Council of Europe, the original vehicle for the intended unification of western Europe, now a protector

of human rights and "knowledge-transfer agent."

- The Nordic Council, an interparliamentary Scandinavian union.
- IEA (International Energy Agency), an offshoot of OECD whose area of responsibility is energy planning and development.

Three other bodies, today of less importance, but still of historical interest, are also treated, but more briefly. These are:

- WEU (Western European Union), a European mutual defense compact.
- Benelux, the three-nation prototype of the Common Market.
- EFTA (the European Free Trade Association), an organization which links non-EC nations in the lowering of trade barriers and which, since 1973, has been de facto a part of the EC trading system.

Subsequent chapters will show how these various institutions relate (or fail to relate) to one another, how they innovate and change, and how the System as a whole works. This chapter discusses the individual bodies as of 1978. The reader may again find it convenient to refer frequently to the charts and text in Appendix B, and to descriptions of each organization in Appendix C.

THE NORTH ATLANTIC TREATY ORGANIZATION

President de Gaulle and his successors attempted to draw a clear distinction between the Atlantic Alliance (commitments of the Treaty of Washington [1949]) and the North Atlantic Treaty Organization (the elaborate structure of political, military and administrative organs set up to give effect to the treaty). The treaty committed members (Article 5) to aid other members if they were attacked. It also bound Alliance members for a period of 20 years, after which any party could opt out after one year's notice (Article 13). Both these provisions differed little, if at all, from classical military alliances of the past. Article 9, however, provided the legal basis for the Alliance's great innovation in international institution building: it established a council (since dubbed "The North Atlantic Council") of the members and granted it power "to set up such subsidiary bodies as may be necessary." This clause is not unique among IGOs, but NATO members have resorted to it extensively to establish an operative, creative political force. The military establishments of the members have been "integrated" to a considerable extent; a far-flung network of radar screens, fuel pipelines, air control systems, airports, and other costly fixed installations (known collectively as "infrastructure") has been set up and jointly paid for; and international committees and working groups in great variety have been created to give the Alliance political and military effect.

This network of institutions, together with the common characteristics shared by its members (see Chapter 2), is precisely what distinguishes NATO commitments from earlier alliances and also what accounts for NATO's surprising durability. Nevertheless, the unfinished state of these institutions devoted to collective security magnifies their political weakness and makes them, and the commitments which underlie them, increasingly vulnerable.

In the three decades since the treaty went into effect and the principal institutions were created, what could be said to be NATO's chief accomplishments?

1. NATO has kept the USSR out of western Europe, which was its prime objective. Not only militarily (and there were some who never believed the Soviet Union intended to march its armies across the Elbe), but more importantly politically, NATO has provided a convincing deterrent to Russian pressures and attempts to extend its influence westward. Although recently the question of whether all of NATO's European members would remain "non-Communist" has become highly topical, it was even more valid and urgent in the Organization's early years.

2. Behind the NATO "shield," the western Europeans

have developed the confidence necessary to permit them to pursue economic expansion and social development. NATO strength established and preserved a diplomatic and political, as well as military balance in Europe without which, for example, the efforts to unite Europe would probably have failed. (In this sense, the "system-icity" of the complex of European, Atlantic, and Atlantic-Pacific organizations can be quite clearly seen: EC and OECD have been greatly dependent on NATO, while NATO probably could not have endured unless OECD and EC had made their contributions to economic development and political stability.)[1]

3. Behind the scenes, the North Atlantic Council, the international NATO Secretariat, and the 15 national delegations in residence at NATO headquarters in Brussels have developed a sophisticated, pervasive, and on the whole unusually effective system of "political consultation" to deal with international problems. NATO itself has little power to act in the field of international politics (although Council resolutions and initiatives by the Secretary General, as in the case of Cyprus, for example, can sometimes make a difference), but it has served extremely well as a clearinghouse. Nations, individually or in small groups, explain to the Council serious foreign policy issues which they face, advise the Council as to their contemplated actions, and often in return receive advice and sometimes various kinds of support. By far the greater part of this activity is undertaken confidentially, out of public view. It is done constantly, however, and for the most part successfully. In the view of many seasoned observers, this is one of NATO's greatest achievements.

4. Beginning in 1967 (with the so-called "Harmel Exercise"), NATO began to undertake the mission which Churchill had foreseen for it: "We arm to parley." Plans were laid for diplomatic initiatives to ameliorate, if not at some point actually end, the Cold War. The allies, in effect, organized a long-term effort in joint diplomacy (some might prefer to say "coordinated" diplomacy), out of which grew the Federal Republic of

Germany's *Ostpolitik,* later the U.S. efforts at détente, and more recently the Helsinki and Belgrade Conferences on Security and Cooperation in Europe (CSCE) and the Vienna talks on Mutual and Balanced Force Reductions. Whether or not these initiatives were timed correctly, mounted with adequate care, or on balance served the cause of peace, only future historians can answer. But at least the effort has been an impressive response to those who earlier accused NATO of an entirely negative aim and stance.

5. Structurally, NATO has developed (often in concert with OEEC in its early years) interesting and effective innovations which have substantially advanced the theory and practice of international organization. The annual review process, "Wise Men" exercises for studying problems and breaking deadlocks, a joint council in continuous session, resident national delegations and an international secretariat, the integrated military headquarters, and the "pilot-country" method of marshalling new knowledge to attack technical problems are a few examples of this ingenuity. Some commentators, in fact, believe that NATO has developed forms of "multibureaucratic decision making" which go far beyond the intergovernmental confines of the treaty (such as the unanimity rule and the claim that sovereignty is maintained). These, noted Kaiser:

> conceal the fact that the national bureaucracies from several countries jointly allocate substantial resources in a process of negotiation and mutual adjustment which is mostly hidden from the public.[2]

6. The Alliance has also shown ingenuity in dealing ad hoc with political problems. In the 1960s, for instance, the question of "whose finger should be kept on the nuclear trigger" threatened to split the Alliance. Eventually, this was resolved, at least for the time being, by working out an institutional means for briefing the principal European allies regularly with regard to U.S. nuclear capabilities and by bringing the allies at least partially

into the U.S. strategic planning process. Ad hoc solutions were similarly found to vexatious problems of financing the stationing of U.S. and British troops on the continent.

7. In nonpolitical but nevertheless important and interesting fields, NATO has organized highly innovative methods for transferring knowledge and experience. In the physical sciences, for example, NATO's "study institutes," fellowships, research grants, and advisory groups for private scientists from both NATO and non-NATO countries have resulted in considerable new stimuli in many branches of the scientific world. NATO's Committee on the Challenges of Modern Society has sponsored similar concentrated transfers of knowledge in the field of environmental management. In both instances, high-pressure methods which had developed out of military practice, coupled with the political importance attached to NATO by its member governments, were instrumental in bringing international cooperation to a surprisingly high pitch of effectiveness.

8. NATO has helped to avert conflict among its members. The multilateral mix of national delegations in residence and the nonpartisan influence of the NATO Secretary General have often proven useful in this regard.

9. A lasting sense of teamwork among military leaders, many of whom have subsequently served in high places, has been fostered by the NATO Defense College and by individual service in the various multinational NATO commands. The efficacy of the College in particular can be shown by the extent to which its French graduates, more than a decade after de Gaulle's withdrawal from the NATO command structure, have continued to cooperate effectively, albeit informally, with their counterparts from other countries in the Alliance.

* * *

The Alliance nevertheless has had some failures and suffers

some weaknesses:

1. The common defense structure, which never was as strong as the generals or some governments would have liked, began in the 1970s to erode perceptibly. Under the pressures of inflation and the weakening of the common perception of danger, it became all too easy for governments, especially the smaller ones, to make economies at NATO's expense. There was some reversal of this trend in the latter part of the decade, but not sufficiently to keep pace with the high rates of expenditure among Warsaw Pact nations.

2. Although ad hoc, temporary solutions were found to the burden-sharing problem, at least insofar as U.S. troops in Europe were concerned, in a broader sense these will certainly not last. Some nations, for example, continue to conscript; others do not. Some pay out 2 or 3 percent of their gross national product annually in defense expenditures; others, up to 6 percent. The situation in 1980 was unsatisfactory, and the future outlook clouded.

3. Nor is the solution developed in the 1960s for letting the Europeans share in U.S. nuclear planning satisfactory for the long run. The nuclear issue will be confronted by Europeans if SALT III talks are mounted. It is also bound to be raised again, for example, when the Europeans seriously confront the implications of their declared aim to create a political union. Can they do so without providing also for the common defense? And can they do that without also developing their own sizeable nuclear arm? This, plus the always present uneasiness of Europeans (and Canadians) at being at the mercy of the United States with respect to the most crucial questions of nuclear war or peace, are virtually certain to threaten NATO's cohesion at some point in the future.

4. Although it is true that the existence of NATO has been

a major factor in preventing armed conflict among its members, there is always the possibility that just such conflict will take place or that the mere prospect of such conflict will force a member to abandon its NATO commitments. The differences between Greece and Turkey over Cyprus and the Icelandic fishing disputes are the two most obvious recent cases.

5. Some Europeans, especially those who also are members of EC, worry because they do not constitute an effective "European identity" inside NATO. Yet, other European countries would obviously prefer the present situation to any visible alternative. The continuing lack of effective unity in Europe is thus also one of NATO's weaknesses.

6. The Alliance in its present form is clearly not a permanent institution in either a political or a legal sense. The French left the NATO military structure in 1966, and the Greeks declared their intention to do so in 1975, leaving their status uncertain. Turkey has threatened a partial withdrawal. It is entirely possible that still other countries, for various reasons, including the possible advent of Communist-dominated governments, will also either opt out of the integrated commands and training structures (which have given the Alliance much of its military credibility, at least insofar as the European contributions are concerned) or leave the Alliance altogether. Article 13 provides a perfectly legal, straightforward means of departure (unlike the EC treaties, which make no provision for de-acession or termination of the compact). The tidiness of the legal arrangements, however, does not mitigate the damage which "opting out," partial or complete, would do to the strategic and political worth of the Alliance.

7. Article 3 of the North Atlantic Treaty limits the geographical scope of the Alliance to the territories or forces of the allies in Europe or North America, or in the North Atlantic Ocean north of the Tropic of Cancer. (Hawaii, incidentally, is interestingly omitted from cov-

erage of the treaty.) This has meant, in practice, that the involvement of U.S. forces in Vietnam, for example, fell outside the treaty commitments. While politically, given the determination of the United States to "do what it had to do" in Vietnam and elsewhere, this limitation of NATO's scope probably kept the Alliance from falling apart at the time, the provision has also had the effect of stimulating a general sense of failure. NATO, or the west more generally, seems unable to cope with any threat other than an immediate one inside Europe. Formally and legally, Soviet and Cuban incursions into Africa are none of NATO's business, even though in 1977 and 1978 steps were taken, under French leadership, to counter rebellions in Zaire.[3] The Middle East most pointedly does not come within the terms of the North Atlantic Treaty. Yet, it is in just that area, where the greatest danger to peace seems to have developed, that the interests of the Allies most glaringly parted company politically in the early seventies. This is primarily a political/psychological problem, but it also has important structural and legal implications for the Alliance.

8. To make the integrated military structure efficient and credible from a defense point of view, as well as financially bearable, the standardization of the arms and equipment of the NATO nations has long been regarded as a compelling necessity. Although some progress in standardization or a lesser, but still important version of it (called "interoperability") has been made, it is disappointingly small. The problem is rooted in nationalism and in the uncertainties surrounding NATO's future. (Why commit oneself to long-term dependence on outside sources of military supply when the Alliance may turn out to have no more than a short-term existence?) The predominance of U.S. manufacturers of aircraft and other military hardware is an especially serious aspect of this problem.

9. NATO, like most of the Atlantic and European institutions, remains remote from the individual taxpayer,

or even from the control or surveillance of his representatives. A parliamentary group called the "North Atlantic Assembly" was organized in 1955 by parliamentarians themselves and has done important work; yet, it is not an official part of the Alliance.[4] Although such bodies are annoying to foreign ministries, from a practical, long-term point of view, NATO is more likely to receive legislative and public support from the various member countries if it also has a parliamentary arm. To some extent, this issue is also bound up with OECD's complete lack of parliamentary activity and with the question of the future of Atlantic and European consultative assemblies in general.[5]

10. There can be no doubt that the removal of NATO forces and commands from France, and France's departure from the integrated structure, have weakened the Alliance's strategic position greatly. Much has been done to compensate (in part) for this deficiency, but the damage cannot be fully repaired without restoring France to full membership and participation in the total NATO complex.

* * *

The twice-weekly *Atlantic News* of Brussels summed up fissiparous tendencies of the members in the Alliance at the end of 1975:

While realising that it is normal that each [member country] pay attention to the specific problems which concern it, one can ask oneself whether the absence of a general attitude regarding the global Alliance situation is due to the fact that the latter offers less and less common political substance, that its cohesion is increasingly undermined by regional or national conflicts and problems and that the common undertaking for which it was created is encountering growing indifference. Although it is true that the governments are increasingly aware of the need to conduct a strong security policy, it must also be noted that only one in two of them has the necessary political support to make a genuine contribution to this policy.[6]

Times have changed since 1949 when the NATO treaty was signed. The perception of an external threat has dimmed, as has the more general social and political consensus within NATO's member countries which must undergird foreign policy. Governments do not generally act today with the same assurance or sense of urgency as they did in the fifties and sixties. Such domestic political uncertainty is bound to affect international institutions, and all the more when the institutions themselves are relatively new and weak to begin with. NATO was never intended to be a supergovernment, nor could it have been endowed with truly strong institutions at the outset. It is rather remarkable, indeed, that it has proven as effective and enduring as it has. There are good reasons for such success as it has enjoyed. The political lessons of two world wars were learned, at least partially. The old enemy, Germany, was made an integral part of the new security system. The United States, which had formerly stood aside in peacetime, this time took the lead. International command and logistical structures, pioneered in both world wars, were elaborated and put on a semipermanent basis. Ingenious new methods of coalition diplomacy produced consensus among governments on a wide variety of important issues. On balance, the achievements have been far more noteworthy than the always conspicuous public failures.

In sum, NATO at the end of the 1970s was a good deal stronger than most of its public critics avowed; yet, the seeds of decay and dissolution seemed ever present. NATO remains fragile and beset by pressures to which it may well succumb unless a new political consensus and improved institutions can be fashioned to produce the necessary reinvigoration and the basis for long-term stability. For several years, NATO has been essentially a West German-U.S. alliance. That kind of arrangement is inherently unstable.

Despite all of its weaknesses, NATO has become the most successful collective defense organization in history. Its inadequacies should not be permitted to overshadow this fact. It has been argued that its actual—as distinguished from its legal—protection extends far beyond the borders of its members and the treaty-protected area. So far, it has seemed to be, from the western point of view at any rate, an indispensable element in preserving a precarious world balance of power. If the NATO alliance had not existed, the United States would almost surely have had a much more difficult time in mobilizing the necessary political and military power to preserve the worldwide balance.

From the point of view of the growing association of developed democracies, it would seem at the very least unwise to allow NATO to disintegrate without trying to determine whether or not it could be recast geographically, given permanence and stronger institutions, and provided with a reformulated role. Until this can be done, NATO will probably remain an unfinished "building block" of the System, with an increasingly finite life span. Until an acceptable universal system can be devised, NATO's greatest challenge is somehow to become collectively what the United States was for the three decades after 1945, the principal trustee of world security.

THE ORGANIZATION FOR ECONOMIC COOPERATION AND DEVELOPMENT (OECD)

The ordinary citizen of one of OECD's member countries has probably never heard of OECD. Buried in the financial pages of his newspaper may occasionally be an article with the headline, "OECD Sees Difficult Economic Outlook for West," but beyond that, OECD is unknown to the public, or at least certainly less known than the Common Market or NATO. Neither OECD nor its predecessor, OEEC (Organization for European Economic Cooperation),[7] has ever enjoyed the straightforward assignment of NATO, to keep the Russians out of Europe, or the glamor of a European Economic Community, billed as Europe's new "supergovernment." Yet, in many ways, of the three, OECD may give the most promise of succeeding.

OECD is not supranational, but relies instead on an expert international staff and national delegations concentrated in one place. It enjoys a far-flung communications and knowledge-gathering capability. Its staff has worked out a well-developed set of techniques for meshing the economic, socioeconomic, and politicoeconomic interests of its members. As a result, OECD accomplishes a good deal more in these fields than the sum of what the individual members could accomplish on their own.

OECD's individual, formal decisions are much less important to its members than the cumulative effect of its continuing process of information sharing and policy formation by osmosis. That is, member countries tend to arrive at the same general policies (not invariably, to be sure, but often) because their own governmental apparatus receives the same information from which to derive decisions. Moreover, the international institution and the domestic apparatus of all of its members are so linked that subtle pressures are inevitable, often pervasive, and on many occasions strong enough to force conformity to a general norm.

One observer, Henry Aubrey, wrote: "The potential of the OECD for joint discussion, and, eventually, for the formulation of specific policies, is unrivalled elsewhere."[8]

OECD is a prime, modern example of the "spin-off" technique. From within the OECD staff, one of the national delegations, or OECD's far-flung coterie of consultants and correspondents, an emerging economic or social problem is first recognized, then defined. Informal discussion in the OECD Paris complex refines the dimensions of the problem. OECD's committees and councils eventually make the decision to set up a special-purpose agency to undertake further study leading to action. In this way, the European Productivity Agency, the European Nuclear Energy Agency, and the OECD Centre for Educational Research and Innovation were set up.[9]

(The Club of Rome and the international environmental movement, to a large extent, were also informal OECD "spin-offs.")

Many OECD agencies operate more or less autonomously, sometimes with membership that is not congruent with that of the parent organization.[10] Thus, OECD has an open-ended and flexible character which most intergovernmental organizations do not possess. Because it is flexible and decentralized, OECD is able to deal with an exceedingly broad range of problems, involving questions related to science policy, education, manpower, social affairs, land-use planning, environment, tourism, transport, industry, energy, demography, trade, fisheries, agriculture and food, the status of women, development aid, productivity, economic policy, international payments and monetary affairs, financial markets, and the gathering of statistics.

OECD serves as an "off-camera" forum where virtually all of the trading, banking, producing, and investing nations of the non-Communist, developed "first world" can discuss their own economic interests, as well as their economic relations with countries outside of the organization. It is most particularly a place where the EC's measures to fashion closer forms of economic unity among its nine members can be reconciled with those of the other 15 OECD members. It also provides a framework for considering how best the industrialized democracies can aid and come to terms with both the oil-rich and the very poor developing countries.[11]

The attitude of OECD is not simply the sum of each member's conception of its national interests; in a very real sense, it has been from the first international in character. In the early years, it was "European," then "Atlantic"; now, it is increasingly "Atlantic-Pacific" and even worldwide.[12]

These characteristics constitute the chief strengths of OECD. But there are also weaknesses.

1. The public hardly knows about OECD; those who do most probably do not adequately understand its work or significance. OECD is technical, abstruse, opaque, remote, and as multifaceted as the compound eye of a housefly. The international secretariat publicizes its activities conscientiously, but the member governments do relatively little to help. This means that beyond government or scientific circles, OECD has few if any special-interest constituencies and virtually no general public support on which to rely.

2. In particular, OECD has no parliamentary sounding board, as do the Council of Europe, the European Communities, WEU, NATO (although in this case of

an informal sort), and even Benelux. It has nevertheless developed and maintained useful links with the Consultative Assembly of the Council of Europe, and its problems and policies are often discussed by the North Atlantic Assembly (NATO's unofficial parliament). But OECD itself has no direct line to influential parliamentarians; both they and OECD are intellectually the poorer for this, and OECD is correspondingly less strong politically.

3. OECD has been rightly criticized for "lack of cohesion." To some extent, this is a problem shared with many IGOs and is bound to be especially acute in the case of a body such as OECD, which must deal with a very wide range of phenomena and activities. As a result, control and surveillance suffer. Yet, as Aubrey pointed out, this may not be only a problem of organization or leadership within the secretariat, but still more: "it may reflect division within the national administrations of the member countries."[13] This is true of the United States more than of any other member. In the United States, the Treasury; the President's Council of Economic Advisers; the Federal Reserve Board; the Departments of State, Commerce, and Agriculture; and others, most importantly in some cases the Congress, must often reconcile divergent views and domestic pressures in order to reach agreement on some significant international economic matter—all of this before the whole government can adopt a single position and represent it abroad. Sometimes, to OECD's detriment, this proves impossible.

4. OECD's lack of supranationality, with decision-making powers which are feeble and in any case usually thrust into the background, also represents a weakness in the view of many. One might respond: "It was never *meant* to do that." But when one looks at the magnitude, complexity, and interrelatedness of the economies of the advanced democracies, it is evident that the situation cries out for stronger joint decision-making capa-

bilities, as well as more cohesion of purpose and vigorous leadership.

5. Some good features of the old OEEC were abandoned when it was reorganized into OECD. It may not be too late to retrieve these; yet the possibility should still be considered. For example, the European Productivity Agency was dismantled, although productivity in many OECD countries is today an even greater problem than it was in the fifties. In another case, the framers of OECD were fearful that if the OEEC Trade Liberalization Code was carried over into the successor organization, the U.S. Senate might not ratify the treaty for fear that its powers over trade would be abridged. With hindsight, eliminating the Trade Liberalization Code now seems particularly unfortunate, as nontariff barriers to trade in particular bedevil the developed world increasingly. In general, OEEC embodied more rules and obligations to which each member was bound; these too have been greatly attenuated under OECD. One could do worse than consider what more might still be learned and incorporated from OEEC experience.[14]

OECD's basic problem is not just one of administrative efficiency (hard to achieve when the scope of work is so vast, the problems so interconnected, and the national actors from such varying cultures and backgrounds), but also one of political effectiveness. OECD is continuously faced with the twin problems of how best to concentrate the attention of governments and get them to act, and of how to develop within the member states constituencies that will influence public opinion and governments effectively.

OECD'S SIGNIFICANT ACCOMPLISHMENTS

OECD deserved substantial credit for insuring that the deep recession of the mid-seventies did not turn into a severe depression like that of the 1930s. To be sure, other international bodies had important roles, and many individual governments pursued generally wise policies; nonetheless, OECD's role was central. As the watchdog of the core economy of the world, OECD prodded and pushed governments, strove to harmonize their policies and actions, and marshalled the objective facts and statistics which were needed. The OECD network functioned well. While few people have been completely satisfied with the state of economic affairs in the 1970s, the situation would have been profoundly worse without OECD and the other international mechanisms for cooperation.

OECD's efforts since 1960 have undoubtedly resulted in a considerable improvement in the overall quality and quantity of western and Japanese aid to the developing countries. Few in either the first or third worlds are satisfied with the mechanisms for providing aid or with the amount provided, but both of these would surely have been even less acceptable, and by a wide margin, were it not for the gadfly operations of the OECD Development Assistance Committee. The glaring failure of the advanced nations to provide adequate assistance to the third world in the 1970s can be blamed largely on the lagging effort of the United States. Ironically, it was U.S. prodding that led most of the other advanced members of OECD to increase their own aid efforts appreciably after 1960.

Much of the thinking and impulse behind the current effort to curb damage to the world environment and conserve resources originated inside OECD. Consequent policy changes in member governments owe a great deal to OECD in this regard. OECD stimulated not only a general change in economic and social goals, but also the practical study of how to implement them.

OECD provided most of the stimulus for the unprecedented level of growth in the western economy during the 1960s. Although it later became fashionable to deplore high economic growth in the west, critics often forgot that the principal effect of this growth was to improve greatly the living standards of ordinary people in the extended Atlantic System, which contained about one-fifth of the world's population. In many OECD countries, poverty in the traditional sense was virtually eliminated. The social and political implications of this transformation were profound. It should not be surprising, of course, that in the 1970s one of the chief goals of developing countries was to emulate their more active and more fortunate partners in the industrial democracies by striving hard for economic growth.

OECD has been a major factor in pressing Japan to withdraw its excessive restrictions on foreign trade and investment (although the process cannot be considered complete). This in turn made it possible for Japan to join the industrial west, gave her new markets in Europe, and will probably exert a constructive influence on her political course in the future. This is a classic case of how OECD can work: An increasingly important potential member of the free world economic community is invited to join the organization; she is asked to make certain adjustments at the outset; but these concessions are worthwhile, because she receives clear advantages and benefits; her accession adds to her sense of international responsibility, to the overall strength of the OECD, and ultimately to world prosperity generally.

OECD was especially creative following the perilous world crisis of 1973. A Financial Support Fund of $25 billion was proposed to underwrite member countries which might find themselves in serious financial straits because of rising oil prices. In the face of the most serious economic difficulties since World War II, the OECD countries, by renewing their trade pledge, refrained from putting restrictions on commerce. Thus, they averted the kind of beggar-thy-neighbor policies which tragically deepened and lengthened the Great Depression. The International Energy Agency was created, further buttressing the capability of the extended Atlantic System to deal with any future oil crisis. The acrimonious debate in 1975, between the advanced countries and the developing countries, over the "division" of world assets and resources was shifted from the UN to a new framework in which OECD played a key role and the Soviets, by choice, stayed on the sidelines. In October 1975, OECD announced the creation of the "McCracken Group," an effort of distinguished economists and thinkers to try to find a way to reconcile noninflationary economic growth with high levels of employment.[15] In 1976, OECD (rather painfully) hammered out a Code of Ethics for multinational business which, although not legally enforceable, had some notable impact on the conduct of large corporations.

Finally, OECD has become increasingly important because it is the only body which groups together all the industrial democracies. If an urgent requirement for new mechanisms or action arises, as it did in the oil crisis of 1974, or if an appropriate forum is needed, OECD is not simply the most logical locus, it is the only locus available. More and more, OECD offers itself as an operating mechanism for serving the interests of the advanced nations. These signs of a continuous dynamism, even momentum, in OECD bode well for the future.

DURABILITY OF OECD

Whereas bodies such as WEU or Benelux may today be chiefly of historic interest, OECD is very much alive, with a considerable future—at least potentially—before it. So far, the OECD is the only important IGO in which the political and economic interests of the industrial democracies are dealt with across the board. OECD has confined itself to economic matters in the past, but is more and more being drawn into the political arena, especially since the Middle East War and the oil boycott of 1973. From its beginning as OEEC, the organization has eschewed any connection with the Cold War, out of respect for its several neutral European members. Early suggestions that OEEC or OECD and NATO might somehow be merged into an Atlantic "superbody" have come to naught. With the incorporation of Japan as an OECD member, this sort of geopolitical orientation has become even more unlikely. Nonetheless, world events have forced the OECD nations to come to grips with the political implications of their irreversible economic interdependence.

Perhaps OECD itself needs some reform. If its members were willing, it might be given some capacity for helping to formulate actual joint policies instead of its present role of simply trying to promote parallel action by its members. Perhaps its present scope is too great and ought to be broken down into a series of "ministries," each with a broader and clearer role and more autonomy than some of the special-purpose OECD agencies that exist today. Maybe OECD also needs some kind of political steering body, along the lines of the Rambouillet summit group, to give it more public visibility and more political direction at high level. Finally, OECD could use an effective parliamentary adjunct.

These and other questions for the future all impinge, in turn, on the futures of the other institutional "building blocks" of the emerging community of developed democracies. In Chapter 7, I shall return to problems of the future. Meanwhile, I feel that it is sufficient to note that OECD today constitutes one of the strongest, most versatile, and most potentially adaptable of all the building blocks of the System.

THE EUROPEAN COMMUNITIES: INSTRUMENT FOR POLITICAL AND ECONOMIC UNIFICATION

The European Communities (EC) consist of three separate, economically oriented organizations which, for all practical purposes, have been merged into one. The European Coal and Steel Community was established in 1952, to provide a far-reaching supranational regime for the coal and ferrous industries of France, Germany, Italy, and the three Benelux countries. The European Economic Community was set up to govern the formation, first, of a customs union and then of a full economic union. EURATOM (the European Atomic Energy Community) was established in 1958, as Europe's counterpart to the U.S. Atomic Energy Commission.

The European Communities were ultimately intended to bring about the political union of Europe. EC has an independent executive body (the Commission), a European Parliament, and a separate judiciary. Whereas all of the other postwar western IGOs have represented simply an elaboration—often ingenious and far-reaching in implication, to be sure—of earlier, cruder models of international organization, the supranational European Communities are truly something different.

Says Miriam Camps, a long-time student of the EC:

The Community is today a mixed system, a construction which is *sui generis*, which cannot be equated with either a

[74]

federal state or an international organization in the conventional sense, although it has some of the attributes of each.[16]

Belgian Prime Minister Léo Tindemans called the EC "a completely new way of international life."[17] It is entirely possible that future historians will conclude that the EC is one of the most important—if not *the* most important—political invention of western man in this century, an innovation to rival that of the nation state.[18] Since the launching of the plans for the first Community (Coal and Steel) in 1950, the community process has been buoyed by powerful European hopes—aspirations that in an earlier day might have been considered foolish. It is a tribute to the framers of the ECSC, and of the later Rome treaties, that a considerable portion of these hopes has since been realized. But it is also true that Europe is not yet unified politically, or even wholly unified economically, and that the process is now beset increasingly by doubts and frustrations. The following observation sums up a common negative view:

> . . . many observers . . . characterize the Community, often with ambivalent feelings, as an evolving technocracy, one whose basic pattern of influence is centered on a hard core of technocrats. . . .[19]

There was, especially during the EC's first decade, a good deal of truth to this charge. British reservations about entry into the Community, to a considerable extent, were based on it. In the seventies, however, the member governments have tended to "take charge." This perhaps has lessened the power of the "faceless Eurocrats" in Brussels, but it also has diminished the supranational potential of the Community. France and Britain—first from outside, and then as members—have both with depressing regularity sabotaged the spirit and the substance of EC's intent. However, the Community, as we shall see, is far from dead and is far from being simply the creature of the governments.

* * *

What has EC achieved, in the quarter century since the Schuman Plan (ECSC) was launched, and less than two decades after the Treaty of Rome?

Even more rapidly than envisaged by the treaties, common markets, first for coal and steel, then for all products (including agricultural) were established. Tariffs and other barriers to trade among members were removed, and a common external tariff was instituted in their place. This alone—the EC's first objective—was enough to mark it off from the majority of past efforts, usually unsuccessful, to create customs unions. In addition, laws of the member countries governing economic and social matters have been harmonized, in fact more so than the treaties had envisaged.[20] There has been a widespread "multinational intermeshing of the political process" among EC members, to such an extent (says Karl Kaiser), that

> Today about two-thirds of all questions of agricultural policy facing the West German Ministry of Agriculture can no longer be made in a purely national context but rather must be made within the decisionmaking structures of the agricultural system of the European Community.[21]

Workers and some professionals move about freely from one member country to another, as does capital.

A strong European Court has taken full advantage of the broad powers given to it under the treaties to make rulings which can be binding on all EC organs, on national governments, and on individuals and business firms. Governments have been forced to change laws and regulations. Without national legislative enactments, both the Court and the Commission of the EC have created much new "community law." The Court's role in fact has been so extensive that some commentators have complained of "government by judges."[22]

The budgetary powers of the European Parliament have been increased modestly. It has used its authority to compel the Commission to answer its questions (but not its bludgeon-like power to vote the Commission out of office). However, in 1975, the EC Council of Ministers finally agreed that members of the parliament would be directly elected by their peoples, beginning in

1978. In 1978, the elections were postponed to 1979. For the first time, the parliament (and EC as a whole) have their own popular base, independent of the member governments. A "Federation of European Liberal Parties," and an "EC Popular Party" [Catholic] were created in anticipation.[23] All-European Socialist and Communist groups were formed as well. Important national political figures, such as Willy Brandt, left their national parliaments and ran for election to the new European legislature.

From the beginning, the ECSC has had its own power to tax iron, coal, and steel enterprises. Recently, the EC also began to generate *its* own financial resources by collecting customs duties. The EC is thus no longer dependent on annual budgets agreed to by the member states.

Not without great travail, to be sure, the EC finally succeeded in enlarging its ranks to include Britain, Ireland, and Denmark; thus, unlike most of the other Atlantic-Pacific institutions, it is not standing still or contracting, but instead continues to expand. (Portugal, Greece, and Spain all applied for membership in the late seventies.)

EC has created a Social Fund and a Regional Fund to help areas in which unemployment is worst. The EC has adopted an "outline energy policy," as well as environmental, transport, and social policies. It has attempted, with some success, to protect the interests of consumers, workers, and the general public. A policy on business competition, buttressed with a series of European Court decisions, has also been successfully instituted, as have provisions for incorporation of business firms as "European companies."

In 1975, the outlines of a "European Community foreign policy" began to appear. At the Helsinki Conference on Security and Cooperation in Europe, in the United Nations, in GATT and IMF meetings, in the Paris meetings between oil consumers and producers, and in meetings on other issues, the nine EC countries managed to adopt a common stand. In addition, an EC policy tying Community aid and future membership for Portugal to the establishment of pluralistic democracy in that country appeared to have a positive, enduring effect.

In its relations with developing countries, the EC has been increasingly generous and successful; first the Yaoundé Convention and later the Lomé Convention extended generalized preferences to the industrial and agricultural goods of 47 countries (as of 1977). Coupled with significant aid provisions, these agreements appear to be the most forthcoming of any arrangements so far profferred by advanced countries to the third world. Such agreements have not found favor with the United States, which looked askance at the "reverse preference" provisions included in earlier "association" agreements. There are other grounds for criticism as well, based on EC quotas on imports of raw materials and the protectiveness of special ties between former colonies and mother countries. Nevertheless, the Lomé Convention surely represents an important advance, perhaps even a model, for wider future arrangements between countries of the first world with those of the third and fourth. The Lomé Convention suggests further, as has much of the work of OECD's Development Assistance Committee, that a joint approach by advanced countries to less-developed nations tends to be *more* liberal, not less so, than bilateral arrangements. Finally, it is especially innovative in that there is a quasiconstitutional structure within which the LDC members have rights of codetermination in various EC development plans.

Measured against the actual accomplishments in the past of nations acting voluntarily together in the fields of peacekeeping, judicial arbitration, economic integration, or international cooperation in general, the attainments of the Communities are significant indeed. The EC's achievements have meant a full economic recovery for Europe from the depths of devastation in 1945; a much better material life for all Europeans; a tremendous increase in trade among the members (sevenfold between 1962 and 1970 alone); two decades of economic and social stability, which—with NATO—provided the security and confidence to begin in earnest the search for détente with the USSR; the creation of dynamic new international models for other regions of the world (there are already two common markets in Latin America); and, finally, a general reconciliation among the proud and contentious nations of western Europe, and most particularly between France and Germany. These are great, historic achievements, even if they do not yet add up to full or irreversible union.

On the other hand, after nearly two decades, the EC still has not managed to achieve the economic or monetary union envisaged by the framers as the objective to be completed after establishment of the customs union. In fact, in April 1975, a special committee headed by Robert Marjolin, former vice president of the Communities and an aide to Jean Monnet, concluded that "discordant and divergent policies" among the nine member nations had made chances for economic and monetary union so dim that "it is not worth attempting now." "As long as the political will is not there, it is useless to plan for EMU," Marjolin was reported as saying; in fact, his report concluded that "there has been backward movement."[24]

EURATOM, the third community created in 1957 alongside ECSC and EEC, was supposed to have put the development of all forms of nuclear energy in EC countries under one authority, just as the AEC had done in the United States. EURATOM has been essentially a failure, principally because France under de Gaulle wished to pursue a strictly nationalistic course in its atomic development.

French nationalism also brought about a number of other setbacks. The voting of the Council of Ministers on certain important kinds of questions had been scheduled, under the Treaty of Rome, to move to decisions by "qualified majority," as contrasted with the rule of unanimity then prevalent in IGOs. When the time came, in 1965, for this "escalation" to take place under the treaty, however, de Gaulle balked; the provision was set on the shelf. It was only in 1974 that the procedure of resolving issues by qualified majority vote was again resurrected and a new start agreed on.

In other matters, the EC has suffered some setbacks as well. The political power of the commission, whose members swore to uphold community law and take no instructions from their respective governments, has lost ground since the "heroic" period of the late fifties and early sixties. A corresponding rise in the power of the Council of Ministers is not the kind of political "strengthening" which the founding fathers envisaged, but it does correlate with the rising nationalism of the seventies.

Among the newer members, there is still an unsettling degree of reserve, of a desire and willingness to "go it alone." Nowhere is this more pronounced than with respect to Britain's new-found oil, which she has pointedly placed out of reach of her partners. Nor has the EC been particularly successful in dealing with "hot" problems on Europe's fringes. Crisis containment in such places as Cyprus and the Middle East has found the members both powerless and lacking in ideas. While the EC has accomplished much that is of historic importance in Europe and worldwide, it still is only half a community. It remains distant from its goal of political union (and even from its objective of full economic union), still riven by nationalistic pressures and old rivalries which slow its pace markedly.

* * *

The European Communities represent perhaps the archetypal postwar IGO. What have been the Communities' principal strengths and weaknesses?

Strengths:

1. The treaties of Paris and Rome have proven their resilience and flexibility. In a few limited, but important cases, they have shown the "supranational expandability" for which they were written. The treaties indeed are a kind of "escalator," making possible a gradual transition from the mere cooperation expected of a standard IGO to the fusion of interests and powers and processes characteristic of a federation. While actual supranationalism is manifestly hard to attain, the treaties grant "real but limited powers" to make progress possible where there is a political will to do so. The institutional framework so far has not been found wanting.

2. The treaties have no ter.ninal date. In other words, members do not have the legal option, as in NATO, to drop out of the European Communities, although practically such a step was at least contemplated in Britain after Labour's return to power in 1973. Psychologically, this

provides an important inducement for nations to resolve their problems of growth and change.

3. The aim of achieving political union through the European Communities has brought with it great popular support. That is, the man in the street has watched his prosperity rise, and he has associated this factor with the efforts of the member nations to create a Common Market. As a result, a "community mentality" has grown up around the EC.

4. The members and organs of the European Communities have shown a surprising political inventiveness. Time after time, just after the EC has been pronounced virtually "dead" by a public figure or by the media, some part of EC has jumped back with new political impulses. For example, after the oil crisis in 1973 and the mounting recession of 1974, when it seemed that not just the EC, but the whole advanced world would relapse into a downward spiral of *sauve qui peut*, the entire EC sprang forward with new energy to show their determination to act as a community. Led by Giscard d'Estaing and Helmut Schmidt, they developed a common approach to foreign policy in the Middle East and elsewhere and agreed on direct elections to the European Parliament; a series of informal meetings of heads of government (since institutionalized as the "European Council") that eschewed the pomp of "summits," but appeared to get down to concrete practicalities; and a series of further measures which moved the entire community ahead visibly.

5. The EC can be expanded and thus made more influential in the world. Although Britain and two other new members were brought in with difficulty, nevertheless, they did enter the EC in 1973, and the new Community of Nine has gradually been consolidated. The entry into the community of such less-developed (politically as well as economically) countries as Portugal, Greece, Turkey, or Spain will be even more difficult, but the task does not appear impossible. This "expandability"

is a great asset, not just to the EC, but to Europe as a whole, and to the expanding Atlantic System as well. Where traditional diplomacy and coalition efforts (as in NATO) may be stymied in damping down conflicts (e.g., Greece-Turkey) or in bringing about essential internal change (Portugal), the EC may offer an alternative way—supranationalism—to deal with the same matters.

Weaknesses:
1. National bureaucracies and political elites still resist ceding power to Brussels.
2. There is still no central means of enforcing decisions made by members of the European Communities. Instead, each member must depend upon its own legal systems for enforcement within its own borders. Perhaps in the future, a member can be made to comply if the other members make a concerted retaliation against that nation. This is potentially at hand.
3. Cultural and national differences still seem to impede unity. The Brussels Eurocracy, until 1973, deferred to the French in most instances when organizational and procedural decisions had to be taken. The Germans acquiesced to this for years, but may no longer be willing to do so. More recently, the British have tried to sieze the leadership of Europe's "bureaucratic culture" from France. The giants of European industry have by and large remained national in terms of production operations and mergers.[25] U.S. firms, in contrast, have taken advantage of transnational opportunities.
4. Some members of the European Communities, most notably Italy, possess governments which are becoming increasingly politically ineffectual. They pose a serious threat to the internal cohesion and growth of the EC. In addition, other nations, most notably Germany, are outstripping their partners economically and politically. Others, such as the United Kingdom are growing weaker economically and socially. Britain is also demonstrably

less "community-minded" than most of its partners. Because of its size, its historical importance, and more recently its oil, Britain seems likely to pose a serious problem for a long time to come, slowing down an already labored process of integration. Swift progress toward unity might mitigate the effects of such differences, whereas delay could bring about an overall failure.

5. There is at least one major flaw in EC machinery; the Commission, which was to have become the supranational executive, has instead lost power and authority. Some claim this was due to the 1966 "Luxembourg accord" with de Gaulle, a series of weak Commissioners, or the merger of the executives. Robertson thinks it is due to the terms of the EEC treaty, which he compares with the earlier ECSC treaty:

> it is significant that the name of "the Commission" is more modest than that of "the High Authority." Secondly, in Article 157 of the Rome Treaty . . . the word "supranational" has been deliberately omitted . . . though it is found in Article 9 of the ECSC Treaty, from which the remainder of the text is copied. More important, the High Authority of the ECSC is "responsible for ensuring the achievement of the purposes stated in this treaty in accordance with the terms thereof." . . . The Commission, on the other hand, shares this responsibility with the other institutions of the Community—and, more particularly, with the Council [of Ministers] . . .[26]

Coombes believes the cause must be sought elsewhere:

> the problem lies not in the Commission's lack of formal powers of decision but in the absence of real political leadership at a Community level. Indeed the more formal the powers that are delegated to the Commission, the more vital will become the

need for such leadership and the greater will be the demands upon it, given the need to provide bureaucracy with a mission and purpose.[27]

It is also possible that part of the difficulty traces back to the decision to merge the executives of the three original communities into the new EC Commission. The new Commission was perhaps too large for quick or easy discussion, let alone decision making. Whatever the reasons, it is clear that the Commission has been losing importance in the supranational scheme of things. This loss has considerably weakened the EC overall.

6. The Common Agricultural Policy (CAP) of the European Communities is seen increasingly as a political and economic failure. It was designed to placate rural voters, principally in France and Germany, while theoretically creating a common market in food. However, the cumbersome equalization funds and customs "levies" on imported foodstuffs have caused increasing hardships for consumers and many farmers inside the EC, and have also distorted market mechanisms unreasonably. The levies are also a constant bone of contention with the United States.

7. Perhaps the most serious shortcoming of the European Communities is one over which EC has no control. Since the birth of the idea of a community in 1950, many of the problems with which the EC was to deal— trade, money, economic policy, investment—have burst their European bounds. These problems require, at the very least, an Atlantic-wide context, and probably a context which includes Japan as well.[28] Newer supranational problem areas, such as the environment, food, resources, and energy, do not lend themselves to policymaking or enforcement by the EC acting alone.

FIGURE 2

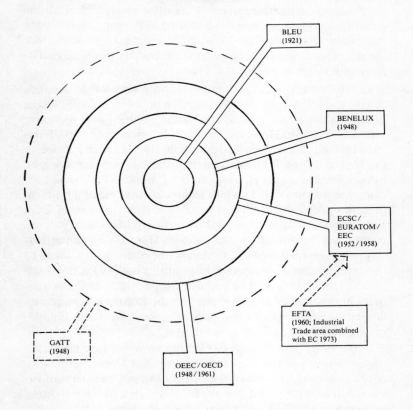

Economic Policy and Trade IGOs

European—Atlantic / Pacific—World

Note: Dates shown are those on which various bodies were established. For details, see Appendices B, C, and (in the cases of BLEU and GATT) D.

On balance, the European Communities have been moderately successful. The EC is clearly still the most promising of all the postwar European-Atlantic institutions. Perhaps, one might more accurately regard the EC as but the pioneering nucleus of a considerably larger (and eventually much more powerful) politicoeconomic grouping.

In the 1960s, it was fashionable on both sides of the Atlantic to talk about "Atlantic Partnership," a union of Europe and the United States which was to follow the political and economic union of Europe. However, no satisfactory description of this "Partnership" was ever set forth publicly, either in Europe or the United States.[29] The partnership may be encouraged again, in part because direct elections to the European Parliament became a reality in 1979. This political reality may mean the advent of true Europe-wide political parties. A strengthening of EC's Parliament could, in turn, lead to further parliamentary development on the Atlantic or Atlantic-Pacific front. The partnership might be furthered as EC aid and membership are linked to the development of democracy in countries such as Portugal and Spain. This effort could be coupled with Council of Europe activity in the field of human rights. As the European community deepens, ethnic antagonisms, such as those in Northern Ireland, in Belgium, and on Cyprus, may diminish.

In the future, the European Communities will face new challenges as they exercise their leadership in the larger community of democracies. (In January 1976, for example, the German Interior Minister proposed that the EC draw up a pact for fighting terrorism as the first step toward a world antiterrorist treaty.[30] In 1978, the big four of the EC and the United States, Canada, and Japan reached a summit agreement that covered the treatment of nations which harbor terrorists and hijackers.) The EC also will need to develop a much more active, responsive, common foreign policy with respect to political events in Asia, Africa, and Latin America. Europe may be faced more and more with the necessity of shouldering the burden of peacekeeping in farway places, with the help of the United States or alone. As Europe's agricultural system continues to modernize and its population stabilizes further, the continent will become more and more able to feed itself and even to export foodstuffs. The present system of agricultural price supports and external duties is not designed, however, to encourage such a role; the Communities will need to place more emphasis on their economic role in light of the potential growth of the agricultural sector.

THE COUNCIL OF EUROPE: COORDINATION, HUMAN RIGHTS, AND THE TRANSFER OF KNOWLEDGE

Both in its makeup and its attempts to achieve things of significance, the Council of Europe reflects all the complexity of modern life and all the frustrations of trying to surmount the obsolescent nation-state system. It was originally set up in 1949 as a diplomatic alliance, but with the broadest political aims, to further the unification of Europe. Although the Council's parliamentary debates, especially in the early years, contributed notably to the unification process (helping to stimulate initiatives such as the Coal and Steel Community), this broad political aim now receives little better than lip service. As the practical political task of "making Europe" moved more and more toward the framework of the EC, the Council tended to concentrate on social, educational, legal, environmental, and other problems which were not being undertaken by the other regional IGOs. Defense had been consigned to NATO and WEU; economic matters rested with the OEEC (later OECD) and the EC; matters of high politics were delegated to any or all of these IGOs; the Council therefore directed its attention to other matters.

The most important of these areas, representing in the opinion of many the outstanding accomplishment of the Council, has been the active protection of human rights. In establishing a Commission and a Court of Human Rights to safeguard civil liberties, in defining those liberties more comprehensively than had been done before, and, particularly, in giving individual citizens in the signatory countries the right to petition supranational bodies directly as individuals, the Council opened up entirely new vistas in international law. Europe, in effect, now has its own "supreme court" in this limited, but critically important field. The results are far from negligible: the Dutch government has been compelled to revise its military discipline rules; Austria has modified its criminal appeal procedures; Belgium has changed its penal code and vagrancy laws; Norway has amended its constitution to guarantee complete religious freedom; and Germany has adopted new legislation regulating detention pending trial. Early in 1976, the European Court of Human Rights overturned a 170-year-old French law which had required that all French babies be named from a government-approved list. In 1978, the court ruled against the old practice of "birching" minor criminals on the Isle of Man.

To be sure, the machinery of the Commision and Court are ponderous. Decisions sometimes take years and there are signs of growing irritation—even exasperation—on the part of governments as the number of cases mount. Yet, it is hard to deny that the aim, the effect, and particularly the potential, are of great significance. Whereas the United Nations can do nothing to give practical effect to the principles set down in its Universal Declaration of Human Rights, the Council of Europe has invented a serviceable instrument for doing just that.[31] The Court is the one truly supranational achievement of the Council.

In other areas, the work of the Council of Europe has not been so impressive. Part of the difficulty in citing achievements lies in their multiplicity and their relative insignificance as individual cases. To badger the national administrations of the 18 member countries to adopt better protective laws regarding the sale of pharmaceutical drugs, to improve social security regulations, or to develop more acceptable leisure programs for youth, or to do more to preserve historic buildings is not the heady stuff of newspaper headlines. Yet, it is the cumulative effect of such areas that has made a truly considerable impact. What are the strengths of the Council's methods, the justification for its continued existence?

First, the Consultative Assembly, over the years, has educated a lot of MPs. Discounting the inevitable criticisms of "junkets" and "talkshop," the Strasbourg assembly can be seen as a valuable instrument for sharing knowledge on various aspects of modern government. Such knowledge transfer between countries has resulted in constructive changes in legislation and governmental procedures.

Second, through other channels—such as studies by experts, conferences of civil servants, or publications of the Secretariat—the Council's headquarters in Strasbourg has disseminated good ideas between governments and also between governments and nongovernmental individuals and institutions.

Third, the Council sometimes has been able to set standards or agree on common action which has moved societies forward. In its early years, for example, the Council was successful in bringing about the elimination of visa requirements throughout western Europe. Sometimes, through gentle pressure, the Council has been able to help a single government ameliorate a difficult domestic situation. There is evidence, for example, that the British government's policies and conduct in attempting to preserve order in Northern Ireland have been influenced in important ways by the recommendations of the Council's Consultative Assembly.[32] A good deal has also been accomplished by harmonizing the national legislation of members in many fields, rather humdrum but, in the aggregate, useful work.

Fourth, by refusing to accept as members any countries which do not have democratic regimes (and, as in the Greek case, by forcing out those which backslide),[33] and by doing something concrete and significant about civil rights, the Council has rendered valuable service to the cause of European—and indeed worldwide—democracy and representative government.

Fifth, although the Council has never been able to develop into an effective political instrument, it nevertheless established its credentials as the forum where "all-European" (or at any rate, all-west-European) opinions could and should be expressed. The OEEC, the OECD, and the European Communities, early recognizing the Council's role in this regard, have regularly submitted reports to its Consultative Assembly. Even the UN's International Labor Organization does so (recognizing implicitly the Council's status as a regional organization under Article 52 of the UN Charter), as do numerous special-purpose European bodies. While such a forum—a "medium of open discussion"—

represents no dramatic new form of supranationalism, neither is its contribution to society negligible in a highly complex world where the right kind of communication between the right people and the right institutions at the right time, can be important. Above all, in its "all-European" role, the Council has symbolic value which cannot be entirely discounted.

One can thus point to a large number of aspects of European life which have probably improved because of the Council's ministrations. It has developed some interesting methods for sharing knowledge and promoting technical cooperation. Yet it remains a weak instrument of international cooperation, in comparison with the European Communities, NATO, or OECD.

Some critics have been harsh. Ernst Haas noted that

> the cultural activities of the Council of Europe lack a focus on intensely experienced wants. Its emergency aid measures have been short-range and its contributions to the solution of political tensions . . . non-repetitive. . . . [The content of the European Conventions only] reflects practices and policies of the member states . . . the Council had to resort to the device of 'partial agreements' to get beyond this level. Conventions which depart from this denominator tend not to be ratified by the country whose standards are below the norms fixed in Strasbourg.[34]

Howard Bliss states: "The Council of Europe provided a forum for expressing the aspirations of the 'European'; it failed to furnish the political means for converting these aspirations into reality."[35] Bliss quotes a British commentator, William Pickles, who labeled the Council of Europe "an immense structure of unrealities" and compared the relationship between its Consultative Assembly and a genuine parliament with an adulterous weekend at Brighton and the institution of marriage: "it offers some of the pleasures but none of the responsibilities."[36]

And yet such criticisms, based on the distance by which the Council of Europe has fallen short of the original dreams for a classic federation of Europe and also perhaps on the biases of political scientists for ideal structures which are "supranational" and entail "giving up sovereignty," at least partially miss the mark. Aside from its Court of Human Rights (which is truly supranational), the Council's value and its accomplishments must be seen as an important, integral part of the social knitting together of western Europe and, on a larger scale, of all the advanced countries. If a chief criterion of power and success in the emerging postindustrial society is indeed to be the acquisition, marshalling, and effective utilization of knowledge, then the Council can lay claim to an important role.

It is true that its budgets are too small for its many tasks, that its Secretariat suffers from overstaffing and the wheel spinning common to many IGOs, that it languishes in the political and geographical backwater of Strasbourg, and that its charter unfortunately denies it either the supranationality of the European Communities or the flexibility of action of NATO or OECD.[37] The Council also suffers from a specific handicap. Although one of its most important roles is the preservation of the west's peculiar civic culture, the Council is not linked directly (out of deference to its neutral members) with NATO, whose function is to defend that culture militarily if necessary. The Council furthermore is controlled by and large by the foreign ministries of its members; this has resulted in an unfortunate and vexing bottleneck. Sharing ideas and "mutual pressuring" could be a very useful tool in all of the important areas of government.

Despite these weaknesses, the Council of Europe obviously has an important role to play in the larger community of industrialized democracies. This role may require expansion of the Council's mandate, to include nonmember countries both within and without the borders of Europe. There are precedents for such an extension: Australia and Canada have sent observers to sessions of the Council's Assembly; in 1951, delegates from the Assembly met with members of the U.S. Congress to discuss common interests.[38]

An important area in which the Council's role could be broadened is in the field of human rights. The idea of "conventions" (agreements by governments to act on their own, but along internationally agreed-upon lines, on a broad range of domestic matters) could be both extended geographically and strengthened so that ratifications would be hastened and progress monitored adequately.

The idea of making the Council the "Trustee of Western Humanism"[39] and, in particular, of its civic tradition has no counterpart elsewhere in the western world. Although the Council's primary function in this arena has been its human rights activities, the declared aim is worth a great deal in an era when the validity of western democracy itself seems questionable to so many. The Council's general aim of promoting social innovation will most certainly be useful in this regard. In the United States, this role has often been exercised by private foundations; in Europe, this has not been the case, except in Great Britain and to a lesser extent in Germany. Therefore, the value of the Council of Europe's "social transfer" activities seems evident. These could perhaps be improved by adapting some of the methods used by the OECD in its socioeconomic activities. Together, the two organizations have been developing valuable methods to move their members forward and upward gradually in terms of human betterment.

THE NORDIC COUNCIL: GENERAL-PURPOSE INTEGRATION IN A HOMOGENEOUS REGION

The cultural and racial homogeneity of the Scandinavian countries is striking and forms a solid backdrop which makes cooperation among them relatively easy, once political aims have been agreed upon. In a wide variety of areas, the five nations (Denmark, Finland, Iceland, Norway, and Sweden) have indeed, since 1952, organized many thoroughgoing joint projects and have agreed on common measures by means of the Nordic Council. Building on the experience gained in the nineteenth and early twentieth centuries from the postal and currency unions between Sweden, Denmark, and Norway, the parliaments and governments of the Scandinavian countries have brought about some notable and highly practical achievements.[40] These were summarized by A.H. Robertson in 1973:

. . . a common labour market [meaning that] a citizen of one Scandinavian country may settle and take up work in another without any special formalities; and he has full social security rights in the country where he is working. Passports are no longer required for Scandinavians travelling in other Nordic countries and customs and currency controls at the frontiers have been abolished. A postal union has been established, which means that internal postal rates apply for correspondence between Scandinavian countries; and telephone and telegraph rates are lower than with the rest of the world. Much has been done to secure uniformity of legislation in both civil and penal law, including a simplified procedure for extradition.[41]

In harmonizing laws and social conditions and in eliminating barriers to free intercourse among peoples, the nations of the Nordic Council have gone much further than any other group of countries in voluntary association. However, their union has never progressed to the level of "high politics" because each country saw its broad security and economic interests somewhat differently from the others. Sweden, for example, has been neutral since 1814 and has sought scrupulously to maintain this position; Norway and Denmark (defenseless and occupied in World War II) decided in 1948 to throw in their lot with continental and U.S. efforts to defend Europe collectively; Iceland gained full independence only in 1944 and was uncertain about what position to take in this regard. For these reasons, the discussions in 1959 to form a Scandinavian Defense Union proved abortive. Similarly, several attempts to bring about a Nordic Common Market have also failed, in view of larger markets promised by EC, EFTA, and (implicitly) OECD. Scandinavian cooperation in the realm of foreign policy (unless confined to less political matters, such as aid to developing countries) has fared no better. Finland's delicate position vis-à-vis the USSR kept her out of the Nordic Council until 1956 and has contributed further to the political weakness of the organization.[42] Like the Council of Europe, the Nordic Council has thus had to content itself with action on a broad range of social, technical, educational, scientific, legal and administrative fronts. Simply because the Scandinavian countries have failed to overcome the issues of national sovereignty and individual commercial interests does not, however, mean that either the quality or the attainments of the Nordic Council can be easily dismissed. It is clear that the possibility of warfare between the five countries is today remote; that cooperation has enhanced the members' standards (already among the highest in the world) of literacy, education, scholarship, penal practices, transport, social welfare, public health, and artistic achievement; and that the frontiers between the Scandinavian countries are virtually nonexistent for the practical, everyday purposes of a large majority of Scandinavians. In an especially significant measure, first implemented in 1976, the Nordic countries agreed to permit immigrants to vote and stand for office in municipal elections, even though they retained citizenship in their countries of origin.

In several ways, the Nordic Council's structure and operation are unique among IGOs. In the first place, the heart of the Council's work lies in interparliamentary cooperation and the harmonizing of national legislation. The original Statute of the Nordic Council (1952), for example, is not a treaty, but rather an identical set of laws which were passed by each of the four original parliaments (and later by the Finnish parliament). Because no international legal obligations were assumed, these individual laws can be amended or repealed unilaterally at any time.

The basis of the Council is mutual trust. Unlike any of the other European IGOs, the Nordic Council seats the governmental representatives and MPs together in its assembly. This practice, suggests Ruth Lawson, "makes possible less tension and more sustained collaboration."[43] The five governments are required (not simply invited, as in most other interparliamentary bodies) to submit reports to the Council about the action which they have taken on its recommendations.[44]

The Nordic Council can be compared in some ways with Benelux, a small group of highly similar neighboring countries with many common interests and historical associations, no great-

'power responsibilities (or pretensions), and a strong inclination towards cooperation. Both groups have worked out pragmatically their own institutions and procedures, which in some ways go further (even if they are less inherently "supranational") than those of the European Communities.

INTERNATIONAL ENERGY AGENCY: SPECIAL-PURPOSE IGO

The most recent agency established under the OEEC and OECD is the International Energy Agency (IEA).[45] IEA was established in November 1974 and thus has had little time to acquire much of a record. The following analysis will therefore concentrate on IEA's chief constitutional features and on the political context within which it will do its work. Because IEA is probably the most dynamic and inherently supranational, as well as the most potentially powerful, of all the IGOs; because not all OECD members are also members of IEA (which implies in itself a certain autonomy); and because in certain crucial respects IEA's powers go far beyond those of OECD (again implying autonomy), I have chosen to show it as a separate body in Chart 6 (Appendix B).

In February 1974, at the request of the United States, most of the OECD countries met in Washington, D.C. to consider some kind of common action in response to the 1973 OPEC oil boycott. Secretary of State Henry Kissinger urged a unified, effective program; France's Foreign Minister, Michel Jobert, just as resolutely opposed any joint measures which might antagonize the oil-producing countries. The conference ended in public bitterness and apparent stalemate, although important basic principles had been established by the majority present. (It was made clear, for example, that France would not be permitted to thwart the will of all the others.)

As a result of months of intense, behind-the-scenes diplomacy; changes in French policy, due in part to the death of Premier Pompidou; and clarification of the world energy situation, it became possible to create a new agency. IEA came into being with

16 initial members. New Zealand, Greece, and Norway joined subsequently, the latter with a "special relationship"; Australia joined in 1979. France did not join the newly created IEA, nor did she block it; France was able to prevent EC membership in the IEA. In practice, however, France has since followed energy policies which are parallel to those of IEA.

Hearings were held before U.S. congressional committees in March 1975 to examine the new agreement. The broad aims of the IEA were described by Assistant Secretary of State Thomas O. Enders. "First, we must find a way to reduce our dependence on imported oil and second we must find a way to acquire the market power necessary to get the price of oil down," under the threat of the OPEC cartel.[46] He told the Congressmen that the United States was compelled to act with the other IEA countries because "unless other countries join us in an effort to change the market balance, then it will be impossible to obtain the better balance of demand and supply that is required to get prices down." He cited further the need for "a balance of advantage and burden among the consuming countries," and finally he described IEA as a "deterrent"—a warning that "an embargo on any one consuming country . . . would be an embargo on all the consuming countries."[47] (This, incidentally, paraphrases Article 5 of the NATO Treaty and the "action clauses" of WEU and other mutual defense arguments within the extended Atlantic System.)

As described by Mr. Enders, the IEA program of action would reduce the demand for oil by establishing agreed-upon conservation measures, coordinate research and development programs for alternative sources of supply, and formulate an agreement that "no country among the consumers would permit oil imported from the OPEC countries to compete with the development of [conventional] domestic energy sources in a destructive manner."[48] In the same hearings, Melvin Conant of the Federal Energy Administration told the Congressmen that "this is the first agreement in peacetime that the United States has entered into with regard to emergency supply."

The IEA's ability to invade the sovereignty of its members is rare in international law. In the event, for example, that the

Governing Board of IEA decides that an oil emergency exists, members are bound to institute previously agreed-upon "emergency reserve commitments" and a system of international allocation (which binds oil companies in the member countries as well). The provisions for this kind of decision (and many others) call for a majority, not unanimity, vote. "Majority," as defined in the IEA Agreement, means 60 percent of the votes of all the members and 50 percent of the votes cast. For some decisions, a "special majority," taking into account the levels of oil consumption of each member, is required.[49] The essential point is this: the member countries have committed themselves in advance to abide by the decision of a majority of all the members, even if, in some cases, they find themselves voting in the minority. Among the IGOs examined in this book, only the European Communities, the Court of Human Rights of the Council of Europe, and (in very special and very limited cases) WEU and EFTA have such powers. It may be the first time that the United States has ever so bound itself internationally. Only an unprecedented situation, as the first successful institution in peacetime of a major resource boycott, could have induced the United States and other industrial countries to adopt such far-reaching measures.

The creation of IEA is also significant in that it appears to signal a reversal of the trend by the western countries not to create new IGOs or to deny any of them real powers. IEA does have the power to induce its member nations to meet international crises through common action.

During its short life thus far, IEA has figured in the news occasionally. Perhaps the most dramatic occasion was the publication of a review of energy conservation measures undertaken by its members. One report of the review in the U.S. press stated that IEA "gave America the poorest rating among 17 of the West's leading industrialized states," and that it was IEA's opinion that "the current American program depends almost entirely on voluntary programs, research and development and public education."[50] The IEA did, in fact, praise some countries and criticize others (including the United States), noting that "not all programmes are of equal impact and countries are not yet sharing the conservation responsibilities equitably." IEA also announced that it had drawn up its own "indicative list of energy conservation measures, each of which has been implemented in one or more countries," and passed these on to all members.[51]

During the same period in which IEA was created and began to operate, EC was also searching for its own ways and means to deal with the energy situation. France, which had long held out on a proposed EC emergency oil-sharing scheme, and Britain, which attempted to reserve its large North Sea oil reserves for itself, blocked EC success on this issue in 1975. The IEA thus appeared to be a more effective mechanism for dealing with the energy crisis than the EC. IEA did not have to involve France in its decision making, and it also had the support of the United States and Canada, the largest energy producers in the Atlantic world but not members of the EC.[52]

Some critics worried that creating still another special interest group formed of "first world" countries, this time to balance OPEC, was not an answer to the world's energy problems. But IEA officials suggested that the agency's work, which took "a global view of energy problems because that is the way energy problems are," could in the end be helpful to developing countries too. J. Wallace Hopkins, IEA's Deputy Executive Director, was quoted as saying: "The basic principle which we think is inescapable is the alleviation of energy problems, or betterment, if you will, of the energy supply/demand balance *anywhere*."[53] Later justification of this philosophy came when IEA was nominated to service the Permanent Commission on Energy which the conference of producers and consumers from the third world created in Paris in December 1975.[54]

* * *

This completes our survey of the six principal IGOs of the extended Atlantic System. Because of their historical importance, three additional IGOs of the Atlantic System, WEU, Benelux, and EFTA, are described briefly below. Seen from the perspective of sheer logic, none of the three seems any longer essential, as the purposes each was set up to serve are either no longer important or the functions are now more successfully performed elsewhere. But something, nevertheless, remains to be learned from each of the three, a lesson or two which might be applied to the strengthening of existing IGOs or to the creation of new organizations in the future.

WESTERN EUROPEAN UNION

The Western European Union (WEU) was preceded by the Treaty of Dunkirk (1947) and the Brussels treaty (1948). WEU was clearly the first organization established to administer Atlantic and Pacific collective defense systems. The Brussels treaty was signed to supplant the Treaty of Dunkirk. It was then substantially modified in 1954 and given the new title of *Western European Union*. Under all of these titles, the pact bound first two, then five, and finally seven key European powers and served as a model for the North Atlantic Treaty, SEATO, and the 1960 Treaty of Mutual Cooperation and Security between the United States and Japan. In substantive terms, WEU had ambitious aims from the beginning. It has covered not only various aspects of military cooperation (including arms control), but also cultural, social, economic, and political matters.

The Brussels Treaty of 1948 assigned the members the task of encouraging the progressive unification of Europe. In the years which followed, foreign ministers, MPs, and civil servants of the seven member nations have met often to try to harmonize positions on various common "European" matters, including items coming up on the agenda of the UN and its affiliates. WEU has been the scene of numerous debates on "how to unify Europe." WEU's proponents can cite numerous instances in which the organization's political good offices were helpful in resolving European problems. For example, WEU offered both a public and a private forum for discussion of Britain's entry into the EC, even when official EC negotiations seemed totally bogged down. WEU also offered a way out when the ill-fated European Defense Community was abandoned by the French in 1954; by recasting the Brussels treaty, the West Germans were given their sovereignty, rearmed within NATO (strengthening that body considerably), and set on a broad path of reconciliation with France. Similarly, the long-disputed Saar territory was an extremely delicate bone of Franco-German contention; WEU played a major role in resolving that matter peacefully. WEU was also the vehicle whereby the British made an historically notable, long-term security commitment to the continent.[55]

There is no denying, however, that the concluding quarter of the twentieth century finds WEU primarily an institution without important tasks. Most of its original goals have been accomplished. Others have been assigned to other bodies; some have become obsolete. Apart from contributing to French psychological feelings of security in the 1950s (and this contribution no doubt was of substantial importance), virtually the only positive WEU accomplishment that can be cited in the field of arms control was its practical technical experience in the area of verified arms surveillance systems. Only the future can tell if this accomplishment can be considered to have been of value.

So long as France remains a member of the Atlantic Alliance, but outside the NATO integrated military structure,[56] WEU probably has a moderately important but distinctly limited role to perform as the main arena for European-level parliamentary and intergovernmental discussions on the defense of Europe.[57] The European Communities have so far shied away from dealing purely or mainly with defense matters (although the parliamentary body of the EC began to touch on defense in the late seventies); these were in any case not included in the terms of the EC treaties. To move from economic to political union, in the minds of not a few observers, will require that EC one day establish a defense union as well. When and if that time arrives, much of WEU's staff, procedures, and traditions could presumably be incorporated into the EC. In 1975, parliamentary resolutions were presented in both the WEU and EC assemblies to this purpose.

Within NATO, there is a so-called "Eurogroup," made up of ten countries[58] which have concerned themselves especially with the need to standardize further NATO armament on a European scale. In the fall of 1975, pressed by budgetary stringencies and the recession, the group members began to talk seriously with the French about creating some sort of "neutral" forum in which joint arms production, accelerated standardization, and "weapons interoperability" could be advanced. The first meetings of the Eurogroup with France were held in February 1976, and a "European Programme Group," with no formal ties to NATO, was subsequently formed. With the institutions and mission of EC itself far from clear or fixed, the eventual outcome of such attempts at rationalization are difficult to foresee.

Some conclusions may be drawn about WEU's record, its strengths and weaknesses, and its possible future role.

1. WEU's chief weakness, aside from having outlived its original mission and having found no new one, is its lack of supranationalism. WEU is in no way independent of its member states; it is bound in its decisions by the "unanimity rule"; and it has no lawmaking functions or sovereign powers of its own. The single (and yet very important) exception is Article 6 Protocol No. II to the treaty, which commits the United Kingdom to maintain a specified level of forces on the continent for the common defense, so long as a majority of WEU members wish it. (From a legal point of view, Protocol III is equally "supranational" in character, as it imposes firm control over German armaments by all the other members; this provision, however, is today of minimal political importance.)

2. The conditions of the Brussels treaty under which the defense clauses of the treaty would become operational are notably stronger provisions than those of the North Atlantic Treaty. The Brussels treaty (Article 5) says: "If any of the . . . Parties should be the object of an armed attack in Europe, the other . . . Parties will . . . afford the Party so attacked all the military and other aid and assistance in their power." While Article 5 of the North Atlantic Treaty states that "the Parties agree that an

armed attack against one or more of them . . . shall be considered an attack against them all," it only binds the members "to assist the Party or Parties so attacked by taking forthwith, individually and in concert with the other Parties, such action as it deems necessary to restore and maintain international peace and security."[59] If WEU were abandoned because of its increasing obsolescence, this important advantage might be lost. However, if the essential provisions of the Brussels treaty, including this one, could be extended to still other countries by incorporating them in some wider scheme for European union, the disadvantages could be outweighed by the gain.

3. Article 8 (3) of the Brussels treaty is equally noteworthy. Whereas there are geographical limitations on the scope of the NATO treaty, the Brussels pact provides that "At the request of any of the . . . Parties the Council shall be immediately convened in order to permit them to consult with regard to any situation which may constitute a threat to peace, in whatever area this threat should arise, or a danger to economic stability." Although this provision has not been greatly used, it again represents a distinct improvement over the machinery of other alliances, past or present. If a "European" foreign policy were to develop sufficiently, it is conceivable that threats to Europe in, say, the Middle East or Africa, might be considered actionable.

These unique legal features aside, WEU no longer appears to have a significant mission. Although the treaty provisions, for important political and legal reasons, cannot be simply discarded, the council, the assembly, and the secretariat (which together cost some $3,000,000 per annum to maintain) are clearly anachronisms. Now and then the council or the assembly can provide the locus for an important debate, when some other forum is not available, as was the case in the 1960s, when WEU was used to discuss the means by which a European nuclear force might be created. Today, however, WEU must simply be considered as one of the historical "building blocks" of a European-Atlantic System.

BENELUX

The initial steps toward the postwar economic unification of Europe were taken in London in 1944, when the governments in exile of the Netherlands, Belgium, and Luxembourg signed the first of approximately 30 different agreements effectuating the Benelux Economic Union.[60] Minor changes and improvements continue to be made in the organization and practices of the union. In 1969, the three member governments broadened their areas of cooperation into foreign policy, science, education, and the administration of justice. In 1970, they discontinued frontier controls among them (a step which the larger European Communities have yet to take).

During the ten years prior to 1958, when customs duties were abolished and the Benelux partners adopted a common external tariff, trade among the three countries almost tripled in value. It is impossible to say to what extent this increase was attributable to Benelux, to wise and active policies of the three governments, or to generally expanding world economic conditions; yet, it represents a growth of commerce which clearly anticipated a later development among other groupings of western countries. Benelux created the first completely free international labor market; free movement of capital and services was also established. Postal and transport rates were standardized; welfare laws were coordinated well in advance of similar EC measures.

Many of the features of the Benelux Union, including the Economic and Social Advisory Council, which links private interest groups with the international secretariat; the Benelux Consultative Interparliamentary Council; and the quasi-judicial organs, were incorporated into the later EC treaties. Benelux was a solid core around which the EC could develop, just as the EC in turn formed a tight nucleus for the EC-EFTA trade group and the even larger, looser grouping of the 24 OECD powers.[61]

Like the EC treaties, the Benelux treaty did not lead to appreciably closer political ties among the participants. The assumptions of the neofunctionalists, such as Haas and Monnet, that economic and other forms of technical cooperation would almost automatically lead to political integration, have so far not been proven in Benelux. National habits of mind, traditions, cultures, and institutions remain too diverse, even within these historically close and socially very similar countries. Nor are the penalities of a failure to complete the union sufficiently obvious to the parties.

The chief failure of Benelux has been its inability to institute a completely free market for agricultural products among its members. In this particular area, the European Economic Community has been more successful.

Benelux, like WEU, has a certain historical importance; also like WEU, it does not seem inclined to "wither away." The three states which comprise it must believe that its activities are still useful to them; in fact, the Benelux functions are probably now so tightly woven into the economic fabric of the member states that to dismantle them would be extraordinarily disruptive. Whether or not Benelux will strike out again, to pioneer significantly for the EC (or perhaps for OECD), is impossible to predict. Meanwhile, its contemporary influence outside the Union is minor indeed, and its practical importance seems destined to diminish still further.

THE EUROPEAN FREE TRADE ASSOCIATION (EFTA)

Of the nine principal IGOs in the extended Atlantic System, EFTA is today the least active, the one with the least perceptible future. Once Britain, Denmark, and Ireland were admitted to the Common Market on January 1, 1973, and a generous free trade agreement linking the EFTA countries with EC was concluded, there was little more for EFTA to do.

Those familiar with the period from 1957 to 1959 in European affairs will find it somewhat ironic that the EC finally did in 1973 what Britain had asked it to do 15 years earlier. The EC created a looser free trade area surrounding the Common Market, under the terms of the General Agreement on Tariffs and Trade. With some reason, the British had feared that, with the advent of a tight, protective Common Market, western Europe would be divided into two economic camps. The members of the Common Market felt that exactly this threat of division would in time force the "outsiders," or at any rate most of them, to seek admittance to the new "club." Both were correct.

Britain, because of her size and power, first temporized and then in excruciating, on-off fashion sought entry to EC for more than ten years before she was admitted in 1973. By the early 1970s, the Common Market had become more or less consolidated, with free trade established internally among the six nations and common tariff barriers to the outside. With the inclusion of the United Kingdom in 1973, the EC was strong enough to make a free trade deal with EFTA members which were not part of the Common Market, Finland, Switzerland, Austria, Sweden, Norway, Iceland, and Portugal. These seven thus virtually became members without a vote of the Common Market. They were accorded all the trade privileges of the nine Common Market nations. In practical terms, however, they would also be required to go along with the provisions of the unified European economy which the nine other nations were in the process of creating. In this case, the "political steamroller" effect, which the framers of the EC had believed the Treaties of Paris and Rome would exert, was working.

EFTA also had worked. Its aims had been to remove all barriers to industrial trade among its members and to strengthen the bargaining power of its members vis-à-vis the Communities. The "free trade area," rather than the "common market" mode (defined by the 1947 General Agreement on Tariffs and Trade [GATT]) was chosen because the EFTA countries each wished to retain its own trade barriers against non-EFTA nations. This involved a complicated system of certifying the national origins of goods traded in EFTA, which skeptics had predicted would never work, but which did prove effective.

With its limited aims, which included no mention of "European unity," EFTA indeed worked so well that all customs barriers among its members were dismantled three years ahead of schedule, on January 1, 1967. And, although agricultural trade had not been covered by the agreement (given the highly disparate farming economies of members), considerable progress was ultimately made in bringing down barriers against trade in this area too, and in such a way that it helped the less- advanced regions of EFTA. Once tariffs were abolished, EFTA paid increasing attention to the other, more difficult obstacles to trade, such as import quotas and terms of competition. In these areas, too, EFTA worked with dispatch and a minimum of constitutional encumberments and regulations. In fact, from an administrative point of view, EFTA was the very model of a streamlined IGO. The international secretariat never numbered more than 100; the EFTA Convention covered a spare 20 pages (whereas the ECSC treaty is 222 pages in length, and that of EEC, 378 pages). Obviously, EFTA was not designed to do all the things that EC would attempt; yet, in retrospect, its founders and movers deserve admiration for the grace, spareness, and efficiency of their effort.

The student of international relations can draw certain useful lessons from the history of EFTA. EFTA proved that free trade was possible among nations. It also showed that a full common market was not necessary to deal successfully with the often intractable nontariff barriers to trade.

Some of EPTA's "constitutional powers" are of interest as well. EFTA has demonstrated that certain decisions can be arrived at by majority vote, Thus, EFTA embodied a slight element of supranationality. These decisions dealt with the implementation of matters already agreed on in substance by the EFTA Council, to be sure; the effect of the "power" was nonetheless to speed business considerably. The Council of EFTA also has powers of a quasi-judicial character. Thus, under Article 31 of the convention, if one member state considered that another had violated or might violate the convention to its detriment, it could lay the dispute before the Council. After examination by a special committee, the Council could then grant legal redress to the member.[62]

There is little likelihood that EFTA will be resuscitated. By the beginning of 1973 it had found itself, in the words of Professor Robertson, ". . . in the unusual situation for an international organization of having achieved its objectives so successfully that its services would no longer be required."[63]

IGOs AS "BUILDING BLOCKS" FOR AN ATLANTIC-PACIFIC SYSTEM

The foregoing analysis has looked at nine different intergovernmental organizations which the west has created since World War II to serve its own special needs, and, more recently, those of three Pacific powers. In every instance, the IGO in question can be seen to have created some new approaches or mechanisms which resolved important international problems or which led to important advances in cooperation with other frameworks. Over the years since 1947, a constant process of institutional and procedural innovation has gone on, with one or more IGOs frequently borrowing from another something that has worked well. This process of innovation and its achievements have the greatest importance, both for those who are seeking to develop new practical ways of international cooperation, and for scholarly observers of the process. In Chapter 4, I shall try to describe some of those innovations which seem to have made an important difference in relations between nations.

FOOTNOTES

1. See pp. V-37/41 in Chapter V for a more detailed treatment.
2. Karl Kaiser, "Transnational Politics:.Towards a Theory of Multinational Politics," *International Organization*, No. XXV, Fall 1971, p. 798.
3. In July 1978, it was reported that NATO had "completed contingency plans to protect the shipping routes around South Africa's Cape of Good Hope." The Secretary General of NATO, Joseph Luns, was cited as the source. See Kingsbury Smith, "NATO Ready to Guard Key Oil Route," *Seattle Post-Intelligencer* (July 29, 1978), p. A-6. See also *Atlantic News*, Brussels (June 1, 1978), No. 1032, p. l.
4. Attempts have been made repeatedly to close this institutional gap. The U.S. declared its strong support in the fall of 1975, when Secretary of State Henry Kissinger sent Prime Minister Harold Wilson a cable including these lines:

. . .our Government recognizes the North Atlantic Assembly as an official international organization, in which the United States

Congress participates. The United States is prepared to consider any suggestion your Government may have with regard to making the Assembly an official part of the Alliance and will note with interest any official statement you may make on the subject.

(Letter to the author from the Secretariat of the North Atlantic Assembly.)

5. See pages V-11/12 and also, for a general discussion of the functions and situation of such parliamentary bodies in the Atlantic world, Allan J. Hovey, Jr., *The Superparliaments: Interparliamentary Consultation and Atlantic Cooperation* (New York: Frederick A. Praeger, Inc., 1966). See also Elliot R. Goodman, *The Fate of the Atlantic Community* (New York: Frederick A. Praeger, 1975), Chapter 11, "Parliamentary Assemblies in the Atlantic Community."

6. No. 787, December 17, 1975.

7. Inasmuch as the bulk of OEEC's objectives, working methods, organization, and staff were taken over by OECD on its establishment in 1961, my observations in this section should be taken to apply, where appropriate, to the historical record of both. From the point of view of the student of international relations, the "line of contribution" from one to the other is unbroken.

8. Henry G. Aubrey, *Atlantic Economic Cooperation: The Case of the OECD* (New York: Frederick A. Praeger, 1967), p. 94.

9. The first two of these agencies are described in Appendix B; IEA is the most recent (1974) of the principal IGOs of the Atlantic System described in Appendix B (see Chart 6).

10. Not all OECD members, for example, participate in the Development Assistance Committee (DAC). Greece, Turkey, and others are themselves underdeveloped and so feel they have little to contribute in a forum concerned with stepping up aid to the Third World. There have been other countries, however, which initially were not OECD members, but which nevertheless participated in one or more of its specialized agencies. Japan, for example, joined DAC in 1961 but did not become a full OECD member until 1964. In more attenuated fashion, Yugoslavia retains "Special Observer status" in several OECD committees and agencies, but gives no indication of seeking full membership.

11. The meetings of first-, third-, and fourth-World countries in Paris during 1975 and later to try to find acceptable formulae for cooperation are a good illustration of the OECD at work (albeit behind the scenes) in this sensitive field.

12. Writing of the early OEEC years (during which the United States, although not a member, contributed a great deal behind the scenes), Lincoln Gordon characterized this spirit: "Their development and refinement [the European Payments Union and OEEC Trade Liberalization Code] at every stage have shown the results of the thinking from a European-wide point of view fostered by the OEEC climate." "The Organization for European Economic Cooperation," *International Organization*, Vol. 10, 1956, p. 6.

13. Aubrey, op. cit., p. 138.

14. Aubrey makes some of these points tellingly. Ibid., pp. 24–25; 29; 34.

15. This, to be sure, does not yet come under the heading of achievement; yet, it well illustrates the OECD capability for "going for the jugular" of the most pressing economic problems.

16. Miriam Camps, *European Unification in the Sixties* (New York: McGraw-Hill, 1966), p. 220.

17. *International Herald Tribune* (November 25, 1975) p. 2.

18. Of the creation of the first European Community, an American political scientist commented:

The Schuman Declaration of 9 May 1950 was one of the most extraordinary political initiatives of the twentieth century. It was an attempt to deal with a resurgent Germany by assimilating it to a European system rather than by seeking guarantees to check its economic progress; it was a means for giving substance to the prevalent wishes for a united Europe, albeit in the limited sectors of coal and steel; and it was a challenge to the traditional organizations that sought to mute but not interfere with the principle of national sovereignty. With the passage of time, it has become increasingly evident that the Schuman Declaration marked a radical change of course in European affairs. . . .

Howard Bliss (ed.), *The Political Development of the European Community: A Documentary Collection* (Waltham, Mass.: Blaisdell Publishing Co., 1970) pp. 5–6.

19. Bliss, ibid., p. 21.

20. See Peter Hay, *Federalism and Supranational Organizations: Patterns for New Legal Structures* (Urbana: University of Illinois Press, 1966), p. 99.

21. Kaiser, op. cit., p. 799.

22. Werner Feld, *The Court of the European Communities: New Di-*

mension in International Adjudication (The Hague: Martinus Nijhoff, 1964), pp. 113–114.

23. Rolf Zundel, "Edging Towards an Elected European Parliament," *Die Zeit* (December 5, 1975) and reprinted in *The German Tribune*, No. 714 (December 14, 1975), p. 2. A "League of Social Democratic Parties of the EC" was established in 1974, but it is apparently less an "international party" than the others.

24. *International Herald Tribune* (April 23, 1975).

25. In Europe, one often hears Americans called "the best Europeans," whether in business or diplomacy.

26. A.H. Robertson, *European Institutions: Cooperation, Integration, Unification* (3rd ed.), (London: Stevens and Sons, Ltd., 1973), p. 183.

27. David Coombes, *Politics and Bureaucracy in the European Community* (London: George Allen and Unwin, Ltd., 1970), p. 292.

28. The inclusion of Japan in the Rambouillet "Big Six" economic summit of November 1975 was a clear indication of this. (Canada was left out of the 1975 summit, but attended subsequent meetings.)

29. For an imaginative private attempt to outline such an arrangement, see Pierre Uri's *Partnership for Progress* (New York: Harper and Row, 1963). Also, on June 1, 1964, the Action Committee for the United States of Europe issued a declaration outlining briefly its proposals for a "Committee of Entente" between the EC and the United States. See also Goodman, op. cit., Chapters 3 and 4.

30. *Christian Science Monitor* (January 6, 1976), p. 2.

31. Eric Stein and Peter Hay, *Law and Institutions in the Atlantic Area; Readings, Cases, and Problems* (Indianapolis: Bobbs-Merrill, 1967), p. 959, point out that the provisions of the European Convention on Human Rights also, at the time of adoption, applied to the colonies of the European signatories. This posed a problem, as the various colonial territories became independent:

> The solution found has been to incorporate in the constitutions of the newly independent countries guarantees of human rights based on the provisions of the European Convention. This has been done in the new constitutions of Nigeria, Sierra Leone, Cyprus, Jamaica, Trinidad and Tobago, Uganda, Kenya, Malawi, and Zambia.

Evidently in some of these countries, the civil rights provisions have been more honored in the breach; yet, it is possible that because of this particular European heritage, the civil rights of the populations of at least some of these new nations have been greater than they might otherwise have been.

32. The London *Times* of April 11, 1972 described the work of a Consultative Assembly Committee of MPs in proposing reforms (some of which were accepted by the Government of the United Kingdom) to "eliminate discrimination and violence."

33. See page 28 for a brief account of Greek expulsion from, then re-acceptance in, the Council of Europe.

34. Ernst B. Haas, "International Integration: The European and the Universal Process," in B. Landheer (ed.), *Limits and Problems of European Integration* (The Hague: Martinus Nijhoff, 1963), pp. 12-13.

35. Howard Bliss (ed.), op. cit., p. 5.

36. Ibid., p. 5.

37. Compare, for example, Article 14 of the Statute of the Council of Europe with the much less restrictive provisions of the OECD Convention (Article 7) and the North Atlantic Treaty (Article 9).

38. Robertson, A.H., *The Council of Europe*, 2nd ed. (New York: Frederick A. Praeger, 1961), pp. 242-243.

39. "Function and Future of the Council of Europe," Council of Europe Consultative Assembly Doc. 2273, Strasbourg, 1967, p. 3.

40. Frantz Wendt, *The Nordic Council and Cooperation in Scandinavia* (Copenhagen: Munksgaard, 1959), pp. 25-26.

41. Robertson, *European Institutions*, pp. 282-283.

42. Wendt (op. cit., p. 105) notes that the Soviet press and radio attacks (in the early 1950s) on the Nordic Council as an "agent of American imperialism" produced Finnish hesitations. When, in the mild warmth of the first postwar détente, the Russian attacks stopped, the Finns felt able to join.

43. Ruth C. Lawson (ed.), *International Regional Organizations: Constitutional Foundations* (New York: Frederick A. Praeger, 1962), p. 198.

44. Robertson, *European Institutions*, pp. 281-282.

45. See Appendix D for descriptions of some of the early OEEC/OECD agencies, including the European Productivity Agency and the European Payments Union. Still active is the European Nuclear Energy Agency (Appendix D).

46. *Legislation on the International Energy Agency*; Hearing before the Subcommittees on International Organizations and on International Resources, Food, and Energy of the Committee on International Relations, House of Representatives, Ninety-Fourth Congress, 1st Ses-

sion, U.S. Government Printing Office, Washington, D.C., 1975, p. 3.

47. Ibid., pp. 4–5.

48. Ibid., pp. 5–6.

49. The text of the agreement containing these provisions will be found appended to the Congressional document cited (ibid., beginning p. 56).

50. UPI dispatch, published in *The Seattle Post Intelligencer* (November 28, 1975).

51. *News from OECD*, No. 10 (December 1975).

52. See, for example, *The Economist* (December 6, 1975), p. 41.

53. Interview in *Development Forum*, Vol. III, No. 9 (December 1975), p. 2.

54. As late as May 1977, however, OPEC was refusing publicly to negotiate with IEA. Ali Jaidah, OPEC's Secretary General, was quoted by *The Times* of London (May 16, 1977) as saying: "The International Energy Agency was formed for a specific purpose: for confrontation with OPEC. We won't deal with it at all."

55. See also Jacques Westhof, "Western European Union," *Memo from Belgium* No. 109 (February 1969), Ministry of Foreign Affairs, Brussels, pp. 11–13.

56. The French—and more recently the Greeks—have made this fine distinction: they continue to regard themselves as legally and morally bound by the mutual defense (Article 5) and other clauses of the North Atlantic Treaty (which ties they refer to as "l'Alliance Atlantique"); but they do not wish to participate (at any rate, fully or formally) in the broad range of common measures such as international commands, frequent joint training exercises, or combined staff planning, which constitute "NATO." The political structure (in which France and Greece do choose to participate) and the military structures (in which they do not) have been formed by the North Atlantic Council, the treaty's highest authority, which under Article 9 was given the power to "set up such subsidiary bodies as may be necessary." It is these subsidiary bodies in the military field which the French and Greeks do not generally recognize, although more and more since President Giscard d'Estaing's assumption of office, France has worked tacitly with its allies on many of these matters. See Goodman, op. cit., pp. 120–123. In 1978, Greece began negotiations with her NATO allies for military reintegration; the discussions became painful and protracted.

57. The quality of many of the reports of WEU's Parliamentary Assembly is indeed noteworthy and, in the opinion of many observers, often superior to that of other interparliamentary assemblies.

58. Members of Eurogroup are the United Kingdom, the Federal Republic of Germany, Italy, Norway, Denmark, Greece, Turkey, and the three Benelux countries.

59. This weaker NATO clause was necessary in order to secure passage of the treaty by the U.S. Senate, which—as usual—promised to look askance at any openended, ironclad overseas commitments. There was, further, the constitutional position of the United States, in which the power to declare war was vested in the Congress.

60. Unless, of course, one wishes to trace the origins of Benelux back still further to BLEU (Belgium-Luxembourg Economic Union of 1921). Interestingly, Benelux's historical origins are linked with the wartime headquarters of General Eisenhower, SHAEF. Each of the three countries had a military mission at SHAEF and it is said that Eisenhower himself had an impact at that period on the formation of the thinking behind Benelux (conversation with Prof. H. Angelo of University of California, Davis, 1976).

61. For a further discussion of Benelux accomplishments, see A. H. Robertson, *European Institutions*, pp. 272–278.

62. Ibid., pp. 230–231.

63. Ibid.

[114]

CHAPTER 4

Innovation: The European-Atlantic Contribution

Each of the nine "European-Atlantic" IGOs whose records were briefly reviewed in the previous chapter has contributed in some significant way to the growing body of institutional structures and practices which has enhanced effective international cooperation. This chapter presents an analysis of a representative number of these innovations and attempts to show their importance and their place in the development of Atlantic-Pacific cooperation.

The specialist will realize that some of the innovations cited were tried out at an earlier time, for example, in the Young and Dawes Plans in the 1920s. The League of Nations Council experimented with the procedure of establishing international policy without requiring a unanimous vote, although under extremely limited circumstances. More recently, IGOs outside the extended Atlantic System have sometimes made use of these techniques. In terms of the range, versatility, and sophistication with which the extended Atlantic System has employed these techniques, the System however is clearly the preeminent innovator and user.

* * *

The innovations described below seem to group themselves logically into ten categories: (1) improvements in consultative

[115]

and decision-making mechanisms, (2) enhancement of international and supranational legal powers, (3) use of country reviews and information transfer mechanisms, (4) improvements in supranational and international parliaments, (5) establishment of supranational taxing powers, (6) development of better means to harmonize divergent national policies, (7) establishment of partial IGO memberships, (8) provision for IGOs to negotiate on behalf of their member countries, (9) development of flexible systems of IGO membership, and (10) creation of international public corporations.

CONSULTATION AND DECISION MAKING

Before this century, diplomatic conferences, involving foreign ministers or ambassadors and occasionally prime ministers, sometimes sat for long periods. But there were no permanent mechanisms for continuous representation in an international body until the League of Nations was formed. It remained for NATO, OEEC and OECD, the European Communities, and other bodies formed after 1945 to develop and refine the mechanism of continuous-session international consultative and decision-making organizations.

The OEEC was the first to institute a system whereby its chief decision-making organ (the Council) could meet at either of two levels: with ministers (cabinet members) representing their countries or with ambassadors accredited to OEEC as permanent representatives. Foreign ministers were understood to be first in rank, but the heads of other ministries, such as finance or trade, could also serve on the Council in place of or in addition to the foreign ministers. The permanent representatives were able to act at the same level of decision making as the ministers, if they were so authorized by their governments. However, it was reasoned that nothing could substitute for face-to-face contact of ministers when there was a crisis, or simply on a periodic basis to preserve good communication at high levels. The Council thus began *regular annual meetings "at the ministerial level."* Very soon after OEEC initiated these practices, NATO adopted and later elaborated on them. The principal NATO innovation was

[116]

the summit meeting, with members represented in the treaty's most important organization, the North Atlantic Council, by the heads of their governments. Although some IGOs have never had summit meetings, NATO and EC in particular have found them useful. Such meetings help bolster public confidence in the work of the IGO and sometimes help resolve diplomatic impasses. In this latter connection, governments have come to realize that their national prestige is at risk in the event of failure and are thus often forced to find a mutually acceptable solution before the summit meeting. The summit meeting itself then is used simply to ratify the solution, even though communiques may represent the decision otherwise.

A variation on the public summits was instituted in 1974, when French President Giscard d'Estaing invited his EC counterparts to join him in Paris for a simple "dîner à neuf." The heads of government were able to review informally and privately the important questions which Giscard d'Estaing laid on the table. Frank exchanges of view, not decisions, were sought. These dinners continued every few months, not replacing the more elaborate and formal summit meetings, but supplementing them.

Another informal summit technique was applied at the Atlantic-Pacific level in November 1975, when President Ford and the heads of the Japanese, British, French, Italian, and West German governments met at Rambouillet for a weekend of informal economic talks. This case differs, however, because the body which met was acting as an ad hoc group of the most economically powerful democracies,[1] rather than the "super council" of an existing IGO. The meetings of this group have subsequently been held annually, with the addition of Canada in 1975 and the President of the EC Commission in a more or less ill-defined status in 1977.

* * *

Not only the composition and powers of the decision-making bodies, but their methods of deliberation as well, have been affected by postwar European-Atlantic practices. Alternatives have been found to the traditional rule of unanimity which has hampered the United Nations Security Council, for example. One alternative is the so-called "qualified majority," which has recently been instituted by the International Energy Agency and, to a great extent, by the European Communities. Both the Treaty of Paris and the Treaty of Rome provide that certain important decisions shall be taken in the Council of Ministers (the highest authority of the institution) by means of weighted voting. In the ECSC, the weights vary between heavy and light producers of coal and steel (Article 28). In the EEC and EURATOM treaties, the weights generally vary according to size and population. There is also a form of weighting on the EC Commission, with two Commissioners for each of the larger countries and one for the smaller countries. Weighting is also reflected in the work of the new, directly elected European Parliament.

The Treaty of Rome (EEC) established the intent of its voting provisions at the outset (Article 148.1): "Except where otherwise provided for in this Treaty, the conclusions of the Council shall be reached by a majority of its members." The exceptions, needless to say, are numerous. The signers agreed at the outset, however, that certain very important voting provisions, such as qualified majority decisions, would not enter into force for a certain number of years. (President de Gaulle's unwillingness to accede to qualified majority decisions threatened for a time to bring about the collapse of the Community.)[2]

In EFTA, quite a number of decisions may be made by a *simple majority* (originally, four votes out of seven). The Convention, however, restricts such decisions to fairly innocuous matters concerning implementation of decisions previously agreed on by unanimous vote. For example, if a member believes itself wronged by another member in violation of the Convention, the EFTA Council can decide by majority vote whether or not a violation has occurred.[3] In a special case, the United Kingdom agreed not to withdraw her forces stationed on the continent under NATO "against the wishes of the majority of the High Contracting Parties."[4] Although this pledge was qualified considerably in later passages, it is nevertheless another instance in which a postwar European IGO provided for less-than-unanimous decisions.

Still another major innovation in decision-making procedures is the provision that allows less than the full membership of an IGO to proceed with some agreed-upon action, providing the remaining members abstain. This practice is codified in the OECD Convention.

> Each member shall have one vote. If a Member abstains from voting on a decision or recommendation, such abstention shall not invalidate the decision or recommendation, which shall be applicable to the other Members but not to the abstaining Member.[5]

Although there was no such provision in the NATO treaty (in fact, the matter of voting was not mentioned at all in the treaty), the North Atlantic Council has considered itself free to move ahead in many areas, even when one or more members did not necessarily agree, but did not wish to go on record as being opposed to a proposal. It is significant that the statutes of the Council of Europe set down in great detail the manner of voting in the Committee of Ministers (the only place in which governments can commit themselves), but did not include provisions for less-than-full-membership decisions.[6] The "less-than-full-membership initiative" enabled members of NATO in 1968 to establish the so-called "Eurogroup." Eurogroup has acted as a kind of caucus that allowed these ten members to concert their government's views on strategy and promote the standardization of weapons.

An "Independent European Programme Group" (IEPG) grew out of the need to establish some larger and more effective grouping dedicated to European-wide arms standardization and "interoperability," as well as more European (as distinguished from U.S.) weapons production. IEPG may eventually supersede Eurogroup. Thus, the initial less-than-unanimous decision allowed work to take place until initial abstainers could be brought aboard.[7]

* * *

[119]

The International Energy Agency was formed in a similar manner in 1974. Largely at U.S. Secretary of State Henry Kissinger's insistence, diplomats of a number (but not all) of the members of OECD met to try to agree upon a policy with regard to the oil crisis of 1973. France chose not to participate; several other countries hesitated as well (Norway, for example, because it was on the verge of becoming a major oil producer). By November 1974, 16 of the 24 members of OECD had created the IEA by a less-than-unanimous decision.

* * *

Another postwar innovation related to the IGOs is the *independent executive organ,* which exists, so far, only in the European Communities, in the form of the Commission.[8] Robertson described its character: "an executive organ . . . which can exercise certain powers . . . in complete independence and in the general interest, without receiving instructions from governments."[9] This independent power has often made it possible for the Commission to initiate measures which, if left entirely to the six- or nine-nation Council of Ministers, might have languished. (The Council, in fact, is specifically *prohibited* from taking initiatives under the treaty.)

Even without supranational executive powers, the secretaries of the IGOs can play strategic roles. Keohane and Nye note the "agenda-setting function" that defined issues to be considered and excluded others, and the "active lobbying" carried on with governments.[10] Cooper, Kaiser, and Kosaka also point out that

the secretaries of [international] institutions can be extremely valuable. Such leaders can propose solutions when no country is able or willing to do so, help galvanize support in individual countries, and implement decisions when everyone else goes on to the next issue. The experience in GATT and the IMF and some other agencies [esp. NATO. ed.] indicates how much can be contributed by strong Secretaries General. They do not need formal authority. Their influence comes from impartiality, integrity, and good political sense, as well as intellectual command of the subject.[11]

* * *

Still another useful device for circumventing the requirement for unanimous decisions is the so-called *"wise men"* technique which was first applied in 1948, when the original 16 European OEEC countries could not agree on a formula for the fair division of forthcoming U.S. Marshall Plan aid. The United States insisted that it would not engage in bilateral negotiations to parcel out some $4 billion to the needy countries; all potential recipients would have to agree among themselves on a formula for "fair shares." Not surprisingly, the negotiations between the 16 became deadlocked. The logjam was broken when the OEEC Council agreed to appoint the heads of four of its national delegations to consider the matter. Sir Eric Roll of Britain, Guillaume Guindey of France, Sr. Stoppani of Italy, and Dirk Spierenburg of the Netherlands withdrew to a small inn in the forest of Chantilly, developed general guidelines for the division of aid, and returned to the Council with a precise formula. Lincoln Gordon observed:

> While certainly no government was fully satisfied [with the result], the process sufficiently equalized the dissatisfactions so that the recommendations were accepted.[12]

A year later, when the task of dividing Marshall Plan monies became even more difficult,

> . . . a special committee of two was appointed to arbitrate . . . So successful was their work that the recommendation they produced was accepted by all the governments as the allocation of aid not only for the year 1949 but also for the subsequent years. . . .[13]

In 1951, during the Korean War, NATO faced a similar crisis. A sense of urgency impelled the allies to augment drastically their defense establishments. General Eisenhower, Supreme Allied Commander in Europe, and his staff thought 100 or more divisions would be needed; the feasibility of accepting such a burden and dividing it fairly was, however, a politically and economically delicate matter. The North Atlantic Council, again not surprisingly, reached a deadlock in its discussion; it was decided to appoint a "wise men's" committee consisting of Jean Monnet, Sir Edwin Plowden, and Averell Harriman to survey the defense needs and resources of other members.[14] The operation was successful, in that a plan considered feasible by all members was adopted.

In 1956, on the heels of the disastrous Suez affair, NATO again employed the same technique, this time not to break a diplomatic logjam, but to build understanding and support among governments and their peoples. Accordingly, three foreign ministers, Gaetano Martino of Italy, Halvard Lange of Norway, and Lester B. Pearson of Canada, were named to study the possibilities of nonmilitary cooperation under the North Atlantic Treaty. Their subsequent report, urging especially that the North Atlantic Council develop and strengthen political consultation, had a long-term and significant effect.[15]

In 1960, the establishment of the two new European Communities and the growing economic interdependence of all the advanced countries posed new problems which OEEC was not equipped to handle. Accordingly, another group of "wise men" consisting of four heads of national delegations to OEEC was appointed to

prepare a report which would examine the most effective methods for ensuring economic cooperation in Europe, submit a draft agreement for an improved organization for economic co-operation and indicate which functions of the OEEC should be continued in the new framework.[16]

Thus, the creation of OECD in 1961 was the result of consigning a subject both complex and vast in its implications to a small group of respected persons. Four men could obviously deal with such matters more expeditiously than a formal council that represented 20 countries.

NEW DEVELOPMENTS IN INTERNATIONAL
AND SUPRANATIONAL LAW

The Council of Europe's Commission and *Court of Human Rights,* which enable individual citizens of the member countries to press claims against national powers, are a truly supranational undertaking.[17] In addition, the Benelux Court of Justice was assigned the task of promoting uniformity in the application of legal rules common to the three member countries, as specified in any of the treaties and agreements among them or in decisions of the Benelux Committee of Ministers.[18] But it is the European Communities which again have made the most impressive contribution in this area, in what Peter Hay described as "the breaking-up of the rigid dichotomy of national and international law."

[European Communities law] is municipal law in effect, federal in structure, but not national in origin.

The legal technique for regional association which the Communities contribute thus is 'supranational' law-making.[19]

Andrew Wilson Green viewed this *supranational lawmaking function* as a significant contribution to the process of political integration among the six (later, nine) EC states:

Six elements used to define political integration have been increased by the [EC] Court of Justice through its jurisprudence. Summarized:

1. The Court of Justice has usually but not always resolved doubts about jurisdiction in favor of the communities . . . .
2. . . . has upheld the authority of the High Authority and the E.E.C. Commission, particularly on substantive questions. . . .
3. . . . has recognized substantive individual rights created by Community Law . . . .

[123]

4. . . . has asserted the supremacy of Community law over national law. . . .
5. . . . is building its own independent system of law distinct from traditional international law and distinct from the legal systems of the member states. . . .
6. . . . has resolved disputes between member states in a number of significant instances. . . .[20]

W.A. Axline went even further:

. . . the Community society is witnessing legal integration along revolutionary lines that surpass all previous examples of international organizations based in conventional international law.[21]

The European Court of Justice (of the EC) exercised jurisdiction across a far wider spectrum of law than had any previous international court, acting not only as an *international tribunal,* but also as a *constitutional tribunal* (interpreting the treaties and ruling on relations between the Communities and the member states), as an *administrative tribunal* (ruling on appeals of private parties) and as a *civil court* (ruling on disputes involving the employees of the Communities).[22]

The Council of Europe and the European Communities, in particular, have both broken significant new legal ground by means of the constitutional provisions which they have assigned to their judicial bodies and in the way in which these powers have been exercised.[23]

COUNTRY REVIEWS AND INFORMATION TRANSFER

In the early days of the Marshall Plan, it became the practice for members of OEEC to lay before their partners each year a review that summarized the accomplishments, problems, and outlooks of their national economies. After the first NATO "wise men's" report in 1952, the NATO countries also adopted the practice of annually examining the defense efforts of individual members. In both institutions, and in OECD as well, *country reviews* of this type have become traditional and, in some cases, greatly elaborated.

Annual reviews have been used by both OECD and NATO in other areas. The Development Aid Committee (DAC) of OECD publishes an annual aid review. OECD conducts reviews by country on science policy, research and development, education, environmental management, and growth policies. The OECD economic reviews have also become more sophisticated. Experts from the Secretariat and from several national delegations other than that of the country under review annually examine the performance and prospects of each country. Such reports have become highly respected sources and are used as the basis for the semiannual *OECD Economic Outlook*, which summarizes the overall situation and projections for all 24 members.

The impact of the annual reviews has been to transform the way in which the participating nations conduct economic planning, make military decisions, and provide assistance to developing countries. In profound ways, the reviews affect the workings of these nations' governments, armed forces, and economies.

* * *

European-Atlantic IGOs disseminate information in other ways by sponsoring conferences of government officials and private specialists, research, translation and publication of reports, and fellowships for scholars.

In NATO, this *information transfer process* has essentially taken two forms: arranging for the interaction of scientists and stimulating action on environmental problems. Under its Assistant Secretary General for Scientific Affairs, NATO has promoted research and the dissemination of knowledge on general scientific matters and defense. NATO's Committee on the Challenges of Modern Society (CCMS) collects and disperses information on environmental management. This program utilizes a highly original procedure known as "*the pilot-country method*," whereby one member country takes over responsibility for a problem which all have agreed is important. The pilot country, helped in some cases by "copilots," collects the information, pays for it, and prepares all the necessary reports. The most striking innovation of this method is CCMS' role in stimulating action in the member countries following the information transfer. The procedure has insured the motivation of the pilot country. A government accepts the substantial responsibilities of "pilot" only if it has serious interest in the work at hand.[24] The International Energy Agency has also used the "pilot country" technique in managing joint research and development efforts.

The Council of Europe has evolved a quite different framework for attacking societal problems. Each year, the Council's Committee of Ministers adopts an *"Intergovernmental Work Programme,"* which sets forth a certain number of tasks which the governments have agreed that they want to accomplish together. Each task is assigned to a committee of experts drawn from member countries' governments. The committee issues reports and sometimes arranges for the drafting of conventions which commit the Council's members to specific action. Tasks have included "reducing river pollution" or "the exchange of war cripples . . . with a view to medical action." Although some projects take several years, the Council's secretariat has stated that "the present rhythm of tasks completed . . . is about forty a year."[25] It is difficult to find out what the publication of reports or the conclusion of conventions has actually accomplished. One may assume that a good many of the recommendations or agreements remain suspended between the covers of increasingly dusty dossiers. Nevertheless, whether direct action is taken or not, it seems evident that to bring so many officials and experts from the governments of western Europe together to concentrate on a set of precise objectives must, at least indirectly, lead to a considerable transfer of knowledge, at least some of it to good purpose.

OECD has also dealt with economic and social questions, but it has relied mostly on its own staff and on outside consultants. OECD has also set up several special-purpose institutes and centers to work more or less autonomously on problems such as development, education, or nuclear energy. OECD has developed a reputation among governments and in academic circles for having up-to-date information on the economic, social, and technical problems of the day. The OECD complex, consisting of the

Council, the International Secretariat, national delegations, working parties and committees, outside consultants, and special agencies, has sponsored a number of important reports, including studies on the relationship of research and development expenditure to economic growth, the ties between educational investment and industrial productivity, the "limits to growth," and the importance of governmental "science policy."

INTERPARLIAMENTARY INNOVATIONS

Prior to 1949, there had never been an *international assembly of members of parliaments* that met regularly and was sanctioned officially by governments.[26] The Consultative Assembly of the Council of Europe (1949) was the first, and in the next few years, many more assemblies were established. The European Coal and Steel Community formed a Common Assembly (later to serve the Economic Community and EURATOM under the title of the European Parliament). The Nordic Council was begun as a body of Scandinavian legislators. When the Brussels treaty was amended to include Germany and Italy, an assembly of parliamentarians also was set up, the Western European Union (1954). Benelux created an Interparliamentary Consultative Council in 1955. EFTA holds a yearly meeting of MPs. A number of MPs from NATO countries created, in 1955, the NATO Parliamentarians Conference (renamed the "North Atlantic Assembly" in 1966). Unofficial at the outset (set up as a charitable association under British law), this body has tenaciously sought recognition and full official standing from the NATO governments. U.S. participation has been authorized by an Act of Congress, and similar validation has been granted by other parliaments, but NAA is not formally or legally a part of the Alliance. In 1975, intergovernmental status seemed somewhat closer, but still elusive.[27] In a more informal and perhaps less satisfactory way, OEEC/OECD has benefited from rather close ties with the Council of Europe Assembly.

Unfortunately, because so many assemblies have been formed by the Atlantic System IGOs, some countries, such as Belgium or the Netherlands, must send delegates to as many as five different international assemblies. This gradually has become a burden which numerous scholars and governments have sought to alleviate by means of various proposals, but no significant action had yet been taken by the late seventies to reduce the number of assemblies.[28]

Among all of these parliamentary bodies, only the European Parliament can lay claim to any supranationality. It can deny a budget to the EC Commission; it also has the power (on paper at least) to force the executive body (the Commission) out of office. These powers, even if weak compared with those of a national parliament, nevertheless are without precedent internationally. They carry with them the seeds of "community building." None of the interparliamentary assemblies, including the EC parliament, however, has yet acquired true legislative power. Until they do, it is doubtful that they can play a truly revolutionary role in the federation of Europe.

When the WEU Assembly was created, it wrote its own charter which was "granted," if somewhat grudgingly, by the Council of Ministers. Like the other interparliamentary assemblies, the WEU Assembly can discuss and criticize the work of the member governments and of WEU itself, express and help to form public opinion, and ask questions and make recommendations. The Assembly also was granted one important power:

A motion to disagree to the content of the report of the Council, or to a part of the report, shall be tabled in writing by at least ten representatives.

This provision actually permits the Assembly to express "no confidence in the executive." The WEU Assembly gained other powers as well. Its president, for example, may call extraordinary sessions without the prior consent of the Council of Ministers, and the president can transmit the Assembly's resolutions directly to other international organizations or to national governments and parliaments.[29] These represent only the most modest level of power, if they are compared with the powers of modern national parliaments. However, measured against the early

IGOs, they represent the kind of power to which only national legislative bodies have so far been accustomed.

The most effective interparliamentary group in terms of substantive accomplishment is the Nordic Council. Its expert committees prepare the texts of laws which the individual governments then submit to their legislatures. A great many of these statutes have been adopted. The Consultative Assembly of the Council of Europe is not quite as powerful as the Nordic Council, because it operates under a restrictive constitution imposed by initially suspicious governments. Nevertheless, this assembly has shown considerable ingenuity in finding ways to exert significant political influence. For example, the Consultative Assembly has devoted much attention to the aim of achieving the unity of Europe. In 1949, the Assembly proclaimed that "the aim and goal of the Council of Europe is the creation of a European political authority with limited functions but real powers." It proved impossible to get the Committee of Ministers to agree, but the phrase was often repeated at crucial points in later debates on the proposed European Communities.[30]

While the postwar interparliamentary assemblies are relatively powerless, they are not without influence. The interparliamentary assemblies of the European-Atlantic System have managed to shape national parliamentary and public opinion on big issues; to review the work of IGOs and try to hold them at least morally, if not legally, accountable; to force participating MPs to see problems within the framework of a wider common interest; to help build a "European" (and in the case of the North Atlantic Assembly, an "Atlantic") "esprit de corps"; to help convert laws and other arrangements made by individual countries or small groupings of countries into the agreements of larger groupings of countries; and to foster and publicize useful new ideas about modern society and its problems.

SUPRANATIONAL TAXING POWERS

Articles 49 and 50 of the European Coal and Steel Community treaty gave the High Authority the power to raise the money necessary to operate the Community. Levies were placed on the production of all coal and steel within the member states, and were payable directly to the High Authority. The two newer Communities now also have the authority to finance their activities from their own sources of income (customs duties and agricultural levies). These truly extraordinary developments not only authorize a supranational body to levy taxes on the citizens of national states, but also make the Communities at least potentially financially independent of the member governments.

Although the European Parliament has only limited budgetary powers, it can use its powers to increase some expenditures in concert with the Commission and against the Council of Ministers. Both the Parliament and the Commission have a common interest in expanding the areas of EC competence. Their limited federal powers may prove in later years to have been among the most important constitutional and practical elements in bringing about a "United States of Europe."

HARMONIZING FOREIGN POLICY

Unprecedented progress has been made by the EC countries and NATO in arriving at common policies with respect to significant questions of external relations.[31] A NATO publication explains the value of the technique in this way:

> the practice of political consultation which has developed over the years is now established as an indispensible element in the functioning of the Alliance. Its significance, not least for the smaller NATO countries, can hardly be overestimated. It provides the opportunity for all member countries to take full part in the shaping of the major policies of the Western world—regardless of size or power.[32]

Such *political consultation* is carried out between members' permanent representatives in Brussels, with the International Secretariat, at twice-yearly meetings of the heads of foreign office planning sections, at periodic meetings of ministers (and occasionally heads of government), and in the North Atlantic Assembly. When necessary, special meetings of senior foreign office or defense officials can also be convened.

As background for talks at all these levels, NATO collects and assesses intelligence provided by various national governments and issues a common statement of facts and their evaluation to all members. In addition, the governments also provide their permanent representatives at NATO headquarters with recommendations and statements of policy. Although the bulk of these exchanges are never reflected in the newspapers (partly because they are secret, but also because of sheer volume), a wide range of policy questions has been successfully handled by NATO. In recent years, a common NATO policy on East-West contacts has been agreed to as well as a series of precise positions which were taken during the long Helsinki negotiations. In addition, the North Atlantic Council has guided the efforts of the various NATO countries to improve their relations with the Soviet Union and has dealt with such matters as German reunification, European security, disarmament, balanced force reductions, and global security.

Since 1970 (when the EC still consisted of six members), some progress also has been made to harmonize the foreign policy of the EC countries by means of the so-called *"Davignon Committee" of the Political Directors of Foreign Offices*. In some non-EC capitals (Washington, D.C., for example), the ambassadors of the nine members stay in especially close touch. As a result, the nine members of the EC have taken common positions in the UN General Assembly and Security Council more often than not.

IGO NEGOTIATION ON BEHALF OF MEMBER COUNTRIES

In 1971, under Article 9 of the NATO treaty,[33] the North Atlantic Council appointed a single envoy to act on behalf of all the members. Manlio Brosio, an Italian statesman who had been Secretary General of NATO, was given a mandate to open exploratory talks with the Soviet government on the reduction of armed forces. Although the mission came to naught, it demonstrated the degree to which mutual trust had developed among the coalition partners. It also demonstrated the development of a perception of common interests among the member countries.

PARTIAL, SPECIAL, AND "ESCALATING" MEMBERSHIPS

European-Atlantic IGOs have invited nonmember countries to participate in specific, limited activities, such as membership in special committees, appointment of observers to some or all activities of an IGO, or associate membership status in the IGO. Finland, Spain, and Portugal all participated in the work of the Council of Europe on nature conservation before they were full members of the Council.[34] Although the Council has attempted to promote similar involvement by eastern European countries, it has not been very successful. In the work of NATO's Committee on the Challenges of Modern Society and also in NATO's science activities, individuals and governments from non-NATO countries have often participated. In these non-military, unclassified activites, NATO has taken the position that to stimulate the free flow of scientific and practical knowledge is in itself good and that much is to be gained on both sides by broadening contacts regardless of nationality.[35] More recently, the IEA has taken this position in sponsoring energy research. Before becoming full members of OECD, both New Zealand and Australia belonged for several years to one of its committees. Japan belonged to OECD's Development Assistance Committee for four years before she became a full member of OECD in 1964. For some years, Finland sent observers to OECD meetings on maritime transport, pulp and paper, industry and machinery, before becoming a full member of OECD in 1969. Yugoslavia has "special status," and (according to the OECD official handbook) is a "full Member for confrontation of economic policies, scientific and technical matters, agricultural and fisheries questions, technical assistance and productivity."[36]

The EC treaties provide for *associate memberships*. The United Kingdom was an associate member of ECSC for some years. Turkey and Greece are associate members of EEC under agreements that can lead to full membership. Portugal and Spain, beginning in 1976, actively sought the same arrangement.

In 1960, Switzerland broke a long-standing policy against participating in IGOs that had even the slightest "political" taint by becoming an observer at the Council of Europe. By 1963, the Swiss had decided that there was much to be gained and nothing to be lost by full membership. Partial membership and even more informal "participation" are often effective means for associating countries with IGOs on a tentative basis when there are reasons, political or otherwise, for eschewing or postponing full membership.

THE SPECIAL-PURPOSE IGO

In a few cases, special organizations have been created by international conventions, but are operated under the laws of the country in which they have their headquarters. EUROCHEMIC and EUROFIMA are two such examples. The former was created by OEEC to build and operate jointly a European plant for the chemical processing of irradiated nuclear fuels.[37] It is an international company of which the shareholders are governments, public or semipublic corporations, and private companies. EUROFIMA is similar; it was set up in Switzerland in 1955 to finance jointly the construction of railway equipment for 16 European countries.[38] Three NATO countries incorporated and operate an international company (Panavia) in Germany, to develop a new fighter plane, the MRCA.[39]

ATTEMPTS AT INNOVATION WHICH DID NOT WORK

The western partners have not always been successful in their efforts to create new forms of international cooperation. The *Atlantic Partnership* was certainly one example. Proposed by President Kennedy in 1962, as a rather vague concept for linking a future 'United Europe" with the United States, the Atlantic Partnership has become a dead issue.[40] The idea, however, had originally attracted Europeans because it offered them "equal status," and Americans because it offered a possible way to ease U.S. burdens in Europe.

[133]

The idea of a *"true Atlantic Community,"* proposed by the Atlantic Convention of the NATO Countries in Paris in 1962, has also not been realized.

In the early 1960s, the U.S. government expended great time and energy in trying to sell its allies on the concept of a *"multilateral force,"* in which naval personnel of the NATO countries would serve together on nuclear-armed ships. The concept was an attempt to take the heat out of the question of whose finger would be on the nuclear trigger, an issue which, at the time, was bedeviling alliance politics. Neither President Kennedy nor President Johnson, however, mustered sufficient political will to convince the doubters among their allies, and the project was scrapped.

The effort to turn the Saarland into a *"European Federal Territory,"* like the District of Columbia, also proved unworkable. The idea depended on the inhabitants of the Saar, who were Germans by birth and culture and who decided in a 1955 referendum that their future, like their past, should lie mainly with the German state.

Still other ideas have been defeated by the spirit of nationalism. The projected *European Defense Community* and *European Political Community* were defeated by the French. The suspension of *majority voting* by the EC in 1965 must also be accounted a definite setback, if not a failure. *The Fouchet Plan* was an effort to circumvent the supranational elements in the EC treaties. In 1961, President de Gaulle pressed on his partners a rather elaborate, cooperative (as distinguished from integrative) system of harmonizing foreign and defense policies. The plan was rejected, after lengthy consideration, by the other five EC governments.

President de Gaulle also tried at least ostensibly to exercise political creativity on the Atlantic front. In 1958, he proposed to Prime Minister Macmillan and President Eisenhower the establishment of a *Political Standing Group*, composed of France, the United Kingdom, and the United States; the group was to act as a kind of executive committee or directorate that could formulate Atlantic Alliance policy and concert "Big Three" actions globally. President Eisenhower agreed consultations would be useful, but rejected the idea of a formal body, ostensibly because of its potentially divisive effect on NATO.

ATLANTIC-PACIFIC IGOS IN A WIDER CONTEXT

In the foregoing account, occasional reference has been made to the provisions of early European treaties which presaged some of the innovations described. Indeed, one might go back even earlier, to the Greek IGOs, for the seeds of important ideas. The main point is not the novelty of all of these developments (and some of them, especially in the revolutionary European Communities, are indeed new), but the combined effect of all the innovations, the ingenious elaborations which have been undertaken, and the relative consistency and continuity with which they have been and are being employed. Furthermore, these efforts have revolutionized relations, not only among the western powers and Japan, but, more indirectly and over a longer time, on a global level. Whether or not these new international "tools" can be applied successfully depends of course entirely on the political will of the nations and leaders who would, or could, use them.

FOOTNOTES

1. See page 117 for further discussion of the Rambouillet meeting, November 1975.

2. In the fall of 1974, the French government agreed on a return to the earlier agreements on qualified majority voting.

3. A.H. Robertson, *European Institutions: Cooperation: Integration: Unification* (3rd edition), (London: Stevens and Sons, Ltd., 1973), p. 231.

4. Article 6 of Protocol II (October 23, 1954) to the Brussels treaty. (For abridged text of the Brussels treaty and subsequent protocols, see Ruth Lawson, *International Regional Organizations: Constitutional Foundations* (New York: Frederick A. Praeger, 1962), pp. 160–161.)

5. Article 6(2), Convention on the Organization for Economic Cooperation and Development, Paris, December 14, 1960 (quoted in Robertson, *European Institutions*, p. 324).

6. See Article 20, Statute of the Council of Europe, London, May 5, 1949 (quoted ibid., pp. 313–314). From a strictly legal point of view,

abstention is allowed in the UN and various other bodies, but vetoes are much more prevalent than in the Euratlantic bodies, where a general permissiveness in this regard is more often than not the rule. Under the League of Nations, separate accords to permit the Council to make majority decisions in a few special cases (but not for its regular work) were undertaken. (See Louis B. Sohn (ed.), *Cases and other Materials on World Law* (Brooklyn, N.Y.: The Foundation Press, 1950), pp. 728-729.

7. For a fairly full account of how IEPG came into being, its functions, etc., see Luciano Radi, "A European Initiative for Cooperation in the Armaments Field," *NATO Review*, no. 3 (June 1977), pp. 8-11. See also *Atlantic News*, no. 974 (November 11, 1977), pp. 1-2.

8. Until the merger of the three EC executives in 1967, the ECSC High Authority exercised even more "supranational" powers than the Commissions of the EEC and EURATOM.

9. Robertson, *European Institutions*, p. 187. Article 10 of the Treaty of Rome states, in part:

> 2. The members of the Commission . . . be completely independent in the performance of their duties. . . . They shall neither seek nor take instructions from any Government or from any other body. . . . Each Member State undertakes to respect this principle and not to seek to influence the members of the Commission in the performance of their tasks.

Upon assuming office, each commissioner makes a "solemn declaration" affirming these principles.

10. Robert O. Keohane and Joseph S. Nye, "Transgovernmental Relations and International Organizations," *World Politics*, vol. 24 (1974), pp. 39-67.

11. Richard N. Cooper, Karl Kaiser, and Masataka Kosaka, *Towards a Renovated International System* (The Triangle Papers: 14), (New York: Trilateral Commission, 1977), pp. 40-41.

12. "The Organization for European Cooperation," *International Organization*, vol. 10 (February 1956), p. 5.

13. Robertson, *European Institutions*, p. 73.

14. Ibid., p. 109.

15. Ibid., p. 109. See also, for the text of the report, *NATO Facts and Figures* (Brussels: NATO Information Service, 1969), pp. 303-313.

16. Robertson, op. cit., p. 82. See also *The Organization for Economic Cooperation and Development* (Paris: OECD Publications, un-

dated), pp. 9–17. It is interesting that the impetus for reconstituting OEEC into something more suitable came from a summit meeting in December 1959 of the presidents of France and the United States, the Federal German chancellor, and the prime minister of the United Kingdom.

17. Robertson (op. cit., pp. 269–270) points out that there is a precedent—although much more restricted in nature than the Council's human rights activities—in the work of the Central Commission for Navigation of the Rhine, which has an international court of lawyers expert in river navigation, and to which nationals convicted by their own courts of offenses against the Rhine navigation rules may appeal. Note also that individuals may also apply to the Court of Justice of the European Communities in certain instances. See Werner Feld, *The Court of the European Communities: New Dimension in International Adjudication* (The Hague: Martinus Nijhoff, 1964), p. 65ff. The case of Costa vs. ENEL (European Court of Justice, No. 6/64, July 15, 1964) was particularly instructive, as the Court ruled that an individual could carry a complaint against an organ of his national government to the EC Court; the Italian government, in this case, had claimed that this was "absolutely inadmissible," but the Court of Justice ruled otherwise (cited in Howard Bliss [ed.], *The Political Development of the European Community: A Documentary Collection* [Waltham, Mass.: Blaisdell Publishing Co., 1970], pp. 71–72).

18. Robertson, op. cit., pp. 277–278.

19. Peter Hay, *Federalism and Supranational Organizations: Patterns for New Legal Structures* (Urbana: University of Illinois Press, 1966), p. 300.

20. A.W. Green, *Political Integration by Jurisprudence* (Leyden: A.W. Sijthoff, 1969), pp. 493–494.

21. Eric Stein, et al., *European Community Law and Organizational Development* (Dobbs Ferry, N.Y.: Oceana Publications, Inc., 1968), p. 165.

22. Feld, op. cit., pp. 34–86. See also Robertson, op. cit., p. 189. In this early period, the European Court's actions are reminiscent of the formative years of the U.S. Supreme Court under Chief Justice John Marshall. In 1979, however, a cloud appeared on the Court's horizon, in the form of the first refusal by a member government to abide by one of its decisions; the case involved a French import quota on British mutton.

23. In other regions of the world, this European experience has animated similar efforts. There is a planned African Court of Human

Rights. Feld (op. cit., p. 122) cites further the plans for an Arab Court of Justice, outlined in E. Foda, *The Projected Arab Court of Justice* (The Hague: Martinus Nijhoff, 1957).

24. See James R. Huntley, *Man's Environment and the Atlantic Alliance*, 2nd ed. (Brussels: NATO Information Service, 1972), pp. 47–48.

25. *Man in a European Society: Intergovernmental Work Programme of the Council of Europe, 1969–1970* (Strasbourg: Directorate of Information of the Council of Europe, 1969), p. 12.

26. The Interparliamentary Union, created in 1889 and still extant, includes MPs from 70 countries, but it has no official sanction from their governments.

27. See page 64, Chapter 3. NAA's status is an unusual one legally; on August 14, 1974, the Belgian Parliament (N.B.: NAA's headquarters is in Brussels) passed a law concerning the Assembly's status. Although there has been no protocol to the NATO treaty or any other agreement among the 15 nations involved, the Belgian statute expressly grants to NAA most of the immunities and privileges accorded an intergovernmental organization. NAA's secretariat members are also granted virtually the same status as international civil servants.

28. For interesting views on the subject, see Kenneth Lindsay, *Towards a European Parliament* (Strasbourg: Secretariat of the Council of Europe, 1958); Joseph Harned and Gerhard Mally, *Atlantic Assembly: Proposals and Prospects* (London: The Hansard Society, 1965); and J. Allan Hovey, Jr., *The Superparliaments: Interparliamentary Consultation and Atlantic Cooperation* (New York: Frederick A. Praeger, 1966); and Elliot R. Goodman, *The Fate of the Atlantic Community* (New York: Frederick A. Praeger, 1975), Chapter 11.

29. Robertson, *European Institutions*, pp. 137–140.

30. Ibid., p. 45.

31. There are, of course, instances of military alliances which were more often than not bilateral which, under the pressure of war, were able to bring about a substantial concerting of policy for a time; OPEC, in the field of economic warfare, is a more modern example. But the NATO and EC experiences are both far more pervasive and better institutionalized than any other. (See also p. 58.)

32. *NATO Facts and Figures*, op. cit., p. 96.

33. Articles containing this provision appear in a number of post-1945 IGO treaties, universal or regional in type. However, the uses to which such articles have been put in NATO and the frequency of use, constitute the unique aspect of this development.

34. Robertson, *European Institutions*, p. 66.

35. See Huntley, *Man's Environment and the Atlantic Alliance* (op. cit.) and *NATO and Science* (op. cit.).

36. *OECD: History, Aims, Structure* (Paris: OECD, 1972), p. 36.

37. See Appendix D, p. 359 and Robertson, op. cit., p. 81. P. Rohn has pointed out to this author the existence of a few interesting precedents for this kind of development: the Constantinople Convention (1888) and the Suez Canal Concession (1854, 1856).

38. Robertson, ibid., p. 81, and *Yearbook of International Organizations*, no. 14 (Brussels: Union of International Organizations, 1972–1973), p. 512.

39. *The Times* (of London), April 1, 1974.

40. See p. 86; also Goodman, op. cit., Chapters 3 and 4.

CHAPTER 5

Action and Interaction Among the Institutions

The aim of this chapter is to clarify the dynamics of the inter-action process within the intergovernmental institutions individ-ually, between the IGOs and member nations, and among the IGOs as a group. The problems of avoiding duplication and co-ordinating the work of IGOs are examined, and improvements suggested.

THE DYNAMICS OF INSTITUTIONS IN COMMUNITY BUILDING

There are important prerequisities to the construction of inter-national communities. Some of these—including shared percep-tions of common purpose; facility of communication; trained manpower available for extranational efforts; and similar social, economic, and political structures—were discussed in Chapter 2. Such factors might be termed collectively the necessary "social infrastructure." Unless they are present to the necessary degree, no amount of goodwill or declarations by heads of government can create the working fabric of international community. Egypt, for example, has expended considerable effort since the 1950s to establish political unions, first between Egypt and Syria, then between Egypt and the Sudan, and Egypt and Yemen, and later between Egypt and Libya. There was no lack of ingenuity in designing common institutions such as joint presidencies, councils of state, interparliamentary assemblies, and ministerial working groups; but the paper institutions and the good intentions of the heads of government involved could not overcome the inertia of national institutions, bureaucratic vested interests, the lack of perception and sophistication, and other problems which characterized the nations involved. Even the European-Atlantic-Pacific institutions have not always been able to overcome the inertia of national institutions or the lack of common perceived interests.

Common institutions, properly designed and launched, can provide a catalyst and the supranational machinery necessary to build an international community. Such common institutions can then gradually acquire a life of their own and an ideological hold on the national institutions and political constituencies involved and thus reinforce that which gave rise to their creation in the first place. Theoretically, the forces of the growing community can, in time, become strong enough to override the special interests and narrow perceptions which might otherwise have frustrated attempts at cooperation, were the institutions not there.

The debate about the importance and efficacy of institutions in such international communities has nowhere been more intense than in postwar (1945) Europe.

Robert Schuman, Foreign Minister of France in the early fifties, recognized both the limitations and the importance of institutions when he proposed the first genuinely supranational European organization, the Coal and Steel Community:

Europe will not be made all at once, or according to a single, general plan. It will be built through concrete achievements, which first create a *de facto* solidarity. . . .[1]

His declaration went on to propose the historic pooling of coal and steel production that was the raison d'etre of the community, asserting:

. . . The solidarity in production thus established will make it plain that any war between France and Germany becomes, not merely unthinkable, but materially impossible.

[142]

In this way there will be realized, simply and speedily, that fusion of interests which is indispensable to the establishment of a common economic system; and that will be the leaven from which may grow a wider and deeper community between countries long opposed to one another by saguinary divisions.[2]

Schuman recognized that the existence of the new framework itself would force men to think in entirely new ways. Ernst Haas elaborated this concept with a theory which rested on the aggrandizing nature of all institutions:

[T]here is no dependable, cumulative process of precedent formation leading to ever more community-oriented organization behavior, unless the task assigned to the institutions is inherently expansive, thus capable of overcoming the built-in autonomy of functional contexts and of surviving changes in the policy aims of member states.[3]

Haas's "unless" clause is the key to the neofunctionalists' theory that European integration would proceed more or less inexorably. Once vital interests were locked together, there could be no going back.

There appear to be gradations in institutional processes, and these can affect efficacy. Haas, in studying the forms of negotiation within international institutions, suggested the prevalence of three types of "compromise," each indicative of a certain stage of development:

1. the least demanding we may call accommodation on the basis of the minimum common denominator . . . the impact of the transaction never goes beyond what the *least* cooperative bargaining partner wishes to concede. . . .

2. Accommodation by 'splitting the difference' carries us a little farther along the path of integration. . . . Con-

flict is resolved, not on the basis of the will of the least cooperative, but somewhere between the final bargaining positions. . . .

3. Finally, accommodation on the basis of deliberately or inadvertently upgrading the common interests of the parties takes us closest to the peaceful change procedures typical of a political community with its full legislative and judicial jurisdictions, lacking in international relations.[4]

The OEEC, in Haas's example, worked on the basis of "splitting the difference" or compromising at the level of the minimum common denominator in all areas except those relating to currency convertibility and the removal of trade quotas; in the latter two, it was possible to raise the common denominator and thus "upgrade the common interests." This process relied heavily on the services of a mediator experienced in working with institutions. Strong secretaries general of NATO, for example, have on occasion performed this role; sometimes it has been accomplished by a board of experts with an autonomous range of powers (as in the High Authority of the Coal and Steel Community). The upgrading process combined intergovernmental negotiation with the participation of independent experts and spokesmen for interest groups, parliaments, and political parties, a combination of interests and institutions that Haas termed "supranational."

The most successful European institutions, the Communities, have employed all three modes of negotiation. Their contribution to "the art of political integration"[5] is surely related to their emphasis on "upgrading the common interest."

The nature and success of the institution are also heavily dependent on the attitudes and behavior of individuals within the institutional framework. A working theory of functionalism in international community building must recognize both the power of institutions to mold thought and behavior and the power of individuals to change institutions.

THE LIMITATIONS OF INSTITUTIONS

Political realities have sometimes placed limitations on an institution, regardless of the constitutional powers of the IGO. A good example of this is found in the Western European Union. WEU's charter granted the Union extensive power to limit and control armaments. Originally, these powers were intended to prevent a resurgent Germany from ever again upsetting the peace of Europe. Yet, their existence has been of little more than historical interest, for these powers were never used and are now moribund.

The Monnet theory of institution building supposed that economic union would inexorably lead to political union. Several recent examples suggest that this may not necessarily be the case. In 1921, Belgium and Luxembourg formed a customs and currency union (BLEU). In 1948, these two states plus the Netherlands dropped customs duties among themselves and formed an economic union (Benelux). Despite these far-reaching economic changes, however, the three states have remained totally separate politically. Political unions of the German states in the nineteenth century did follow from the creation of customs unions, but other factors were present. (Cultural nationalism was a powerful component, and the example and might of Prussia, the unifier, an even greater one.) The Nordic Council also appears to have brought about some unity between the Scandinavian countries (although Haas believes that these changes might well have taken place even without the Council because "they are so deeply rooted in the Scandinavian setting" and therefore "lack the stimulus of controversy and debate"[6]). In any case, there is no evidence that the participating countries are moving in the direction of political union.

Certainly, the practical significance of international institutions is severely limited by their obscurity, facelessness, remoteness, and complexity, as well as by the esoteric nature of their operations. The proliferation of IGOs is a further limitation. Wallace and Singer have documented the growth of IGOs worldwide, from the first in 1815 (Central Commission for the Navigation of the Rhine) to a total of 192 in 1960.[7] By and large, IGOs are unknown to the public; in those few cases in which they are known, their image is usually unfavorable. Fortunately, the latter is not true of the European Communities. Monnet, Hallstein, and other EC leaders saw to it that the progress of "making Europe" was a public matter. The typical European responded positively, and usually strongly, to the idea of European unification. The Communities were recognized as the chief symbol of such unification. NATO has also been accepted publicly as the symbol of an "Atlantic community." But public acceptance of EC and NATO has given them only a relative advantage over other IGOs. In general, they too are unknown. Public ignorance still poses one of the most severe limitations on the use of institutions to achieve supranational integration.

In Coombes's study of the EC, he maintained that the Commission had been forced more and more into a "bureaucratic" role, whereas the need was evident for political leadership to "sell" further integration and to "legitimize measures by [the Commission's] uniquely European character and defining the common interest."[8] He admitted that "bureaucratic activity in the Communities may have been re-oriented in many important respects on to a European axis," but asserted that this meant nothing in terms of political support. "Power in all essentials still rests in the national capitals of Europe." Only by "legitimizing effective leadership at a federal level" would Europe put itself on the true path to integration.[9] To "work" in a political sense, the EC institutions (or any other important IGOs) require a more political framework. Popular elections (which were held for the EC Parliament in 1979) will probably in time make a difference. But the IGOs must also be able to evoke popular appeal, so that people will transfer to them the kind of loyalty which they have traditionally given to their nations. This will be difficult to achieve and is thus a further limitation.

Still another limitation is the lack of suitable personnel. The most technically perfect constitutional schemes will be of no avail unless the institutions reflect the values and behavior patterns of those who make the decisions and of those who carry them out.

Not only are such questions as the commitment of the chief "Eurocrats" to the principle of an ultimate federation at issue, but also such mundane questions as what sort of filing system to use or how to draw up an agenda for a meeting. We shall have more to say later about "supranational personnel," and especially those in leadership categories.

INSTITUTIONAL TECHNIQUES AND PROCEDURES

Henry Aubrey has provided a good description of the mechanics of an important IGO.

The OEEC was an innovator of institutional procedures. It was ingenious in solving crises with the help of special, small working groups of outstanding experts who had sufficient authority and negotiating skill to work out acceptable compromise solutions, such as the guidelines for the division of American aid and the devaluation of 1949.

What proved equally important was the development of techniques of cooperation that were later taken over, adapted, and expanded by the OECD. Actually, the 'technique' does not adequately describe this achievement, because it covers not only an institutional device but also a climate of mutual influence based on 'a sense of corporate responsibility' for a joint undertaking. It is in this general area that we find the enduring success of the OEEC, as well as the somewhat intangible influence of the OECD in its more extensive and diffuse tasks.[10]

The character of meetings is important, because it is here that the general spirit of the IGO can be most notably expressed. Monnet often urged statesmen and "Eurocrats" alike to eschew conventional meetings in conducting diplomacy. Instead of confronting one another around a table and trying to "make points" for their respective countries, they should, said Monnet, sit with one another on *one* side of the table and confront the problem on the *other*: this was the heart of the "Community method."

Aubrey lauded off-the-record "talk-shop" meetings, in which views and information were simply shared. "When talks are plainly a part of the bargaining process proper, the participants will state their positions rather than speak their minds."[11] More informal meetings afford opportunities to try out future policy alternatives. As a former diplomat with years of experience in IGOs noted, "the *real* meeting is over dinner, or on the telephone, or in the corridors." Ultimately, it is the most informal, person-to-person contacts which seem to determine the quality and durability of the work of IGOs, because mutual trust seems to develop best—in fact, some might say *only*—as a result of such relationships.

The interparliamentary bodies connected with IGOs offer yet another set of techniques and relationships. Many, but not all, of the European-Atlantic IGOs have their own parliamentary bodies or are served by legislators from the parliaments of member nations. In either case, a continuing organization or secretariat organizes committee work and public plenaries. Frequent debates and agreed-upon rules of procedure govern these bodies, and there are procedures for reaching conclusions, usually couched in formal resolutions arrived at by some kind of majority vote. Such parliamentary diplomacy rarely settles international questions, but it can be of tremendous value in setting the limits within which eventual settlement is reached. When it works well, an international parliament "mobilizes political mediatory forces—the uncommitted states, parties, groups, or persons—whose voice in the settlement process is given volume by the reluctance of the parties to the dispute to annoy the mediating forces."[12] In contrast, traditional diplomacy greatly reduces the maneuvering room and tends to channel negotiations within a rigid framework controlled by the agents of foreign ministries.

Another interesting technique of IGOs is the "origin of initiatives." Nearly all of the action in the Council of Europe is originally "proposed" from the Secretariat or the Consultative Assembly; the ministers who do hold a strict power of veto are thus consigned to the role of "disposers." In OECD, action must originate in the national capitals. As a result, governments' permanent delegations to OECD have been much larger than those of the Council of Europe, which in some cases does not even have permanent delegations.[13] In NATO, as in OECD, the permanent delegations have played an especially important role. Formally, the permanent delegations work within elaborate committee structures superintended by the Secretariat. Informally, the delegations and secretariats, working closely together, form a "club" which, in both OECD and NATO, has worked surprisingly well. Meetings of ministers or heads of governments actually reflect months of continuing work to prepare the ground before the meeting and then afterwards to see that decisions are subsequently implemented. Overall, the effect is considerable.

THE HUMAN ELEMENT IN INTEGRATION AND COOPERATION

Fortunately, during their formative years, the European Communities and other major IGOs were able to hire efficient and multilingual clerical and staff personnel. There was, of course, a special need for leaders in all important fields (including the business world and the mass communications media) to achieve the necessary degree of unity across national borders. The efforts to create effective European and Atlantic communities since 1945 have rested to a crucial extent on the availability and the capability of such multinational leadership. I believe that, where integration or cooperation has failed significantly, it has done so primarily because of the inability of the people involved to operate in this multinational fashion. The heads of government and leaders at both the highest and the secondary levels of leadership in government and in other crucial fields must have this ability.

Such men as Paul-Henri Spaak, whose sensitivity and ability to think as a "European" rather than as a Belgian was singular, have been instrumental in pushing forward the processes of integration. On the negative side, the lack of this multinational sensitivity by Secretary of the Treasury John Connally probably contributed significantly to the drift away from the ideals of transatlantic partnership and community in the early 1970s. Similarly, Ambassador Arthur J. Goldberg, a former Justice of the U.S. Supreme Court, was criticized for his lack of understanding of America's European allies during the Belgrade Conference in 1977. "We seem to have spent more time negotiating with Arthur Goldberg than negotiating with the Russians," a member of one NATO delegation was quoted as saying.[14]

The factor of multinational capability is even more critical at the level Mosca called "the secondary stratum" of leadership.

> Below the highest stratum in the ruling class there is always, even in autocratic systems, another that is much more numerous and comprises all the capacities for leadership in the country. Without such a class any sort of social organization would be impossible. The higher stratum would not in itself be sufficient for leading and directing the activities of the masses. In the last analysis, therefore, the stability of any political organism depends on the level of morality, intelligence and activity that this second stratum has attained; and this soundness is commonly the greater in proportion as a sense of the collective interests of nation or class succeeds in exerting pressure on the individual ambitions or greeds of the members of this class. Any intellectual or moral deficiencies in this second stratum, accordingly, represent a graver danger to the political structure, and one that is harder to repair, than the presence of similar deficiencies in the few dozen persons who control the workings of the state machine.[15]

This level of leadership generally includes the people who create and present new ideas to the upper levels of leadership and then execute them once top leadership has made its decision. In the army, this level includes those officers whose relations with ordinary soldiers are direct, those who must lead them in battle. In business, it includes that important level of leadership called middle management. In the building of an international community, this group's contribution is vital.

In this sense, integration in the European-Atlantic context has worked in two directions. The requisite minimum number of "European-" and "Atlantic-minded" and linguistically-operational leaders was available to mold, influence, and run the new institutions. In addition, by the very token of serving in the institutions or in a national capacity related to them, many of those in leadership positions "learned on the job." The two processes appear to be mutually reinforcing.[16] However, a critical mass of persons does need to be involved.

Factors present at the conclusion of World War II were uniquely favorable to the creation of such a multinational elite:

1. The wartime experience forged a common bond, not only among the British and Americans and other Allied participants, but even in many cases between the Germans and those they had conquered; Continental Europeans on both sides were profoundly conscious in 1945 of having "lost the war"; there was widespread resolve that never again should Europeans fight brother Europeans in murderous civil conflict.
2. There existed a common philosophical and educational base among the key European elites.
3. The economic prostration of Europe plus the Soviet menace produced a conviction among leadership in the United States and Europe that a united Europe was a necessity; world conditions—not only European conditions—were favorable for the exercise of a new kind of leadership.[17]

The myriad personal bonds, the common emotional experiences, the shared goals, the perceptions of common interests, and a demonstrated capacity for conciliation and compromise that had been necessary to win the war could also be used to unify Europe. The generation of leadership forged in World War II is disappearing today. But the impetus that they gave to international integration and/or effective cooperation has been great. They are being replaced with junior national and international civil servants, some internationally minded members of parliaments and cabinet members, military leaders, journalists who have followed developments internationally, and top executives of multinational and other big corporations. A fair number of these persons have studied in multinational institutions such as the College of Europe, the INSEAD European Business School, or the NATO Defense College. Others have simply learned by serving together in international programs. Such ties were never formed between the Japanese and American leadership following the war, although the quality of rapport could not be termed negligible. Between Japan and Europe, ties of this kind remain extremely tenuous. This fact, coupled with the need of Australia and New Zealand to develop new ties to replace the old ones with Mother Britain, constitute an entirely new set of challenges for the future of the emerging Atlantic-Pacific System.

THE EFFECT OF THE SYSTEM ON THE PARTICIPATING NATIONS

Arthur S. Hoffman has described the impact of the System on a member nation:

> If a country belongs to the system, its freedom of action is circumscribed, its thought processes channeled. In conducting foreign policy it becomes automatic to think of the effect of any action on the system, its other members, one's role in the system as one of its members. Even before that, many of the foreign (and domestic) policy decisions one has to face are shaped by the functioning of the system.[18]

Elliot R. Goodman has described the same phenomenon, with emphasis on the economic impact:

> The fact that the countries of the Atlantic Community are concerned with a common and interrelated set of problems makes it natural for them to share an interest in each other's economic policies; in fact, that these problems are so interdependent practically compels such interest. At the same time, mutual knowledge of each other's institutions has increased mutual confidence, which has in turn contributed to the breakdown of the psychological barriers which in the past have coincided with national borders. In short, the advanced industrial countries are becoming more 'integrated.'[19]

Efforts to cope with this interdependence may in turn further broaden the scope of the common agenda and provide increased occasions for interstate relations. Yet, such interdependence can lead, as Keohane and Nye note, to "a continuing struggle between groups favoring transgovernmental policy patterns and those supporting a return to strategies of national assertion or national protection.[20] For example, in the early 1960s, de Gaulle determined to reverse the course of U.S. business penetration into France. His government denied numerous attempts by U.S. multinational enterprises to purchase French firms or otherwise to establish manufacturing operations inside France. By reason of French membership in the Common Market, however, and indirectly because the process of general interdependence with the rest of the Atlantic countries had proceeded so far, even de Gaulle had to concede ultimate defeat in this policy. Generally speaking, U.S. business has since been welcome in France, as has French business in the United States.

What are some of the specific ways in which IGOs affect the policies of members states?

"The organizations' definitions of which issues cluster together and which should be considered separately may help to determine the nature of interdepartmental committees and other arrangements within governments. In the long run, therefore, international organizations will affect how government officials define 'issue areas.' "[21] Officials of IGOs also can exert personal influence.

Participating officials who work at, or close to, the policy level are influenced by the explanations of events and objectives given by their counterparts, men whom they have come to know and trust. They, in turn, can extend this educational process from the OECD meetings to other government circles at home. And the foreign policy interest can be used to promote, perhaps to open up, new approaches to old issues.[22]

The IGOs can also confront member nations over their policies.

There is no doubt, for example, that such confrontation in the early days of OECD's Development Assistance Group (later Committee) served to increase substantially the level of foreign aid by some European countries and Japan and also made possible more generous terms of loans to less-developed countries.[23]

NATO as well can significantly affect the internal politics of its members. Led by a nonconformist lawyer, Mogens Glistrup, the Danish Progress Party declared its intention of reducing government bureaucracy and abolishing the income tax. However, whereas Glistrup would also have dismantled Denmark's defense establishment (quite justified, he said, because the Soviet Union could "take the country with a telephone call"), the Progress Party's platform was forced to acknowledge that so long as a majority in the Danish parliament favored NATO, "it is hardly possible to cut down the total volume of the defense budget."[24] Because the large majority of Danes obviously believed that the existence of NATO depended in part on their country's participation and constituted a credible guarantee of Denmark's security, the platform of the Progress Party—and perhaps of other Danish parties—had to be significantly changed.

In certain instances, the very existence of IGOs can bring about changes in the policies of even those governments which are not members of the IGO. In July 1976, for example, when a new government took office in Lisbon, its ministers announced that the thrust of its foreign policy would be aimed toward Europe rather than the Third World. The government further announced its intention of asking for immediate admission to the Council of Europe and of opening negotiations for its "integration into the Common Market."[25] A month later, an interview with Premier Constantine Caramanlis of Greece also indicated his feeling that only the shock of competing against the Common Market could do the job of modernizing the Greek economy. Seeing Europe as the "natural and effective guarantor" of Greece's territory and democratic institutions, Caramanlis' efforts reportedly were bent towards integrating his country "politically, culturally and ideologically" with Europe. The prospects of joining EC, and the efforts which would be necessary to make Greece an acceptable member, have clearly been a dominating theme since the restoration of Greek democracy in 1975.[26]

In a quite different way, the EC may have had a considerable indirect effect on the internal politics of another nonmember, Canada. Not long after René Levesque became Premier of Quebec in the upset elections of 1976, he announced that, while his party would seek independence for the province, it would also try to arrange a common market for Quebec and the rest of Canada. Newspaper reports in April 1978 indicated that the premier had been "often in Brussels in recent months, to study the example of the European Communities, to determine whether or not this could also be a model for Canada."[27] Aside from the obvious shock (to the vast majority of North Americans) at the thought of dismantling Canada, the possibility of using the economic union model of the European Common Market for what the British call "devolution of powers" from a central government, in this case to make an existing union less unitary, is nevertheless an intriguing one.

Obviously, IGOs can affect both participating and nonparticipating nations and their governments. The reverse is also true and deserves some comment. In times of crisis, and under the influence of unusual leaders with international vision and the personal power to dominate events, national governments have given impetus to IGOs—in some instances, creating IGOs out of nothing; in others, giving established IGOs wider scope or greater powers. General Marshall in 1947, Robert Schuman in 1950, Paul-Henri Spaak in 1956, and Henry Kissinger in 1974, for example, changed the course of the System positively by the force of their leadership. Sometimes, however, governments retard integration and inhibit cooperation. For example, the EC's new plan for a European Monetary System was held up by the French government in 1979 until agricultural support concessions could be won from Germany. In 1971, the United States "shut the gold window" and devalued the dollar without consulting its chief partners in the System. These potentially negative effects, however, tend to be counterbalanced and over time outweighed by the cumulative impact of the Atlantic-Pacific System. The System has had more than three decades to stabilize and develop a strong life of its own. Whether it will survive is still an unanswerable question.

Before moving on to analyze the interaction of IGOs within

the Atlantic-Pacific System, it might be well to summarize what can be concluded so far about the dynamics of the integration cum cooperation process.

- Institutions alone cannot bring about desired levels of international cooperation, nor will their existence necessarily or automatically lead to political integration.
- "Upgrading the common interest" of the parties in an IGO brings the process of integration closest to the ideal of a true community.
- The integrating effect of international institutions is limited by a variety of factors: how well they are known by the general public, the extent to which their activity is bureaucratic rather than political in nature, and whether there are "supranational-minded" personnel available to operate them.
- Effective IGOs employ numerous procedures and techniques, including working parties, specialized meetings, and interparliamentary diplomacy.
- IGOs cannot work well unless their leaders and clerical staff are skilled in cross-cultural communication and share values and cultural coordinates which make international teamwork possible.
- The domestic and foreign behavior of nations can be modified significantly by their involvement in an IGO.
- IGOs can also affect nations which are not members.
- The nation state itself is still a strong force within the System.

THE EFFECT OF THE SYSTEM ON IGOs

The various European, Atlantic, and Atlantic-Pacific IGOs have influenced one another considerably. They have borrowed structural or procedural innovations from one another; in a few cases, IGOs have preempted an entire field of work from others. The results have not always been beneficent, but this borrowing process is further evidence of a developing System. The more intricate the extended Atlantic System becomes, the more opportunity there will be for such borrowing.

One of the most singular achievements of the OEEC, for example, was the removal of virtually all quantitative restrictions on trade among its members in 1950 under the Code of Liberalization. The initial aim had been to create greater equality in European trade; the final result was a 95 percent liberalization of trade in Europe. Although the code lapsed, the new European Communities in effect reinstituted it by agreeing on rules to cover reimposition of quotas. The code was also incorporated more or less wholesale into the EFTA treaty of 1960. As a result, all quantitative restrictions on trade had been abolished among EFTA members by the middle of 1965. The OEEC precedent and the experience of OEEC members under the code obviously had a direct effect on both the EEC and the EFTA treaties.

An annual review of the economies of OEEC members was begun in the late 1940s, as part of the administration of Marshall Plan funds. The practice was not long thereafter adopted by NATO, as a means of insuring that members' defense expenditure plans were adequate in terms of overall NATO plans.[28] This review process was elaborated greatly in the 1960s by OECD, which applied it to a wide variety of fields—environmental affairs, science policy, education, and energy policy among them. EFTA also adopted the practice and conducted a continuous review of the economic and financial policies of all of its members, "their effects on the others and on the Association as a whole."[29]

The transfer of information and techniques between IGOs in the System is helped by the fact that, in many cases, the same national civil servants are themselves tied in with the process of two or more IGOs. These civil servants can easily take a procedure which works well in one IGO and apply it in another.

In some cases, an IGO has simply served as the model for a new IGO. This was certainly the case with the European Communities. There is no doubt that the prior experiences of political leaders and senior civil servants in designing and operating Benelux and its various components influenced greatly the development of the larger Coal and Steel Community, the European Economic Community, and EURATOM.

The European Communities began in 1952 with the integration of a single economic sector, that of coal, iron, and steel. When IEA was created in 1974, it covered all sources and uses of energy. With IEA, however, the joint exercise of sovereignty by its members was on a much larger, Atlantic-Pacific basis with the United States, Canada, Japan, and others as members. There is no doubt that IEA is a lineal descendant of ECSC.[30]

But borrowing has not always worked. The North Atlantic Assembly's attempt to establish the "Atlantic Conventions," modelled on the European Conventions of the Council of Europe, ended in failure. Borrowing has also inevitably led to a proliferation of activity and to some duplication of effort. This effect can be especially taxing to small countries. If, for example, the EC, the Council of Europe, and OECD decided more or less simultaneously to deal with the problem of worker migration in Europe, their decision would undoubtedly have a significant negative impact on Denmark or Ireland because of the small pool of experts on the subject in those countries: to which organization would they go?

CONSTITUTIONAL BORROWING

Extensive borrowing has been done to draft the various treaties and conventions concluded among the members. Those clauses of the Benelux, ECSC, EEC, and EFTA treaties dealing with free trade, for example, show a clear family relationship, as do the casus foederis clauses of the Dunkirk, Brussels, and NATO treaties. A comparison of the references to democracy in several treaties of the System illustrates the point.

The first postwar treaty in the Atlantic System, the "collective self-defense" pact signed in Brussels on March 17, 1948, affirmed the ideal of democracy. On April 16, 1948, 16 nations signed the Convention for European Economic Co-operation, which also reflected this ideal.

Considering that a strong and prosperous European economy is essential for the attainment of the purposes of the United Nations, the preservation of individual liberty and the increase of general well-being, and that it will contribute to the maintenance of peace. . . .

The Treaty of Washington, which established the North Atlantic Alliance, reaffirmed in similar language the same points.

> [The signatories] are determined to safeguard the freedom, common heritage and civilisation of their peoples, founded on the principles of democracy, individual liberty and the rule of law.

The preamble of the Statute of the Council of Europe (signed one month after the NATO treaty) referred first to "the pursuit of peace based upon justice and international cooperation," then restated the ideal of democracy.

> Reaffirming their devotion to the spiritual and moral values which are the common heritage of their peoples and the true source of individual freedom, political liberty and the rule of law, principles which form the basis of all genuine democracy.

In Article 1(a), the signatories declared their aim "to achieve a greater unity between [the Council's] Members for the purpose of safeguarding and realising the ideals and principles which are their common heritage. . . ." The Council of Europe statute, incidentally, is the only such document which goes on to limit membership to states which uphold such democratic principles and aims; Article 3 states:

> Every Member of the Council of Europe must accept the principles of the rule of law and of the enjoyment by all persons within its jurisdiction of human rights and fundamental freedoms, and collaborate sincerely and effectively in the realisation of the aim of the Council. . . .

When the European Economic Community treaty (Rome, 1957) was drawn up, the preamble also contained a reference to the democratic ideal.

Resolved by thus pooling their resources to preserve and strengthen peace and liberty, and calling upon the other peoples of Europe who share their ideal to join in their efforts. . . .

In 1978, the European Council of the EC countries adopted a statement amplifying this provision of the treaty:

They solemnly declare that respect for and maintenance of representative democracy and human rights in each Member State are essential elements of membership of the European Communities.

DUPLICATION AND OVERLAPPING FUNCTIONS

Table 2 shows 56 separate functions, falling into 12 categories, which are presently performed by some 9 IGOs in the Atlantic-Pacific System. Some of the 56 functions are undertaken by several of the IGOs. The table is inevitably incomplete, as some IGOs perform functions, at least on paper, which they might consider important but which I consider insufficiently important to include. Also, for the sake of simplicity, some related functions which might well be considered separately have been grouped under a single heading. The table is thus not for purposes of exhaustive reference, but is meant to represent the broad spread, occasional bunching, and overlapping of functions. Aubrey has pointed out that:

OECD activities overlap with those of other bodies, such as the World Bank in aid, the International Monetary Fund (IMF) in monetary problems, and the General Agreement on Tariffs and Trade in trade matters. Initially, some observers felt that the OECD, not having a clear-cut field of action, was not needed. . . . the OECD has some tasks that are not preempted by other bodies. But even a manifest overlap should not lead inevitably to the verdict of redundance.[31]

Table 2. The Functions of IGOs In the Atlantic-Pacific System. 1978

Category	Function	BENELUX	COUNCIL OF EUROPE	EUROPEAN COMMUNITIES	EUROPEAN FREE TRADE ASS'N	INTERNATIONAL ENERGY AGENCY	N.A.T.O.	NORDIC COUNCIL	O.E.C.D.	WESTERN EUROPEAN UNION
Foreign Policy	Political Consultation, Foreign Policy	X	X				X	X		X
	Coordinate International Negotiations		X	X				X	X	
	Conduct International Negotiations			X					X	
Economic Policy and Activity	Economic Policy Harmonization	X	X						X	X
	Establishment of a Customs Union	X		X						
	Establishment of a Free Trade Area				X					
	Economic Projections and Forecasts			X					X	
	Monetary Consultation, Coordination	X		X					X	
	Joint Monetary Policy and Action			X						
	Trade Policy Harmonization				X				X	
	Fiscal Policy Harmonization	X		X					X	
	Joint Industrial Policy and Action			X						
	Industrial Policy Studies, Coordination			X					X	
	Judicial Regulation of Competition			X						
	Mitigation of Distortions of Competition			X	X					
	Multinational Enterprise, Studies, Harmonization			X					X	
	Joint Patent Registration			X						
	Patent Harmonization		X	X						
	Joint Agricultural Policy	X		X						
	Agricultural Policy Harmonization			X						
	Agricultural and Fisheries Research							X		
	Study and Promotion of Tourism			X				X	X	
	Transport Policy Harmonization			X				X	X	
Defense	Defense Policy Harmonization						X			X
	Joint Military Commands						X			
	Joint Military Staff Structure, Plans						X			
	Joint Military Exercises and Training						X			
	Joint Military Infrastructure						X			
	Cooperative Defense Equipment Programs						X			
	Control of Armaments						X			X
Social and Cultural	Social Research, Plans, Coordination			X					X	X
	Cultural Protection, Cooperation		X						X	
	Public Health Promotion, Harmonization		X						X	
	Movement of Persons, Harmonization and Promotion		X	X					X	
Education	Educational Research and Planning	X	X						X	X
	Educational Cooperation	X	X	X					X	
	Manpower Research, Policy Promotion			X					X	X
Environment	Environmental Research		X						X	
	Environmental Policy Harmonization		X	X					X	X
	Environmental Policy Promotion		X	X					X	X
Energy	Energy Research		X			X			X	X
	Energy Consultation, Planning, Promotion		X			X		X	X	
	Joint Energy Policies		X			X				
	Joint Nuclear Research		X							X
	Parliamentary Discussions, Debates, Studies	X	X	X	X		X		X	X
Development	Development Aid, Study and Promotion		X							X
	Joint Development Aid Programs		X	X						
	Development Aid Programs for Members		X	X						
Science	Science Policy Study and Promotion		X					X	X	X
	Science Policy Harmonization		X					X		
Communication	Postal Union (Domestic Rates for Members)		X						X	
	Broadcasting Coordination		X						X	
Civic Matters	Protection of Human Rights		X							
	Defense, Promotion of Liberal Democracy		X							
	Legal and Administrative Harmonization	X	X						X	
	Adjudication, Fact Finding in Trade Disputes									
Missing or Inadequately Discharged Functions	Rule-Making for Multinational Enterprises									X
	Joint Operations to Control Terrorism			X						
	Joint Operations to Cope with Natural Disasters							X		
	Overall Political Direction of System									
	Coordination of Atlantic and Pacific Defense									
	Coordination of Pacific Economic Interests									
	Parliamentary Control of IGOs			X						
	Systematic Coordination of IGOs									
	Fully International Currency, Reserves									
	Educational Program-Community Ideals									

Aubrey commented further:

> Since OECD activities in some fields overlap with those of other organizations, we may ask what would constitute a meaningful demarcation. Yet, is this the right question to ask? It seems to assume that there is but one "proper" conduit through which all policies on a particular matter must be funneled. This is clearly an unrealistic concept for the conduct of foreign relations. A variety of instrumentalities, used pragmatically and flexibly, provides a range of options; moreover, several can be used, simultaneously or alternately, as the situation demands. And always, there are the conventional and enduring methods of bilateral talks and negotiations.[32]

Within the Atlantic-Pacific System, for example, environmental affairs are treated by four, and possibly more, of the System's IGOs. OECD funds technical studies and has tended to concentrate on the market distortions which arise when countries adopt different regulations to control pollution. NATO, in its "Challenges to Modern Society" program, has attempted to integrate the results of research and the best practices in environmental control into policy for its members. The Council of Europe sees to it that signatory nations adopt and carry out policies and action with respect to specific environmental hazards (e.g., pollution in the Rhine). The European Communities have duplicated virtually all of these activities as they have gradually become concerned with the relationship of the environment to the Common Market. Certainly, the performance of all of these functions differs according to the capabilities and more or less unique working methods of each individual institution.

Indeed, IGOs with small, more homogeneous memberships (such as the Nordic Council) are sometimes able to accomplish more, faster than the larger IGOs (such as OECD). Nonetheless, there is a good argument for using both, because a particular IGO may carry special political "punch." The scattered, incongruent pattern of membership in the various IGOs is also a factor, since some countries might be left out of the work of one, but be reachable through others.

Although at the outset of establishing a function several IGOs may duplicate efforts, eventually functions tend to be distributed more rationally, with an overall result that is usually satisfactory and beneficial. But not all duplication can be explained or rationalized satisfactorily. There is a need for better coordination in many fields. There could be some pruning and adjusting of functions. There are some functions which affect only some of the members of the System. There are also important international functions which no IGO or combination of national efforts has yet performed well or, in some cases, at all.

RELATIONS AMONG IGOs

There is already a good deal of informal cooperation and coordination among the secretariats of Euratlantic IGOs. For example, one IGO might request another to undertake a study of a particular problem. Thus, the Council of Europe has often asked the OECD to study a problem because OECD possessed staff and access to outside experts (especially U.S.), while the Council of Europe did not. On the other hand, the Council of Europe has an active parliamentary assembly, while OECD has none. Therefore, the expert conclusions reached by OECD on a particular matter stand a better chance of gaining publicity and public support through the Council's Assembly than through OECD's Council of Ministers. The Council of Europe and OECD maintain a standing agreement to consult on technical questions. Socini has pointed out that, as international problems often have both a technical and a political aspect, an IGO whose character is primarily political may usefully collaborate with another whose character is technical, to design and to implement a particular project.[33]

Some IGOs have been empowered to send recommendations to other bodies for action. Thus, the Assembly of the Council of Europe receives reports from the ministerial councils of EFTA and OECD and from the High Authority of ECSC. When EEC and EURATOM were created in 1958, arrangements were made to communicate their commissions' annual reports along with that of the EC's European Parliament to the Consultative Assembly of the Council of Europe.[34] Socini felt that all these reporting activities and interactions, centering on the Council, implied "a certain right of supervision," with the Council more or less thrust into a coordinating role.

The symbiosis between NATO and the European Communities has been especially important. "While NATO does not form part of the movement for European unity," observed Robertson, "it is a condition of its success."[35] Many observers have referred similarly to NATO's role in the early postwar years, as the shield behind which western Europe's economic reconstruction and political consolidation could take place. In recent years, NATO membership has also been considered advantageous for nations, such as Portugal, which wanted to enter the EC. In October 1977, the President of the European Commission, in an interview reported in *Atlantic News*, pointed out NATO's dependency on the EC: "NATO is older than the European Community, but I doubt very much that it could continue after a break-up of the Community." Economic success and security "cannot be divorced. If we do not succeed within the Community to re-establish and improve our economic cohesion, this will endanger our external security."[36]

The EC and NATO have sometimes worked in tandem in the foreign policy field. In January 1978, a working group of the EC countries met in Copenhagen and traveled to Brussels for a meeting with the NATO countries to prepare a common position for the Belgrade conference on European security.[37]

This kind of interaction has been evident for several years in the role played by the Western European Union in its attempts to bridge the gap between EC and the EFTA countries. WEU's importance stemmed from the composition of its membership: the six EC countries plus Great Britain. The WEU Assembly in June 1960 urged the United Kingdom's accession to EURATOM; in November 1960, it proposed British membership in all three Community institutions. The British government responded positively, but carefully. In May 1961, when the WEU Assembly met in London, Prime Minister Harold Macmillan gave the idea encouragement in an address to the parliamentarians. Two months later, he announced in the House of Commons that the U.K. would apply to join the EEC. Between 1963 and 1971, there were three successive British applications and two French vetoes; WEU helped to maintain hope and pressure until the United Kingdom was finally accepted for membership. Of all the European-Atlantic IGOs, WEU is today the obvious first candidate, along with EFTA, for the scrap heap; yet, at various times and in various ways, it has performed needed tasks.[38]

There are many arguments for a greater consolidation of the functions of the many IGOs. However, it might be well to take stock of the virtues of this somewhat excessive pluralism. The present decentralized system, with a number of more or less independent bodies, lends itself more readily to "pruning," including the elimination of IGOs such as WEU, for example, than if there were just one or two large, comprehensive IGOs which encompassed all functions. Within the Atlantic-Pacific System, if one organization weakens, others are available to supplant it quickly, and the System goes on.[39]

The interaction between a particular IGO and nonmembers which are nevertheless part of the larger System is also an interesting phenomenon, especially so in the case of the European Communities and the United States. The so-called "Kennedy Round" of trade negotiations, begun under GATT in 1962, was organized largely at the initiative of the United States. While one United States motive was to pressure the EC to keep its new common external tariff low, another American aim—and more important—was to give EC a strong incentive to complete the common market and reach agreement on common policies, so that a greater degree of European political unity, which the United States as well as the Europeans wished to see, would tend to come about.

Coordination among IGOs, in a few cases, has been specifically encouraged by international statutes. The EURATOM treaty specified close collaboration with the OEEC. The OECD treaty (Article 12) also provided specifically for cooperation with other IGOs and nonmember nations:

Upon such terms and conditions as the Council may determine, the Organization may: (a) address communications to nonmember States or organizations; (b) establish and maintain relations with nonmember States or organizations; and (c) invite nonmember Governments or organizations to participate in activities of the Organization.

Although there is no analogous provision in the North Atlantic Treaty, the NATO Assistant Secretary General for Political Affairs has nevertheless coordinated the activities of NATO with other IGOs. The Council of Europe has an External Relations Service to do the same.[40]

Cooperative, even symbiotic, relationships between IGOs and nongovernmental international bodies are also frequent within the Atlantic-Pacific System. In 1976, as a result of the so-called "Lockheed Scandal," OECD worked out a voluntary code of conduct for multinational corporations which was published widely in OECD member countries. Subsequently, the International Chamber of Commerce came out with its own code of conduct. OECD has worked on many international problems in concert with two private groups set up specifically for the purpose: the Trade Union Advisory Committee (TUAC) and the Business and Industry Advisory Committee (BIAC). Nongovernmental international instruments of this kind are reminders that IGOs and the extended Atlantic System as a whole do not have a life apart from that of the larger international community.

Improving Coordination and Rationalizing the System

Overall, the record of the European-Atlantic-Pacific IGOs has been generally satisfactory. Nevertheless, improvement in the System is desirable. The mounting public concern for "inflated bureaucracies" and inefficient government should provide ample grounds, in and of itself. Effective reform may be the price of preserving the System.

The task of devising concrete measures is not easy. Socini has pointed out that most IGOs in the Atlantic System were created under difficult, special, or even contradictory political circumstances. At the time, no thought was given to the question of liaison with other IGOs (except in the case of OECD). Lately, IGOs have tried to "enlarge their domains of competence" and "exceed their terms of reference" without worrying about "invading" areas reserved to other IGOs. In addition, most states belong to several IGOs whose programs may well differ or conflict, and these states sometimes act in one IGO in a manner which may not square with their actions in another.[41] All these factors complicate the task of improving coordination among the IGOs.

Such coordination may be approached in two ways: (1) by attempting to prevent and eliminate conflict and duplication, or (2) by developing cooperation among IGOs active in the same fields. Probably a combination of these approaches is called for. A number of measures, suggested by Socini and others, might be employed. Several IGOs could use the same central agency (such as an international court) to fulfill similar functions, but for different purposes. The three European Communities did this on a large scale, even before they merged their administrative/executive functions. The same individuals or groups of individuals could serve in two or more IGOs; for example, members of parliament might be represented in several international assemblies, as is done in the assemblies of the ECSC, the Council of Europe, and WEU. A country which is not a member of a particular IGO might nevertheless send observers to the IGO's meetings. By this means, the EFTA countries might, for instance, be represented on the Council of the European Communities, which adopts economic measures that often affect their vital interests as participants in the same free trade area.

The number of assemblies should be reduced. With great patience, complicated plans for "three-tier" or "back-to-back" assemblies have been suggested in the past, but have not been put into effect.[42] The advent of a directly elected European Parliament, in 1979, could provide a convenient excuse to begin coordinating this function.

There is also something to be said for trying to center the headquarters of all European, Atlantic, and Atlantic-Pacific bodies in one city. Not only could cooperation among IGOs be expected to improve, but member governments could combine their delegations. This would also make it possible for representatives of one IGO to participate as observers at meetings of others, enable IGOs to present regular reports of their activities to other IGOs, and make it easier for all IGOs to exchange agendas for major meetings and planned work programs. Finally, such centralization would make possible joint meetings of the organs of several IGOs; this could be of particular value with respect to the parliamentary assemblies.

IGOs should be willing to recommend actions to other IGOs. IGOs should also be able to request other IGOs to undertake studies of a particular subject.

How could these and other improvements in IGO machinery be effected? Socini has proposed an agreement between all states which are members of at least one European IGO (presumably this could be extended geographically to include the United States, Canada, Japan, Australia, and New Zealand). The agreement would commit the IGOs to exchange information and documents, to send observers to other IGOs as appropriate, to consult one another's experts, and to hold joint sessions of their various organs. Socini has also proposed that the member states create a "European Committee of Coordination," composed of one representative of each "supreme directing organ" of every European IGO; this committee would designate one IGO to undertake the "executive work of coordination."[43] However, after setting forth these probably useful, but rather mechanical plans, Socini has concluded that "in the last analysis, one must count on the careful preparation and the goodwill of the international civil servants" to make coordination work. Again, the value of common training, experiences, and associations among such personnel is evident.[44]

THE WORKING OF THE SYSTEM AS A WHOLE

The IGOs of the Atlantic-Pacific System constitute, in effect, a panoply of instruments which can be used in concert to undertake large, complex international tasks. On occasion, other regional organizations or universal bodies from the UN "family" will also be involved. There are three good historical examples of such coordination.

The Helsinki Agreements of 1975 on Cooperation and Security in Europe, the parallel MBFR (mutual and balanced force reduction) negotiations and the subsequent Belgrade conference (1977–78) were all part of an ongoing process. In 1969, the new Brandt government in West Germany had initiated a policy of "Ostpolitik," designed to open up relations with the East. Under the new Nixon administration, the United States took leadership in the process of "détente," but always with consultation in NATO. Meanwhile, as a result of an initiative by President Pompidou, the European Community countries had begun systematic regular consultation on their foreign policies in 1970; this mechanism inserted itself increasingly into the détente process and later in the preparations for and conduct of the Helsinki negotiations. Thus, all of the various efforts toward détente were "coordinated" within NATO, but with a special and central role for the EC foreign policy group.

Similarly, the Dillon, Kennedy, and Tokyo Rounds of trade negotiations involved several IGOs, most notably the OEEC (which became OECD during the Dillon Round), the European Economic Community (later, simply EC), and the General Agreement on Tariffs and Trade (GATT). The actual negotiations took place within GATT, an 83-member organization; the western allies sorted out their general approach in OEEC/OECD; and the six (later, nine) members of EC adopted a common position and negotiated through their European Commission.

The international energy crisis, beginning with the oil boycott of October 1973, also called for coordinated measures over a wide front. One can argue that the crisis was only partly, or inadequately, met; yet, a considerable international effort, involving several existing instruments plus new ones created for the purpose, was made. Without that effort, the situation would undoubtedly have been much more critical than it was; in the event, the System held.

In such situations and others, the extended Atlantic System has worked reasonably well. The growing interdependence of the members has virtually compelled their participation on the basis of their interests as they have perceived them. Activity among the individual IGOs and in the System as a whole has constantly increased. This, in turn, has contributed to the confidence of the members in each other and in the System. The System, however, in its present form, has distinct limits. In the interests of improving its capabilities and lowering costs to taxpayers, beneficial changes could be made.

FOOTNOTES

1. May 9, 1950; quoted in Howard Bliss (ed.), *The Political Development of The European Community: A Documentary Collection* (Waltham, Mass.: Blaisdell Publishing Co., 1970), p. 31.

2. Ibid., pp. 31–32.

3. Ernst B. Haas, "International Integration: the European and the Universal Process," in B. Landheer (ed.), *Limits and Problems of European Integration* (The Hague: Martinus Nijhoff, 1963), p. 17.

4. Ibid., p. 8.

5. Ibid., pp. 9–11.

6. Ibid., p. 12.

7. Michael Wallace and J. David Singer, "Intergovernmental Organization in the Global System, 1815–1964," *International Organization*, XXIV (Spring 1970), pp. 239–287.

8. David Coombes, *Politics and Bureaucracy in the European Community* (London: George Allen and Unwin, Ltd., 1970), p. 296ff.

9. Ibid., pp. 307–308, 320.

10. Henry G. Aubrey, *Atlantic Economic Cooperation: The Case of the OECD* (New York: Frederick A. Praeger, 1967), p. 27. The same spirit obtained in NATO as well, from its earliest days. "The practice of finding the *right* answer, regardless of [foreign ministry] instructions, informal, off-the-record sessions and then getting the respective governments to adopt has been very valuable [in NATO]." (Personal letter to the author from Ambassador T.C. Achilles, one of the drafters of the North Atlantic Treaty, September 11, 1978.)

11. Aubrey, op. cit., p. 144.

12. Haas, op. cit., p. 9. In practice, the OECD Secretariat does sometimes take informal policy initiatives, but usually restricts these to matters connected with discrete tasks assigned to it.

13. Robertson, *European Institutions*, pp. 74–75.

14. Don Cook, "Making America Look Foolish: The Case of the Bungling Diplomat," *Saturday Review* (May 13, 1978), pp. 8–11.

15. Gaetano Mosca, *The Ruling Class* (English title; translated by

Hannah D. Kahn from the original, *Elementi di Scienza Politica),* (New York: McGraw Hill, 1939), pp. 404–405. Mosca was a member of the Italian Parliament and a professor of constitutional law whose theories on the social functions of elites have had a pervasive influence on modern scholarship in the field.

16. Psychological research has provided evidence that barriers between groups can best be broken down by means of common work towards shared goals. Applying the lessons of his experiments internationally, Joseph de Rivera noted "that attempts at European integration failed as long as they were structured in terms of global ideals and politics. It was simply impossible to get enough consensus and enough willingness to give up national power. The Schuman plan for a coal and steel community had the advantage of being a concrete plan to accomplish a definite task." See Joseph de Rivera, *The Psychological Dimension of Foreign Policy* (Columbus, Ohio: Charles Merrill, 1968).

17. For a more detailed discussion of leadership in this historical context, see James R. Huntley, "The Role of Leadership in Rebuilding the Atlantic System," *Orbis*, vol. X, no. 1 (Spring 1966).

18. Arthur S. Hoffman, in a note to J.R. Huntley, August, 1975.

19. "The Impact of the Multinational Enterprise upon the Atlantic Community," *Atlantic Community Quarterly*, (Fall 1972), p. 357.

20. Robert O. Keohane and Joseph S. Nye, "Transgovernmental Relations and International Organizations," *World Politics*, vol. 27 (1974), p. 61.

21. Ibid., pp. 50–51.

22. Aubrey, op. cit., p. 103.

23. Ibid., p. 105.

24. *Christian Science Monitor* (June 17, 1976), p. 19.

25. *International Herald Tribune*(July 27, 1976), p. 2.

26. *International Herald Tribune* (August 28–29, 1976), p. 4.

27. *Frankfurter Allgemeine*, Frankfurt (April 3, 1978), p. 14.

28. The origins and mechanisms of the country review are described in some detail in Chapter 4.

29. *The European Free Trade Association: Structure, Rules, and Operation* (Geneva: EFTA Secretariat, 1976), p. 63.

30. The writer is indebted to Joseph Harned of the Atlantic Council of the United States for this insight.

31. Aubrey, op. cit., p. 7.

32. Ibid., pp. 83–84.

33. Roberto Socini, *Rapports et Conflits entre Organisations européenes* (Leiden: A.W. Sythoff, 1960), p. 49.

34. See in this connection, A.H. Robertson, op. cit., pp. 171, 201–202, 231; and Socini, op. cit., pp. 76, 85–86, 150ff.

35. Robertson, op. cit., p. vii.

36. *Atlantic News*, no. 966 (October 12, 1977), p. 4.

37. *Atlantic News*, no. 992 (January 13, 1978), p. 1.

38. Robertson, op. cit., p. 143ff.

39. Haas, op. cit., p. 13.

40. Socini, op. cit., p. 51.

41. Ibid., pp. 43–44, 47.

42. See especially, J. Allan Hovey, Jr., *The Superparliaments: Interparliamentary Consultation and Atlantic Cooperation* (New York: Frederick A. Praeger, 1966); various reports of the Council of Europe, beginning in 1956; various publications of WEU, from 1957 to 1962; and Joseph Harned and Gerhard Mally, *Atlantic Assembly: Proposals and Prospects* (London: Hansard Society, 1965); Joseph Harned, "Atlantic Assembly—A Genesis," *Atlantic Community Quarterly*, vol. 3, no. 1 (Spring 1965).

43. Socini, op. cit., pp. 163–164.

44. Ibid., p. 56. See also Resolution 607 of the Consultative Assembly of the Council of Europe (November 27, 1975), Strasbourg, which recommended "complementary, not competitive" activity by the various IGOs and improved coordination.

CHAPTER 6

Comparisons With Other Regional and World Systems

The extended Atlantic System, while in some ways similar to other regional systems, is also fundamentally different from all of them. It is characterized by its voluntary character. In some, but not all the regional systems, for example, states may join in the various activities or not, or leave once they have joined, if they wish. The System's members are united in achieving common goals through relatively advanced, effective agencies and methods. The System is useful, not only to its members, but also to other nations. The basic difference between the extended Atlantic System and all other systems is this: the Atlantic System has many of the attributes of an international community as defined in Appendix A (pp. 324–325); the others possess few, if any.

The present chapter examines some of the other international systems, both regional and universal, in order to clarify the characteristics of the extended Atlantic System. The relationships between the Atlantic System and other systems will be treated. A general trend toward regional organization in various parts of the world will be reviewed.

THE UNIVERSAL INTERNATIONAL SYSTEM: THE UN "FAMILY"

More of the world's governmental work is being administered

by intergovernmental bodies. Certainly, no others are more active or more in the public eye than those of the United Nations. The origins and detailed workings of the UN have been explained elsewhere, with great competence.[1] I shall try simply to point out some salient features of the so-called "universal system," compare it with the extended Atlantic System, and briefly discuss its future. At the end of this chapter, I will examine the future, possible relationship of the nascent Atlantic-Pacific community with the universal system.

In 1978, the United Nations had more than 150 members, but it was still not fully "universal" in its make-up. A number of very new or small countries did not belong to the UN, nor did such large nations as South Korea, North Korea, the Socialist Republic of Vietnam, or the Republic of China (Taiwan).

Two bodies, loosely tied to the UN, GATT (General Agreement on Tariffs and Trade) and IAEA (International Atomic Energy Agency), had substantially fewer members than the UN itself: GATT had 83 in 1978, and IAEA had 109. This same type of membership pattern has prevailed in the "specialized agencies" of the UN. There is, thus, within the UN family an untidy pattern of memberships, not dissimilar from that within the Atlantic System. Some countries must evidently believe that membership in one or the other UN body will not be of substantial benefit to them; others will not, or cannot for political reasons, belong to certain organizations. Some may simply not be able to afford membership and all that it entails in financial or representational terms. The less-than-universal character of the UN system, despite its aspirations, is evident. Yet, it is paradoxical that the effort to include all nations also restricts the UN's effectiveness.

United Nations Peacekeeping

The most crucial task of the UN, when it was set up in 1945 as the successor to the League of Nations, was to maintain international peace and security. The attempt to discharge this task has represented the UN's most singular failure and revealed its most glaring weaknesses. The problem arose out of the lack of cooperation among the major powers. The wartime "Big Four"—the USSR on the one hand and the United States plus the United Kingdom and China, on the other—could not agree on the conditions of peace.[2] The differences between the United States and the USSR in particular proved especially fateful and eventually erupted in what came to be known as the Cold War. Goodrich and Simons have described the factors underlying this standoff and the consequent inability of the UN to keep the peace in a major sense:

> Although [the United States and the USSR] had been allies in the war against the Axis, differences in their accepted values, their historical experiences, their economic and political systems, their guiding principles and purposes, their general outlooks on the world made intimate association unlikely and placed serious obstacles in the way of cooperation. The fact that they were thrown into close contact with each other in many unsettled areas under conditions of great stress and strain made cooperation even more difficult. The awesome fact of the atomic bomb, the circumstances in which it was developed and used, the profound ideological conflict and suspicions and distrusts of long standing probably made it impossible.[3]

In the late sixties and seventies, the Cold War might be said to have diminished somewhat in intensity and acerbity. At least at times and in certain places, a condition ensued which was generally described as "détente" (which means only "a lessening of tension"[4] and not, as many have surmised, an accommodation or settlement). Nevertheless, the basic differences between the two superpowers and their close allies remained.

There have been times when the two Cold War contenders have agreed that conditions in a particular area such as the Middle East were so potentially volatile that it behooved them to set the international peace-keeping machinery of the UN Security Council in motion. In other cases, they have acquiesced in UN peacekeeping operations (as in the India-Pakistan War of 1965), because their own interests suggested that status quo in an important area was better than any new, but unstable equilibrium which might emerge from further conflict. On one occasion only (Korea, 1950) has the Security Council authorized collective UN intervention to halt aggression, and that instance happened under very special circumstances. The absence of the Soviet delegate to the Security Council (because his country was "boycotting" that body), and the ability and willingness of the United States to commit substantial armed forces for the UN action, enabled the Security Council to act in the case of Korea. In all other cases, no U.S. or Soviet troops have been directly involved in UN peacekeeping operations. The nations which have provided combat-ready troops have tended to be neutral nations or those (such as Canada) considered not sufficiently powerful to upset the Cold War balance. In cases where the forces of the USSR and the United States have confronted one another over a border which both have held to be of vital interest, as in Europe, the UN's efforts have been completely unavailing.

The old League of Nations was the first important worldwide attempt to organize what was called "collective security." Under the Charter of the League, members were pledged to act together against an aggressor, but it was never possible to define "aggression." Furthermore, the failure of the United States to join the League insured that its collective security machinery, however inadequate, could not function effectively. In 1945, the United States took a very different course and joined with its wartime allies to create a United Nations which they believed embodied a more realistic set of structures and procedures than the old League.

In the United Nations, the job of dealing with threats to the peace was given to the Security Council, which had five permanent members (Britain, France, China, the United States, and the USSR) and six (later increased to ten) non-permanent members. Any of the five permanent members could cast a negative vote, the celebrated veto. It was assumed—wrongly, as it turned out—that the allied powers which had won the war would maintain a general identity of interests in peacetime and that therefore the Big Five would be able to find agreement when it was necessary for the Security Council to act. However, at critical times, when no identity of interest between the Security Council's Permanent Members could be found, the UN has been paralyzed. Arthur S. Banks and his colleagues have characterized the situation:

> Since the requisite measure of unity has seldom proved attainable in practice, the organization, in its dealing with peace and security matters, has been effective only to the degree that political accord has been possible in relation to specific international disputes, and that the parties to such conflicts have been willing to allow the UN to play its intended role.[5]

In a perceptive work on collective security, Pick and Critchley concluded:

> The management of power can only be centralized where there is an identifiable and identified range of common interests. This correlation cannot be found at the universal, global level. This is a pity, but it is also a fact.[6]

The UN's intervention, therefore, can only be relied on to cope with limited situations. Even in those situations, the force of the world community, such as it is, is never certain. Much more reliance than the framers of the UN Charter had hoped has thus been put on national armed forces and on regional or bilateral alliances, such as NATO, ANZUS, CENTO, the Japanese-U.S. Mutual Security Treaty, and the Warsaw Pact. The United Nations, like the League of Nations, possesses inadequate machinery for collective security. Nonetheless, its failure has been essentially political, a reflection of its constitutional weaknesses.

Arms Regulation

The UN has also failed in the field of arms control, mandated to it by its Charter. (In this area, too, the League of Nations had tried and failed.) The UN Security Council in 1945 was given the responsibility of formulating plans for "a system for the regulation of armaments." To succeed, these plans would have had to fit within the framework of a larger system of regularized intervention in international disputes by UN forces. Such a system was never developed fully.

During and after the Korean War, responsibility for arms control was placed in the UN General Assembly, an even weaker body than the Security Council. Special commissions and committees on disarmament and arms control were created. A General UN Conference on Disarmament, which was held in 1978, concluded its work in an atmosphere of perhaps greater pessimism than that in which it had begun. Once more, the dispute between the superpowers and the more fundamental cleavage it symbolized between rival conceptions of human society and world order, overshadowed the situation.

In the period between 1945 and 1978, whatever limited success in arms regulation was achieved came very largely as a result of direct negotiations between the Soviet Union and the United States. The first postwar arms control agreement was reached in October 1963, when the two superpowers signed the Nuclear Test Ban Treaty; the UN General Assembly subsequently "ratified" this treaty by resolution. In 1968, a nuclear nonproliferation treaty was first signed by the USSR and the United States and then opened to others for signature. Several countries which did not have nuclear weapons, but did have the capability to manufacture them refused to sign. (India later exploded its own first nuclear device.)

In 1971, the United States, USSR, and the United Kingdom agreed on a new limitation of biological weapons (amplifying a 1925 Convention). Again, the General Assembly approved the treaty, but it was the superpowers, not the UN, which had brought it about because they had believed it served their interests to do so. Although the UN's Disarmament Commission had spent endless hours discussing these matters, preparing draft agreements, and authorizing technical studies, it could not press the matter forward. Significant progress came only when the two big powers were able to reach an accord. Other minor agreements followed, but with the successful conclusion of the first Strategic Arms Limitation Talks (SALT) in 1971, the de facto assumption of initiative and responsibility by the two superpowers for really important collective arms control and disarmament decisions was made explicit. The UN at times had played a useful role, but always a minor one; the deep conflict between the United States and USSR and their respective coalitions had effectively emasculated any possible UN role in arms regulation. It is most likely that even if the Cold War and the uncertain times which have followed it had not existed, other rivalries, conflicting perceptions of interests, and misunderstandings would have precluded effective world action through the UN.

With respect to keeping what one might call "the Big Peace"—that is, direct, effective measures that prevented the outbreak of World War III—by far the major responsibility has been borne by the United States unilaterally, by NATO collectively, and by a few subsidiary alliance systems on the western side. For the past three decades, these have maintained a combination of nuclear and conventional, as well as strategic and tactical, forces that appear to have had the necessary "balancing" (and therefore deterrent) effect.

For those who worry about the possibility of large-scale conflict and who wish for a more effective, universal system of collective security, the record of the UN is depressing. Again, Goodrich and Simons have stated what appears to be the only realistic conclusion:

> In looking to the foreseeable future, therefore, it would seem that Members of the United Nations will have to rely primarily on their national armed forces and the forces that are made available under special defense agreements permitted by the Charter to meet major military attacks.[7]

Still, there have been numerous occasions when, through the good offices of the UN Secretary General or General Assembly or by means of the informal "corridor" network among national delegations to the UN, powers which might otherwise have gone to war have been induced instead to talk and to find a way to resolve their differences or forestall open conflict. If only as a forum of this kind, the UN is probably worth the expense and effort entailed.

Initially the UN had 51 members. Of these, more than half were close allies or protégés of the United States in western Europe or Latin America. In the UN General Assembly, therefore, the United States, and its two closest wartime allies, Britain and France, could count on a handy majority in support of their views in most debates. The tensions of the Cold War, however, soon manifested themselves and were greatly exacerbated with the advent of wholesale "decolonization" in the 1950s. The western majority was rather quickly swamped in the flood of new Asian and African members.[8] In the same period and increasingly in the 1960s, most of the Latin American countries also began to revise their positions and to align themselves in the UN with other underdeveloped nations.

Collectively, the developing countries came to be known as the "Third World," and they formed various blocs, such as the Bandung Conference and later the Group of 77. These regional groups and blocs gradually turned the General Assembly into a quite different body from that which its framers had envisaged. Among other things, it became highly politicized, as did certain of the specialized agencies, such as UNESCO and the International Labor Organization. For their own purposes, the Soviet Union and, to a lesser extent, the Peoples' Republic of China after its admission in 1971 attempted, often with considerable success, to play off the less-developed countries against the western powers within the UN. In recent years, UN political debates (plus many that would not ordinarily be thought of as political) have been dominated by such issues as the Palestinian conflict, the Vietnam War, the general turmoil in Africa, and such general ideas about "North-South" relations and underdevelopment as "the New International Economic Order" or "the New International Information Order." Since at least the early 1960s, the western powers, who are also the members of the extended Atlantic System as defined in this book, have been consistently on the defensive within the UN.

The United States has tended to react strongly at times to what is often referred to as a "tyranny of the majority" in the United Nations. In the early seventies, U.S. Permanent Representative

Daniel Patrick Moynihan took the offensive frequently to attack nations which criticized others in the UN for their disregard for human rights, but which obviously had less than clean hands in respect to their own domestic affairs. In December 1974, his successor, Ambassador John Scali, returned to the fray; Scali warned the General Assembly that its stream of resolutions, passed over U.S. objections, was rapidly eroding U.S. support for the UN. He was followed by representatives of Britain, West Germany, France, Belgium, and Sweden, all echoing the same theme: forcing through one-sided, unrealistic, polemic and unenforceable resolutions was undermining the UN's credibility and authority.[9]

In November 1975, an Asian-African coalition forced through the General Assembly a resolution declaring that "Zionism is a form of racism." Western reaction was pronounced. Both houses of the U.S. Congress unanimously adopted resolutions calling for a reassessment of the United States' relationship to the UN. The Swedish Prime Minister, whose country was among those voting against the resolution, told the press he feared the vote "may be the start of a period of trouble for the United Nations." The President of the General Assembly, Premier Gaston Thorn of Luxembourg, called for a "reversal" of the resolution. Arab governments and the Palestine Liberation Organization, however, hailed their "victory over the United States" and the progress they saw in furthering "the just struggle of the Palestinians."[10] In May 1976, the UN Human Rights Commission approved a resolution asserting that the security of the state was of higher value than the protection of the individual from abuse by the state. The U.S. and British delegates once again protested.[11]

The trend to play politics at surprising times and places was also apparent in the conversion of the UN's Habitat Conference on Human Settlements in June 1976 into an anti-Israel platform and a forum for a "new international economic order" desired by some less-developed countries. At the conference, a Panamanian resolution attacking U.S. control of the Panama Canal Zone was introduced and adopted. Canada, the United States, Israel, and other countries protested, but to no avail.[12] Polemics in the General Assembly subsided somewhat in 1977 and 1978, but the general trend towards politicization of the UN as a whole has persisted.

The public and press reactions in the United States have often contrasted the size of the U.S. financial contribution to the UN (25 percent of its budget) with the growing impotence of the United States under the General Assembly's one-nation, one-vote system. If one considers the extent of the contributions provided by all western interests, the disproportion of financial support to political power is even more striking. The "Summit Seven" industrial democracies (Canada, France, Germany, Italy, Japan, the United Kingdom, and the United States) together contribute almost 60 percent of the United Nations budget.[13]

Reflecting the rising criticism of the UN throughout the west, Edwin O. Reischauer, in his book *Toward the 21st Century: Education for a Changing World*, summed up the prevailing opinion as he saw it:

In short, the United Nations as it now operates produces the bitterness we know in the domestic political process but not the necessary political decisions.

But, he hastened to add:

I do not mean to suggest that the United Nations is useless. It remains a symbol of the hope that man can someday achieve a stable world order. Around it also have grown up a large number of institutions for worldwide cooperation in the less controversial areas of human activity, and these probably do contribute to the creation of a sense of world community.[14]

Early in 1976, the UN Secretary General, Kurt Waldheim, warned Americans against "disproportionate and excessive disillusionment" with the United Nations. He said: "For all the criticism which is directed at the world organization, there seems, in the minds of governments at least, to be no alternative in times of trouble to its admittedly imperfect procedures."[15] In an earlier interview, Mr. Waldheim had warned that the devel-

[182]

oping nations could not accept a situation in which only the west had a voice and made the decisions, as it had done for centuries. "One should not see and watch things only from the angle of the Western world. This is our part of the globe, but it isn't everything."[16] There was little assurance, however, that western mistrust, or what many viewed as nonwestern misuse, of the UN would soon dissipate.

The International Court of Justice (ICJ)

One of the greatest hopes of the internationalists has been to create world law by means of international adjudication and arbitration. The International Court of Justice, an integral part of the United Nations, is the successor to the League of Nations' Permanent Court of International Justice. The latter, between 1922 and 1938, had 79 cases referred to it by states and 28 by the League; the ICJ has rendered only 14 opinions in the 30 years from 1946 to 1976. The difference probably reflects a growing, modern disillusionment with the efficacy of quasi-judicial procedures for resolving the "tough cases," which in any case are usually highly political in nature.

Among the most celebrated of ICJ's opinions was its determination in 1962 that the expenses of the UN peacekeeping forces in the Congo and in the Middle East were "expenses of the [UN] Organization" within the meaning of the UN Charter. The charter stipulated that "the expenses of the Organization shall be borne by the members as apportioned by the General Assembly." The USSR had contended that members could not be assessed for peacekeeping operations. If the USSR's point of view had prevailed, it would have completely gutted the UN's already weak power in this area. The ICJ's decision was an important victory for international law.

Other notable opinions have concerned South Africa's administration of the trust territory now known as Namibia. South Africa, however, has regularly ignored the court's opinions when it considered them unsatisfactory. Major powers have tended more and more to question the court's jurisdiction when they believed that a decision would be unfavorable to their interests. In 1970, the Canadian government notified the UN Secretary General that it rejected in advance the ICJ's jurisdiction in any disputes which might arise in connection with its new Arctic anti-pollution law. France rejected ICJ jurisdiction when Australia and New Zealand sought an injunction to stop French nuclear tests in the Pacific in 1970. In the same year, Iceland ignored an ICJ opinion that it could not bar foreign vessels from fishing within 12 miles of its coast.[17] By means of the Connally Reservation (1946), the United States has assured that its government alone would determine, in each case, what matters lay within its domestic jurisdiction.

Law, to be effective, must reflect the values and standards of the community it is meant to encompass; international law is no exception. Courts such as the ICJ can only operate to the extent that nations trust the court and the other members of the community. An international community as wide as the entire world obviously has trouble defining even a minimum number of mutually acceptable standards or values. In fact, the lack of use and consequent ineffectiveness of the ICJ are strong evidence that a "world community" does not really exist in any meaningful sense.

The Efficiency of the United Nations

Quite apart from the question of international high politics, the United Nations is hindered by its own intergovernmental machinery. With few exceptions, the United Nations Secretariat and those of the specialized agencies are relatively inefficient in the discharge of their tasks. Deplorable as this may be, the reasons are due, in part, to a so-called "quota system" governing employment in the UN family. The quota system assures that each member nation, large or small, is given a proportional share of places on the UN staff. Thus, if a vacancy occurs, the UN personnel office is obliged to hire, not the most qualified person available, but a person from a country whose "turn" it is to occupy a position. A recent article about UNESCO cited charges that "such a quota system . . . allows lazy and sometimes incompetent workers to be hired purely on the basis that their countries must be allotted some jobs;" a UNESCO professional worker noted, ". . . There are a lot of unqualified people running around here."[18]

A second reason for the lack of efficiency is the diversity of background among UN staff members. The full variety of the world's cultures is reflected among the personnel of the UN. In our analysis of the Atlantic-Pacific IGO system, we referred to the importance of the "human element." Great as the problem of language and cultural differences is in a multi-state European body such as the Common Market or in an Atlantic-Pacific IGO such as the OECD, nothing can begin to rival the complexity of the UN in this regard. Communication is rendered extremely difficult by the diversity of tongues—six official languages (Arabic, Chinese, English, French, Russian, and Spanish) represent only the beginning of the problem. Except for the numerous Spanish-speaking nations, the large English-speaking group, and a few smaller language groups, virtually every other member country ... one or more languages peculiar to itself. If the UN delegate or Secretariat member does not speak one of the official UN languages as his mother tongue, he must nevertheless have a sufficiently good working knowledge of at least one of them to perform effectively. English is the closest thing to a lingua franca for the UN, but even that language is not universal. The possibilities for linguistically based misunderstanding and confusion within the UN framework are therefore endless.

On the cultural level, ranging from workaday questions of etiquette and manners to the most complex ones involving conflicts in value systems, the difficulties of doing the UN's business are serious. Even national loyalties are sometimes difficult to inspire. Effective performance in the United Nations Secretariat requires a special kind of loyalty: loyalty to a nebulous "world community." Needless to say, people capable of holding such a loyalty can sometimes be found. But international civil servants tend, with time, to become alienated from, and often to be disowned by, their home societies to such an extent that they become ineffective as national representatives. One problem common to all IGOs, in fact, is that this alienation factor tends to create a group of cosmopolitans who in some cases may truly feel and act (insofar as it is possible) like "citizens of the world," but who more often than not are simply rootless beings, completely out of touch with the people and the domestic affairs of their home country or of the world. In any case, the problem of eliciting the necessary degree of institutional loyalty from a high international civil servant, while still insuring that he does not become totally uncoupled from his home culture, is not one that can ever be fully resolved, especially in so large and loose a body as the UN. It is noteworthy that the record of the old League of Nations in this regard was a good deal better than that of the UN or of most other contemporary IGOs.

Finally, at higher levels of the UN Secretariat and those of the related and specialized agencies, the personnel problem tends to become politicized. There must always, for example, be at least one national from the Soviet Union and the United States among the under secretaries of the UN. Nationals of China and other Communist countries, as well as those of the main NATO countries, also are often appointed to key UN jobs.

The Specialized Agencies

The UN constitutionally includes the Security Council, the General Assembly and its commissions and other bodies, the Economic and Social Council, and the International Court of Justice. But there are also within the UN specialized agencies which have been established by inter-governmental agreement; these are legally autonomous international entities with their own staffs. For purposes of "coordination," these IGOs are considered part of the framework of the United Nations. Three such agencies—the International Monetary Fund, the International Bank for Reconstruction and Development, and the General Agreement on Tariffs and Trade—are of special importance for the Atlantic System.

Perhaps the most successful of the specialized agencies has been the International Monetary Fund (IMF), created in 1945, only a few months after the UN itself, to facilitate trade, to promote exchange stability, and to make loans to members by means of "machinery for consultation and collaboration." The IMF is unusual among IGOs because voting power is roughly equated with monetary strength. Individual members are assigned quotas based on the size and strength of their economies. These quotas determine both the amount a member may borrow under IMF rules and its approximate voting strength on policy matters. In practice, most of the powers of the Board of Governors (one governor and an alternate appointed by each member) are delegated to the Board of Executive Directors. This body, having 20 members and meeting at least once per week, is responsible for the day-to-day operation of the agency. Five of the twenty executive directors are appointed by the five members having the largest quotas (the Federal Republic of Germany, France, Japan, the United Kingdom, and the United States); the others represent the remaining members and are elected by the Board of Governors. Each of the 15 elected directors casts as a unit all of the votes of the states that elected him.

A considerable share of the credit for the steady reconstruction and expansion of the world economy since World War II and for the prevention of a worldwide depression, must go to the IMF. By helping members with short-term balance-of-payment difficulties, by renovating the exchange-rate system, and by taking the steps necessary to create the greater liquidity required to finance growing world trade, the IMF has carved out an indispensable role for itself. The creation of the so-called "Special Drawing Rights" (SDRs) in 1969 might accurately be termed the first instance of "international money." This new system created rights of credit beyond a member's quotas; its use so far is limited to central banks. The absence of all but one Communist state from the IMF has meant a relatively greater consensus than in the UN on fundamental issues. The IMF voting system has also insured domination by the five largest industrial democracies. But, in most cases where significant reforms in world monetary affairs have been carried through, the conception and planning began in the Atlantic-Pacific System, and not in the IMF.

Critics, especially from (or on behalf of) the third world, have complained about western domination of the IMF. Yet, it is extremely doubtful if the world monetary system could have worked as well, or indeed worked at all in any meaningful sense, had the principal developed countries been unable to take the initiative and accept the responsibilities commensurate with their power and wealth. Among all of the economically oriented IGOs, the IMF probably represents the most advanced form of governance, because in it, power and responsibility are most nearly matched.

The International Bank for Reconstruction and Development (IBRD), often known as the World Bank, is the companion organization of IMF. IBRD's original task was to complete post-World War II economic reconstruction. Its main function since then has been to lend money on generous terms to less-developed members for projects which will increase their productive capacities. The World Bank has earned a reputation for strict professionalism, competence, and a relatively politics-free operation.

IBRD's structure is similar to that of IMF. Most of its powers are exercised by 20 executive directors, five of whom are appointed by the members holding the largest number of shares of the World Bank's capital stock. As these five include the chief western powers plus Japan, the Atlantic-Pacific System inevitably has a major influence on the World Bank's policies and programs. The pattern of memberships of the World Bank and the IMF are virtually identical. Again, the absence of Communist participation in the Bank, with the single exception of Romania, has insured a relative absence of ideological wrangling. The fact that the majority of IBRD members are developing countries who stand most to benefit from the Bank's largesse has also served to bring about a fairly high consensus with the other members.

IBRD has tended in recent years to assume a more activist role. It has organized its own staff college, the Economic Development Institute, to train senior officials of less-developed countries in development techniques. It has also approached the solution of the development problems of particular less-developed countries by organizing donor countries to work out long-range, comprehensive plans for assistance; such consortia do not confine their help to loans.

The General Agreement on Tariffs and Trade (GATT) is the third of the organizations which are closely linked to the Atlantic System. When the U.S. Senate refused to ratify the 1947 treaty that would have created an international trade organization, the trading nations fell back on GATT, which had been signed earlier. As a result, an international agreement became an IGO and developed its own secretariat, principles and codes, resident delegations in Geneva, and all the other accoutrements of an IGO. In a series of seven negotiating conferences beginning in 1947, GATT has substantially reduced tariffs and other barriers to international trade.

As have IBRD and IMF, GATT has relied for its stability and drive on the dynamism and sophistication of the leading nations of the Atlantic-Pacific System. Initially, GATT's members were drawn almost exclusively from Europe, North America, and Latin America. By 1978, there were 83 members, including six Communist nations (Cuba, Czechoslovakia, Hungary, Poland, Romania, and Kampuchea). The advantages of membership included so-called "most-favored-nation" treatment among its members. The exception to this rule is embedded in the original GATT provisions for customs unions and free trade areas, which permit discrimination in trade under agreed-upon rules. The United States in particular has used GATT to reconcile such politically desirable developments as the European Communities (a customs union) with the economic objective of maintaining as liberal a general trading system as possible.

Within IMF, IBRD, and GATT, small groups of advanced nations have exercised powerful influence and leadership. Indeed, without the leadership and commitment of these developed democracies, none of the three—IMF, IBRD, or GATT— would have been likely to accomplish anything more than have other UN agencies. The operation of the three has proven absolutely essential to the well-being of the Atlantic-Pacific System and has served as a vital link between that System and the rest of the world.

* * *

The International Labor Organization (ILO), another specialized agency, has had a long and honorable history. The ILO was created at the same time as the League of Nations (1919) as an autonomous, but related body. Its aims are unexceptional: "To promote international action aimed at achieving full employment, the raising of living standards, and improvement in the conditions of labor." But the ILO, in the last quarter of the century, has encountered grave problems, stemming from its structural vulnerability to politicization along ideological lines.

The ILO's structural vulnerability arises from the fact that its membership includes not only representatives of governments, but of employers and employees as well. National delegations to the ILO Conference are composed of two delegates named by governments and one each from management and labor. In the case of the United States, for example, the employees' representative is chosen by the A.F.L.-C.I.O., while that of the employers is selected in agreement with the National Association of Manufacturers and the U.S. Chamber of Commerce. This structure is appropriate for pluralistic countries in which these three social groups are autonomous. But, in the case of Communist countries or those with monolithic or authoritarian social structures, labor unions and management are organs of the state, and the ideological orientation and monolithic character of the national delegations are usually their distinguishing features. These delegations generally vote as a bloc, whereas the delegations from free enterprise, pluralistic countries often split their votes. If the ILO was intended to encourage among social interest groups an international solidarity which would arch over national borders, it has failed to do so largely because of the composition and behavior of the Communist states' delegations.

In its early years, the ILO was able to establish a number of forward-looking international conventions that defined the length of the work day, the conditions under which women could work underground, and the liability of shipowners for sick and injured seamen. It also called for the abolition of forced labor and dealt with the treatment of indigenous and tribal populations in the work force. In 1969, the ILO directed attention to the problem of providing enough jobs for the world's burgeoning population. The ILO has defended the rights of labor unions, when they appeared subject to infringement by member states. The ILO has provided technical assistance to members in the fields of labor organizing and labor-management relations.

But in the 1970s, the ILO began to break down. The Soviet Union and its east European allies, aided frequently by the delegations of some of the developing countries, began to use ILO meetings to promote their own ideologies. In 1975, when the ILO Conference granted observer status to the Palestine Liberation Organization, the United States government filed an intention to withdraw from the organization. Secretary of State Kissinger gave four principal reasons for the action:

1. The United States could not accept a growing tendency for workers' and employers' groups to fall "under the domination of governments."
2. The ILO for some years had shown "an appallingly selective concern" for human rights.
3. The Organization had abandoned its earlier record of objectivity in considering violations of basic human rights by member states.
4. There was a trend toward "increasing politicization of the Organization."[19]

The withdrawal became effective in 1977 (following expiration of the required two-year period). An immediate ILO budgetary crisis ensued, because the United States had historically provided 25 percent of ILO's budget. Although several other countries threatened to withdraw at the same time, none did. In any case, the future of the Organization is distinctly unclear.

UNESCO (the United National Educational, Scientific and Cultural Organization) is probably the most nobly conceived of all the UN family;[20] yet, it was also subject to the same processes of politicization in the 1970s as the ILO had been. In 1974, UNESCO's General Conference voted to exclude Israel from the European regional UNESCO grouping, making Israel the only member that belonged to no regional affiliate. At the same time, under pressure from the Arab countries, the Conference voted to withhold UNESCO aid from Israel on grounds that Israel had persisted "in altering the historical features" of Jerusalem during archaeological excavations. In protest, the United States withheld its annual UNESCO contribution for a time. In November 1976, Israel's membership in the European regional grouping was restored, but the process of politicization was by no means over.

In July 1976, a number of third-world members of UNESCO attempted to create a "New International Information Order," presumably to complement the "New International Economic Order" that had been demanded earlier in the UN proper. Governments of some developing countries had complained that the bulk of the news dispatches provided by the large western wire services and purchased by the newspapers of many third-world countries were scanty and biased in their coverage of events in developing areas.[21] A draft statement asserted that "states are responsible for the mass news media under their jurisdiction." Under strong protest from the west, the draft was amended to read that states must "encourage the mass media under their jurisdiction to act in conformity with the principles of this declaration." UNESCO sponsored a colloquium of journalists in Florence in April 1977. In papers presented at the colloquium, journalists themselves elaborated more new principles for the role of journalism. For example, they declared that:

- "News media must 'participate in the liberation of national economies.' "
- "News media have a role in 'decolonization.' "
- "Journalists should assume moral and legal responsibility for their treatment of information."[22]

All of these activities raised reservations among western leaders as to the political biases of some of UNESCO's staff and of the organization itself. UNESCO's real accomplishments in such important areas as the reduction of illiteracy and the protection of internationally important monuments were in danger of being devalued in the heat of a burgeoning ideological conflict.

* * *

Various UN agencies have performed extremely important international work which has seldom made headlines. In most cases, they have done so without involving ideological or political issues. The World Bank has approached with great professional skill and sensitivity the needs of the developing countries to promote economic growth; so far, there has been no hint of ideological struggle in the Bank's operations. The World Health Organization, the International Civil Aviation Organization, and the International Telecommunication Union are examples of technical agencies that work for the most part quite successfully out of both the public view and the political arena. The conquering of smallpox under WHO leadership, for example, is no mean achievement. In assessing the continuing worth of the UN, the political turmoil and ideological manipulation must be balanced against the painstaking, useful, sometimes indispensable, and generally competent work that the world organization has accomplished.

Inefficiency, waste, and duplication are inevitable in the loose, ill-controlled, and essentially unaccountable bodies of the UN family. Specialized or dependent agencies of the General Assembly often do not accomplish what they were set up to do. Instead of reforming or abolishing these agencies, however, the responsible governing bodies generally continue to oversee them, with payrolls and overheads lumbering on, and instead create a new agency to do what the old one could not. The Food and Agriculture Organization (FAO), a case in point, was created in 1945, along with the UN itself, to solve food, agricultural, and farm problems. Its charter was bold and comprehensive. Yet, a new organization, the World Food Council, was created in 1974 at the World Food Conference held under the auspices of the UN General Assembly. By 1977, the World Food Council appeared to be on the way to becoming still another specialized agency.[23] Similar criticism could be levied at the UN's Economic and Social Council, which has done such a desultory job that responsibilities which logically should have come under its purview have been given to other existing bodies or to new ones created specially for the purpose.[24]

Edvard Hambro tried to sum up the pros and cons of the United Nations:

> Denunciations and accusations fill the air. Financial crises follow each other with frightening regularity. Dissatisfaction is ripe, voices of doom are heard. Yet far more important is the fact that year after year the leading statesmen of

the world flock to New York because the United Nations continues to be the dominant world forum, the focal point of the hopes and longings of humanity, and the best machinery for peace devised in our world of today despite all setbacks. . . . How the machinery is used will determine whether 'we shall nobly save or meanly lose the last best hope on earth.'[25]

The United Nations system is assuredly a vital component of the entire international system, even with all its shortcomings. The chances for peace and prosperity would be much less did it not exist. In an age when interdependence is not just a catchword, but a sober reality, the existence of international machinery which is universal in scope and which can encourage cooperation and understanding among nations is extremely important. The toughest problems requiring international action must still somehow be resolved.

The idea of a world government providing such machinery seems unlikely in the foreseeable future. Nonetheless, there are tasks, beginning with the simple matter of assuring cooperative, efficient, worldwide communications systems, that require intergovernmental organization on a universal basis. Other tasks, such as monetary coordination and collective defense, touch on areas of national sovereignty. In these cases, regional IGOs are often able to do the job. For a variety of reasons, the developed democracies of the Atlantic and Pacific seem best prepared and most willing, at this juncture in history, to undertake the more vital international community-building tasks.

THE SOVIET INTERNATIONAL SYSTEM

The examination of Communist international systems which follows is meant to highlight the characteristics and capabilities of the extended Atlantic System by contrasting it with a sharply different kind of international system. It also is meant to describe the relationships between the Soviet international system and the Atlantic System, and to discuss the difficulties inherent in relating different systems in general, and these two in particular. Finally, it is meant to describe the competitive struggle being waged by the two as alternative models of regional or universal systems.

With some success, the USSR has tried to emulate U.S. leadership in the Atlantic-Pacific System by creating its own international system. The USSR's efforts, initiated during World War II, to erect a series of buffer states on the western approaches to the Soviet Union gradually evolved into a highly coordinated system of military alliances, trade relationships, ideological and political control mechanisms, and socialist-style economic integration. Soviet and eastern European leaders have referred to this system as "The Socialist Commonwealth" (Sotsialisticheskoe Sodruzhestvo), although by definition it is hardly either a commonwealth or socialist.[26], [27] In this book, however, I shall refer to it as "The Soviet International System" and try to let those facts which can be ascertained, rather than the "codewords" in the Russian title, explain the phenomenon. (Because the grouping does not include China, it cannot properly be called "the Communist System." The Soviet International System was created almost entirely at the initiative of, and remains under the control of, the Soviet Union.)

A comparative chronology of the evolution of the Atlantic System and the Soviet International System is instructive. Below are the dates of establishment of the important IGOs in each grouping:

Table 3. Dates of Establishment of Important IGOs of the
Atlantic and Soviet International Systems

Atlantic System		Soviet International System	
OEEC	1948	Comecon[28]	1949
Brussels Pact, NATO, WEU	1948–54	Warsaw Treaty Organization	1955
CERN (European Organization for Nuclear Research)	1953	Joint Institute for Nuclear Research	1956

European Investment Bank	1957		
[Inter-American Development Bank]	[1959]	International Investment Bank	1970
ESRO and ELDO (precursors of European Space Agency)	1964	Intercosmos	1969 or 1970 (?)
INTELSAT	1965	Intersputnik	1971

The list provides strong circumstantial evidence that the creation of each of the organs of the Soviet International System was undertaken as a response to an earlier development in the west. The case for this theory is persuasively documented in Richard Szawlowski's *The System of International Organizations of the Communist Countries.*[29] There were 30 intergovernmental bodies in the Soviet System in 1976. "All these organizations are tightly knit together, representing a formidable combination of military and economic power. In spite of all the difficulties and shortcomings, they represent a dynamically growing potential."[30] Szawlowski classified the 30 IGOs into five groupings: (1) the two "key organizations," the Warsaw Treaty Organization (WTO) and Comecon; (2) third in order of creation and alone in its class, the Joint Institute for Nuclear Research; (3) two international banks and several industrial combines; (4) international laboratories and training centers; and (5) minor bodies without international secretariats.[31] The entire System is, according to Szawlowski, completely dominated by the USSR. The USSR supplies two-thirds of the armed forces and is twice as powerful economically as all the other Warsaw Pact nations together.[32] Furthermore, "no top WTO position is held by any East European."[33] In almost all the IGOs, Russian is the only working language.[34]

The Warsaw Treaty Organization

The Warsaw treaty was signed on May 14, 1955, by Albania, Bulgaria, Czechoslovakia, East Germany, Hungary, Poland,

Romania, and the USSR. The ostensible public justification was the western decision to rearm West Germany and bring her into NATO, under the October 1954 WEU agreements. The more likely reason had to do with the USSR's need for continuing control of her European satellites.

> the creation of the Communist regional defense alliance reflected the Soviet Union's conviction that . . . its past methods of ruling East Europe had become inadequate. Subsequently, the Warsaw Pact was to be a new mechanism for modernizing Soviet management of East Europe. . . .[35]

Staar cited ". . . the USSR's desire to obtain legal justification for stationing its troops in East-Central Europe,"[36] while Remington pointed out that

> the [Warsaw] treaty formalized Soviet influence in East Europe without sacrificing the outward equality of East European Community states. It accomplished this by conveniently limiting independent foreign policy maneuver on the part of the people's democracies in that (1) the members pledged not to join other conflicting alliances, and (2) no withdrawal procedures were specific.[37]

The Russians had other goals in mind as well, for on the day following the signing of the Warsaw Pact, the state treaty was concluded with Austria, ending ten years of allied occupation in return for permanent Austrian neutrality. U.S., British, and French forces were subsequently removed from Austria, with the result that NATO's formerly solid defense corridor from West Germany to Italy was cut. There was, however, a corresponding disadvantage for the USSR; with the withdrawal of Soviet troops from Austria, there no longer seemed any justification for continuing to station Russian forces in Romania or Hungary. However, the subsequent Warsaw treaty provided a framework to do so, an "ever closer, uniform, and internationally institutionalized control over the military and political life of the 'people's democracies.' "[38] The treaty even permitted the Russians to introduce troops where they had not been (for example, in Czechoslovakia in 1968).

With respect to both the Warsaw Pact and the economic organizations which the Soviet Union established as part of its "Socialist Commonwealth" in eastern Europe, the substance was derived not from the stated aims, but from the nature of the political system of the member states and the necessity, above all, for the Soviet Union to maintain its regime intact.[39] The crucial question was, "What is an acceptable model of socialist construction and who decides—the country in question, Moscow, or a collectivity in which the Soviets have the loudest but not the only voice?"[40]

Kolcowicz sums up "the several key roles the Warsaw Pact plays in Soviet policy":

> *Symbolically,* the Pact legitimizes the Soviet presence in Eastern Europe and provides a device for unifying the member states under Soviet domination. *Politically,* it provides a focal point for the eroding community of socialist nations and a 'proper' mechanism for rallying dissenters around Moscow; further, it defines the limits of Soviet tolerance of nationalistic pressures within Pact countries. *Militarily,* the Pact augments the Soviet military posture and capabilities in continental Europe, and enables Soviet military leaders to exercise effective influence and control over the indigenous East European military establishments.
>
> The Warsaw Pact, then is seen as an entangling alliance by which the Soviet leaders seek to enmesh their frequently unwilling allies in the web of Soviet national interests. . . . the Pact's present purpose is primarily internal: to contain under Moscow's influence, a group of turbulent and disruptive countries and thereby maintain stability in Eastern and Central Europe.[41]

Structurally, the WTO developed agencies which, in many respects, seemed to parallel those of NATO. There are a Political

Consultative Committee, a Unified Command, and a supranational general staff. Despite the provisions of the WTO statutes, the bodies appear to have functioned only sporadically. The Political Consultative Committee, for example, met only 15 times between 1956 and the end of 1976, although the statutes called for two meetings per year.[42] During the same period, only two summit meetings of the First Secretaries of the Communist parties of the respective members were held.[43] By contrast, the North Atlantic Council (NATO's supreme authority) was in continuous session in Brussels at the level of the permanent representatives, met frequently at the ministerial level, and has held summit sessions more or less annually in recent years.

At least in the early years, the WTO international staff seemed insubstantial, consisting "of a skeleton crew whose functions were ill-defined."[44] (However, virtually all the important command and staff posts of WTO appear to be held by Russians.) Between 1955 and 1960, the Warsaw Pact nations carried out no joint war games, but have conducted them since 1961 with increasing regularity, giving the impression that the USSR is bent on perfecting the military mechanisms of WTO.[45] WTO's accelerated buildup in the 1970s presented a formidable challenge to NATO in numbers of tanks, tactical aircraft, soldiers on the central front, and certain other important respects.[46]

The political balance also seems to have leaned in WTO's favor: ". . . as the vitality and influence of NATO declined in the 1960s, the Warsaw Pact has assumed a new and growing role in the politics of Eastern Europe."[47] The vulnerability of the Warsaw Pact, however, lies principally in the character and quality of those political relationships with its east European allies which it deems vital. From the outset, the Soviets never could be sure that the armies of their socialist allies could be counted on in either a major defensive or offensive action.

The Soviet Union has good reason to be concerned about the reliability of its allies. Albania, for example, withdrew from the alliance in protest at the Warsaw Pact invasion of Czechoslovakia in 1968. (Albania's membership, however, had been a dead letter from 1961, when she was "locked out" of WTO activities by the USSR as a result of ideological disputes between the two nations.) On October 31, 1956, when the Hungarian government announced that it was pulling out of WTO, Soviet troops intervened, put down the growing rebellion, and restored a regime congenial to the USSR, thereby effectively cancelling Hungary's withdrawal. Romania can be considered only a partial or associate member of WTO (a status not unlike that of France or Greece in the Atlantic Alliance). Since 1962, Romania has permitted no WTO joint maneuvers on her soil; her forces did not participate in putting down the Czech defection in 1968; in 1970, Romania sent only a group of officers to participate in WTO maneuvers in East Germany.[48] The Soviet interventions in Hungary and Czechoslovakia violated both the Preamble and Article 8 of the Warsaw treaty, which cites "the principles of respect for the independence and sovereignty of States and of nonintervention in their domestic affairs." Yet, the Warsaw Pact was used as ex post facto justification for both interventions.[49]

Remington has termed the Warsaw Pact a Communist "conflict resolution system." Of course, the Soviet Union's method of "conflict resolution" differs from that of the western powers. Whereas WTO has been used to impose "solutions" on its members, as in the case of Hungary, NATO has never been used in this fashion, even though some of its members, such as Greece and Turkey or Iceland and Britain, have had considerable differences during the period in which the treaty has been in force. When France withdrew from the NATO military structure in 1965, she was careful to say that she would still honor the obligations of the treaty, and the other members of the Alliance acquiesced and withdrew NATO's political and military headquarters and foreign units promptly from French soil. (French withdrawal was deemed by many Alliance professionals to constitute a serious impairment of NATO's strategic position).

The differences between the two systems are considerable. Pick and Critchley have characterized NATO as follows:

The North Atlantic Treaty provided, from the beginning, for a political alliance rather than a military bloc. Its military organization was and is subordinate to civil authority, the multi-national North Atlantic Council. The national policies of European countries of NATO are not dependent on the presence or absence of United States military forces on their territories. [50]

Bernard Brodie has also pointed out major differences between NATO and WTO:
• The United States is a non-European power geographically, and thus gains only "derivative protection" and not direct defense from its European allies. The USSR is afforded a "direct, strategic buffer zone" by its allies.
• NATO contains some big powers of the "second tier," France, West Germany, and Britain, for example. WTO has none, and thus, the USSR tends to dwarf the other members.
• "Unique to the Western alliance . . . [is] the wide range of difference in the degree of dependence on NATO and the need for its protection which exists among the partners. . . . West Germany has the greatest need of the alliance . . . [and Canada the least]." In WTO, the relationships between members are much more uniform. [51]

Kintner has also contrasted the two alliances. He observed that "WTO had a more fundamentally political character than a security character." The USSR does not depend on WTO for its security; "WTO serves a purely political function." WTO officers receive ideological indoctrination; in NATO, there is no unity of outlook or attempt to impose one. Kintner allowed that sometimes the United States "is guilty of an overzealous attempt to dominate NATO's policy, but it is nothing like the complete domination of strategy imposed by the Soviets on the Warsaw Pact countries." [52]

Manlio Brosio, the former Secretary General of NATO, contrasted the precisely circumscribed geographical limits of the North Atlantic Treaty (essentially western Europe and North America) with those of the Warsaw Pact. In practice, Warsaw Pact nations have extended not only "consultation," but also "real military cooperation" to such non-European areas as Indochina, the Middle Eastern countries, and the Horn of Africa. [53]

Finally, as Pick and Critchley have pointed out, there were significant differences in the circumstances under which the two alliances were created:

> The North Atlantic Treaty was freely negotiated by its signatories; the Treaty was ratified after full, and in some cases animated, debate in parliaments during which all political tendencies had a chance to express their views. Thus the North Atlantic Alliance is on the whole the product of normal democratic processes. This statement is generally true despite the existence of authoritarian regimes on the periphery of the alliance. [Portugal especially at the time.] The Warsaw Pact, on the other hand, was imposed by the Soviet Union, two years after Stalin's death, upon a number of Eastern European countries whose one-party Communist governments did not permit the free exchange of domestic political opinion. Nor were these countries in a position to negotiate freely with the Soviet Union as to whether it was in their interest to join the Pact.[54]

Regardless of such differences, the two alliances together have performed a function of great importance for stability in Europe and world peace generally: they have maintained the security equilibrium in Europe. Those nations in NATO like to point out that since the Alliance was formed, not one square inch of "free" European territory has passed to the Soviets. On their side, the Communists aver that it is the Warsaw treaty which has preserved the "Socialist Commonwealth" from the aggressive designs of the "imperialists and revanchists." Regardless of the truth or justice of these claims, the NATO-WTO equilibrium has undoubtedly done more than the UN ever could have done to preserve peace in Europe and prevent World War III.

The Council for Mutual Economic Assistance (Comecon)

Comecon was essentially a Soviet riposte to the initiation of the Marshall Plan: to "prove that the Communist bloc is not 'worse' than the West with its OEEC."[55],[56] The USSR and its east European allies had all been offered the opportunity to participate in the Marshall Plan in 1947, but had declined on grounds that it would violate their sovereignty. By 1949, the OEEC had begun its work, and the Marshall Plan appeared well on its way to achieving its ambitious objectives. Comecon was rather hastily organized at that point, with the explanation that the Communist bloc had come together because "these countries did not consider it appropriate that they should submit themselves to the dictatorship of the Marshall Plan."[57] From 1949 until Stalin's death in 1953, Comecon remained essentially inactive, and then became active only slowly. A proper charter and convention for Comecon were not signed, for example, until December 1969.

From the outset, Comecon has had to cope with the dichotomy of independent sovereignty on the part of its members and "unity" for the organizational whole. An official Soviet publication, by the USSR Minister for Foreign Trade in 1971, showed clearly this anomaly:

> A new type of economic relations came into existence between the Soviet Union and the countries that embarked on the path of socialist construction after the Second World War. It is based on *complete equality**, strict observance of the *national interests* and *sovereign rights* of each state, comprehensive and mutually profitable cooperation and fraternal assistance.

> The countries of the world socialist community, in coping with the task of building up quickly their productive forces, encounter complex problems which are related to their level of development in the past, the socioeconomic structure, the availability of natural resources and geographic conditions. Successful solution of these problems largely depends on the *strengthening of economic ties* between the socialist countries, their *cohesion* and *unity*.[58]

---

*I have supplied the italics in the quotation to emphasize the contradictions.

Cohesion, unity, and the strengthening of economic ties between sovereign nations cannot go far today without sacrificing some of the independent powers of decision making and sovereign rights which have previously stood in the way of full economic interdependence among groups of nations. In contrast with Comecon, the European Communities have acknowledged this contradiction and set its resolution as a positive goal, although there have been many setbacks and the final goal of political unification remains elusive. Comecon has been unwilling to face this contradiction, let alone find ways to resolve it. This remains a basic, significant flaw in the Comecon system.

In 1962, Krushchev proposed a "united planning organ for Comecon, but Romania objected (others might have), and the proposal was dropped." Schaefer believed that the smaller Comecon nations were wary of an integration which "might weaken [their] longer-run economic and political independence."[59] The word "integration" was finally used for the first time in a public Comecon document in April 1969. The 1971 "Comecon Comprehensive Programme" called for "the formation of deep and lasting links [among members] in the basic branches of the economy, science, and technology," but then hastened to assure readers that "socialist economic integration takes place on the basis of full free will and does not lead to the creation of supranational organs."[60]

It has been easier for the USSR to define Comecon in negative than in positive terms:

> It apparently didn't want economic relations among East European members to become significantly closer unless the Soviet Union was also included. It didn't want Comecon members to become too economically involved with Western countries or to develop relations with the EEC. . . . [It] did not want Comecon reform to lead the domestic reform movement or to help to provide its members with the means to slip out from under the Comecon yoke.[61]

Just as the primary function of the Warsaw Pact has seemed to be to serve as a framework within which the USSR could more easily exercise control over its socialist neighbors, Comecon's primary function has also seemed to be political.

The original members of Comecon were the USSR, Poland, Czechoslovakia, Romania, Hungary, and Bulgaria. Albania joined a month after the others, although it never became a member of any of Comecon's specialized agencies and has not participated in Comecon since 1961. East Germany became a member in 1950. In 1964, Yugoslavia became an associate of Comecon, participating in a few activities only.[62] Finland and Comecon concluded an agreement of "cooperation" in 1973, after Finland had initialled an agreement with EC in 1972. Mongolia became a member in 1962, Cuba in 1972, and the Socialist Republic of Vietnam in 1978; these three memberships would appear to be prima facie illegal under the Comecon Charter registered with the UN. The Charter states that "Membership . . . shall be open to other European countries," and any change to the Charter requires unanimous consent of all members.

North Korea, and Vietnam before it joined, have frequently sent observers to Comecon meetings; China did so until the mid-sixties. Angola and Laos sent observers to the July 1976 Comecon session in East Berlin. In addition, possible "association" between Comecon and such countries as India, South Yemen, Iran, and Argentina has been reported at various times. The first Comecon agreement for cooperation with a developing country was signed with Iraq in July 1965; a similar pact was signed with Mexico a month later.[63] Thus, at the same time that OECD was broadening its membership outside the Atlantic Community with Japan in 1964, and that the EC was developing special relationships with countries in Africa and Asia through the Yaoundé Convention in 1964, Comecon was branching out as well.

* * *

Comecon decisions have generally been made on the basis of unanimity. If any members wished to declare a "non-interest" in the question at hand, however, the vote could be taken without them, but they might still join later in a consequent activity if they changed their minds. In a few fields and under limited circumstances, some specialized Comecon agencies apparently

have made decisions by majority vote (the International Investment Bank, Interatominstrument, Intersputnik, for example).[64]
For all intents and purposes, however, Comecon has remained
the antithesis of a supranational organization. It has a plethora
of formal organs, commissions, committees, and the like, but
their roles are "purely advisory" according to Jozef Brabant.
"In no way do they have the ability to impose forms of rationalization, specialization, and integration in a particular field."[65]

> . . . national communist parties have not only the final say,
> but also the initial and intermediate say on important mat-
> ters of principles and methodology of socialist coopera-
> tion.[66]

The really important Comecon decisions appear to be made at
the occasional meetings of heads of state and top Communist
party functionaries. Schaefer has suggested that Comecon suffered precisely because it was "interstate" and not an "interpar-
ty" organ: "a truly effective Comecon would be 'supraparty'
not supranational as non-Communists understand the term."[67]
By comparison with the international secretariats of OECD
and EC, the Comecon staff (about 1,000 members in the Moscow headquarters) appears to be rudimentary. Neither Comecon
nor its affiliates have anything approaching an international
civil service with tenure and independence. National governments appoint members to the Comecon Secretariat for terms of
four years, but may recall them at any time. The chief positions
in Comecon and the subsidiary agencies appear to be held almost overwhelmingly by Russians.[68]
Economists in the socialist countries insist that Comecon en-
courages trade among its members in preference to commerce
with the "capitalist world," but in actual practice, the percentage of trade with non-Comecon countries expanded in the 1970s
for most members. (Nonetheless, Comecon cannot be considered an important trading bloc. In 1974, its share of world trade
was only 8.5 percent, an actual decrease from 9.5 percent in
1973, and 11.4 percent in 1966.[69] The share of world trade of the
chief industrial democracies, minus the less-developed countries

of Europe, in the same period remained more or less constant at around 67 percent.) Comecon instead has striven to arrange a "socialist division of labor" among its members, to the end that each would specialize in the production of different manufactures. The 1975 Comecon plan, for example, called for the USSR and Romania to build small trucks, Czechoslovakia to construct medium-sized ones, and the Soviet Union to build very large trucks.[70] Such industrial agreements are also typical of regional integration plans like those of the Central American Common Market and ASEAN. Another form of Comecon economic cooperation is for all or most members to join in the construction and financing of a very large project from which all would presumably benefit. There have been, for example, the "Friendship" oil pipeline, the "Peace" electric power distribution system, and the "Brotherhood" natural gas pipeline. Still another Comecon method of collaboration is for one member to finance projects in the territory of another; the project is owned by the government on whose territory it has been constructed.[71]

Agencies Related to Comecon

Some 30 international organizations have been developed by Comecon since 1956. After Comecon itself, the Joint Institute for Nuclear Research, founded in 1956, is the oldest. Located at Dubna, in the Moscow region, the Institute was reported in 1974 to have approximately 3,000 staff members, including more than 600 scientists. The Institute's function is apparently similar to the EURATOM joint laboratories in Italy, Germany, and Belgium. The Institute has collaborated with CERN in Geneva and with the U.S. Atomic Energy Commission.[72]

Two banking institutions, the International Bank for Economic Cooperation (IBEC) in 1964 and the International Investment Bank (IIB) in 1970, have been created under Comecon. Nine Comecon countries belong to both.

The International Bank was meant to facilitate payments in the manner of the European Payments Union, an OEEC agency between 1950 and 1958. Apparently, however, IBEC has only been involved at the level of bilateral settlements. Brabant believed that IBEC had become more and more a bookkeeping agency, granting and accommodating seasonal credits, rather than spurring trade expansion and specialization, as had been anticipated.[73] The IIB grants long-term credits to "enhance the national economies of member states" and loans and credits to developing countries.[74] IIB might be considered Comecon's answer to the IMF and World Bank; certainly, the names of both suggest an aspiration to universalism.

In 1963, an East European (Railway) Waggon Pool was created, a decade after the creation of a parallel body in western Europe. Intermetal was established in 1965 in part to emulate the European Coal and Steel Community. Its task is to modernize Comecon steel industries; "Intermetal can pass resolutions that are binding on all members."[75] Intersputnik was created in 1975, as the counterpart of INTELSAT, the western-sponsored organization which provides international public satellite telecommunications services. As of 1977, the Intersputnik system was described as still under active development;[76] Szawlowski could find no evidence that Intersputnik was anything but "a paper organization."[77]

Of particular interest is the "International Institute for the Economic Problems of the World Socialist System," established by Comecon in 1970. The Institute's task has been officially described as the "preparation of theoretical, methodological, and applied problems of the development of the world socialist system, economic cooperation between socialist countries, and the problems of socialist economic integration."[78] This ambitious aim is quite in keeping with Marxist-Leninist ideas about providing an alternate world model to capitalism. There is no intergovernmental counterpart in the west, but the private Atlantic Institute for International Affairs (Paris), which has close informal links to OECD, NATO, EC, and other IGOs of the extended Atlantic System, might be considered in some ways analogous; there are also parallels in the work of the private Trilateral Commission.

Evaluation of the Comecon System

While the purpose of Comecon may seem to be economic integration, that is probably not its main goal. Like the Warsaw

Treaty Organization, Comecon seems meant primarily to serve political and ideological ends. The Soviet Union has seemed determined to use Comecon as a means of pressing its economic model on the other members.[79] Comecon documents devote great attention to the "coordination of plans" as the "principal method of socialist integration."

Suspicion and nationalism also have interfered with the success of Comecon. "The national states remain unwilling to accept the recommendation of the CMEA [Comecon] coordinating agencies with respect to the necessary revisions to be introduced in the national plans in order to eliminate CMEA-wide inconsistencies."[80] Comecon's repeated efforts to promote commodity specialization under the "international socialist division of labor principle" have also met with obvious distrust. Bilateral trade policies, which restrict trade and unnecessarily limit international specialization, have prevailed over the multilateral systems and tariff-reduction programs common under GATT, EC, EFTA, Benelux, and other western schemes. Paradoxically, the Comecon countries have experienced rapid economic growth over the past 20 years, especially in heavy manufactures. This growth in production "has not been accompanied, as in other world economic groups, by a relatively more extensive international division of labor, either among its members or with the rest of the world. . . . it is the very disparity between growth and trade which is striking."[81]

Comecon has suffered other deficiencies. Kaser has noted the absence of criteria that would allow the Soviet economy to measure its own goals and its own performance. In his opinion, this has been "the crucial issue on which Comecon integration has foundered."[82] He has also cited the crucial problem of national planning—the selection of economic priorities.[83] Szawlowski has added to Kaser's list: "Comecon group is faced with serious, extremely frustrating, and almost perpetual problems, such as the lack of realistic 'uniform' exchange rates, of a convertible currency and of developed multilateral settlements of accounts, problems of pricing and economic modernization in general." Comecon's economic and geographic heterogeneity arising from the inclusion of Mongolia, Vietnam, and Cuba have made matters worse; "in this respect the priority of purely political considerations is obvious."[84]

As Brabant has observed, "the usefulness of IGOs in general seems to be determined by the initiative of those actually working there." Experience in such bodies as OECD and NATO certainly bears this out. In contrast, the staff of Comecon has not been allowed this flexibility; in fact, the staff itself is accustomed to traditional planning systems and rigid bureaucratic controls. How can one then assume that the same functionaries would exercise initiative, even if they were allowed to, within the Comecon framework?[85]

Apparently, just as does the extended Atlantic System, the Soviet International System has coordination problems. Szawlowski reports that in the early 1970s, conferences and other means to better coordinate the secretariats of the 30 institutions of the Comecon family were undertaken.[86]

In summary, Comecon has been caught up in the contradictions of socialist economics which stress national self-sufficiency, heavy manufactures, and rigid planning. In Comecon, as well as in the Warsaw Pact, any desire to achieve interdependence has been discouraged by the feelings of suspicion, sovereignty, and independence on the part of the member states. Furthermore, the use of Comecon more as an ideological model and a means of political control than as a practical tool for increasing trade and living standards has limited its role. To surmount these difficulties under Soviet policy requires a further contradiction: iron control administered from above. This is the antithesis of "international community" spirit.

As an exercise in modern *economic integration*, Comecon must so far be counted a failure. However, as a means of holding together the eastern bloc of nations under Soviet direction, it is a political success, albeit with an uncertain future. Despite the failure of economic integration, the phenomenal increases in aggregate industrial production of the Comecon countries cannot be ignored. Industrial development in the Soviet international system does go forward, and living standards have risen. The progress of a few nations within the socialist commonwealth, such as East German, has been prodigious indeed. By comparison with the integrated Atlantic-Pacific System, the Soviet system in economic terms comes off a very poor second. But for some developing countries it nevertheless has attractions.

This Soviet-Comecon model of a tightly planned economy and a one-party state can exert a powerful pull on hard-pressed, relatively inexperienced political leaders and bureaucrats in new countries. Even though its main asset today is great military force, and its ideological appeal is waning, the Soviet International System on balance is a strong competitor of the Atlantic-Pacific System for world leadership.

Interactions and Comparisons: The Soviet International System and the Atlantic-Pacific System

Manlio Brosio viewed the comparatively monolithic Soviet system with mixed pride and envy.

> Actually, the Warsaw Treaty and Comecon are two organizations that integrate perfectly, one in the military and political field, the other in the economic field. It is evident that Comecon works essentially as an economic instrument, if not an economic weapon in the communist world, in close connection with the Soviet Union and under its dominant direction. The OECD, on the other hand, is totally different, in its composition and functions, from the Atlantic Alliance. This organization includes many European and non-European countries which do not have and do not want to have any connection with [NATO]. We could legitimately add that the predominant feeling in the OECD is one of complete detachment from whatever is related to the military and political interest of NATO; whoever has been in contact, as I have been with the Atlantic Alliance, vividly felt this detachment, which does not signify hostility, but a very rigid will to maintain distances.[87]

Brosio concluded that this dichotomy underlined a "great deficiency" of NATO, the failure to apply Article 2 of the treaty which had provided for economic cooperation among the allies. But, in truth, the fact that OECD was not a political instrument, and particularly not a political instrument for use in the Cold War, has been a source of strength for the Atlantic-Pacific System. It was much easier, for example, for OECD to muster all the advanced economies of the industrial democracies for a program of increased aid to the less-developed countries than it would have been for NATO to do so, because both OECD's purpose and its image were and remain essentially economic. OECD can be further contrasted with Comecon by citing the different methods employed by the two in postwar economic reconstruction and development in Europe. "Even Albania put a steel smelter into its 1951–55 plan. . . . The contemporary round of OEEC long-term plans . . . were in revealing contrast: Norway and Greece were rebuked for wanting steel plants."[88] When Comecon did finally get around to adopting an "integration program" in 1971, there was apparently little substance to it.

There was now little prospect of integration becoming essentially an economic process based to a large degree on a devolution of decision-making. . . . There was also less prospect of integration becoming a superstate process.[89]

In terms of future trends, the countries on the margins of the two systems are of special interest. In 1974, one-third of Yugoslavia's trade was with Comecon countries, whereas more than 50 percent was with western Europe. Yugoslavia has held observer status in several OECD committees, as well as full membership status in the Bank for International Settlements, the European Conference of Ministers of Transport, and the European Conference of Posts and Telecommunications (none of which contains other "east bloc" countries) and associate membership status in the European Civil Aviation Conference and CERN. She has also maintained a permanent mission to the EC in Brussels and holds a most-favored-nation trade agreement with the Communities. But Yugoslavia's links with Comecon are likewise strong and growing. She was granted affiliated status with Comecon in 1965 and has participated in a number of the permanent commissions (foreign trade, monetary-financial, ferrous industry, nonferrous industry, machine construction, chemical, scientific and technological development, among others). She has also attended Comecon council sessions with an "advisory" vote,[90] and has a permanent mission to Comecon in Moscow. She has participated in commodity specialization agreements with Comecon,[91] in a Comecon program for the protection of the environment,[92] and in the Comecon-related agency, Intermetal.[93] She has an agreement with Comecon's International Investment Bank[94] and is involved with a variety of minor Comecon affiliates. Economically, it seems clear that Yugoslavia is not in one "camp" or the other; she has kept her options open and developed close links with both, securing as much national advantage as possible in the process. Ideologically, Yugoslavia's internal system is clearly Communist, although there have been serious doctrinal and even greater political differences with Moscow over the growing divergencies in the two regimes.

Finland is also a country caught on the frontiers between east and west, but her situation has been quite different from Yugoslavia's. The orientation of her people and political system is thoroughly "modern western," but she has also had a long history of closeness to Russia. Finland secured independence from Russia in 1918 and has since fought two bitter wars with the USSR. Since 1945, the Soviet Union has sought, with great success, to neutralize Finland completely and to make her as dependent as possible on the USSR for both markets and raw materials. Finland has had no choice but to acquiesce, although she has striven nevertheless to maintain her economic and cultural ties with Scandinavia especially and with the rest of the western countries. Gradually, she has been able to join several IGOs of the Atlantic System—most importantly the Nordic Council, OECD, and EFTA (the latter as an associate member).

A brief history of Finnish negotiations with both Comecon and the EC illustrates the delicate nature of her position. In the summer of 1972, along with other EFTA members, Finland initialled an agreement with the EC for free trade in industrial products. Fifteen months transpired, however, between the time Finland initialled the agreement and signed it. In the interval, intensive discussions with the USSR and Comecon resulted in a draft agreement providing for Finnish-Comecon cooperation in various economic, scientific, and technological endeavors. This framework treaty, later extended to cover several other fields, was buttressed by a number of bilateral, long-term trade agreements with various other Comecon members. Simultaneous with ratification of the EC agreements, the parliament passed a declaration affirming that the EC agreements implied no political connection and had no influence on any treaties previously concluded by Finland. If the EC agreement "were to damage closer relations with the USSR, Finland would give notice of withdrawal." Observed Szawlowski, "The agreement with Comecon was evidently the price the country had to pay for Moscow's 'fiat' to the treaty with Brussels."[95]

One would do well to watch both Finland and Yugoslavia for signs of any change in the sensitive balance of their relations with east and west. Whether they lean more toward one or the other in the future could be an important indication of the growing strength or weakness of the two systems.

* * *

While relations between the Atlantic and the Soviet systems have been conducted mainly between states, there have been instances of IGO-to-IGO contact. In the seventies, Comecon showed increasing interest in developing ties with the EC, although the EC maintained its distance. EC members had ceded to Brussels the negotiating authority for trade relations with third countries, but most of them had reserved the right to deal bilaterally with members of the Comecon and China. Part of the reason for this reservation stemmed from a distinct difference in the character of economic relations with Communist countries. (These generally consist of block purchases of food and industrial cooperation arrangements for substantial western manufacturing investments in the east in return for a share of the goods produced. Such agreements usually allow the eastern government involved to buy the investment back gradually.) In addition, none of the western countries or Russia's east European satellites seem anxious to help strengthen Comecon through IGO-to-IGO agreements, because this practice could tighten Soviet control over its Comecon partners. EC and Comecon have agreed to a limited, formal relationship, one confined to exchanges of information on production and trade and possible technical collaboration. For the USSR in particular, this is an important development.

The Future of the Soviet International System

What are the prospects for the Soviet International System? It could evolve in any one of several directions.

1. The System might advance on a continuum suggested by present trends, with a moderate, socialist-style integration proceeding among Comecon members and a further drawing together of military forces (with common Soviet doctrines, standardized equipment, joint training, and the like). Occasional non-European members could be added to the System, to display the worldwide appeal of Communism. The Soviets would continue to control their allies, while allowing varying, but always gradual, degrees of liberalization.

2. The Soviet International System might gradually disintegrate for a number of reasons. It could be endangered if the political contradictions became too great or if the Soviet leaders ever lost their sense of conviction and belief in the System. It could disintegrate if Communist successes in developing countries eventually evaporated (as a few already have) and the "Red tide" perceptibly receded. It might deteriorate if Comecon and the individual regimes could not cope with growing economic disjointedness at the same time that modernization urgently demanded market economies and a flexibility which Soviet Marxist doctrine could not allow. Sooner or later, given any of these trends, a member of the System will defect; a successful defection would probably be the beginning of the end for the System.

3. With younger and possibly more pragmatic, open-minded, and worldly wise Soviet leaders, a very gradual liberalization might take place in the USSR, and the

[215]

political floodgates could then open within the System. The way might then be cleared for a great deal more serious cooperation with the extended Atlantic and UN systems. This possibility would probably entail a period of considerable turbulence first.

4. The deterioration of the Soviet System might come suddenly, as a popular explosion, rather than gradually. It might affect all countries of the System, including the USSR itself. Such a cataclysmic development might also lead to general war.

5. The USSR might gradually dominate western Europe through political blackmail based on superior military power, as it has done with Finland. This scenario would assume a withdrawal of U.S. forces from Europe, the disintegration of NATO, and the political or military inability of western Europeans to fill the vacuum and resist.

6. The Soviet Union might decide to consolidate its System, in the full sense of the word. Szawlowski, among others, has suggested that this is the most likely course of events. As Lenin said:

We are internationalists. We stand for the close union and the complete amalgamation of the workers and peasants of all nations in a single world Soviet republic![96]

Other Soviet declarations have echoed these words. The 1928 Comintern Statute called for "the formation of a world union of Soviet Socialist Republics." Brezhnev's 1974 message to the 28th Session of Comecon stated, "The historic process of the rapprochement of the socialist states, the strengthening of their cohesion, continues to gather momentum." The first deputy chairman of the Bulgarian Council of Ministers also declared:

. . . Bulgaria will develop as a constituent and inseparable part of a single world socialist cooperative, will strengthen all-round fraternal cooperation with the country of the Soviets, together with which, speaking in the words of the

[216]

First Secretary of the CC of the BCP, T. Zhivkov, we will "act as one organism, which has one set of lungs and one blood system."[97]

The future is impossible to predict, but one thing seems certain: the most critical determinant of change is the Soviet Union itself. Substantive political changes among the other members of the Soviet System seem highly unlikely unless the USSR concurs and/or changes too. Outside forces are not likely to bring about major changes. Very slow, painstaking western efforts, such as the Helsinki accords (1975), may influence the internal situation in the USSR; but such efforts probably can never be decisive. The future of the Soviet International System ultimately depends on the world view of Soviet leaders.

REGIONAL SYSTEMS IN THE THIRD AND FOURTH WORLDS

United Nations Authority for Regional Organizations

Articles 51 through 54 of the United Nations Charter provide a basis in "universal" law for regional security treaties. Article 51, established the "inherent right of individual or collective self-defense" and provided a basis for immediate response.[98] Most less-than-global postwar security treaties, including NATO and WTO, have cited Article 51 as their authority. Articles 52 through 54, however, contain apparent defects. They refer specifically to "regional arrangements" (and thereby require definition of what consititutes a region). They raise questions of the respective primacy of obligations under the UN Charter or under more limited security agreements. Finally, these articles expressly forbid regional agencies from taking any enforcement action without authorization by the Security Council. Only the Treaty of Dunkirk (1947) and the treaties of alliance between the USSR and various transitory allies, such as the United Kingdom, France, and China, have cited these "regional arrangements" articles.[99]

The UN Charter contains no mention (either for or against) of

[217]

independent, regional economic or social organizations. The United Nations itself has set up regional agencies, such as the Economic Commissions for Europe, Latin America, and other continents; but the ineffectiveness of these organizations and the parent body has led nations to create their own organizations, outside of the UN framework. Such organizations have proliferated. The statutes of most of the principal Atlantic, European, and Atlantic-Pacific IGOs contain some reference to the United Nations.[100] Some have actually antedated the United Nations; for example, the predecessor of the Organization of American States was the "International Union of American Republics" (1890).

Latin American Regional Organizations

Generally speaking, integration has not worked well in Latin America, although new attempts are continually being made. The Organization of American States (OAS) is the oldest and most comprehensive of the Latin American organizations. It includes a wide variety of subsidiary organs (General Assembly, Permanent Council, Economic and Social Council, Juridical Committee, Commission on Human Rights, and others). OAS grew principally out of security considerations arising from the Second World War. The Rio treaty of September 1947 antedated all the western security treaties but that of Dunkirk; the casus foederis clause can be considered a forerunner of the NATO clause. Gradually, economic and social cooperation within OAS came to assume greater importance than concerns for security. The most publicized endeavor was perhaps the launching of the so-called "Alliance for Progress" in 1961, although the Alliance ultimately failed to meet the hopes of either the Latin American countries or the United States, which had sponsored it. In general terms, relations between the United States and the Latin American states have gradually deteriorated since that time. Overall, the experience of the OAS suggests the difficulties facing a regional arrangement in which one very large, powerful state overshadowed all the other members.

One interesting feature of the OAS is its provision for "Permanent Observer" nations. In 1977, there were 11 of these, all but two (Canada and Guyana) from outside the western hemisphere. Belgium, France, the Federal Republic of Germany, Israel, Italy, Japan, the Netherlands, Portugal, and Spain all took part in OAS as permanent observers. Correspondingly, the Inter-American Development Bank (IADB) has many nonregional members; the bank is an organization complementary, but not directly related, to OAS. Virtually all the highly developed west European countries as well as Israel belong to the bank, which has a total of 40 members. The IADB is similar to 12 other development banks which were set up between 1958 and 1977. The European Investment Bank, created under the Treaty of Rome, was the first, and in many ways the model, for all the others; IADB was the second of these banks.

In 1961, convinced that a regional economic approach without the United States might offer fresh possibilities for progress, nine Latin American countries took a cue from the EC and EFTA and set up the Latin American Free Trade Association (LAFTA). The current number of members is 11. The organization adopted an ambitious program for the elimination of tariffs among members by 1973, but postponed the date to 1980. Two members, Colombia and Venezuela, failed to ratify the extension agreement, and the future of LAFTA became questionable.[101] A rather optimistic view of LAFTA's future had been common in the mid-sixties; Business International of New York, for example, maintained that integration for Latin America was inevitable:

> LAFTA will progress toward its goals, if sometimes at a slow pace, because it must. The absolute necessity for the creation of a single market for most goods in Latin America became increasingly evident in the 1950s. The hard facts of economics left no other recourse.[102]

A few years later, however, the situation looked different. Wrote Sidney Dell:

> It was inevitable that the process of reducing trade barriers [in LAFTA] should grind to a halt so long as no agreement

was reached on a distribution of industrial policy for the region. The lack of such a policy means that the weak countries . . . have no assurance that their own infant industries will not be overwhelmed by the more advanced industries of their stronger neighbors; and still less do they have any assurance of a fair share of any new industrial capacity, whether financed out of external or local resources.[103]

Feeling this disparity acutely, six members subsequently formed the Andean Group within LAFTA (1969) and attempted to increase the rate of integration among themselves.[104] Four years later, however, the Institute for Latin American Integration could only report that "the undeniable success obtained in the formal design of certain mechanisms . . . must be followed by an implementation stage;" this stage had not yet been reached. In the same year, the incorporation of Venezuela into the pact introduced further complications and required a "redefining of some negotiations."[105] In 1976, one of the original members, Chile, withdrew, complaining that the Andean Pact emphasized economic nationalism, whereas Chile wanted more foreign investment.[106] A scheme for distributing industrial assignments among the members was also foundering, with only two out of ten industrial agreements for petrochemicals and metals concluded and no mention of implementation. Nor was there any reported progress on the fixing of a common external tariff.[107]

The Organization of Central American States (ODECA), a forerunner of CACM and CESC, was formed in 1952. Its founders (Costa Rica, El Salvador, Guatemala, Honduras, and Nicaragua) established a fairly elaborate structure and proclaimed extremely broad aims, but ODECA appeared to be moribund by the mid-seventies. The post of secretary general was abolished in 1973; there has been virtually no activity since that time.[108]

The Central American Common Market (CACM) was established by Costa Rica, El Salvador, Guatemala, Honduras, and Nicaragua in 1960, although Honduras withdrew from active participation in 1969. By 1977, the four remaining participants had removed most internal barriers to trade among themselves and had agreed on nearly all of the items in the regional customs classification (a prerequisite to instituting the common external tariff of a customs union). Whereas early dynamism had led to "a rapid and smooth implementation of the principal integration instruments," the Institute for Latin American Integration concluded nevertheless that

> it was the very success of that implementation that led to such basic problems as, for example, the inequitable distribution of the results of the Common Market.[109]

Tariff reduction alone was an insufficient program for CACM. A "serious industrial policy" was also needed.

> The benefits of the tariff reduction program seem to have accrued mainly to the big foreign companies that have had the strength and resources to move in and take advantage of the program. Local enterprise appears to have gained very little. Moreover, new industry has tended to gravitate to the more advanced centers in El Salvador, Costa Rica, and Guatemala, bypassing the two less developed countries, Honduras and Nicaragua.[110]

In fact, this disparity in benefits threatened the CACM in 1966. Nicaragua demanded preferential treatment; El Salvador threatened to withdraw from CACM if Nicaragua's demands were granted.[111] The CACM case underlines the proposition that the general expansion of trade expected from a common market does not necessarily carry the weakest members along on "the rising tide," especially among a group of less-developed countries.

> The CACM was to have been replaced by the Economic and Social Community of Central America [Spanish acronym: CESC]. . . . However, the new organization's draft treaty, which was published on March 25, 1976, still awaits ratification by the five potential members. None was pleased with the draft, and all appeared eager to postpone the CESC's establishment when renewed hostilities broke out between Honduras and El Salvador in mid-1976.[112]

Despite CACM's difficulties, all the CACM countries enjoyed relative monetary stability; comparative ease of transport via the Inter-American Highway; and, with the exception of the dispute between Honduras and El Salvador, no long-standing enmities.[113] However, after 1973, countries of the CACM incurred payment deficits, due to the increase in the price of oil. They encountered further difficulties when they attempted to establish commodity specialization agreements. The total market was too small, and the effect on existing plants in other member countries proved dire.[114]

The Caribbean Free Trade Association (CARIFTA), formed in 1968, was converted into the "Caribbean Community and Common Market" (CARICOM) in 1973. Again, despite complex machinery and elaborate schemes for integration, no substantial progress has been recorded.[115] The Institute for Latin American Integration noted that ". . . tariff reduction as a basic instrument of the integration process has revealed its inability to accelerate the development of the member countries" and suggested that it was "necessary to replace the implicit integration model."[116] The most recent instrument of Latin American integration (1975) is SELA, the Latin American Economic System. Initiated by Mexico and Venezuela "as a means of halting diminishing terms of trade," SELA has attempted "to recast the entire pattern of multilateral economic diplomacy and to respond immediately to changing world economic conditions." Of SELA's first year, the *Political Handbook of the World: 1977* adjudged: ". . . undistinguished performance."[117]

Still another new Latin American IGO has been proposed. This one would bridge the South Atlantic Ocean. The South Atlantic Treaty Organization (SATO) was proposed in 1976, "in response to the Soviet military buildup in Africa and the South Atlantic." SATO would comprise Argentina, Brazil, and South Africa. However, early negotiation of such a treaty seemed unlikely because of unresolved conflicts between Argentina and Brazil, plus the latter's unwillingness to offend former Portuguese territories in Africa.[118]

Regional integration has had a poor record in Latin America for a number of reasons. Despite the considerable cultural and linguistic affinities of the Latin American countries, the most fundamental psychological factor is missing. These countries lack an historical sense of, and commitment to, continental unity. The nineteenth-century Spanish colonies had practically no loyalty to one another. Nationalism is strong, and the gap between blacks, Indians, and whites remains great. Although nationalism historically seems to be a prerequisite for industrial development, it also stands in the way of supranational integration. Perhaps development and integration cannot both be undertaken successfully at the same time. Indeed, scarcely any of the Latin American countries have managed to integrate their own states or societies. "People who have difficulty in identifying themselves with their own country . . . [will have difficulty identifying] themselves with a continent of which they know little or nothing."[119]

Integration can be speeded up if there is an external enemy. In recent western European integration, the Soviet Union has served in this role. In Latin America, the United States has played the "enemy" role, but ambiguously, for the hate in the relationship is mixed with affection and respect. A further ambiguity is the Latin American Marxist propaganda that integration will help mainly the United States and the multinational corporations. How can one unite against the enemy when unification will only play into its hands?[120]

Integration requires an appropriate regional transportation network. The Inter-American Highway provides some, but not all of this requirment. Geography and lack of capital both militate against repairing this defect soon, if ever.

If the disparities in development are too great between nations, and the disproportion between the more-developed and the less-developed members favors the latter, integration is virtually stopped before it can begin, as has been the case with LAFTA.[121] A great burst of economic growth would ease the inevitable growing pains of integration and is thus highly desirable. But the lack of "technological initiative and versatility in the use of resources" and "a deep-seated cultural apathy toward invention and discovery, or what has now become organized research and development,"[122] in most Latin American countries make this an unlikely factor in the integration of that continent.

Nor were factors external to Latin America in the late seventies (especially the world price of oil, but also the terms of trade for the continent's raw materials generally) favorable to integration. In contrast, much of the lowering of trade barriers in the EC and EFTA took place before the quintupling of energy prices and the general disruption of world markets.

The factors noted above would themselves more than have explained the failure of integration in Latin America, but other prerequisites for integration were missing as well. There was virtually no feeling of interdependence with respect to external security. There were no well-developed civic cultures, bringing with them the capability for self-government and contributing to responsible international government. The education systems of these countries were essentially not modern, and the research system was inadequate. As a result, there was a paucity of available, skilled, educated persons to staff sophisticated international institutions and a relatively high incidence of friction among some of the members of those institutions.

The essential problem in Latin America is development—the development not only of backward economies, but of societies, of political structures and habits, and most importantly of human resources. Stubborn cultural and social factors block change. Without the prior resolution of such deep-seated and contradictory problems, efforts at integration in Latin America will probably continue to produce at least as much tension as they relieve. The repeated frustration of well-meaning attempts simply adds to a record of mediocre performance and compounds the dissatisfactions. Integration has not worked in Latin America: so far, it has been largely a fad; certainly, it has proven to be no panacea.

ASEAN: The Association of Southeast Asian Nations

Efforts were made in the late 1950s and early 1960s to create a framework of regional cooperation in Southeast Asia. One security-oriented IGO, SEATO (Southeast Asia Treaty Organization) was initiated by powers outside the area (notably the United States, Britain, and France); SEATO was, however, dropped following the collapse of the western position in Indochina. An abortive Association of Southeast Asia was established in 1961 by Malaya, the Philippines, and Thailand. In 1963, Indonesia, Malaya, and the Philippines created the short-lived Maphilindo. The 1965 change in government in Indonesia opened the way for a somewhat broader association; and in August 1967, the foreign ministers of Indonesia, Malaysia, Thailand, the Philippines, and Singapore established the Association of Southeast Asian Nations (ASEAN). Little of consequence, however, was accomplished until February 1976, when a Treaty of Amity and Cooperation, a Declaration of ASEAN Concord, and an Agreement for the Establishment of an ASEAN Secretariat (subsequently set up in Djakarta) were all signed at the organization's first meeting. The Treaty of Amity and Cooperation was the first legally binding agreement among Southeast Asian countries in the history of the region. It has remained open to other countries in the area, although the Indochinese nations, (the principal potential members) have so far declined to participate, and indeed have displayed hostility towards ASEAN.[123] The Declaration of Concord has attempted to provide a foundation for expanded cooperation in political, economic, social, and cultural fields, although a proposal for the arbitration of territorial disputes among members was turned down.

ASEAN was revitalized in 1976, after the takeover of South Vietnam by North Vietnam (April 1975). This renewal of the organization was no accident: it was obvious that some members hoped that ASEAN could be used to pull the region together in the face of expected new Communist pressures from Indochina, China, and the USSR. This certainly was a principal motive of Indonesia, and apparently paramount in the mind of Singapore's Prime Minister Lee Kuan Yew when he was interviewed a few days after the historic ASEAN heads of state meeting in February 1976. In response to the question, "What is your [ASEAN's] most serious problem?" he replied, "It is post-Vietnam." He went on to predict that increased help from both Russian and China would add to the economic strength and "all other things—including political clout" of the states of Indochina.[124] The communiqués issued from the 1976 Denpara meeting contained no reference to Indochina or Communism. By the next summit meeting in August 1977, ASEAN's leaders were ready to say outright that they were threatened by the "hostile challenge" from Indochina,[125] and the Vietnamese invasion of Cambodia in 1979 appeared to alarm ASEAN leaders even more. The main effort of ASEAN however, has been to put fear in the background and to portray ASEAN simply as an attempt by friendly, contiguous countries to deal with underdevelopment, a problem common to all of them. The search for practical ways of implementing a program of cooperation has been neither easy nor particularly fruitful.

Development of a free trade zone or a common market has been hampered by economic disparities and the absence of significant trade and other economic relations among members. Singapore ranks with some of the middle-level western European nations in living standards and industrial production; Indonesia's per capita GNP is among the world's lowest. And less than 15 percent of ASEAN trade is among member nations. As *The Economic Bulletin* of Kuala Lumpur observed, ". . . it is doubtful that the members would be eager to disturb the 85 percent of the trade with non-ASEAN countries by having a customs union."[126] Nevertheless, a modest start in this direction has been made; a schedule of tariff reductions on 71 products traded among the five countries was accepted for implementation not later than January 1, 1978 by the 1977 ASEAN Summit Conference. Singapore, Thailand, and the Philippines but not Malaysia and Indonesia, had already approved a 10 percent reduction on a further list of 1,700 items.[127] Each of the five countries did agree to take the lead in developing one major industrial project. A diesel engine factory was envisaged for Singapore (which has the trained manpower at hand), a soda ash fertilizer plant for Thailand, a phosphate plant for the Philippines, and urea fertilizer complexes for Indonesia and Malaysia. But a year and a half later, the only progress which could be reported was completion of a feasibility study for Indonesia's urea factory.[128] This lack of progress made it difficult for ASEAN to request specific aid from such countries as Japan, which had hinted that it might give as much as $1 billion in assistance. Such offers were contingent upon the completion of feasibility studies.[129,130]

ASEAN's relationship with the big developed countries of the Pacific, especially the United States, Japan, and Australia, has been both critical and delicate. These countries are the only likely sources of substantial capital and technical assistance. Japan has been more or less eager to help ASEAN, but does not want to accept too many light manufacturing imports from the area. Also, she has encountered attitudes of mistrust (dating from World War II), mixed with envy and hope, on the part of the ASEAN peoples. In July 1977, Lee Kuan Yew reportedly told the ASEAN foreign ministers:

Together we must establish closer, more constructive and complementary relationships with Japan and perhaps also with Australia and New Zealand. [131]

The "perhaps" was significant. While Australia agreed to double its aid to the ASEAN countries (from $100 to $208 million) [132] and obviously wanted ASEAN's goodwill, she was extremely reluctant to entertain the idea of tariff reductions for ASEAN goods, which "will only add to Australia's already severe unemployment problem." [133]

At the time of the 1977 ASEAN summit, a State Department official in Washington, D.C., was quoted as saying: "ASEAN is an idea whose time has come." [134] A few weeks later, U.S. Undersecretary of State Richard Cooper met with ASEAN foreign ministers in Manila. ASEAN's spokesman, Carlos Romulo of the Philippines, told the ensuing press conference:

It was an historic dialogue—the first time that the United States dealt with an Asian group. In the past the United States dealt with the nations bilaterally.

He reported that ASEAN and the United States had agreed that "all countries should reject protectionism," and that the United States had "declared readiness to participate with ASEAN in developing cooperation supplementary to the assistance extended bilaterally to ASEAN countries. . . ." [135] The United States was less forthcoming than Japan had been. But these were still positive indications, suggesting the potential importance that the U.S. government saw in ASEAN. Dr. Cooper spoke of ASEAN as "a pragmatic force, intent on pursuing a constructive rather than a confrontational role in international economic forums...." If the United States was also cautious, there was good reason. Washington wanted to avoid, if possible, any aura of renewed confrontation in Southeast Asia.

In 1977, the ASEAN foreign ministers also decided to "establish joint consultative groups with the European Economic Community and other developed countries."[136] They apparently feared that the EC, still affected by the recession that followed the oil boycott, might begin to erect higher barriers to ASEAN goods.

Of all the attempts at regional cooperation among various groups of developing countries, ASEAN certainly is one of the most hopeful. ASEAN's leaders have seemed to realize that grandiose plans for economic integration would be distinctly premature, but that there are many ways in which members can help one another to build strong economies. ASEAN has also challenged the developed democracies, especially those bordering the Pacific, to find suitable methods of providing effective development aid and to find common interests around which an equal partnership might be built.

Asia also has a regional bank, the Asian Development Bank (ADB), which is modelled on the Inter-American Development Bank and the European Investment Bank. In 1977, there were 42 members of the Bank, 28 of which were from the region. The ADB serves as a channel for development loans from Japan (principally), the United States, and Europe to the Asian countries. The role of the ADB in the general scheme of things is not large (lending commitments in its first decade were less than $4 billion),[137] but it could have a useful future as a model for practical, nonpolemical cooperation between developed and less-developed countries.

Other Regional Systems
Certain of the so-called "commodity organizations" can also

be categorized as IGOs. The most notable of these is the Organization of Petroleum Exporting Countries (OPEC). Composed of nations generally regarded as "less developed," OPEC electrified the world in 1973 with its successful imposition of doubled oil prices and an oil boycott. Some observers have cautioned that OPEC is a forerunner of things to come, but other attempts to create commodity organizations have failed. However, OPEC does bear watching as one possible model of future international organizations. Certainly, its relationship with the Atlantic-Pacific System is of paramount importance.

The Commonwealth (formerly the "British Commonwealth of Nations") also deserves special, if brief, mention. Evolving out of the old British Empire, the Commonwealth originally was a voluntary association of the self-governing, largely white Dominions and the United Kingdom; all members were equal and united only by their common allegiance to the British Crown. As the process of decolonization accelerated after 1945, the membership of the Commonwealth grew to include 35 nations which were strung around the globe and which represented a wide variety of cultures, ethnic backgrounds, and stages of development. While the Commonwealth had undertaken a good deal of useful activity in scientific, educational, technical, developmental, and athletic areas, it had lost much of its meaning by the late 1970s. Such figures as Idi Amin, President of Uganda, were a distinct embarrassment to the other members; many members had become republics and no longer shared the symbolism of the Crown; Britain's weakness limited its ability to give life and direction to the whole. On balance, the Commonwealth's work still seemed useful, but its future appeared extremely cloudy.

* * *

I have not treated Middle Eastern or African intergovernmental organizations. Although there are a number of regional groupings in those areas, virtually all of them have so far proven to be ephemeral or ineffectual. Their schemes have been grandiose, but little has been accomplished.

THE ATLANTIC-PACIFIC SYSTEM AND ALL THE OTHERS

Over the past few decades, new varieties of intergovernmental organizations have grown up everywhere. There seems to have been literally no end to the numbers of special-purpose and general-purpose IGOs that have been created to serve the needs of an increasingly interdependent world. Yet, man has not yet solved the basic problems of creating or operating such institutions successfully. To continue their headlong growth unchecked ultimately limits the usefulness and viability of all IGOs. Many IGOs are not really systems or parts of systems at all, but are simply organizations whose aims had little validity to begin with or which have outlived their original importance. Others continue to be needed and to grow with the emergence of fresh tasks. In the interest of all the inhabitants of the globe, IGOs should be used to attain security, increased prosperity, social justice, a more decent environment, and the other goals shared by an interdependent world. Above all, then, the purposes and the working methods of IGOs must be consonant with those of others; they must dovetail, rather than conflict with one another. In a world torn by sharp ideological and power conflicts, this may seem an idle dream, but is one still worth striving for, step by small step if necessary.

Interlocking Systems and Special-Purpose IGOs

One way to work for a more stable world security system would be to encourage cooperation among IGOs with similar tasks and, when possible, congruent aims. Even though the cultural or ideological framework differs sharply between the EC and Comecon, there is value, for example, in supporting discussions between the two in such technical fields as the environment, transport, or communication. There is also value in encouraging overlapping memberships in IGOs (e.g., Finland and Yugoslavia are both associate memebers of Comecon and OECD; the Socialist Republic of Vietnam is a member of both Comecon and the Asian Development Bank). "Bridge" organizations can also be useful to some degree, because they often include members of more than one IGO (e.g., the UN's Economic

Commission for Europe contains practically all the members of both OECD and Comecon).

Special-purpose IGOs, such as the regional development banks and the Conference on International Economic Cooperation, also have promise. These organizations generally comprise both developed and less-developed countries from several continents. They help insure the transfer of information and expertise from one group or system to another. If their purposes, methods, and structures are sufficiently apolitical, they can even help overcome differences that arise in the UN General Assembly. The Yaoundé and Lomé Conventions for example, between groups of less-developed countries and the European Communities, offer still more possibilities for cooperation which can gradually build global trust and capabilities.

The UN System and the Atlantic-Pacific System

The relationship between the UN System and the Atlantic-Pacific System is especially important. Some of the IGOs of the Atlantic-Pacific System were set up because the UN was clearly unable to do an important job.

> The North Atlantic Treaty is not so much a derivative or a logical consequence of the provisions of the UN Charter; it is rather an attempt to fill a gap or to provide new machinery for the maintenance of peace and security in a case where the Security Council would not be able to act because of disagreement between the permanent members.[138]

OECD assumed a variety of economic tasks which the UN was patently not equipped to perform. These included the coordination of advanced economies to give more and better aid to the less-developed countries and the more recent establishment of a caucus of the principal oil-consuming nations under IEA. Other IGOs in the Atlantic-Pacific System, strictly regional in character, were intended to perform tasks which were never part of the UN's mandate.

Most institutions of the extended Atlantic System work a good deal better than those of the UN family. As nations become disillusioned with the "one-nation, one-vote" UN System and the increasing politicization of the UN and its agencies, they may cause a gradual reconstitution of international mechanisms. If more countries joined the growing Atlantic-Pacific System, they could build alongside the UN System another international system, but one more pragmatic and effective because its tasks were more carefully matched to its members' capabilities. A strong, capable Atlantic-Pacific System could be a powerful stabilizing force, undertaking what the UN could not.

There must always be universal organizations, but the impossible should not be expected of them. Such expectations have been the source of much of the disillusionment and cynicism about the UN. In the long run, the world's nations may be able to create a much more effective UN System. A stronger UN could build on the achievements of the Atlantic-Pacific System and might eventually envelop and supersede the System. If, on the other hand, the UN System does not grow and prosper, a vital Atlantic-Pacific System would offer an obvious alternative.

Of the UN, Haas wrote:

> The United Nations system represents the cohabitation of enemies, the institutionalized attack-and-retreat of hostile forces seeking to get the better of each other by peaceful means, but without any intention of deliberately emphasizing what they may share in common. . . . [Although the UN is not] irretrievably impotent . . . *successful* UN action has *always* been based on the minimum common denominator, success being judged on the degree of implementation given to UN resolutions.[139]

On occasion, the UN Secretary General has received new powers and responsibilities that contained "a dose of supranationalism," but such changes have turned out to be ephemeral. By contrast,

> in the European context such efforts often resulted in a permanent growth of community-oriented procedures; in the UN . . . issues which appeared settled reappear a few years

later, including major constitutional questions.[140]

Plainly stated, the UN System is today essentially impotent and unreliable. There is no reason to believe that this situation will improve in the foreseeable future; and, in fact, the reverse is more probable. The Atlantic-Pacific System could undoubtedly do much that would strengthen other systems in the international community, simply by following the outline that Cooper, Kaiser, and Kosaka suggested for the Trilateral Commission:

> . . . fostering an effective, working concensus [sic] among the advanced trilateral countries will be a positive contribution to renovating the international order in the interest of all. But the trilateral approach cannot be exclusive or parochial. These countries have no mandate to determine what is right or wrong for the rest of the world. They must be responsive to the interests and concerns of others and take them into account. Yet the trilateral nations will often serve the interests of wide cooperation if they can agree among themselves on proposals for consideration and negotiation with other nations or groups.[141]

Alternative World Systems

To strengthen the cause, the mechanisms, and the understanding of practical international cooperation is a positive task, and one for which the Atlantic-Pacific nations are reasonably well equipped. With one exception, no other nation or group of nations aspires to this role. The exception, of course, is the USSR. The Soviet International System is the current working model of the USSR's alternative framework for international cooperation. According to Soviet philosophy, this model is also historically inevitable. In 1920, Lenin wrote of "directing the international tactics of the revolutionary proletariat in its struggle for a world Soviet republic."[142] The speeches of subsequent Soviet leaders, from Stalin to Brezhnev, are replete with similar references. Lenin also spoke to the historical inevitability of this development.

[233]

. . . all the primary features of our revolution and many of its secondary features, are of international significance in the meaning of its effect on all countries. I am speaking of it in the narrowest sense of the word, taking international significance to mean the international validity or the historical inevitability of a repetition on an international scale, of what has taken place in our country.[143]

In 1972, the Soviet theoretician E.T. Usenko stated:

Integration processes . . . should end in the merging of states and nations into one world economy. . . . The solving of the above-mentioned task of the development of human society is the historical mission of socialism. "The aim of socialism," said Lenin, "is not only the elimination of the splitting up of mankind into small states and of all isolation of nations, not only the rapprochement of nations, but also their merging."—Such is the ultimate aim of socialism, such is the ultimate point in the general process of integration, after the attainment of which the process will exhaust itself and leave the historical scene. It is necessary to keep in mind this ultimate aim of integration as the general perspective.[144]

No matter what label is put on East-West relations (Cold War, détente, Ostopolitik, etc.), it is evident that the epoch-making contest between two international systems—the Soviet and the Atlantic-Pacific—will remain a predominant feature of the international scene for some years to come.

FOOTNOTES

1. Perhaps the most authoritative American commentary is Leland M. Goodrich, Edvard Hambro, and Anne P. Simons, *Charter of the United Nations: Commentary and Documents* (3rd and rev. ed.), (New York: Columbia University Press, 1969). See also, Ruth B. Russell and

J.E. Muther, *History of the United Nations Charter: The Role of the United States, 1940-1945* (Washington, D.C.: The Brookings Institution, 1969).

2. Long after the end of the Second World War, for example, there were still no peace treaties between some of the key participants in the conflict. In 1971, the peace treaty between the Federal Republic of Germany and the USSR was finally ratified. As of 1978, however, peace agreements between Japan and the USSR and China had still not been concluded.

3. Goodrich and Simons, op. cit., pp. 28–29.

4. Originally from the French word which described the lessening of tension in the string of a crossbow after the bolt was fired.

5. Arthur S. Banks, *Political Handbook of the World: 1977* (New York: McGraw-Hill, 1977), p. 546.

6. Otto Pick and Julian Critchley, *Collective Security* (London: Macmillan, 1974), p. 46.

7. Banks, op. cit., p. 620.

8. Hambro points out that the framers of the Charter inserted certain criteria for membership: applicant states would have to demonstrate both their willingness and their ability to fulfill the obligations of membership before being admitted. "This part of the Charter is today a dead letter." (In the Foreword to Goodrich, Hambro, and Simons, op. cit., p. vi.)

9. See *Encyclopaedia Britannica Book of the Year: 1974,* pp. 710–712, and "Tyranny of Majority in UN?" *Christian Science Monitor* (December 9, 1974).

10. *Seattle Post-Intelligencer* (November 12, 1975), p. A/1.

11. *International Herald Tribune* (May 3, 1976).

12. *Seattle Post-Intelligencer* (June 13, 1976).

13. Banks, op. cit., p. 555.

14. Ibid., p. 89.

15. *Seattle Post-Intelligencer* (January 26, 1976).

16. *Christian Science Monitor* (December 27, 1974), p. 2.

17. Banks, op. cit., pp. 553–555.

18. *International Herald Tribune* (March 8–9, 1975), p. 2.

19. Banks, op. cit., pp. 562–563.

20. The preamble to UNESCO's Charter begins: "As wars begin in the minds of men, it is there that the defenses of peace must be constructed." UNESCO's lineal ancestor was the League of Nations agency known as the International Institute of Intellectual Cooperation.

21. *Freedom at Issue,* no. 44 (January-February 1978) p. 21.

22. Ibid., p. 26.

23. Banks, op. cit., p. 546.

24. Ibid., pp. 548–549.

25. Goodrich and Simons, op. cit., p. viii.

26. *Webster's Third New International Dictionary,* vol. I, p. 458.

27. To Marxist-Leninist socialists, the word "socialist" signifies a political system in which the state owns and manages the means of production and controls the distribution of the goods. The process is dominated by "the dictatorship of the proletariat" until such time as reeducation and conditioning have produced "socialist man." At this point, socialism, under which there has been necessarily unequal distribution of goods and payments to individuals according to their ability, is superseded by communism, under which the state withers away and each individual produces according to his ability and receives according to his needs. The USSR is a "Union of Soviet Socialist Republics" in this sense, but is run by a Communist Party of the Soviet Union. Modern social democrats in such countries as Norway or West Germany would not accept these definitions of socialism, even though many of them might favor more state ownership of industry. Social democrats and many other "socialists" in the west stand for liberal, parliamentary, pluralist democracy and reject the dictatorship of the proletariat; many do not consider themselves Marxists, and the vast majority do not accept Lenin's teachings. These fairly complex differences render any use of the word "socialist" ambiguous at best and deliberately obfuscating at worst.

28. Comecon is the Soviet International System's counterpart to the OEEC and OECD and the European Communities; the term has been employed in Communist literature for western consumption, as a shortening of the full title: "Council for Mutual Economic Assistance." Sometimes it is denominated by its acronym: CMEA.

29. Richard Szawlowski, *The System of the International Organizations of the Communist Countries* (Leyden: A.W. Sijthoff, 1976).

30. Ibid., p. xvi.

31. Ibid., pp. xxiv–xxvi.

32. Ibid., p. xvii.

33. Richard F. Staar, *Communist Regimes in Eastern Europe* (3rd. ed.), (Stanford: Hoover Institution Press, 1977), p. 223.

34. Szawlowski, op. cit., p. xvii.

35. Roman Kolkowicz (ed.), *The Warsaw Pact* (Arlington, Va.: Institute for Defense Analysis, 1969), p. 12.

36. Staar, op. cit., p. 213.

37. Robin Alison Remington, *The Warsaw Pact: Case Studies in Communist Conflict Resolution* (Cambridge, Mass.: M.I.T. Press, 1971), p. 165.

38. Szawlowski, op. cit., p. 3.

39. Remington, op. cit., p.173.

40. Ibid., p. 172.

41. Kolkowicz, op. cit., p.3.

42. Staar, op. cit., p. 222.

43. Szawlowski, op. cit., p. 16.

44. Kolkowicz, op. cit., p. 13.

45. Remington, op. cit., p. 184.

46. See, e.g., *The Military Balance* (London: International Institute for Strategic Studies, 1978); *Jane's All the World's Aircraft,* London, 1977–78 edition; Arnaud de Borchgrave, "Nightmare for NATO," *Newsweek* (February 7, 1977), pp. 36–38.

47. Kolkowicz, op. cit., p. v.

48. See Szawlowski, op. cit., pp. 6, 9, and 32; Staar, op.cit., p. 216.

49. Remington, op. cit., pp. 166, 185–187.

50. Pick and Critchley, op. cit., p. 43.

51. In Kolkowicz, op. cit., p. 87.

52. William R. Kintner, in Kolkowicz, op. cit., pp. 91, 93.

53. In Preface to Szawlowski, op. cit., p. xi.

54. Pick and Critchley, op. cit., p. 42.

55. Michael Kaser, *COMECON: Integration Problems of the Planned Economies* (London: Oxford University Press, 1967), p. 9.

56. Szawlowski, op. cit., p. 148.

57. Quoted in Kaser, op. cit., pp. 11–12.

58. Nikolai Patolichev, *Foreign Trade* (Moscow: Novosti Press Agency Publishing House, ?1971), p. 36.

59. Henry Wilcox Schaefer, *Comecon and the Politics of Integration* (New York: Praeger, 1972), p. 3.

60. Quoted in Szawlowski, op. cit., pp. 74–75.

61. Ibid., p. 7.

62. Szawlowski, op. cit., pp. 51–52.

63. Ibid., p. 53.

64. Ibid., p. 65.

65. Jozef M.P. Van Brabant, *Essays on Planning, Trade, and Integration in Eastern Europe* (Rotterdam: Rotterdam University Press, 1974), pp. 14–15.

66. Ibid., pp. 8–9.

67. Schaefer, op. cit., p. 192.

[237]

68. Szawlowski, op. cit., p. 67.
69. Ibid., p. 94.
70. Ibid., p. 79.
71. Staar, op. cit., pp. 243-247.
72. Szawlowski, op. cit., pp. 131-135.
73. Brabant, op. cit., pp. 12-13.
74. Szawlowski, op. cit., pp. 120-123.
75. Staar, op. cit., p. 245.
76. Banks, op. cit., p. 518.
77. Szawlowski, op. cit., p. 140.
78. Ibid., pp. 70-71.
79. Shaefer, op. cit., p. 193.
80. Brabant, op. cit., p. 33.
81. Kaser, op. cit., p. 16.
82. Ibid., p. 26.
83. Ibid., p. 1.
84. Szawlowski, op. cit., p. 95.
85. Brabant, op. cit., p. 16.
86. Szawlowski, op. cit., p. 105.
87. Ibid., pp. xii-xiii.
88. Kaser, op. cit., p. 19.
89. Schaefer, op. cit., p. 191.
90. Staar, op. cit., p. 250.
91. Szawlowski, op. cit., p. 79.
92. Ibid., p. 83.
93. Ibid., p. 114.
94. Ibid., p. 120.
95. Ibid., pp. 54-56.
96. *Collected Works,* (Moscow: Lawrence and Wishart, London-Progress Publishers, 1965), vol. 30, p. 293.
97. Ibid., pp. 152-156.
98. Goodrich, Hambro, and Simons, op. cit., p. 352.
99. Ibid., pp. 354-369.
WEU treaties all contained reference to "the principles of the United Nations" or similar language; the EFTA, Benelux, ECSC, and Nordic Council agreements did not mention the UN, nor did the statutes of the many, more limited European bodies, such as the Conference of European Ministers of Transport and others listed in Appendix D.
101. *The Latin American Integration Process in 1973* (Washington, D.C.: Institute for Latin American Integration, 1973), pp. 9-11. See also, Banks, op. cit., pp. 519-520.

102. *LAFTA: Key to Latin America's 200 Million Customers* (New York: Business International of New York, 1966), p. 4.

103. Writing in Ronald Hilton (ed.) *The Movement Toward Latin American Unity* (New York: Frederick A. Praeger, 1969), p. 65.

104. Banks, op. cit., p. 488.

105. *The Latin American Integration Process in 1973*, op. cit., p. 6.

106. Banks, op. cit., p. 488.

107. *International Herald Tribune* (August 23, 1976), p. 6. Cf. also ASEAN's "complementary industrialization" scheme, pp. 226–227.

108. Banks, op. cit., p. 527.

109. *The Latin American Integration Process in 1973*, op. cit., p. 5.

110. Sidney Dell, in Hilton, op. cit., p. 64.

111. R. D. Hausen in Hilton, ibid., p. 23.

112. Banks, op. cit., p. 495.

113. Robert W. Bradbury in Hilton, ibid., p. 76.

114. Dell, in Hilton, ibid., p. 64.

115. Banks, op. cit., p. 493.

116. *The Latin American Integration Process in 1973*, op. cit., p. 7.

117. Banks, op. cit., p. 474.

118. Ibid., p. 475.

119. Dell in Hilton, op. cit., p. 69.

120. Hilton, ibid., pp. 5–6.

121. In western Europe, the Common Market so far has been reasonably successful because most of the nine members have enjoyed relatively high levels of development in at least a preponderance of the regions within their own countries. Italy is the most marginal case, and has had the greatest difficulty adjusting. Ireland, England, and Scotland also pose problems in this regard. However, it remains to be seen if EC will find the underdeveloped economies of Greece, Portugal, or Spain fully "digestible," should they become members. The problem of underdevelopment in Latin America is much greater.

122. James H. Street in Hilton, ibid., p. 43.

123. Banks, op. cit., p. 490; *Regional Politics* (Vol. 2), (Washington, D.C.: National Defense University/National War College, November 17–December 15, 1977), pp. 4–5.

124. *Newsweek* (International Edition), (March 15, 1976), p. 56.

125. *International Herald Tribune* (August 6–7, 1977) p. 2.

126. *The Economic Bulletin* (Kuala Lumpur), February, 1976, p. 37.

127. *Christian Science Monitor* (August 8, 1977).

128. Ibid.

129. *International Herald Tribune* (August 8, 1977), p. 1.

130. *Christian Science Monitor,* (August 8, 1977).

131. *Far Eastern Economic Review* (July 15, 1977), p. 14.

132. *International Herald Tribune* (August 8, 1977), p. 2.

133. *Christian Science Monitor* (August 8, 1977).

134. *Far Eastern Economic Review* (August 12, 1977), p. 10.

135. *Department of State Bulletin* (October 31, 1977), p. 599.

136. *Far Eastern Economic Review* (July 22, 1977), p. 39.

137. "Asian Development Bank: Searching for a Role," *Far Eastern Economic Review* (April 22, 1977), p. 47.

138. A.H. Robertson, *European Institutions: Cooperation: Integration: Unification* (3rd ed.), (London: Stevens and Sons, 1973), p. 95.

139. Ernst B. Haas, "International Integration: The European and the Universal Process," in B. Landheer (ed.), *Limits and Problems of European Integration* (The Hague: Martinus Nijhoff, 1963), p. 26.

140. Ibid., p. 27. Even though Hammersköld received and used sweeping powers in the Congo and was able, with the help of the main western nations, to set matters as straight as they could be set, the USSR—sensing that it had let matters get out of hand—made sure that Hammarsköld or his successors would never again have such a free hand.

141. Richard N. Cooper, Karl Kaiser, and Masataka Kosaka, *Towards a Renovated International System* (The Triangle Papers: 14), (New York: Trilateral Commission, 1977), p. 4.

142. V.I. Lenin, *"Left-Wing" Communism* (Moscow: 1920), reprinted in Robert C. Tucker (ed.), *The Lenin Anthology* (New York: W. W. Norton and Co., 1975), p. 608.

143. Ibid., pp. 550–551.

144. Quoted by Szawlowski, op. cit., p. 160, from: E.T. Usenko, "International Legal Problems of Socialist Economic Integration," in *Sovetskij Yezhogodnik Mezhdunarodnovo Prava* (Moscow: Izdatel'stvo "Nauka," 1972), pp. 16–17.

CHAPTER 7

The Future of the Extended Atlantic System: Towards a Community of the Developed Democracies

This concluding chapter will summarize the accomplishments and shortcomings of the extended Atlantic System, review the factors and conditions which made the achievements possible, draw from this experience whatever theoretical conclusions seem evident, assess the major problems and challenges facing the System, and examine its possible future development.

THE EFFECT OF THE SYSTEM

Modern life more and more requires interdependence among nations. Indeed, a large number of thinking persons have begun to believe that society should transcend the nation state. To a significant extent, the industrial democracies of the extended Atlantic System have managed to do so in the third quarter of the twentieth century. Their effort, the evolution of an advanced international system of unprecedented power, scope, and sophistication, constitutes an important chapter in the history of mankind. What is the net effect of the extended Atlantic System?

1. *In security terms, the Atlantic-Pacific System deserves the main credit for preventing World War III.* For the west—and for Japan and her main Pacific neighbors too—the core of the

world security problem still lies iñ Europe, where the two great power complexes contend most directly. Europe now has a system that Pick and Critchley have called "regional collective self-defence" because of the balance (admittedly somewhat unstable) between the Warsaw Pact and NATO nations. This is neither "collective security" in the sense of the League of Nations or the UN Security Council, nor an old-fashioned "balance of power."

> The regional collective self-defence represents a conceptual compromise between the old balance of power, which became uncontrollable in an industrialized world, and universal collective security. . . . The ideals of universalism, culminating in world government, are obviously not within the realm of practical politics, and as it is impossible to diffuse collective security across the whole wide world, the next best thing is to try and maintain it on a regional basis.[1]

Pick and Critchley have correctly assessed the existing system:

> On the available evidence, the present system is simply more reliable than the purists' idea of collective security, although it would be a serious, and possibly fatal, error of judgement to regard it as infallible.[2]

The Atlantic-Pacific security system represents a marked advance on anything which has gone before, but still has defects.

2. *In economic terms, the System represents at least as great an improvement over the past as does the security achievement.* Because of the quality and sophistication of the numerous linkages, there has not been a repetition of 1933, when the world economy literally collapsed. Four decades after that collapse, Joseph C. Harsch commented on the improved state of affairs:

> Men and governments do remember the mistakes of the past and can improve their responses to problems. True, the responses of 1975 have fallen short of the ideal. More might have been done, and sooner . . . Yet the essential fact is that

the community of the modern industrial democracies has not broken into national fragments. It has held together. There has not been a hasty building of tariff walls. There has been no panic and no disaster. People, money, and goods still flow freely among the industrial consumers and between them and the raw-material producers. The Western economic community has weathered the worst of the storm and is essentially intact.[3]

Political will alone did not make the difference although it was indispensable. New institutions, innovative procedures, human capabilities, and new habits of working together internationally had been fashioned with intelligence, great effort and sacrifice. A major contribution to the economic success of the System has been the internationalizing of production, an achievement largely of the private sector. The vast new network of international investment through multinational enterprises is primarily concentrated in the countries of the Atlantic-Pacific System and insures that every country has a vested interest in the working of every other country's economy.

3. *Politically, the System has displayed surprising durability and resilience.* Numerous crises have taken a severe toll, but the System has held. That the institutions and the System do still work should offer reassurance and cause for hope, if not always for optimism.

4. *The very existence of the Atlantic-Pacific institutions and arrangements represents truly radical change in the methods and possibilities of working toward world order.* For example, the advent of the European Communities has replaced the notorious balance-of-power system in western Europe with a cooperative, community-oriented system of relations among its member nations and virtually eliminated the possibility of war in western Europe. The EC has aided and abetted an astounding economic surge from the postwar period to today's high levels of economic growth and prosperity. EC's organs and procedures represent unprecedented departures in international decision making. However, Monnet asked for more than could be delivered—a "United States of Europe"—and many Europeans (and Ameri-

cans too) are unhappy at what they consider to be the "failure" of the EC. The present EC is less than Monnet and other leaders wanted, but much more than would have been achieved had no attempt been made or their goals been more modest. That the EC has been consciously imitated throughout the world suggests that its great significance has been recognized, intuitively and practically, everywhere.

5. *The System has protected, preserved, and in many ways strengthened western-style liberal democracy.* This was indeed a chief result and an original aim of NATO. The EC, OECD, and other economic organs of the System also have promoted social peace by insuring a high degree of economic growth and employment and rising living standards. Democratic regimes have been installed in Greece, Portugal, and Spain, no doubt in part to gain fuller membership in the System. The Council of Europe's Court of Human Rights has enhanced the political security of the individual. The various interparliamentary assemblies have also contributed to the strengthening of the common civic culture. On this theme, one might quote EC Commissioner Christopher Tugendhat, speaking in December 1977:

> One of the great and guiding insights of the Founding Fathers—of men like Robert Schuman, Alcide di Gasperi, Jean Monnet and Konrad Adenauer—was their recognition that if leading democratic nations of Europe dared to transcend their ancestral rivalries, and to enter an entirely new relationship, in which each brought the best of its individual traditions to bear upon the construction of a greater whole, then, in addition to eliminating the prospect of armed conflict between them, those nations would also immeasurably fortify the individual freedoms and rights which each of them cherished.[4]

Shortcomings

The Atlantic System has shortcomings as well. There appears to be a growing uncertainty about the nature of the challenges facing the System and a consequent lack of consensus as to what should be done. The most critical weakness lies in the realm of leadership. The United States appears no longer able or willing to exercise the role of a powerful leader, even primus inter pares, although its leadership remains essential. While certain other powers in the System (especially Germany and Japan) have grown much more powerful, they are not yet candidates for leadership of the System. The only answer seems to be a new form of collective leadership, but no one has a clear idea of how it could or should work. At the end of the 1970s, there appeared to be other weaknesses in the System.

1. *The System had failed to maintain its early momentum in building creative institutions.* Since the establishment of OECD in 1961, only one other major organ and one incipient organ have been created: the International Energy Agency and the Seven-Power Summits. The world trading and money systems have neither come apart nor progressed substantially. The Bretton Woods arrangments were effectively nullified after 1970, and there was still no general agreement for the long term. The Tokyo Round of GATT negotiations took six years to complete, but resulted in no new or remarkable achievements in trade. There were complaints about the adequacy of the political machinery.[5] In most cases, the process of integration, which had been expected to lead to true community, had given way to cooperation that was not always effective or willing.

2. *The NATO System showed definite signs of deterioration.* Most observers agree that the overall balance in Europe has tilted toward the Warsaw Pact nations. NATO still has serious problems related to command, control, and weapons standardization and procurement.[6] The Soviet challenge to both the Atlantic and the Pacific powers increased geographically in the late 1970s to include Africa and the Middle East. The response was uncertain and called NATO's old, carefully circumscribed treaty perimeters into serious question.

3. *Few of the OECD countries had by the late seventies adopted, let alone implemented, a visibly effective energy policy.* The idea of a collective policy, or a least a set of consistent policies for all of them, was still problematical.

4. *European union had not been achieved.*

5. *Relations with the less-developed countries worsened, putting the Atlantic and Pacific powers increasingly on the defensive.*

6. *The west's sense of purpose, political will, and discipline appeared to be declining.* [7]

7. *The political framework of the System was patently inadequate to carry its economic burdens.* Enterprises and unions had in many ways outgrown both the nation state and the rules and structures that would permit them to carry on worldwide business in an orderly, reasonably predictable way. The economies of the advanced nations, moreover, had grown much more vulnerable to outside pressures and events. Inflation seemed out of control.

8. *The System had not overcome the residues of nationalism;* chauvinistic attitudes, distrust of "foreigners," and cultural myopia were still strong.

Monetary Costs and Benefits.

In an era of inflation and ever-expanding governmental influence, institutions are often judged by some sort of cost-benefit ratio. In the United States particularly, taxpayers questioned many governmental expenditures in the late 1970s. In these terms, the cost of maintaining the Atlantic-Pacific System returned few direct benefits to U.S. taxpayers, with the exception of those costs levied for collective self-defense systems. Yet, the United States did derive certain indirect benefits from the various IGOs of the extended Atlantic System. And, despite the very real concerns of taxpayers, the actual costs borne by any of the advanced countries in maintaining such System components as NATO, OECD, or the minor IGO secretariats and activities have been miniscule in comparison with the expenses of local and national governments in the advanced countries.

In Fiscal Year 1975, for example, the U.S. federal budget was approximately $365 billion; U.S. contributions to all international organizations (minus direct or indirect NATO military expenditures) were approximately $1.26 billion, or less than one-third of one percent of the total federal budget. Of this $1.26 billion, approximately $844 million was channelled through the World Bank, IMF, and other international lending institutions as foreign aid loans and grants. The remainder went for operating expenses of all the IGOs, including the UN, to which the United States belonged. In the same year, the U.S. contribution to IGOs of the extended Atlantic System, including NATO's civilian budget, was around $28 million.[8] Thus, of the approximately $416 million paid by the United States in direct funds, as its share of the operating expenses of all IGOs to which it belonged, only $28 million, or less than 7 percent, went to support the Atlantic-Pacific System. There were, of course, other costs, notably the expenses of various departments and agencies within the U.S. government, which might be attributed to work in support of or in connection with these IGOs. By 1978, the estimated U.S. contribution to extended Atlantic System IGOs had increased by approximately 25 percent, to about $35 million. The increase was largely due to local inflation and the sharp decline of the dollar in relation to the Belgian and French Francs.

Alliance members spent comparatively more on the military agencies of NATO, ANZUS, WEU, and the U.S.-Japanese Mutual Security Pact. U.S. military contributions to NATO are difficult to separate from the nation's general defense expenditures, but approximately one-fourth to one-third of the annual defense budget of the United States appears to go to NATO. These sums comprise the direct costs of maintaining U.S. forces in Europe and the cost of a portion of U.S. strategic nuclear and conventional forces. Similar comparisons can be related to U.S. defense commitments in the Pacific. In 1979, about 2 to 3 percent of the U.S. GNP was spent to back up security commitments to allies. This percentage compared favorably with those of the NATO allies (from 2 to 5 percent) and Japan (1 to 2 percent).

In their report to the Trilateral Commission, Richard Cooper, Karl Kaiser, and Mosataka Kosaka suggested that the cost-benefit ratio of the work of Atlantic-Pacific IGOs to all the nations of the world was extremely favorable.

First, [trilateral cooperation] can produce a more coherent approach by countries whose cooperation is essential to the evolving character of the world order. Second, it can produce better management of important global problems in some areas, notably overall macro-economic management. Third, it is more likely to result in more adequate assistance for the alleviation of world poverty and promotion of economic development in the poorer parts of the world.[9]

The development of a workable system of international cooperation is of historic importance because it demonstrates convincingly that the nation state is not the only mechanism available to carry the heavy load of government. But transcending the nation state has required the industrial democracies to integrate at least some important aspects and functions of their separate national systems.

How far has international integration really come in the three decades since the Treaty of Dunkirk and the beginning of the Marshall Plan? The answer is necessarily imprecise. Compared with what has gone before, integration has come surprisingly far; measured by the aspirations of theorists and idealists and the challenges that lie ahead, it has not come far enough. In fact, in the past decade or so, the future of integration has been considerably weakened as integration tended to give way to cooperation; in the long run, this is an inadequate state of affairs if the goal is community.

How did integration come about in the first place? Conditions favorable to integration must have obtained. These included both external and internal factors. The external factors had their basis in common interests. In 1945, there were both general and rather strong feelings about the need to develop organs that could undertake international tasks, especially the preservation of peace. The creation of public international organizations reflected a disposition to seek new techniques and improved facilities for coping with the new tasks of government under the increasingly complex circumstances of the modern era. In particular, the ancient moral ideal of world peace and the urgent practical requirement of avoiding the devastating results of modern war produced an emphasis upon the peace-preserving function of intergovernmental organizations.[10]

Such motives underlay the creation of the United Nations and its ancillaries. But among the Atlantic powers, additional factors were at work. The "new tasks of government under the increasingly complex circumstances" had special meaning for these countries, inasmuch as they had already moved into an era dominated by every-increasing applications of science and technological development. Interdependence had already, by 1945, become far more of a practical reality for them than it had for the rest of the world.

A. H. Robertson acknowledged the "practical needs for concerted action between many countries," and cited two additional, perhaps more important reasons for the development of a proportionately large number of international institutions in postwar Europe:

- The increased importance attached to the principle of regionalism.
- The widely held belief in the need for European unity.[11]

He went on to explain the "more dynamic political idea" that inspired many of the postwar European institutions:

. . . an idea usually expressed in [the] words "integration" or "unity;" this gave them an evolutionary character of a special nature, for the process of integration and achievement of unity postulate not only cooperation between the participating states, but also the gradual transformation of their mutual relations and the acquisition of new loyalties.[12]

The constituent nations had recently been involved in a world war of unprecedentedly destructive magnitude, preceded by another, almost equally horrible global conflict only 20 years earlier. Memories of these horrifying experiences had united two generations in their determination to "bury the hatchet" forever, and above all between the French and Germans. To do so would ultimately require the development of a superior international system.[13] The Japanese, faced with the general consciousness of having made "a horrible mistake" in initiating the conflict they called the "Pacific War," were equally determined to win an honored place in the world community.

The goal of European integrationists was well expressed by members of the various national parliaments during the first session of the Council of Europe's Consultative Assembly in September 1949.

> The Assembly considers that the aim and goal of the Council of Europe is the creation of a European political authority with limited functions but real powers.[14]

While this aim was never really approached by the Council, it was at least partially realized later in the three European Communities. U.S. encouragement of European unification and attempts to apply the principle in organizing Atlantic relations also lent support to the concept.

From the outset, the U.S. government encouraged and fostered the idea of unity among the Europeans. Shortly after the European Congress of The Hague met in September 1948, the U.S. Department of State publicly declared that "the United States Government strongly favors the progressively closer integration of the free nations of Western Europe."[15] Marshall Plan aid was later made contingent on satisfactory European progress toward unification. The U.S. government played a considerable role in negotiations for the abortive European Defense and European Political Communities (so much so that some observers believe that the overeagerness of the United States was an important factor in the demise of the two Communities). The United States helped bring about the first European Community (for coal and steel), as well as EURATOM and the Common Market. U.S. preoccupation with Vietnam and a general deterioration of the world economy conspired to take the edge off of U.S. support, but the United States nevertheless sought frequent opportunities to declare public support of European integration.[16] The U.S. government clearly encouraged European unity, but the process of unification was nevertheless the Europeans' show.

The European Communities are, for example, European and not "Atlantic" bodies.

In a more global sense, the imperatives of economic interdependence had also been present in the minds of the chief actors of the extended Atlantic System. All had suffered deeply in the World Depression of the 1930s, and all were convinced that the Depression had been a major factor in bringing on the Second World War. After 1945, they were firmly resolved to "do it differently." Thus, the combination of economic necessity and bitter experience propelled west Europeans, other western countries, and Japan in the direction of cooperation and unity.

Another strong integrative force has been the external threat of world Communism, or "Soviet imperialism." The Brussels treaty, NATO, and WEU were all created solely to counter Soviet pressure on western Europe. The ANZUS and U.S.-Japanese security treaties also grew out of the threat posed by the USSR and, perhaps at the time of their inception, Communist China.

Integration also required certain internal prerequisites. To a high degree, the western industrial democracies shared a basic set of attributes. They were modern, pluralistic, democratic political regimes in which Communist parties did not play dominant roles. They were dependent on one another for their security. All possessed advanced, highly industrialized market economies and were active in foreign trade and investment. All had developed science and technology research and development programs and had sophisticated and well-established educational systems. All of these countries had embraced western or parawestern culture and value systems: and all maintained reasonably civilized standards for the conduct of their international relations. Finally, these countries were sufficiently integrated domestically so that a significant portion of their energies could be devoted to international integration.[17]

All of the above prerequisites were important, but the single most important catalyst for European integration was top leadership. Unusual, gifted men of vision and transnational understanding were available in extraordinary supply at the right time.

Such institutions as NATO, OEEC/OECD, or the European Communities could never have been launched without the talents of such men as Ernest Bevin, Harry Truman, George Marshall, Halvard Lange, Paul-Henri Spaak, Alcide de Gasperi, Robert Schuman, or Konrad Adenauer.

Extension of the Atlantic-Pacific System

Supranationalism and international integration occurred first in the North Atlantic region, between the countries of western Europe and the United States. Japan was the next to be included in the extended Atlantic System. In western Europe and in Japan, the proper social and cultural conditions, appropriate value systems, and modern behavior patterns were at hand to enable this kind of international cooperation.

The countries of the Arab world or those of Latin America, for example, would appear to be more unified than those of the extended Atlantic System, by virtue of a common language and religion as well as general cultural patterns. Yet, the less-developed countries of Latin America, the Arab world, Africa, and Asia have all lacked the building blocks necessary for economic, political, or social integration. Nearly all of the internal prerequisites for integration are missing among these countries, as apparently also are any perceptions of common interests that could be met by integration. Perceptions of common interests and the right social capabilities both seem to be indispensable requirements for supranational integration.

The Atlantic-Pacific System is a useful model for states and peoples contemplating the establishment of more effective international linkages, such as "common markets" or regional "communities." Even though the System's integration is by no means complete nor its permanence assured, the System is viable and it does work. Unfortunately, the experience in some areas—notably Latin America—suggests that development may require more impetus than the goal of integration 'Euratlantic style" offers. Even in the Atlantic-Pacific System, the pace of international integration has slowed.

THE THEORETICAL SIGNIFICANCE OF THE SYSTEM

The Atlantic-Pacific System, in its development and current operation, has illustrated rather well a number of theories about international relations and international organizations.[18]

Coercion vs. Contract in Interstate Relations

Henry Maine, Max Weber, Herbert Spencer, Georg Simmel, and others have maintained that society is evolving from traditional forms based on status and coercion toward new forms based on contracts, free association, and mutual interests.[19] This idea has its counterpart today at the level of interstate relations which must evolve from the two well-known international systems, imperialism and the nation state, to a system in which states voluntarily and contractually integrate their sovereignty in order to harmonize and further their interests. The Atlantic System has tended in this direction of supranationalism, although overall progress has not been great, measured against the standard of unification or "pooled sovereignty." The nation state is still the chief political reality; and, as Henry Aubrey pointed out, "Bilateral contacts through conventional or personal diplomacy remain the workaday instruments of policy."[20] Yet, Aubrey also asserted that

> the postwar era marks the emergence of a still proliferating variety of intergovernmental and international institutions. Most of them are not supranational; rather they are places where sovereign nations, which retain their autonomy of decision and implementation, can meet. Various modest degrees of delegation in decision-making have, however, been vested in some institutions. Even where there is no formal transfer of authority, the effectiveness of moral suasion has been growing; these . . . are important stimulants to, and characteristics of, cooperation.[21]

The System has indeed altered the practice of international relations, especially among the Atlantic powers. There has been an important, history-making movement, away from coercion, and toward voluntary assocation, at least among the industrial democracies.

Neofunctionalism

In formulating the concept of European community, Monnet and his associates embellished David Mitrany's concepts of "functionalism."[22] Karl Deutsch explored the idea that "mutual responsiveness" and "pluralism" led to political integration.[23] Later, Ernst Haas set forth the theory of "neofunctionalism" in some detail in *The Uniting of Europe*.[24] Haas captured the essence of "the art of manipulated integration" which

> consists of isolating functional areas which produce converging interests among moderately hostile states, and capitalizing upon those which, while not being immediately political, nevertheless very soon spill over into the realm of politics when specific programs are envisaged by strong international institutions.[25]

Whereas Mitrany had theorized that the formation of a political community would be a natural consequence of technical cooperation, Monnet and the neofunctionalists realized that a political system would still require some impetus and thus advocated a strong "Eurocracy" that would be in a position to lead or influence governments.[26]

There is a good deal of neofunctionalism behind what has happened in the Atlantic-Pacific area since 1947. Technical cooperation, true to functionalist theories, has led to more and more cooperation at the technical level and, at least in the case of the European Communities and to a limited extent, also at the political level. The processes of "developing pluralism" and "heightened mutual responsiveness", as theorized by Deutsch, have seemed both to make possible the various attempts at political integration and, in some respects, to make them necessary. The similarity of the socioeconomic problems faced by OECD members, for example, has required ever-widening arenas and forms of information sharing and cooperation. At the same time, their common social and cultural characteristics and the constant communication between and among them have undoubtedly enhanced the development of intricate and increasingly sophisticated methods of international cooperation. However, the idea of the neofunctionalist theory, that properly designed international institutions would lead inexorably to supranationality[27], failed to account for extraneous factors, such as General de Gaulle, which could interfere with goals. The pace of European unification has not been as rapid as the neofunctionalists and their adherents had hoped and expected. Yet the neofunctionalist theories, in their essence, have not been proven wrong; they have simply taken longer to bear fruit than anyone had estimated.[28]

Cooperation and Altruism

The theories and hopes of such men as Monnet reflected a profound truth about human beings, that there is more to political relationships than the lust and competition for power. Another reality of human behavior, an especially well-developed trait in some western subcultures, is altruism. Some social psychologists have suggested that altruistic behavior—benevolence, humanitarianism, mutual aid, and other forms of "helping" behavior—has some basis beyond sheer philosophical idealism or religious fervor, that there is a "human propensity to cooperate."[29] The deliberate liberation and cultivation of that propensity could serve as a much-needed anchor for international political integration based on consent. Indeed, the history of the Atlantic-Pacific System suggests that altruism is already operative.

THE EFFECT OF INSTITUTIONS ON INTERNATIONAL BEHAVIOR

Institutions are indispensable in building international systems and communities. However, some observers believe that IGOs have been created in most cases simply to legitimize what the principal member nations wanted. The case of Comecon would seem to validate this theory; and certainly the Treaty of

Washington (1949) was extremely important in legitimizing an alliance which the United States and its principal European allies were determined to conclude. But the North Atlantic Treaty, and the subsequent North Atlantic Treaty Organization which grew out of it, have turned out to be a great deal more than "rubber stamp" institutions. Not only have they regulated the collective self-defense of Europe, they have also molded and changed the people and governments involved in strategic ways.[30]

Other observers believe that the role of institutions in international relations is relatively minor. Unwritten law, custom, the exercise of power, the interplay of interests, and the cumulative establishment of precedents determine major events in the course of international behavior, they contend, and institutions are more or less irrelevant.

After studying the IGOs of the Atlantic-Pacific System, however, I have concluded that institutions can, and often do, have a profound and sometimes lasting influence on international affairs. Just as the U.S. federal system is much more than the constitution, so have most of these IGOs become much more than their charters. A few are but facades; they were either set up that way in the first place or became hollow shells through disuse or misuse. But others have evolved into significant institutions which have a substantial impact on world affairs. To imagine the state of the contemporary world without them is to imagine a world much less secure, orderly, prosperous, or viable. Some of the tasks they have successfully undertaken might have been accomplished in other ways, but most would surely have remained undone, to our great peril.[31]

Objective and Subjective Aspects of Government

I am indebted to Georges Berthoin for the following concept, which helps explain the present degree of integration represented by the new European/Atlantic/Pacific institutions: *All government has a subjective as well as an objective aspect.*

All of the technical accomplishments of government, such as providing social welfare, building roads, stimulating employment, organizing education, or conducting foreign relations, are objective functions. Government's subjective, and its most "political," activity has to do with the ephemeral, but absolutely basic, stuff of public emotions and loyalties. General de Gaulle, perhaps better than any modern political figure, understood this and sought to satisy the deep psychological cravings of his people by stressing French *gloire* and national pride. Such behavior may appear to be intellectually deplorable; yet, without emotions and attachments in some form, human communities can hardly exist.

So far, most intergovernmental organizations have served entirely the objective aspects of government; OECD is a prime example. The European Communities, however, were designed in part to deal also with the subjective, to foster an emotional attachment on the part of Europeans to the idea of "One Europe." However limited the success of this effort, the ideas of Jean Monnet and his colleagues nevertheless represented an original and potentially effective approach to international government.

In order for the subjective function of international government to evolve adequately, the corresponding objective mechanisms must be sufficiently developed so that they are effective and reliable. Thus, it is especially important to strengthen the technical and functional capabilities of the IGOs so that members and nonmembers alike can increasingly rely on the technical expertise and services of the IGOs. It will also be important to publicize the work of such IGOs so that the electorates of the member countries will recognize how much the organizations are needed and how much they accomplish in practical, human terms.

If one wished to characterize the degree of progress which the institutions of the extended Atlantic System had attained, one could measure the distance from the "subjectivity barrier." While the IGOs of the System had moved a good distance toward this barrier, in the late 1970s, no IGO had yet broken the "subjectivity barrier." The series of decisions made between 1975 and 1977 to move forward on the direct election of delegates to the EC's European Parliament, as well as the decision made in 1976 to issue "European Passports" to citizens of EC countries, are two concrete steps which eventually might have important subjective consequences for the System, at least in Europe. But in the extended Atlantic System, the "subjectivity barrier" remained high.

Toward a Community of the Developed Democracies

It is my contention that the Atlantic-Pacific System is evolving toward an *international community.* The advanced democracies have so far created a functioning *international system,* described in this book, but it would be premature to call it a "community."

It is largely to the German scholar Tönnies, who originated the concept which contrasts *Gemeinschaft* (roughly translated, community) with *Gesellschaft* (society), that we are indebted for our understanding of "community" in an international context.[32] Tönnies referred to a community of feeling *(Gemeinschaft)* that characterized the simpler, preindustrial cultures based on links of kinship and shared life experiences. In *Gesellschaft* relationships, however, said Tönnies, "everybody is by himself and isolated, and there exists a condition of tension against all others . . . intrusions are regarded as hostile acts . . . nobody wants to grant and produce anything for another individual . . . all goods are conceived to be separate, as are their owners."[33]

Modern U.S. sociologists, wrote Polsby, have taken a much more limited view of community.

> For the most part, a conventional perspective has been adopted and a 'community' has been defined as a population living within legally established city limits.[34]

Students of international politics and organizations have considered the definition of community in relation to what has been happening in Europe, and more generally in the North Atlantic area, since World War II.[35] They have used "community" to refer to a set of close, historical relationships and a political idea, as in the expression, "Atlantic community."[36] Others have concentrated on its application in the precise legal context of the three European Communities. Haas contended that the work of earlier political scientists, with its emphasis on sovereignty and the conditions under which a federation could be created, was inadequate to explain what was happening after 1945, and what might happen, in Europe. [37]

> Since the institutional forms associated with this [new European] development defied traditional constitutional classifications and tended to change *de facto* with the accretion of new tasks, the discussion of 'federation' as the technique for regional integration gave way to the terms 'community' and 'community formation.'[38]

Others have seen this kind of community as characterized by a sense of solidarity that is diffused among the constituent peoples, a perception of common challenges to be met, and a desire to "do great things together."[39]

> [A] 'sense of community' was much more than simply verbal attachment to any number of similar or identical values. Rather it was a matter of mutual sympathy and loyalties; of 'we-feeling,' trust, and consideration; of at least partial identification in terms of self-images and interests; of ability to predict each other's behavior and ability to act in accordance with that prediction. In short, it was a matter of perpetual attention, communication, perception of needs, and responsiveness.[40]

A community implies *collective leadership, collective responsibility,* and *mutual loyalty.* A community is not the same as a coalition or an IGO in which the member nations retain all sovereignty and decision-making powers. Thus, a community implies a certain degree of integration.[41] Above all, a true community displays those subjective aspects of government which we examined above.

A de jure European community has been created; an historical and de facto Atlantic community is more or less a practical reality. It is the thesis of this book that *an international community which includes the main industrial democracies of the world is in a nascent, rudimentary stage. This international community is based on intergovernmental cooperation and, ultimately, integration.* The new community, if indeed it does coalesce sufficiently, will undoubtedly bear some resemblance to earlier communities, but it will also be unlike them in many ways, just as they are different from one another. The community will require unusual, new acts of political creativity and a second generation of "allied statesmen." Large cultural gaps will have to be filled or bridged, to a far greater degree than was the case for either the European or the Atlantic communities. Value systems will have to be modified; perceptions will have to be broadened. Yet, it is quite uncertain if all this can be done.

THE FUTURE OF THE ATLANTIC-PACIFIC SYSTEM: INTERNAL CHALLENGES

This book so far has been devoted to an examination of what we have called "the extended Atlantic System" or "the Atlantic-Pacific System." The former term describes the network of relationships which developed mainly in the three decades beginning in 1947 among the advanced democracies; the latter term is meant to characterize the System as it has now become, and as it may continue to develop in the future. But does the System have a future? The remainder of this chapter concentrates on that question.

The Inertia of Institutions

As do all large organizations, IGOs suffer from the inherent weight of their bureaucracies. In the initial burst of creativity following the Marshall Plan, many of the European and Atlantic IGOs were manned by generally capable, and in some cases brilliant, staffs. A sense of constant achievement, of coping successfully with the main problems, was high for at least the first decade. As time wore on, however, the true dimensions of some of the challenges which faced the System began to emerge. They were often vast; they were often of a much more long-term nature than had originally been assumed; in some cases, they were virtually insoluble. Learning to live with a problem rather than solving it required a different set of human skills than had been involved in creating the IGOs. Many of the initiators and early civil servants of these new IGOs had looked on the IGOs simply as the precursors of much closer associations (political unions and federations of one sort or another). These people, plus many fervent supporters of the IGOs, inevitably became disillusioned. The subsequent social, economic, and political turmoil of the 1960s and 1970s only added to their disillusionment. This mood, on top of the general inertia which eventually overwhelms all institutions, produced a serious internal challenge to the Atlantic-Pacific System, one for which the System was unprepared.

> A problem requiring special attention is the apparent resistance of international institutions to evolutionary change—a characteristic not unlike that found in domestic governmental institutions. It appears that international institutions can seldom be relied upon for originating formal changes in the relevant systems.[42]

The impulses and the ingenuity in most cases will probably have to come from outside the IGOs of the Atlantic-Pacific System if they are to meet the challenges ahead. Without some forward movement—change, adaptation, or innovation, but still more, a shaping of events—the alternative cannot be for very long that of status quo. Especially in the case of tenuous bodies such as IGOs, movement must either go forward, or it will surely drift backward, to eventual oblivion.

In describing the state of OECD in the mid-seventies, Miriam Camps observed: "If no attempts are made to improve the functioning of the partial and imperfect system that already links economies there will be further deterioration."[43] A U.S. Permanent Representative to NATO, in his farewell speech to the North Atlantic Council, warned: "NATO cannot tarry in its present, nondescript state. . . Standing military alliances that have not evolved into political federation have always fallen apart."[44] So far, the IGOs of the System have continually acquired more and more tasks, especially those which fell under the heading of interdependence. But there are inherent dangers in such a process:

> The forces of progress . . . further a multinationalization of previously domestic activities and intensify the intermeshing of decisionmaking in multinational frameworks. This inherently expansive process could in the name of economic advancement, efficiency, and interdependence ultimately undermine our Western systems of democracy unless we develop new forms of democratic control.[45]

Thus, the intergovernmental organizations must be made more responsive to the governments which created and support them. At the same time, they must be encouraged to develop their own power of initiative, so that they can become "operational." Finally, they must be accountable, directly wherever possible, to the electorates of their constituent countries.

National Rivalries and Cultural Clashes

Residual cultural and national egocentrisms pose an even more serious threat to the System than institutional inertia. Not only the proximity, but also the suddenness, of this development has produced shock to all man-made systems. Masses of tourists and commercial travelers swarm over the world; the transistor radio is ubiquitous; the great upsurge in scholarly globetrotting and student exchanges is paralleled only by the intercourse of diplomats, bureaucrats, and technicians. These and other powerful forces make for a certain, unmistakable sameness in modern societies. But the sameness is misleading; profound cultural differences remain and are likely to persist indefinitely among the peoples of the world.

The internal, hidden structures and values of industrial life dictate the way workers and management interact, the way decisions are made in and for a firm or factory, the relationship of government to management, the role of trade unions, the place of a worker's job in his family's scheme of things, the complex ties of worker to worker. These and most other key aspects of industrial life differ sharply from country to country. This difference is significantly heightened when western and nonwestern patterns are compared. Men and women live by the value systems implanted in them as children. Such value systems are constantly reinforced throughout life by the surrounding culture, and they affect everything. Each culture is different, and the differences often cause serious conflict when cultures collide.

Few people recognize the problem in the terms described above; indeed, few even recognize that there *is* a problem. They simply describe the other fellow as odd, or just plain wrong, in many of the strange things he does. Often, such judgments are drawn subconsciously, but nonetheless firmly. Today, one can make them not just at the time of direct contact, but thousands of miles away from a foreign culture, on the basis of things read or seen on television or in a movie. These cultural conflicts most certainly constitute one of the greatest obstacles to cooperation between peoples and governments.

At the heart of many classic clashes of "national interest" are these differences in cultures and ways of doing things. It is all too easy for the parties to a dispute over conflicting national interests to withdraw, and usually quite unconsciously, into their cultural or "national" shells, where it is possible to assume that "our way" is necessarily the "right way," because it is known and comfortable, while "their way" is "different" and therefore "wrong."

In 1974, Secretary of State Kissinger "told a large gathering of women . . . that America's biggest problem is dealing with her allies, not her enemies. . ."[46] The Secretary might have been at least partially forgiven his frustration. His proposals for a new "Atlantic Charter" had been deliberated by the Europeans for months and finally, not long before he made the remarks quoted above, rejected by the North Atlantic Council. But the irony cannot be lost. A European-born Secretary of State, whose entire academic career had brought him constantly in touch with European people, values, ideas, behavior, and history, felt completely stymied by the procedural and stylistic problems of conducting complex business with the Europeans. Neither Kissinger nor his European counterparts could have had much doubt about the general congruence of European and U.S. interests.

However, when it comes down to resolving discrete political issues, the Kissingers of this world and all their cohorts must give way to solid phalanxes of entrenched national bureaucracies and a plethora of national differences. The more domestic affairs intrude on foreign affairs, and vice versa, the more opportunities there are for such conflict and frustration.

Stylistic clashes abound, of course, but there are often seriously fundamental and real differences in national attitudes about world affairs, and about the place of one's nation in the world. These also impede the functioning of an international system. An American political scientist, after a series of long interviews with leading Japanese about key world questions, came to the following conclusion.

> In the Japanese conception, power politics means the pursuit by the great powers of their own interests and the conclusion of agreements among the great powers at the expense of the lesser powers.[47]

His observation may or may not be true, although many observers, Japanese and foreign, would tend to agree with him, but it does suggest an attitude which he believes is a serious obstacle to the conduct of coalition diplomacy with Japan. His experience is repeated constantly, and on a large scale, and acts as an important impediment in contact situations which count heavily in the conduct of international affairs.

National cultural differences are sometimes based on historical experiences which run counter to international cooperation. French attitudes in this respect have posed an especially large stumbling block to the "construction of Europe." Robert Lemaignen, himself French and one of the first EEC Commissioners, is quoted by Bliss:

> Why is it thus in France, especially, that this fear of the "supranational" predominates? . . . because . . . our country . . . holds the idea that a European State will be the simple pantographic extension of the French State and will impose its heavy—and, what's aggravating, multinational—

tutelage through an omnipresent and omnipotent central power.[48]

In short, most Frenchmen believe that a new level of government, even one on the European plane, would operate just like every government of France has always done. The nationals of other countries are not immune from this kind of ethnocentric notion. For example, Clarence Streit's plan for a federal union of the Atlantic democracies was based on the U.S. Constitution of 1787.[49]

Certainly one of the most powerful forces against European—or any wider form of—integration is the opposition of national bureaucracies and politicians. They fear that international integration will inevitably mean their displacement. Three different authorities have commented on this point.

[My] reflections all add up to a view which does not see economic integration gradually and painlessly moving towards political integration. This derives from an assessment of the behavior of national governments as impeding such an evolution. Indeed for this to occur far more positive and deliberate actions on the part of governments would be necessary. Their negative attitudes have not prevented political leaders from embracing apparently progressive positions on the development of the Communities—the Werner Plan is an outstanding example. The contradiction lies in the gap between the adoption of broad proposals and their translation into practice in a heavily mutilated version.[50]

One sometimes wonders whether the opposition to the "Community method" in certain circles is not inspired by the mistrust of national officials and diplomats for the "Europeans" and "Eurocrats," whom they consider as less well-qualified than themselves for the conduct of international affairs.[51]

What are the principal causes of this internal resistance by the national parties to the formation of European political parties? . . . All political parties will show the same opposition when it comes to the point, and everyone realizes that the formation of European political parties means that national party congresses will no longer have the last word. Perhaps this factor will not seem so very important to the ordinary member who attends congresses, but it may appear vital to the party executive which often uses the decision-making process at the party congress to force through its own opinions and override its opponents.[52]

The weakness and immaturity of the IGO bureaucracies also stand in the way of integration. Although the secretariats of the European Communities, OECD, and NATO contain many able, dedicated professionals, the necessary international codes of behavior are still in the developmental stage. The problem that exists in this area is one of the most intractable of all the problems facing the Atlantic-Pacific System. It is also one that is paid little attention by governments and others. The best answer to the problem is assuredly a long-term one and undoubtedly lies in some form of education.

States of the Nations
It is paradoxical that, although nationalism remains collectively an important obstacle to achieving international community, the domestic health of each nation is nevertheless essential to the process of integration. Relatively high levels of social peace, economic well-being, governmental efficiency, internal security, civic health, and generally good morale throughout the nation must obtain if the nation is to integrate successfully with other nations. Such equilibrium is not easy to attain, let alone maintain. Indeed, the seeds of disintegration can be seen in every society. Sometimes nations delude themselves as to their general health and power (cf. Britain in 1945); sometimes they do not appreciate the degree to which their societies are well integrated and internally secure (cf. contemporary Japan). It is extremely difficult for a nation facing severe internal tensions to play a constructive international role.

The Balance of the Nations Within the System

If national states are indeed the most basic building blocks of the System and if IGOs grow but gradually, what will be the place of the nations within the System?

From the beginning of the Age of Discovery virtually until the Second World War, Europe dominated the globe, but recent wars changed that relationship.

> Europe had for a very long time been the center of world politics and all international problems, without exception, could not be resolved without the concurrence of the European powers. This era of the absolute international hegemony of the Old Continent, which marked its golden age with the coincidental emergence of the Rights of Man and of European public law, entered a phase of decline at the beginning of the 20th century, and this came to a conclusion only after the 1939–45 war. In effect, the first indications of this decline were apparent with the Spanish-American War (1898) and the Russo-Japanese War of 1904, which both concluded, unthinkably, with a debacle—of Spain before the United States of America and of Russia before Japan, that is to say, two European powers [humbled] before two non-European powers.[53]

In the First World War, American power was required to prevent German hegemony in Europe; when that war was over, the United States retreated into political and economic isolation. But after 1945, the United States unquestionably emerged as the most powerful nation in the world, and this time she proceeded to play a much more responsible role. Inevitably, since then, the United States has tended to dominate western European affairs generally and the Atlantic Alliance specifically.

The emergence of the European Communities in the 1950s has helped restore the transatlantic balance to some extent, and the U.S. defeat in Indochina furthered the shift. In addition, Japan has begun to emerge from defeat and is now the world's number three economic power, after the United States and the USSR.

Thus, in the quarter century from 1945 to 1970, a greater balance has been achieved among the three main powers of the extended Atlantic System, although the United States still remained dominant both in economic and military, and thus in political, terms.[54]

There had been talk since 1957, when the Treaty of Rome was signed, of an "Atlantic Partnership" between the new European communities and the United States. But this scheme never satisfactorily included Canada or Japan. In order to achieve some form of union with these two countries, at least in the economic sphere, the United States took the lead in bringing about the creation of OECD (1960). But plans for European economic union did not proceed as rapidly as had been anticipated; political unification of the continent, which virtually everyone agreed would be a good thing, seemed much further off by 1970 than it had a decade earlier. And there was a fundamental dilemma for the Europeans in the security equation:

> It is being increasingly acknowledged that the long-term plan of a European Union is not conceivable without this Union being endowed with the means for guaranteeing its security.[55]

Some recommended resurrecting the ill-fated European Defense Community;[56] but, in general, Europeans were not yet ready to make the economic or political sacrifices necessary to create their own fully independent defense system. The United States commitment to European security, through NATO, was needed more than ever. Europeans, indeed, appeared no more eager to establish economic union than they were to provide military security. Even if it were possible to carry out the projections for a European currency or to unify macroeconomic planning and fiscal policy for all of EC's members, it would still be necessary to do virtually the same things on a transatlantic, and perhaps transpacific, scale.

The Question of Collective Leadership

In 1974, Secretary of State Kissinger commented on what he

felt were some of the long-term problems of the advanced nations.

If we do not get a recognition of our interdependence, the Western civilization that we now have is almost certain to disintegrate because it will first lead to a series of rivalries in which each region will try to maximize its own special advantages. That inevitably will lead to tests of strength of one sort or another. These will magnify domestic crises in many countries, and they will then move more and more to authoritarian models. . . I would expect then that we will certainly have crises which no leadership is able to deal with, and probably military confrontations.

Looking toward the end of the century, I would hope that Western Europe, Japan and the United States would have found a way of not just overcoming the current economic crisis, but turning it into something positive by understanding the responsibilities they share for each other's progress and for developing cooperative policies that are explicitly directed towards world interests. This means a degree of financial solidarity, a degree of equalizing burdens, and a degree of ability to set common goals that cannot be done on a purely national basis.

In 1961, Governor Rockefeller had proposed some "new concepts of confederation in the West." Kissinger noted that one now hears nothing about these concepts.

Because we have reached the paradoxical position that at the moment when the need for cooperative action is greatest, the national and regional sense of identity has also grown. Thus any attempt to institutionalize a new structure, within, for example, a confederal framework, would meet resistance out of proportion to what it could achieve. . . Nevertheless, while the organization or the institution of a confederation may be more than the traffic will bear, the need for cooperative action is absolutely imperative.[57]

J. Robert Schaetzel agreed on the need for cooperation as well: "We [the United States] either are going to have to withdraw from responsibilities or join with the West Europeans and the Japanese."[58]

The basic problem raised by both men and by other serious observers too was that, in a world in which the United States had lost power and prestige, at least in a relative sense, and in which the American people appeared to have no stomach for exercising strong leadership or taking risks in exotic places, the only alternative appeared to be a form of *collective leadership* with one's allies. Cooper and his colleagues, for example, commented:

> Some group of nations will have to take the responsibility for insuring that the international system functions effectively. No single nation appears to be likely to assume this role in the near term. The United States no longer seems willing to play it fully. Japan and the European Community are not yet ready to assume such leadership. Accordingly, it can only be done collectively for some time by the members of the trilateral region and notably some of its key states. They must act to provide the initiatives and proposals for wider acceptance. They must be on the watch to assure that the system does not break down as a result of the various tensions and pressures.[59]

This idea of "collective leadership" had been applied, if somewhat tentatively, among the OECD countries, to resolve economic problems following the oil boycott and the ensuing recession in 1973. In the political sphere, European nations joined together in 1973 to help Portugal after a coup had tenuously restored democratic government to that nation. In an earlier day, the burden of trying to uphold a new, democratic government against the threat of a local Communist Party takeover would have fallen on the United States. The new pattern of collective leadership enabled several European powers, and social democratic political parties in particular, to provide collectively the technical assistance, loans, and other forms of aid and encouragement needed to help Portugal attain political and economic recovery. In the summer of 1978, four European nations and the United States joined forces to prevent a takeover in Zaire by externally supported rebels. Both of these situations illustrated the need for a more reasonable alternative to the previous pattern of hegemonial leadership by one large power in the western coalition. The kind of interdependence that bound Europe, Canada, Japan, the United States, Australia, and New Zealand firmly together required a more solid, more durable, more flexible framework.

The Need for Integration

There is lots of international activity going on, but no government of it.[60]

Genuine interdependence is growing, the institutions are not.[61]

In an alliance, you are pledged to come to the defense of an ally whose policy you had no hand in formulating.[62]

With one exception, there has been no outstanding act of political creation at the international level in the Atlantic-Pacific System since 1961. The creation of the International Energy Agency in 1974 marked the single exception during this period. Within the System, there appeared to be no sense of direction or purpose, no sense of confidence, and no sense of movement. Although interdependence was real, it had inadequate support; the parameters within which appropriate action might be taken were extremely narrow. Nonetheless, there still remained the possibility of cooperation:

There is hope for a *"a united front"* among the industrialized nations, but it will have to emerge as an expedient coalition rather than a permanent alliance. The difference is important. We negotiated and advanced common policies in the postwar era largely through formal treaties and arrangements that were perceived early on to be enduring. Those days are gone, and with them the remnants of concensus [sic]; the best we can hope for now are working arrangements, of considerable flexibility, that encourage the nations of the West to cooperate in shaping the means to achieve a particular end. We shall see more deviations among all of us, but policies governed by self-interest can converge when very large issues are at stake.[63]

One problem with this kind of view was that the issues of the late seventies and the eighties were more likely to develop gradually, so that the long lead time necessary to prepare an adequate response would not be available.

Miriam Camps took a more positive view. "It seems likely to be true that a *really* efficient international economic system requires either strong leadership by a single dominant country willing and able to underwrite the system, or strong 'supranational' institutions endowed with real powers."[64] She favored some form of collective leadership; but she had no illusions about the time frame; it would take a long time. There were other requirements as well.

The key advanced countries now need to be willing to discuss with one another virtually all aspects of their macro-economic policy. . . . Multilateral surveillance in the OECD, as in other international organizations, has been one of the most useful techniques of the post-war world. But in several areas—macro-economic policy being perhaps the most important—the advanced countries now need to push beyond surveillance into the much more difficult area of prior consultation.[65]

Max Kohnstamm has also suggested requirements for establishing a better system of interdependence.

Interdependence has to be given a political, and hence ultimately an institutional, framework. . . It demands joint international decisions on who produces what—taken deliberately, and not as the result of competitive dumping of each other's subsidized products, and the inevitable quantitative restrictions which are its results. It demands establishing common and accepted standards for making exceptions (which mean saddling others with the consequences), standards which should distinguish between socially and purely mercantalistically motivated distortions. It involves accepting a *droit de regard* of others on internal policy making, and the right of other nations to suggest alternative strategies to achieve [one's] national objectives: this being a reasonable requirement of those outside national borders who have to share the burden of policies taken within these borders. This is a far cry from the present practice of declaring one's internal policies non-negotiable. It may mean, eventually, positive steps of joint policy making: indicative planning for investment threatened by overcapacity and an orderly transfer of capacity in certain industries to less developed countries. These tasks go far beyond those actually assumed by the international institutions designed to maintain economic order both between the industrialized countries of Europe and America, and in the world in general.[66]

Cooper, Kaiser, and Kosaka analyzed the principles of "effective international-decision-making," as they might be applied to a variety of international institutions.

First, decision-making should adequately involve those needed for solutions and take into account the views of others affected. Second, it should seek to reconcile national policies in interdependent relationships through a system of consultative procedures and mutual commitments. Third, decision-making arrangements should allow for flexible action in times of crisis and emergency. Fourth, these arrangements should secure an adequate distribution of gains from interdependence.[67]

The burden for accomplishing these tasks will realistically fall on the industrialized democracies.

Some group of nations will have to take the responsibility for insuring that the international system functions effectively . . . it can only be done collectively for some time by the members of the trilateral region and notably some of its key states. They must act to provide the initiatives and proposals for wider acceptance.[68]

At the conclusion of the Second World War, Emery Reves summed up the fundamental requirements for "collective security." His words, more than three decades later, still apply to the question of collective leadership, and the ultimate need for integration.

Collective security without collective sovereignty is meaningless. The insecurity of the individual as well as of groups of individuals is the direct result of the nonexistence of law to govern their relations. Allowing sovereign sources of law to reside, not in the community but in the eighty-odd [at that time the sum of nations in the world] separate nation-states forming that community; attempting to make their coexistence peaceful, not by establishing institutions with sovereign power to create law binding all members of the collectivity but by agreements and treaties between the divided sovereign units, can never, under any condition, create security for that collectivity. Only a legal order can bring security. Consequently, without constitutional institutions to express the sovereignty of the community and to create law for the collectivity, there can be no security for that collectivity.[69]

The continued existence of NATO might be said at least superficially to belie Reve's rather dogmatic, constitutionalist approach. Yet, in essence, I believe that he is still correct. As a long-term prescription, his logic was irrefutable. The problem of the Atlantic-Pacific System, and the smaller subgroups within it, was to promote "law for the collectivity" and a program working in that direction, but capable of dealing with problems in the interim.

EXTERNAL CHALLENGES

The Quest for Security

"States pursue interests and they only act in concert when some of their interests overlap with those of other states."[70] If the nations of the Atlantic-Pacific System had not perceived many overlapping interests, they would never have established the System. Conditions and perceptions change. Nonetheless, the most important common interest in 1945 was also the most important in the decades that followed. At its most basic, the quest for security boiled down to what offered the best chance for survival; and working in concert rather than separately seemed to be the most logical way to pursue that quest. The challenge by the Soviet Union, in terms of growing military strength and geographical positions, was the most obvious threat to security in the System. But the threat to survival also included such challenges as the kidnapping of national figures and general acts of terrorism.

Other challenges did not so directly affect the survival of the industrial democracies, but could conceivably become threatening if they were not contained. The uncertainty of war or peace in the Middle East was a prime example. Another, no less important, challenge was the attempt to prevent the spread of nuclear weapons. These two examples indicate the range and complexity of the challenges to the survival of the countries of the Atlantic-Pacific System.

The Problem of a Common Economy

As early as the 1950s, the economic health of even the largest nation in the System had become indivisible from that of its main partners. The economies of the industrial democracies were plainly interconnected; yet, the individual governments still took unilateral decisions on such matters as trade barriers, currency supplies, tax policies, the regulation of multinational enterprises, unemployment, inflation, and economic growth. Interdependence had dictated some coordination on these measures, especially within the Common Market, but the System had not yet fully faced its economic challenge. A system of truly effective international management for the common economy of the industrialized world had not yet been worked out.

Unemployment and inflation were not the only economic problems that the System faced during the seventies. The oil boycott of 1973 revealed a serious, long-term shortage of an industrially indispensable commodity. Such shortages had been faced during the war, but the boycott challenged the peacetime economies of the extended Atlantic System and of other countries as well. The quadrupling of oil prices radically changed the terms under which modern industry had to operate and necessitated a wide variety of major adjustments in both economies and lifestyles. Predictions of energy and other essential raw material shortages had been made for some time, but, in 1973, the members of the System were essentially unprepared for the effect of the oil crisis.

Many of the primary resources and raw materials vital to modern industry are located in the less-developed countries. These countries have begun to express their own views about how such materials should be allocated. The advanced countries had already attempted to develop new forms of relationships with the less-developed countries, but, during the 1970s, large groups of less-developed countries were not satisfied with existing relationships. They were demanding a "New International Economic Order" and insisting that "more justice" be accorded them by means of a radical redistribution of the wealth of the industrial democracies, including

a general restructuring of . . . economic relations for the purpose of creating a more just and workable world economic order . . . [including] . . . greater attention by both developed and developing countries to their growing interdependence, greater respect for the equal rights of all members of the world community under international law, the abolition of "spheres of influence," greater recognition of the differing needs and capabilities of different developing countries, the pursuit of cooperation rather than confrontation, the focusing of development efforts on the poorest segment of populations in developing countries, new rules and arrangements governing access to supplies as well as access to markets, and a restructuring of international economic institutions in the light of new political and economic realities.[71]

The challenge of reorganizing such relationships was a formidable and extremely delicate one. Much had been done by the developed democracies to provide substantial flows of capital aid (from 1960 to 1975, approximately $260 billion worth), to make concessional trade arrangements for less-developed countries in the markets of the developed world, and to provide large amounts of technical assistance.[72] The challenge was global, but it was also very precisely directed at the developed countries, on whom the burden of remedial action would mainly fall.[73]

Societal Growth and Development

Quite apart from their role in helping the so-called developing countries become stable, the "developed" countries also needed to be concerned with their own stability and future development. While the challenge usually had a somewhat different face from one advanced country to another, and while the response to this challenge was mainly the problem of the individual domestic government of each country, interdependence had definitely become a factor that governed the growth and stability of the advanced countries by the 1960s.

The link between geographical distance and intensity of social inter-action, communication, and exercise of control had been decisively weakened.[74]

As positive as interdependence was for the developed world, it also had its negative side.

Interdependence also means that the various actors in one part of the system of interdependence will become more vulnerable to disturbances that originate in other parts of it.[75]

Such disturbances ranged from technological change to the problems of cities. They included moral and ethical issues arising out of scientific advances; problems of urban growth and decay; rising crime rates; environmental issues; the conflicting needs of international trade unions and multinational corporations; the commercialization of recreation and leisure pursuits; and the increasing difficulties involved in land-use planning. The population problems of the developed world differed from those of the less-developed world, but they were nevertheless real, and they too had cross-national ramifications. They included the struggles of youth, minorities, and other groups to overcome disadvantaged conditions or positions in society; problems related to aging among a population whose mean age was slowly but steadily rising; and crises in health care. Nor does this rather long recitation exhaust the list of challenges to society during the 1970s. Even between countries which were widely separated geographically, the impact of such problems could be felt, and the effects were sometimes remarkable.[76]

There was also the question of the future of democracy. In the late 1970s, all of the Atlantic-Pacific countries were functioning, western-style, liberal democracies; but virtually all of them had faced some crisis in governability during the 1970s.[77] Not only was the relevancy of the civic culture as it had developed in the west and in Japan at issue, but its appropriateness as a way of life in other parts of the world was also much debated.[78] President Carter had made "human rights" a cornerstone of his foreign policy; but the issue complicated his relations with the U.S. Congress as well as with the world at large. Despite these difficulties, the European organizations of the Atlantic-Pacific System remained forthright and active in their public attachment to the principles and institutions of democracy. The existence of a European Court of Human Rights was practical evidence of the importance which Europe attached to those principles and institutions, as was the insistence that new members of the European Communities be democratic states. The issue was one which seemed to go to the very heart of all the alliances and treaties and informal agreements which held the System together. The concept of survival itself, if one analyzed it profoundly, led back to the question of "Survival of what, and for what?" One side of the west's civic culture stressed human rights, liberty, and decisions by "the people" or their elected representatives; the other side had to do with responsibility and "the rule of law." A noted Australian jurist, Julius Stone, related the two principles in another way.

> The essence of the rule of law ideally lies . . . not in technical law as such, but rather in the supremacy of certain ethical convictions, certain rules of decency prevalent in the community, and in the psychological fact that those who are at the apex of power share those convictions and feel bound to conform to them[79]

The very essence of the modern concept of democracy gives every person the right to define his or her ideals and his or her conception of the good society. The only caveat is that those ideas or ideals are not to be pursued at the expense of others. The question can be viewed in a philosophical sense or as a practical matter of governance—as an internal matter for the Atlantic-Pacific System or as a question that affects all mankind; as an issue of domestic policy and practice for the industrial democracies individually or as a matter for which they are strictly accountable to one another, to their joint institutions, and to their peoples. However, it is viewed, the question of "democracy" will ultimately pervade the relationships of the members of the System at every level, preoccupy their peoples in the future, and indeed remain *the* public issue. That the question pertained to interdependence as well as seemed undeniable. In the end, the question was simply whether "democracy" would serve as the cement or the solvent of the System.

* * *

Without further embellishment, this list of external challenges to the Atlantic-Pacific System seems a reasonably accurate—and forbidding—statement of the challenges which the Atlantic-Pacific System faced at the end of the 1970s. Perhaps greatest of all was the challenge to confront and accommodate to the demands of interdependence. Conflicts and contradictions, both real and perceived, muddied the waters of common interests. But somehow the preeminence and urgency of the common interest was, in most cases, still greater than the individual or national interests.

The Challenge of Extending the System

What began as a Euratlantic System in the 1940s and became a nascent Atlantic-Pacific Community in the 1960s and 1970s will no doubt undergo many more changes before this century closes. Such factors as the balance of power between the Atlantic-Pacific Community and the Soviet System, the changing fortunes of regimes and unstable countries, the shortages or perceived shortages of various resources, the directions of social evolution in advanced nations, the pace of scientific and technological development, and the changing perceptions of vital national interests will all condition and shape what the Atlantic-Pacific System can become. Large, sudden changes, many of them unforeseeable, such as the timing and circumstances of the U.S. entente with China or the 1973 oil boycott, can disrupt the Atlantic-Pacific System, sometimes setting it back and occasionally spurring it towards common action.

The Addition of Japan

Of all the problematical factors which might seriously affect the System in the next two or three decades, Japan should head the list. Inevitably, this economic giant will once again acquire military and political power commensurate with its place in Asia and its impact on world economic affairs. China's future influence and behavior are also of prime importance, but they seem conditioned and balanced, at least for some decades to come, by what the Japanese can and will do. China's industrial power, and hence its political and strategic power, cannot be fully developed in the future without Japan's partnership. The terms of this partnership, of the west's own relations with China, and of the west's ties with Japan are thus of the utmost consequence. Japan is the key, the most dynamic and the most problematical factor in the world political equation. The future of Japan is more difficult to predict than, for example, the consequences of Soviet global military superiority or the failure to unify Europe.

Japan is like no other modern nation. Her cultural and spiritual formation developed in a much more isolated environment. Even her relationships with China and Korea came too late to alter fundamentally the values and social structures of the Japanese, as the wandering tribes of Europe had done on that continent. The Straits of Japan are 120 miles wide. There were long periods, centuries at times, when communication between Japan and all other continents was virtually nil. In short, Japan's highly homogeneous people have evolved as nearly unique a set of cultural patterns as can be imagined. This uniqueness means that "belonging" to any kind of an international community will require a spiritual and social wrenching that may cause great pain and psychic difficulty for the Japanese people, and for other members of the new community as well.

Japan is a powerful and increasingly innovative industrial nation. She is a prime factor, along with China, in any future association of nations in the Pacific or in eastern Asia. She is a major element in the world economy which, if it is to continue to function along its present continuum, must have Japan's consent and commitment. To isolate Japan is unthinkable, and probably cannot be done today. Yet, the attitudes of most Europeans and many Americans suggest that they believe and hope that Japan's current prominence is ephemeral. There is no safe or constructive alternative to bringing Japan fully into what formerly was a closed western system. Japan should be accepted in the community of advanced nations, and in turn should accept her full role in that community.

This seems to me to be the most difficult challenge faced by the extended Atlantic System, precisely because the dimensions of this challenge are neither understood nor fully appreciated, either in Japan or in the west. Clearly, however, the future of any viable system—Atlantic, Atlantic-Pacific, or world—depends, to a very large extent, on a successful resolution of this challenge.

The Addition of Other Democracies and Other Systems.
Within the UN family, a caucus of the developed democracies is now a fact. The developed democracies have certainly not es-

chewed coordination of this kind nor shied away from their collective leadership responsibilities in such vital organs as IMF, the World Bank, or the Security Council. Even so, this collectivity could be refined and improved, and other democracies could be included as well. More importantly, and perhaps more feasibly as well, the Atlantic-Pacific System should be linked with other systems. A strategy should be developed to extend the System by strengthening global cooperation, through the UN system insofar as possible, but not necessarily always; strengthening the Atlantic-Pacific System so that it can absorb the necessary shocks of expansion; and developing ties between the Atlantic-Pacific System and all other systems.

Within the Atlantic-Pacific System itself, ties could be strengthened in part by completing the pattern of concentric circles of association and membership among the various IGOs (Appendix B, Chart 6). On the whole, continuing growth by accretion seemed all to the good, simply as a matter of principle. For example, Spain shed her totalitarian past at the same time that she was needed in NATO for sound strategic reasons; her ability to enter the System will benefit both Spain and her European neighbors. In the late 1970s, Spain, Portugal, and Greece all applied for admission to the EC; their membership made particularly good sense, economically as well as politically.

In 1975, half of Greek and Portuguese exports and 45% of Spanish exports went to the European Community and this partly explains why these three countries wish to join the Nine. In applying for membership after a long period of dictatorship, Spain, Portugal and Greece have also made a basic choice which expresses their desire to consolidate their democracies and put their faith in the future of a united Europe.[80]

However, the "enlargement" process also posed severe problems, particularly to the EC. In 1978, integration of the nine member economies was by no means complete, and the addition of more members would increase the difficulties of integration.

The economies of the applicant nations were a good deal less developed than those of the nine EC members; thus, financial aid to the potential new members would be essential, but not easily provided. The addition of three predominantly agricultural economies would put further strains on the EC's agricultural sector and the policies designed to protect it. Under conditions obtaining in 1978, membership for the three applicants would also mean that the EC would absorb more unemployed workers and, in the cases of Portugal and Spain, at very high levels. Nevertheless, the consensus was that, with careful planning, the expansion would in the long run help all concerned. Finally, if the idea of a "United Europe" still meant anything, the EC simply could not refuse.

There were other possible candidates for EC membership. Most of the members of EFTA were already more or less de facto EC members by reason of the industrial free trade agreements concluded in 1972, when the EC accepted three EFTA members—the United Kingdom, Denmark, and Ireland—for EC membership. Such countries as Sweden, Norway, Switzerland, and possibly Austria seemed likely to become full EC members. Turkey, which had had an association agreement since 1963 with the EC, also looked forward to eventual membership. Even such tiny countries as Malta, Cyprus, and Iceland might likewise be pulled into the EC—indeed, how could such countries afford to stay out?

The International Energy Agency was a dynamic and expandable IGO within the System. In 1978, Australia joined, while France might also overcome her initial misgivings about the political implications of IEA.

The Council of Europe, which strong partisans of the European Communities had never taken too seriously, nevertheless continued over the years to take on and complete new tasks. The Council's record of transferring knowledge and ideas about the improvement of modern societies and its contribution to the broad pattern of Europewide cooperation were cumulatively impressive. The Council was especially important as a symbol of democratic Europe, and largely for this reason continued to attract new members in the 1970s (Greece rejoined in 1974, and Portugal and Spain became members in 1976 and 1977, respectively). Finland also appeared to show interest in Council membership, although such a step might be viewed by the Soviet Union, and perhaps by her European neighbors as well, as taking sides in the Cold War. There is also the possibility of Council membership for such non-European countries as the United States, Canada, Australia, New Zealand, or Japan. The reasoning for such memberships would be threefold: (1) the Council complemented OECD as an information-transfer mechanism in the social fields; (2) OECD was handicapped by its lack of a parliament, while the Council had an active assembly which was already in the habit of examining OECD-related questions and reports; coordinating the membership of the two organizations would provide a parliamentary forum for all of the nonmilitary questions that faced the industrial democracies; and (3) accession of five important democratic states to the Council would have great symbolic importance, in terms of a unified stance of all the functioning democracies and in terms of a worldwide approach to human rights. Broadening the scope of Council membership allowed the possibility of still more democratic members: India, Costa Rica, Israel, Venezuela, and a few small island countries were at least theoretically qualified candidates. Just as OEEC had expanded geographically as OECD, to incorporate countries from three continents, so the Council of Europe might someday serve as a civic and cultural bridge from the west to other civilizations.

The possibility of expanding OECD also represented challenges to the System. The larger an IGO becomes, and the more culturally disparate its membership, the more complex is its management and the more difficult are the problems of communication among members and within the secretariat. Inasmuch as OECD had already expanded geographically to include Australia, New Zealand, and Japan, however, there could be no good reasons beyond managerial considerations and perhaps occasionally highly political ones to deny membership to any other well-developed and industrialized democracy. OECD had never made democracy an explicit requirement for membership (Spain, Portugal, and Greece all had been members under dictatorships); yet, by 1978, all OECD members were democratic states.

Welcoming to OECD every power which had passed from developing status to the ranks of the developed also seemed advantageous. Such a policy would help prevent the emergence of regional and ideological blocs; it would help insure that newly developed nations would do their part in aiding those still underdeveloped; and it would also enable newly developed nations to participate in responsible decision making with respect to the world's main free market economies. Finally, it would help lessen the "ex-colonial" and "European" image of OECD and bridge still more effectively the geographic and historical gaps in a particularistic world. Part of OECD's attractiveness as an IGO has been its flexibility; an interested country can participate on a tentative basis by association or by membership in one or more of those committees which seem to meet a country's particular needs. Japan, for example, initiated its membership in OECD with membership on a single committee. Possible candidates for eventual OECD membership were those countries which *The Economist* called "NICS" (newly industrializing countries): Brazil, Hong Kong, Israel, Mexico, Singapore, South Korea, Taiwan, and Venezuela.[81] Of the list, Israel stood out as the most immediately qualified; all the others were still developing politically, economically, and/or socially. On May 2, 1975, a *Wall Street Journal* editorial raised the interesting possibility of Brazilian membership in OECD:

> The greatest shortcoming of U.S. policy toward Latin America, in our view, is that there has been little serious effort to distinguish among the many nations of vastly different size, potential, culture, and outlook. There seems to be a lack of appreciation that there cannot be any such thing as an effective "Latin American" foreign policy for the entire hemisphere; there can only be a foreign policy toward individual nations in Latin America.

In partial recognition of this fundamental but important point, at least one scholar has raised the possibility of Brazilian membership in the Organization of [sic] Economic Co-operation and Development. Roger Fontaine, of Georgetown University's Center for Strategic and International Studies, notes that this would allow South America's largest nation to join with the U.S. and Europe and Japan in working out the economic and political problems that all four will soon share. Moreover, helping to integrate Brazil into the developed, neo-capitalist Atlantic Community could prevent it from allying itself with some of the more troublesome tendencies of the Third World.[82]

In support of this idea of Brazilian membership, it should be noted that on February 21, 1976, Brazil and the United States signed an agreement to consult twice a year on global issues. "This is the sort of treatment the United States extends to such powers as Japan, and Brazil is the first nation in Latin America to receive it."[83] By 1975, Brazil had become the tenth largest economy in the world and ranked seventh in population and fifth in area.

OECD might consider still another line of development which could be used to link some of the candidate countries, at least indirectly. Elsewhere, I have proposed the formation of a "Pacific Caucus of OECD," composed of Australia, Canada, Japan, New Zealand, and the United States.[84] Such a group could take the lead in promoting and smoothing trade relations in the Pacific area and might also rationalize and promote more sensible patterns of international investment and development of resources. It could also promote among nations in the Pacific area cooperation on problems of the advanced industrial societies and provide more coordinated and effective development aid to less-developed countries in the Pacific region. A Pacific Caucus could well form gradual associations with such countries as Singapore, the entire ASEAN group, South Korea, Hong Kong, and Taiwan, thus smoothing the way for at least some of them to participate eventually in OECD. Together, the five Pacific Caucus powers might organized a "Pacific Marshall Plan." Over two or three decades, the Caucus might develop from an economic and social body into one with political and mutual defense capabilities and commitments—a kind of Pacific NATO that incorporated ANZUS, the U.S.-Japanese mutual security arrangements, and even the U.S.-Canadian defense arrangements. (Robert Brand has suggested a title for the new alliance: JACANANZUS.) As time went on, other Pacific nations might be asked to join. In this way, a more viable "Pacific Community" could very gradually be built on foundations more solid than those envisaged by some.[85]

There are other possibilities for linking the Atlantic-Pacific System with other sytems. The so-called Conference on International Economic Cooperation (CIEC) was established in 1975, following the near panic which accompanied the 1973 oil boycott. President Giscard d'Estaing had proposed establishing a wider "economic dialogue" between developing and industrialized nations. CIEC represented twelve less-developed countries, seven oil-producing nations, and seven non-EEC industrial countries, as well as the members of the EC. The Conference set up a permanent secretariat; and, although little progress has been recorded, the idea of a group representative of all but the Communist nations, yet a good deal smaller than the entire UN, was still an attractive one. CIEC could conceivably provide a valuable bridge to the future.[86]

The regional development banks provided opportunities for developed and underdeveloped nations to work together in a less politically charged setting. By 1976, nine nations from outside the western hemisphere had joined the Inter-American Development Bank, and four more had indicated their intention to do so.[87] Similarly, by 1977, the Asian Development Bank had fourteen nonregional members, and the Caribbean Development Bank had two.[88]

In considering future membership in the System, neither the size nor the economic, political, or social potential of a country can be ignored. Of course, it is not at all certain that qualified candidates would race to join the System if asked. But certainly the members of the Atlantic-Pacific System ought to be thinking in terms of enlargement and considering the purposes, strategies, and criteria of such expansion.

A universal world government often seems the only panacea to those who yearn for a more orderly world. While probably true, this solution seems unattainable for many generations to come, if ever. As Crane Brinton wrote, it might only "be glimpsed by the eye of faith."[89] Meanwhile, the world will still have to make do with such international and regional systems as exist, gradually reshaping them as best it can. By far the most substantial and effective of these, with all its shortcomings, is the contemporary Atlantic-Pacific System.

WHAT KIND OF FUTURE?

Negative and Positive Scenarios

Which way is the Atlantic-Pacific System likely to go in the next 20 to 30 years? There appear to be only a few models, although with many possible variations; a combination of scenarios is also possible, and indeed likely.

The most negative scenario, for the west at any rate, would be the failure of the extended Atlantic System. This scenario would end the drive for European unity and see the withdrawal of U.S. troops from Europe and Japan, leaving the hollow shell of paper commitments which could not be fulfilled. Trade wars would intensify; nations would go their own separate ways, in terms of both economics and security, and some—especially the United States—would try to make isolation and independence work by arming to the teeth. The Soviet Union would achieve its goal of domination in Europe and among less-developed countries. The UN would become a Soviet tool, with probable western withdrawal. Western governments would keep to the forms of democracy in most cases, but would become increasingly authoritarian as a result of fear. There might be general chaos, then possibly a Third World War, before or after which a strong power, such as the USSR, would try to impose its own version of a global system. (Dr. Kissinger's "worst case" is similar to this scenario.)

In the second scenario, the Atlantic Community would manage to hold together, but the Japanese—rejected because no way could be found to accommodate their economic dynamism—

would leave the System and seek other partners in east Asia. This scenario would exclude the west, and foremost the United States, from Asia. China, partly in response to Japanese rearmament, would resume an expansionist role and initiate war with the USSR. The disintegration of the global system would then be well on the way. The Atlantic rump of the former Atlantic-Pacific System would be imperilled, either drawn into the conflict or isolated and beleaguered, and would eventually fall.

In the third scenario, "trilateralism" would win out as the principal strategy, but the nations of the new system would vacillate between developing a strong partnership of the European Community, Japan, and the United States, on the one hand, or, on the other hand, forming a weak partnership which would try not to assert too much trilateral leadership, because both the global community and its smaller partners in Europe and the Far East resented it. The Japanese would feel somewhat exposed without Australia (in particular) as a full Pacific partner. The mantle of leadership would fall on Japan. The trilateral community would work fairly well in economic affairs, for a time at least, but would break down ultimately over the question of security. Neither Japan nor the United States would be willing to act as the sole defender for the Pacific leg of a broad Atlantic-Pacific security alliance; and NATO, because it could not be integrated into a trilateral mechanism, would languish. Thus, it would become evident, although perhaps too late, that trilateralism was a convenient way at one time of helping Japan develop a sense of international responsibility, but could not be translated into a dominant policy, much less provide the basis for a fully reorganized Atlantic System.

In the fourth scenario, the old brand of hegemonial multilateralism would fail, because the United States refused to take a role of individual leadership, but was also unable to participate in devising a new system of collective leadership. The European nations would no longer regard U.S. defense pledges as credible, but could not fill the political and military gaps either collectively or singly. The old Atlantic Community would gradually disintegrate while NATO developed into an alliance of Germany and the United States alone, an allliance which would put too much weight on the Germans. As a result, the old fear of the German nation would again become pervasive in Europe. Finally, the Soviet Union would find it easy to renew the Cold War and to proceed with "Finlandization" of the continent. The United States and Japan would be able to maintain a bilateral relationship for a time, but at the expense of the larger multilateral trading and money system. Germany, Japan, and the United States would try unsuccessfully to provide a nucleus for a world currency system which would fail because others resented it. The ultimate effect of scenario number four would thus be very close to that of number one and possibly number two.

During the fifth scenario, the present System would hold for a few years, long enough for statesmen and planners to bring about something vastly better. A series of "lucky" economic and security crises, to which the System was able to respond—but just barely—would convince the European countries that they must finally unify politically. Joining with Japan, Canada, Australia, the United States, and New Zealand, the European Communities (and a few small European democracies which had not yet joined the EC) would form an Atlantic-Pacific Confederation, with a common security ministry and the minimum number of organizations required for effective economic policy-making and management. The confederation would establish a common currency and central banking system and would impose common taxes for defense and development aid. The Confederation would ultimately become a federation. Gradually, other countries would join, and over a period of many decades—more probably, several centuries—the federation would merge with the UN and become a world-wide organization.

Finally, in the sixth scenario, the Atlantic-Pacific System would be restructured as a loose, but still effective organization. This scenario would take somewhat longer to achieve than scenario number five, but the final results would be much the same. The organization would make good use of the trilateral psychology described above, but its membership and its purposes would both become broader than the early trilateral concept. Such an organization could come about because the leading statesmen of the principal countries (roughly, the Summit Seven) would agree that it was necessary, and would be willing to formulate clear, long-term goals and a very flexible strategy for such an organization. The process of design would involve still another major innovation in the creation of political institutions, equal to the highly original creation of the European Communities. Technically, the new system would be neither a confederation nor a federation, but would gradually evolve to embrace supranationalism.

Policies of drift could bring about any of the first four scenarios, and all of them would lead inevitably in the same direction, directly opposite to the fifth and sixth, to the eventual breakdown of the Atlantic-Pacific System. The end result would be go-it-alone policies for the members of the System, breakdown of the global systems, international anarchy, possible general war, and certain world depression, with some very large power—and, at this stage, the USSR remains the prime candidate—picking up all the pieces. In such dire circumstances, a new global system would probably be one which we former democrats—and by that time we should all be *former* western-style democrats—would have a hard time recognizing or accepting.

I consider the fifth scenario, although highly attractive and surely the most effective potentially, to be the least likely of all the six to come about, at least directly. Therefore, in the few pages remaining, I should like to concentrate on various aspects of the sixth, which I believe to be both attainable and necessary, and a way of eventually getting to the fifth.

The Requirements of International Community

Earlier, we examined the concept of "international community." A true community requires internationally minded men and women who would construct and operate its mechanisms and who themselves have a pervasive sense of belonging to the community, a powerful will to cooperate, and a well-developed social capacity for intercultural teamwork. It also requires, among the general populace of the participating countries, a minimum tolerance, acceptance, and appreciation of their partners in the community and a general willingness to let their statesmen make the experiment work; wild enthusiasm is not necessary, but reasonably good-natured acquiescence is.

In their book, *The Crisis of Democracy*, Crozier, Huntington, and Watanuki described the direction in which the industrial countries were heading as

> anomic democracy, in which democratic politics becomes more an arena for the assertion of conflicting interests than a process for the building of common purposes.[90]

They further asserted that

> What is in short supply in democratic societies today is thus not consensus on the rules of the game but a sense of purpose as to what one should achieve by playing the game. In the past, people have found their purposes in religion, in nationalism, and in ideology. But neither church, nor state, nor class now commands people's loyalties.[91]

A modicum of loyalty to a united Europe, an Atlantic Community, a larger Atlantic-Pacific Community, or eventually to a world community would probably not be out of place. Such loyalties in the past have required the creation of popular myths; in our era, the idea of finding an international equivalent to "Vive l'Empereur!" or the "Star-Spangled Banner" seems implausible. A subjective component must be present in any workable international community, but it will probably have to be based on rationality and an appeal to the common sense and good will of the ordinary man. The knowledge that creating a better international community is one way of working concretely for peace and a better life for everyone becomes a potentially animating psychological force. But these are not exactly rallying cries. Nor is "liberty" a sufficient motivator; although always highly emotional and certainly important, liberty cannot be defined to everyone's satisfaction. One must inevitably ask, "Liberty for *what*?" "Liberty!" becomes a good rallying cry only in defiance against some tyranny, real or supposed; it is not a slogan for the positive but painstaking job of community building.

A group of Eastern European exiles and Western intellectuals met in Paris in 1977, to contemplate the state of society on either side of the Iron Curtain. Eugene Ionesco cautiously concluded that he thought he could detect some signs of an ideal of *caritas* in the soul of *l' homme occidental*. This is no new idea; in the form of humanitarianism, it was the chief British contribution to civilization in the nineteenth century. In the establishment of the Peace Corps by Kennedy or the offer of the Marshall Plan by Truman, one saw the broad vision of brotherhood and social responsibility. The creation of the welfare state, the billions which have been poured out by the advanced countries for "foreign aid," the donations of the great foundations of the twentieth century, and the helping hand of countless small, voluntary charities and individuals throughout the Western world are all evidence of the same central idea: Men have been placed on earth to help others; "no man is an island. . . ."

The basic requirement for building any community remains the will to help others in some collective way. If this is so, then there are two basic questions which must be asked of the System at this time. Does the world need a community? If so, what kind of community, and what would its purpose be?

Structure and Strategy for an Atlantic-Pacific Community

Rien ne marche dans un système politique où les mots jurent avec les choses.

—Napoléon

A political system will not work unless the rhetoric of that system corresponds with the actual state of affairs. The key challenge to the Atlantic-Pacific powers is to agree on long-term goals which are both inspiring and attainable, as well as appealing, yet concrete. Such goals require a practical, step-by-step program that will assure their completion. A strategy is called for, one whose rhetoric corresponds with perceived reality. There must also be a structure to enable the strategy to unfold. Many things could conceivably be done to restructure and reform the present Atlantic-Pacific System.[92]

Initially, more emphasis could be put on summit coordination and leadership. Beginning in 1975, the heads of government of the seven nations which comprised the "power core" of the Atlantic-Pacific System met annually to discuss world economic affairs, and presumably politics as well.[93] The first meeting seemed to avert a serious crisis, if not a collapse, in the coordination of the industrial democracies' economic policies.[94] A more institutionalized summit could perhaps act as a steering mechanism for the whole System, including its chief IGOs. As far as is known, the consultations of the current group have not concerned security because Japan is not a member of NATO. However, this topic may be of more concern in the next decade or so. A working summit mechanism could also serve a useful purpose in this context. There are other problems with the summit meetings as they are currently constituted. There has been a distinct lack of follow through on issues discussed at the summit meetings. "Summits" themselves seem willy-nilly on the way to becoming institutions. Yet, the summits do not appear to acknowledge existing IGOs or smaller nations within the System. To make the summit meetings effective will require a number of basic decisions; the effort would seem worthwhile.

A second step in structuring the community would be to rationalize and strengthen the democratic control of the institutions which tie the System together. There are currently seven interparliamentary bodies that serve the IGOs and constituent national legislatures of the System. The new procedure for direct elections to EC's European Parliament illustrates one possible avenue for bringing the System and its constituency closer together.

Still another step would be to eliminate outmoded structures and shift and/or modernize the functions of the System. WEU, Eurogroup, and the Independent European Programme Group are all examples of an attempt to make an effective caucus of European powers within the Atlantic Alliance. Old habits of thinking need not forever determine the functioning of an organization. IGOs should be seen afresh, and their functions readjusted where necessary. A few IGOs might simply be eliminated, to good effect. The present IGOs of the System should be thought of as building blocks that can be reshaped or replaced as necessary so that, over time, they can be fitted into a more rational, comprehensive structure. IEA, for example, might be remodeled along the lines of the original ECSC.

Fourth, the IGOs should be opened up to additional members, in cases in which both the applicant and the purposes of the IGO could obviously be better served. This step could take place on two levels: (1) present members of the System might be encouraged to join more of the IGOs in the System, thus developing a tighter overall pattern of membership and participation; and (2) new members could be brought into the System by permitting them to join one or more of the IGOs in the System, or by encouraging their participation in the System by other variations in membership (for example, associate membership or observer status).

Fifth, the formation of a "Pacific Caucus" should be studied seriously. In one respect or another, relationships among the developed countries of the Pacific should be strengthened, as a possible prelude to some sort of Pacific Community. Indirectly, this could also lead to strengthened ties between Europe and the Pacific Countries (e.g., Japan and Australia), not only on economic matters, but eventually on defense questions as well.

A sixth step might be to add still another IGO which could serve as a capstone organization for the whole System. This IGO might be called "The Community of Developed Democracies," or the "Atlantic-Pacific Community." The Community would simply act as an umbrella organization for all the intergovernmental activity in the System, rather than attempting to plan or supervise everything that goes on. It would coordinate and do strategic planning. It might later be given limited, but concrete powers for major security or economic decisions. Organs of the Community might include *a council of governments,* representing all of the nations of the System; *a steering group,* comprising the present seven "Economic Summit" countries (Canada, France, Germany, Japan, Italy, the United Kingdom, and the United States), which would propose broad strategies and oversee the implementation of decisions; *a single parliamentary assembly,* elected directly by voters of the member states; and *an IGO Conference* comprising all the IGOs in the Community, which would reduce duplication, deal with matters cutting across the competencies of several IGO's, and monitor the development of the System overall.

A seventh step in structuring the Atlantic-Pacific System would be to establish a reformed GATT as a permanent body. This body would work best if the Atlantic-Pacific nations formed their own subgroup within it and then brought other GATT members into the more complex schemes as they were ready to participate.[95]

The next step would be to set up a "federal reserve system" for the Community. Such a program would imply capital markets as large as the entire Atlantic-Pacific System, but eventually worldwide, as well as a genuine international currency. The Trilateral Commission has considered this possibility.[96] William McChesney Martin, former Chairman of the U.S. Federal Reserve Board, has also proposed it publicly.

An important step in structuring the System would be to revise the defense system and possibly restructure it with three major regional components: North America (Canada and the United States; possibly Mexico at some future time); western Europe (the European Communities, the other European members of NATO, and perhaps later some of the nations that are currently neutral); and the "Pacific Caucus" (Japan, Australia, New Zealand, Canada, and the United States; with eventual links to such groups as ASEAN or to individual countries, such as South Korea). Because of the way in which membership patterns in the System have developed in the past, some memberships would overlap (for example, the United States and Canada might be members in both the Pacific and the Atlantic groupings). A council of the whole, corresponding to the present North Atlantic Council, but with a worldwide geographic spread and corresponding decentralization, should also be established. The essence of the new alliance would be to regard all major threats to peace as global in character and to view the creation of effective deterrents to aggression as matters not only for regional action, but also for intercontinental coordination.

A further step in devising a strategy for the System would be to preserve, defend, and improve the western democratic civic culture. Common goals for action could be adopted, and various implementing mechanisms worked out. "Human rights" programs, for example, would fit more easily into a general strategy of helping members and nonmembers of the community modernize and update their political cultures and systems of government. As long as everyone was helping everyone else, there would be nothing invidious or patronizing about such programs. Even such prosaic but highly important matters as the improved training of civil servants might find a place in this kind of program. Countries which had not yet joined the European Court of Human Rights might do so.

Another step would be to create an international productivity agency. The earlier European Productivity Agency could be used as a basis. For a variety of reasons, associated with almost every important aspect of contemporary life, the growth of productivity has lagged badly in most countries of the System in recent years. New breakthroughs in science, business efficiency, and public attitudes are badly needed. A central body, perhaps linked with OECD, could usefully study and promote better productivity.

Finally, the System should institute a broad program for building community ideals and interpersonal relations. No community, from the very small to the grandly multinational, can be brought into being or continue to exist without the "subjective" component of government. The existing international exchange programs sponsored by many governments and organizations; the activities of such bodies as the British Council and the French, German, and U.S. information and cultural services; and the work of many private organizations could all be brought more effectively into a general scheme that pointed specifically at the goal of an expanding consciousness of community among the developed democracies. A subsidiary aim, more humble, but no less important, would be to provide the citizenry with compelling evidence that the System also met the objective needs of the community for security, prosperity, and continuing freedom.

CONCLUSION

The construction thus far of the Atlantic-Pacific System, even in its half-finished state, is one of the great achievements of this or any other century. The System functions well, if not perfectly. Neither a state nor an empire, but a voluntary association of states, the System is a nascent international community. At least for the present, the System is not a federation, but it is much more cohesive and holds more promise than any other international system, regional or universal. The Atlantic-Pacific System forms a likely precursor for an even closer, much more dynamic future union and ultimately for a viable world community. But the way ahead is neither easy nor simple.

By the late 1970s, it seemed that the west and its new partner, Japan, were more or less "stuck on dead center." After a surge of unparalleled political creativity in the 1950s, the nations (rather naturally) rested on their oars. The noble and practical ideal of international community had been born, but the job remained unfinished. The student of international affairs and concerned citizens of the world should be aware of the magnitude of what has been accomplished and of the even greater challenges which lie ahead so that they can muster the courage to complete the job of building an international community.

FOOTNOTES

1. Otto Pick and Julian Critchley, *Collective Security* (London: Macmillan, 1974), p. 45.
2. Ibid., p. 50.
3. "West breathes easier as inflation tide ebbs," *The Christian Science Monitor* (October 17, 1975).
4. Quoted by Bernard Levin in *The Times* (of London), (December 7, 1977), p. 18.
5. In an interview with Arnaud de Borchgrave in *Newsweek,* on May 29, 1978, Chancellor Helmut Schmidt commented on the problems of working with the United States: "We have to deal with Congress directly more than ever before. Our embassy is not enough. Members of our Paliament go over to Washington more and more to talk to the new generation in American politics who have neither emotional ties toward Europe nor specific experience in American-European co-operation. Thus the whole process of inter-allied decision-making becomes far more complex than in the past—in strategy, energy, trade, and monetary policies. Horrendously complicated. Cooperation between democracies is becoming more and more difficult to manage."

6. See especially, John W. Vogt, *Improving NATO Force Capabilities,* Policy Paper of the Atlantic Council of the United States (Washington, D.C., 1977).

7. See the debate sparked by A. Solzhenitsyn's Harvard commencement address in June 1978.

8. These calculations are based on figures taken from *U.S. Participation in International Organizations,* Committee on Government Operations, U.S. Senate, 95th Congress, 1st Session (Washington, D.C.: U.S. Government Printing Office, February 1977); and The Secretary of State's Report to the Congress: *United States Contributions to International Organizations,* Department of State, Washington, D.C.: December 1977. The bulk of U.S. contributions to IGOs in 1975 (nearly 85%) was to IGOs affiliated with the UN "family."

9. Richard N. Cooper, et al., *Towards a Renovated International System,* The Triangle Papers, no. 14 (New York: Trilateral Commission, 1977), p. 18.

10. *The Encyclopedia Britannica,* vol. 12 (1967 ed tion5, pm 428.

11. A.H. Robertson, *European Institutions* (London: Stevens and Sons, Ltd., 1973), pp. 1–4.

12. Ibid., p. 1.

13. American feelings on this point were epitomized by Senator H. Alexander Smith, when he stated in the Senate (March 4, 1948): "We all know that the small compartments of Europe for hundreds of years have made difficulties that prevented humane understanding between people by which they could move forward" (quoted by Max Beloff, *The United States and the Unity of Europe* [Washington, D.C.: The Brookings Institution, 1963], p. 27).

14. Texts adopted by the Assembly, September 1949, Resolution 2.

15. Quoted by Robertson, *European Institutions,* op. cit., p. 12. The story of the early years of U.S. support is well told by Max Beloff, op. cit.

16. Succeeding U.S. administrations, from 1972 to 1977, supported the European Communities. On January 22, 1972, President Nixon lauded the signing of the treaty to enlarge the European Communities to include the United Kingdom, Ireland, Denmark, and Norway. The President emphasized the United States' continuing, strong support of the EC. In December 1975, President Ford remarked that "the European Community is heading toward political unity and a greater European role in both political and economic issues. We welcome and support these trends." In 1977, President Carter pleged the support of his administration to a strengthening of the European Community itself

and a close interrelationship among the nations of Europe, the European Community in particular. Furthermore, he suggested the absorption within the European Communities of Portugal and Spain.

17. Crane Brinton, *From Many One* (Cambridge, Mass.: Harvard University Press, 1948), pp. 83–85, succinctly sets forth the "experience of the past in the maintenance of peace by political integration." Not all of the pre-conditions he cites obtain among the powers of the Atlantic-Pacific System, and to that extent, the durability, closeness, and efficacy of their association may be in doubt. His main points are that,

> first of all, it is certain that we of Western society have never, in our five thousand years of recorded history, kept peace for long within an area save by bringing that area within the authority of a single government. . . . Second, the authority of a single government has, in the past, been extended territorially in a variety of ways, which for purposes of analysis can be sorted into a polarity of force and consent, of imperialism and federalism. . . . Third, . . . it is possible to distinguish certain general characteristics of any international or supranational state in our own time. These . . . are: a) a symbolic head of state . . . ; b) an elite, not always an aristocracy in the conventional European sense of the word, an elite commonly charged with responsibility for administration, for setting the tone of society and education, conditioned morally as well as intellectually to the service of the integrated state, thoroughly cosmopolitan or international in outlook; c) at least some loyalty on the part of the masses who live under its authority, though this loyalty would seem both more widespread and deeper in such examples of integration as the modern nation-state than it was in the really international Roman Empire; d) some degree of local autonomy, especially where there is among the constituent units a tradition of self-rule; e) an absence of groups, and especially of groups with a territorial basis, which feel that the existence of the integrated state is compatible with their own existence. . . . Finally, in the past the process of political integration has almost invariably been a slow one, whether it came about imperialistically or federally.

18. See also Chapter 5, in which the community-building process was examined from a different perspective, and Appendix A, in which these concepts are further defined.

19. For example, Sir Henry Maine, *Ancient Law: Its Connection with the Early History of Society and its Relation to Modern Ideas* (Boston: Beacon Press, 1963 [first published, 1861]), p. 168:

> Starting as from one terminus of history, from a condition of society in which all the relations of persons are summed up in relations of a family, we seem to have steadily moved toward a phase of social order in which all these relations arise from the free agreement of individuals.

20. H.G. Aubrey, *Atlantic Economic Cooperation: The Case of the OECD* (New York: Frederick A. Praeger, 1967), p. 6.

21. Ibid., p. 6.

22. Mitrany's concepts are well set forth in David Mitrany, *A Working Peace System* (4th ed.), (London: National Peace Council, 1946). They were considerably different in many respects from the ideas of the neofunctionalists, and it is the latter with which we are particularly concerned in this book. See Appendix A, footnote 21, p. 328.

23. Karl W. Deutsch, et al., *Political Community and the North Atlantic Area* (Princeton, N.J.: Princeton University Press, 1957), pp. 199–201.

24. E. Haas, (Stanford: Stanford University Press, 1958).

25. "International Integration: The European and the Universal Process," in B. Landheer, ed., *Limits and Problems of European Integration* (The Hague: Martinus Nijhoff, 1963), pp. 30–31.

26. Michael Banks, "Systems Analysis and the Study of Regions," *International Studies Quarterly,* vol. 13, no. 4 (December 1969), p. 355.

27. ". . . the term 'spill-over' describes the accretion of new powers and tasks to a central institutional structure, based on changing demands and expectations on the part of such political actors as interest groups, political parties, and bureaucracies." See Ernst Haas, in *International Encyclopedia of the Social Sciences* (New York: Crowell, Collier, and Macmillan, 1968), vol. 7, p. 523.

28. For a further discussion of functionalist theories, see Appendix A, pp. 320–322. Professor Elliot Goodman of Brown University, in a letter to the author in 1978, elaborated on the most important differences between functionalists and neofunctionalists:

> Functionalism seeks to work largely outside of the state and political organs, neo-functionalism consciously works with political

elites and organs of state; functionalism works basically with economic forces (and is really Marxist to the extent that it relies on economic determinism), neo-functionalism mixes economics with politics (although it prefers low to high politics); functionalism does not look to regionalism but to universalism, since regional political blocs are held to be a threat to global functional integration and to world peace; neo-functionalism tries to construct regional poltical units as the most likely way to move toward political integration—that is, Mitrany does *not* like the idea of a European federation, while Monnet and Schuman do; functionalism relies upon voluntary cooperation and is rather naive in the way society operates, while neo-functionalism takes account of competition and cross-cutting conflicts and builds its integration theory upon them.

29. See C.H. Waddington, *The Ethical Animal* (London: Allen and Unwin, 1960); William McDougall, *Outline of Psychology* (New York: Scribner, 1973); T. Dobzhansky, in *International Encyclopedia of the Social Sciences*, op. cit., vol. 5, p. 238; and Joseph de Rivera, *The Psychological Dimension of Foreign Policy* (Columbus, Ohio: Charles Merrill, 1968). pp. 410–415.

30. See page 152 for the opinion of a diplomat on the effect of international institutions on the behavior of governments.

31. William D. Coplin has commented on the relationship of international law to the international "political culture;" one did not, he wrote, follow the other; they were interdependent "because law represents a quasi-authoritative statement of the nature of the culture . . . [but] international law represents a crucial element in providing continuity . . . the study of international law becomes the study of part of the process through which the international poltical culture is maintained and developed." See "Studies of the Functions of International Law," *Political Science Annual*, vol. 2 (Indianapolis: Bobbs-Merrill, 1970), p. 195.

32. Ferdinand Tönnies, *Gemeinschaft und Gesellschaft* (1887); translated and edited by C.P. Loomis, *Community and Society* (New York: Harper and Row, 1963).

33. Op. cit., p. 65.

34. Nelson W. Polsby, in *International Encyclopedia of the Social Sciences,* op. cit., vol. 3, p. 157.

35. See, e.g., Ernst Haas, *The Uniting of Europe* (Stanford: Stanford University Press, 1958), Karl W. Deutsch, et al., *Political Com-

munity and the North Atlantic Area, op. cit., footnote 23; and Karl W. Deutsch, et al., *Political Community at the International Level: Problems of Definition and Managment* (Princeton, N.J.: Princeton University Press, 1953).

36. Robert Strausz-Hupé, James E. Dougherty, and William R. Kinter, *Building the Atlantic World* (New York: Harper and Row, 1963), chapter I.

37. Haas, in *The Uniting of Europe,* op. cit., for example.

38. Haas, in *International Encyclopedia of the Social Sciences,* op. cit., vol. 7, p. 524.

39. "A community of peoples exists only in so far as it does great things together." See Robert Strausz-Hupé, "Maxims," *Encounter* (March 1975).

40. See Deutsch, et al., *Political Community in the North Atlantic Area,* op. cit., p. 129.

41. For a treatment of the concept of integration, at both domestic and international levels, see Appendix A. For a discussion of community, see also Appendix A, and Lippmann's formulation (pp. 4–5, this work).

42. Richard N. Cooper, Karl Kaiser, and Masataka Kosaka, *Towards a Renovated International System,* The Triangle Papers, no. 14 (New York: Trilateral Commission, 1977), p. 39.

43. Miriam Camps, *"First World" Relationships: The Role of the OECD* (New York: Council on Foreign Relations, 1975), p. 38.

44. Robert Strausz-Hupé, "On NATO and the Realities of World Politics," *The New Federalist* (Washington, D.C.: Federal Union, Inc., 1978), p. 5.

45. Karl Kaiser, "Transnational Politics: Toward a Theory of Multinational Politics," *International Organization,* No. XXV (Fall 1971), p. 817.

46. Reporting on a reputedly "off-the-record" address to the wives of U.S. Congressmen, *New York Times* (March 13, 1974).

47. Robert L. Pfaltzgraff, Jr., "Notes: Trip to Hong Kong, Republic of Korea, Japan, and Thailand," unpublished paper (Boston: July 1974), pp. 16–17.

48. Howard Bliss, ed., *The Political Development of the European Community: A Documentary Collection* (Waltham, Mass: Blaisdell Publishing Co., 1970),p. 103.

49. See Clarence Streit, *Union Now* (New York: Harper and Row, 1939).

50. Helen S. Wallace, "The Impact of the European Communities

on National Policy-Making," in G. Ionescu (ed.), *The New Politics of European Integration*, London: Macmillan, 1972, p. 214.

51. Robertson, *European Institutions*, op. cit., pp. 307–308.

52. Vredeling, H., "The Common Market of Political Parties," in G. Ionescu, op. cit., p. 129.

53. Socini, Roberto, *Rapports et Conflits entre Organisations Européennes*, Leiden: A. W. Sythoff, 1960, p. 20 (translated by J. Huntley for this citation).

54. The delicate quality of the European-U.S. relationship at the time is well illustrated by the following quote from *The Times* (of London), December 11, 1973:

If [the United States] wishes to preserve her leadership she has to go on working for it. Her moral and political authority have been severely shaken in recent times, and not only by Watergate. She needs the support of Europe as much as Europe needs her protection.

55. *Atlantic News,* Brussels, December 24, 1975, p. 2.

56. See, for example, François Duchêne, "The Strategic Consequences of the Enlarged European Community," *Survival,* vol. XV, no. 1, Jan./Feb. 1973, pp. 2–7.

57. "Kissinger Sees the World on Verge of Historic Era," *The New York Times,* October 13, 1974, p. 1.

58. "Kissinger's Adversary Mentality," *Newsweek,* September 8, 1975, p. 56.

59. Deutsch, et al., *Political Community in the North Atlantic Area,* op. cit., p. 42.

60. C. K. Streit, personal conversation with the author, 1975.

61. Sir Kenneth Younger, personal conversation with the author, 1975.

62. Former Congressman Walter H. Judd, testifying at a hearing of the U.S. House of Representatives Subcommittee on International Organizations, September 8, 1975. ("Atlantic Convention Resolution," Hearing before the Subcommittee on International Organizations of the Committee on International Relations, House of Representatives, 94th Congress, First Session on H.J. Res. 606, September 8, 1975.) Washington, DC: U.S. Government Printing Office, 1975.

63. *Newsweek* (January 6, 1975).

64. Camps, op. cit., p. 37.

65. Ibid., p. 21.

66. "Institutions for Interdependence," in Gerhard Mally, ed., *The*

New Europe and the United States (Lexington, Mass.: D.C. Heath, 1974), pp. 141–142.

67. Cooper, et al., op. cit., p. 11.

68. Ibid., p. 42.

69. Emery Reves, *The Anatomy of Peace* (New York: Harper Brothers, 1945), p. 210.

70. Pick and Critchley, op. cit., p. 46.

71. Richard N. Gardner, Saburo Okita, and B.J. Udink, *A Turning Point in North-South Economic Relations* ⁵³The Triangle Papers, no. 3 New York: The Trilateral Commission, 1974), p. 9.

72. Note especially the Yaoundé and Lomé Conventions of the European Communities, the work of the Organization of American States, and the various regional development banks, the activities of the World Bank and IMF in the development field, and the efforts—on the whole, successful—of OECD's Development Assistance Committee to stimulate greater aid giving.

73. See also, Camps, op. cit., pp. 33–36.

74. Kaiser, op. cit., p. 808.

75. Ibid., p. 816.

76. In the spring of 1978, the author was asked by an academic friend to assist a Japanese researcher, who had a contract to explore the public reactions of other countries to the development of large modern airports. The problem related directly to the inability of the Japanese government, over several years, to open the new Tokyo airport at Narita because of the strength and vehemence of protesters. The Japanese researcher was put in touch with a firm specializing in public opinion research; the firm made a study of attitudes of people who had been affected by the growth of a large metropolitan airport in the United States.

77. See, especially, Michel J. Crozier, Samuel P. Huntington, and Jojo Watanuki, *The Crisis of Democracy: Report on the Governability of Democracies to the Trilateral Commission,* Triangle Paper, no. 8 (New York: New York University Press, 1975).

78. See, for example, the monthly publication *Freedom at Issue* (New York: Freedom House), and a book by the same publisher: Raymond D. Gastil, *Freedom in the World: Political Rights and Civil Liberties* (1978, 1979).

79. *Quest for Survival: The Role of Law and Foreign Policy* (Cambridge, Mass.: Harvard University Press, 1961), p. 4.

80. *Euroforum* (weekly), European Communities, Directorate General of Information, Brussels, no. 20/78 (May 23, 1978), Annex 2, p. 1.

81. *The Economist* (June 10–16, 1978), pp. 84–85.

82. *The Wall Street Journal* (May 2, 1975).

83. *The Christian Science Monitor* (February 23, 1976).

84. James R. Huntley, *Japanese-Western Relations: Reflections After a Study Visit to Japan,* unpublished monograph (Seattle: The Battelle Memorial Institute, 1975), pp. 25–27.

85. See, for instance, Endel J. Kolde, *Pacific Quest* (Lexington, Mass.: D.C. Heath, 1976).

86. Arthur S. Banks, ed., *Political Handbook of the World: 1977* (New York: McGraw-Hill, 1977), pp. 503–504; "Rich, Poor Nations Build Cooperation Bridge," *Christian Science Monitor* (December 22, 1975), p. 3.

87. *Atlantic Community News* (September 1976).

88. Banks, op. cit., p. 530.

89. *From Many One,* op. cit., p. 114.

90. M.J. Crozier, et al., op. cit., p. 161.

91. Ibid., p. 159.

92. For analyses of the main structural problems of the Atlantic and Atlantic-Pacific Systems, the reader is referred primarily to the publications of three private organizations, some of which have already been cited in this book. These are the Atlantic Institute for International Affairs, 120 rue de Longchamps, Paris 75016; the Trilateral Commission, 345 East 46th Street, New York, New York 10017; and the Atlantic Council of the United States, 1616 "H" Street NW, Washington, D.C. 20006. Similar analyses bearing on this general subject matter, too numerous to mention specifically (except insofar as they have already been cited in this book's footnotes) are published by other organizations, such as the International Institute for Strategic Studies (London) and the various private national institutes which study world affairs (for example, the Council on Foreign Relations [New York] and the Royal Institute of International Affairs [London]).

93. The 1975 summit brought together the United States, Japan, the United Kingdom, Germany, France, and Italy. Canada has participated since 1976. In 1977, the president of the EC Commission was asked to sit in on some of the summit sessions. An even more restricted summit was held in January 1979, by the heads of government of the United Kingdom, France, Germany, and the United States, to consider primarily political and strategic matters.

94. See, especially, *Harmonizing Economic Policy,* op. cit., pp. 16–17, 28, 32–33; Cooper, et al., op. cit., pp. 5 and 41; and "Economic Summit will be held in Bonn," Atlantic Community News (May 1978), p. 3.

95. See *GATT-Plus, A Proposal for Trade Reform,* (Washington: Atlantic Council of the United States, 1975).

96. See, for example, Motoo Kaji, Richard N. Cooper, and Claudio Segré, *Towards a Renovated World Monetary System,* Triangle Papers, no. 1 (New York: The Trilateral Commission, 1973), p. 21. The authors recommended placement of SDRs by a unit called "baricor," and its eventual circulation as a "genuine international currency." See also Robert Solomon, rapporteur, William McChesney Martin, Jr., and Frank A. Southard, Jr., Cochairmen, *The International Monetary System: Progress and Prospects* (Boulder, Colorado: Westview Press, 1977).

APPENDIX A

Concepts and Definitions Related to the Extended Atlantic System

The key words and concepts in this book are:

> System
> Intergovernmental organization (IGO)
> Supranationality
> Federation and Confederation
> Sovereignty
> Functionalism
> Integration
> Community

SYSTEM

In recent years, the "systems" concept has gained increasing attention because it helps in the analysis and explanation of highly complex and interrelated phenomena. The systems approach to problem solving is usually interdisciplinary; its principal inspiration seems to have come from biological or cybernetic analogies. Today, the systems approach is applied to virtually all branches of knowledge—natural sciences, life sciences, engineering and technology, economics, politics, and many other fields as well. There are now experts in "general systems theory" and in "systems analysis" who attempt to train their special methodology on almost any kind of problem that can be characterized by separable parts, interaction between those parts, and dynamic processes at work.

Michael Banks has described *systems analysis* as

merely the more formalised version of clear thinking about complicated problems which education teaches us to use daily; we divide a large problem into sections, concentrate our attention separately and singly on each section in turn or on a group of sections, and as we explain each part to ourselves, rebuild the whole piece by piece in order to reconstruct the phenomenon mentally in a form in which we feel we can understand it.[1]

Systems theory goes further, although there is less consensus as to what exactly it is. Systems theory postulates the existence of a series of abstract systems to which all knowledge can, in theory, be reduced.[2] According to Thomas Robinson, the strength of systems theory in the study of international politics lies

. . . in its ability to permit us to see phenomena in a balanced perspective which is not otherwise obvious. It stresses, for instance, factors of stability as well as instability and this is particularly valuable at a time when the latter set of factors would seem to dominate. It stresses both static-structural features and dynamic growth and decay features. It reminds us that political systems evolve. . . And it places emphasis upon relations with the environment as well as intra-systemic variables operating autonomously. Last, general systems theory frees us, to some extent, from the bonds of traditional categories of analysis; it slices the pie in a different way (in fact, in many different ways) and in so doing it may uncover facts and relationships which may have been hidden by the overlayer of those traditional categories.[3]

Some writers in international politics refer to "the international system"[4] and, for some purposes, such a vast scale may have meaning. But it is also clear that the concept of *an* international system, drastically reduced in size, can be posited. For example, the various continuing ties between two or three individual countries, as in the three-nation Benelux Economic Union, certainly constitute *an* international system. In short, almost any grouping of countries can be regarded as a "system" if the grouping consists of parts which interact with one another on a sustained basis, if it has a recognizable structure, and if it involves processes whereby the system is either sustained or changed.

The *Oxford English Dictionary* defines "system," in part, as:

> a set or assemblage of things connected, associated, or interdependent, so as to form a complex unity; a whole composed of parts in orderly arrangement according to some scheme or plan. . . .[5]

Webster's states:

> SYSTEM may imply that the component units of an aggregate exist and operate in unison or concord according to a coherent plan for smooth functioning.[6]

By employing the noun "system," with the adjective "Atlantic" (or sometimes "Atlantic-Pacific") before it, I mean to characterize a precise group of nations, peoples, and international institutions which are intimately connected with one another; which interact with one another on a sustained basis; which are subject collectively to processes which sustain or change the system; and which are arranged, at any rate to some significant degree, in their grouping according to a general scheme. I could not go so far as *Webster's* definition and suggest that this "Atlantic system" results from a "coherent plan" or that it is invariably or even predominantly "smooth functioning." But that an "Atlantic system" exists, that it is of profound importance to its members, and that today it is in the process of dynamic expansion beyond its original Atlantic confines, should be reasonably clear to the careful observer.

Robinson maintains that systems theory can be used "to slice the pie in different ways." In respect to the *Atlantic System*, this book aims at precisely such varied "slicings of the pie."

INTERGOVERNMENTAL ORGANIZATION (IGO)

One way to slice the pie of the Atlantic System is to consider the interactions of the nation states which are its members. Another is to consider the international institutions which have been established by those members, and to look at how the institutions interact with one another and with their members. The principal institutions with which this book is concerned are those international institutions known as *intergovernmental organizations* (IGOs). According to the United Nations Economic and Social Council, IGOs include any bodies "established by intergovernmental agreement."[7] Banks and Jordan defined an intergovernmental organization as

> an organization whose membership is comprised of more than two states, whose governing body meets with some degree of regularity, and which possesses a permanent secretariat or at least some sort of permanent headquarters arrangement for the collective implementation of collective decisions.[8].

By omission, this last definition recognizes that numerous IGOs represent only intentions on the part of the signatories and either never become active at all or soon lapse into inaction. The large majority of the IGOs to be considered in this book are still active; some, such as the European Payments Union, have been rendered obsolete by events; a few, such as the Balkan Union, were virtually moribund from the start. The surprising thing indeed about the postwar development of IGOs in the Atlantic area is that such a high percentage have prospered and have played significant roles over long periods. The low "drop-out" rate seems to be one distinguishing feature of the IGOs of the Atlantic System, as contrasted with those in other regions.

The most essential point in definition, however, is to distinguish IGOs which are formed by a decision of the governments of states from a host of other international bodies of a nongovernmental character.[9]

Some intergovernmental bodies have elements of "supranationality" that are meant to lift them above and beyond the total control of the governments which created them. It is to this smaller species within the genus "IGO" that we now turn, and to the idea of "supranationality" itself.

SUPRANATIONALITY

The concept of supranationality has come into vogue only since the Second World War and has been used primarily by those seeking to create a form of union between some or all of the western European powers. Whereas a concept such as "federation" (see below) has acquired a fairly concrete and precise meaning, "supranationality" is more difficult to define.

Robert Schuman and others who were instrumental in forming the European Coal and Steel Community (1952), which is generally regarded as the first "supranational" body in Europe, sought to break away from the older model of intergovernmental organizations which depended on the continuing acquiescence of every member state for every action. The avid "pan-Europeans" wanted to introduce organizations which would be more independent of governments and, for example, could make decisions with less than unanimity. The treaties establishing each of the three European Communities (ECSC, EEC, and EURATOM) contained a provision for majority voting in certain cases.

Peter Hay suggests that "supranationalism is a political quality, rather than a power or a right. It does not depend on express stipulation, but follows from powers and functions actually accorded an organization."[10] Hay goes on to list "the criteria of supranationalism":

1. Independence of the organization and of its institutions from the member states. [He points out that this is only a matter of degree as compared with traditional intergovernmental organizations.]

2. . . . . the ability of an organization to bind its member states by majority or weighted majority vote.

3. . . . . the direct binding effect of law emanating from the organization on natural and legal persons in the member states.

4. . . . . a transfer of sovereign powers from the member states to the organization. . . . [This point, says Hay, is hotly disputed by some experts.]

5. . . . . supranationalism depends on the extent of functions, powers, and the jurisdiction attributed to the organization.

6. Finally, supranationalism has been defined in terms of the institutions with which the European Communities have been equipped. [Here, Hay cites especially the judiciary and the parliament of the European Communities, and in particular their jurisdiction and scope, which are considerably greater than such bodies in other international organizations.][11]

The vagueness of the concept of supranationality is evident. Yet, supranationality was an effective device, used in the formative years of the European Communities to indicate the desire of their creators somehow to rise above the limitations of the nation state without going too far. There was a conflict between those zealous Europeans who wished to move quickly to a federation and those, like Jean Monnet and Robert Schuman, who believed in a more pragmatic approach along "supranational" lines. There was also a conflict—and a much more important one—between the pragmatists and the nationalists. In the early years of European integration between 1950 and 1960, Belgium, the Federal Republic of Germany, France, Italy, Luxembourg, and the Netherlands accepted the supranational approach; but when General de Gaulle became President of France, he insisted that supranationalism be played down. His government put forward a set of proposals in 1962 (known as the Fouchet Plan) for a Union of European States, which subsequently was voted down by the other five EC governments. A.H. Robertson describes the division over the Fouchet Plan:

The Coal and Steel Community, Euratom and the Economic Community incorporate an idea of European integration commonly known as "supranational." Their architects believed that the needs of modern Europe cannot be met by intergovernmental conferences where each State has a veto that can block the common interests of its partners; rather it is necessary to set up certain Community institutions, acting in cooperation with the governments, but not subject to their day-to-day control and not requiring their unanimous agreement for every measure taken. . . . The other political philosophy is that attributed to General de Gaulle. . . . This holds that it is only national states and governments which give reality to international actions and that they must preserve their independent characters, their power and their sovereignty; any attempted supranational structure which departs from this principle is said to be vain, illusory and doomed to failure.[12]

The dispute continued until General de Gaulle's resignation in 1969. By that time, a decade later, the earlier enthusiasm for supranationalism seemed to be on the wane as well.

The European Communities were not the only supranational bodies created in the postwar period. The Western European Union treaty, signed in October 1954, brought the Federal Republic of Germany into the European and NATO defense system. At that time, the British government had pledged itself not to reduce the strength of its forces then in Germany "if such action is against the wishes of the majority of its partners." M. Bohy of the Belgian Parliament described the "epoch-making step" of Britain in the debates of the Council of Europe: "It is scarcely possible to overestimate its importance. . . . By taking this 'formidable' decision the United Kingdom turned its back on its traditional policy and threw in its lot with the Continent. The importance of this move lies not only in the commitment to maintain British forces on the Continent but much more in the willingness to accept a majority decision as to the length of time they will be stationed there."[13] A quarter century later, British forces were still in Germany; recently, under the "overseas emergency'' clause of the WEU treaty, units have been withdrawn for service in Northern Ireland, but subsequently returned to Germany.

The Court of Human Rights of the Council of Europe also possesses elements of supranationality. Individuals can and do bring certain kinds of legal actions against their own governments in that tribunal. Most of the postwar Atlantic and European institutions, however, have been the conventional intergovernmental organization. Of the Organization for European Economic Cooperation, Robertson said, for example:

> . . . there was no question of supranational powers or of limitations of sovereignty, except in the restricted sense that the mere fact of participation in an international organisation presupposes obligations (and the willingness to submit to a constant pressure towards conformity), which in practice if not in theory, can hardly be disregarded. In point of fact, the right of veto was hardly ever used and the history of OEEC may be seen as the history of the mutual concessions which the several governments made in order to reach agreement and make progress on problems vital to them all.[14]

Formally, OEEC was not supranational, because each member state retained the right of veto. Yet, Robertson has suggested that, in effect, simply by taking part in the activities of a vital intergovernmental body, all the members abridged their sovereign rights in practical terms. In bodies like OEEC and NATO, there are practical commitments to interdependence of action, but no legal ones. Nevertheless, the members of such bodies undoubtedly are cajoled, pressured, or perhaps even sometimes shamed into taking actions which they would not have taken, had they not been members. Both bodies have also established precedent, in a manner not unlike the growth of the English constitution, and have laid down principles which have affected all other Atlantic and European IGOs. The OEEC, for example, established the principle that members should consult with one another, at least after, if not before, taking sovereign domestic actions which might affect the others.

At the other end of the scale of supranationality are the European Communities. The most "supranationally advanced" of these, in theory if not in practice, is the Coal and Steel Community. In these cases, the treaties that established these organizations were, at least in part, also constitutions of sovereign bodies; the Communities were given the right to exercise some of their own powers.

Federation is a step still further along the scale of supranationalism.

FEDERATION AND CONFEDERATION

Robertson has pointed out the vague border between mere supranationalism and federalism. The essence of the Coal and Steel Community's supranationality was, he says, that "it had the power to give orders that were directly binding on the enterprises concerned [in whatever member country they were located]." But the High Authority of ECSC itself did not have the means of enforcing such decisions. "Indeed, if its powers also included those of enforcement they would have been more in the nature of those of a federal government."[15] So far, all three European Communities have been dependent on the individual constituent governments to see that their supranational judgments and decrees have been carried out or followed. And so far, the governments have faithfully done this, but one can envisage some future "constitutional crisis" in which the weakness of the Communities—the absence of the means of imposing the federal will on the member states—would become all too evident. It is significant that in the cases of Switzerland and the United States, the two most long-lasting federations, civil wars were fought before the power of the federal governments was confirmed.

Andrew Axline[16] has presented some of the other attributes of federations:

1. In a federation, not only states have rights, but individuals and other social groups as well.[17].
2. Federal decisions are binding on the component states and individuals.
3. Decisions are made by majority vote, by representatives

[317]

of the society as a whole, not of component governments.

4. There is usually citizenship common to all individuals within the geographical area of the federation.
5. The federal structure is permanent, and secession is forbidden.
6. The central government is sovereign, having the power as well as the right of ultimate determination of jurisdictional conflicts between it and the local governments.

Implied also in these criteria is the existence of a federal judiciary to judge the validity of federal law. Hay believes that, while the European Communities may not be called a "federation," they "display federal attributes" and that "community law," such as it is, may rightly be termed "federal law."[18]

In a *federation*, the constituent states, while they may (and must, by definition) have their own powers and areas of competence, are not truly independent. In a *confederation*, the member states are clearly sovereign, even though their union may be strong and even considered permanent. Confederations are established by treaty, federations by a "constitutive act." Thus in a confederation, the *states* are the controlling elements. It is they who vote and take decisions, not the constituent *peoples*, as in a federation. Confederations do not, therefore, have direct power over the citizens of the associated states, much less over the states themselves. Member states of a confederation however usually prohibit war between themselves. There is little that is "supranational" about a confederation, although confederations historically have sometimes evolved into federations (as in the case of the United States, Canada, and Germany).

It is interesting that, in January 1971, President Pompidou of France appeared to call for the gradual establishment of a kind of "European confederation."[19] In his mind, this kind of union seemed to represent a tighter organization than that already furnished by the European Communities, although, as we have seen above, the Communities in some respects go beyond confederal power to establish certain federal elements. This suggests that, in the minds of the Gaullists, who have shown extreme reluctance

[318]

to abridge French national prerogatives for the sake of European unity, the creation of a "confederation" might somehow permit them to have their cake and eat it too.

* * *

This discussion has so far pointed out some of the semantic traps lurking in the postwar European political vocabulary. Terms such as "federation" and "supranationalism" have become symbols and slogans for those who want stronger European institutions. It is important to know the various meanings accorded these terms if one is to understand what has been happening by way of institutionalizing the western world. But it is even more important not to be trapped by the terms, and to try to understand the realities.

SOVEREIGNTY

In the debates about moves to unify Europe, as well as in those concerning closer forms of Atlantic political association, the concept of *sovereignty* has usually figured prominently.

Political theorists and legal experts do not agree on the meaning of the term.[20] In the eighteenth century, the theory of federalism was put forward to contradict that of sovereignty. In western democracies, there seems to be a widespread belief today that "all government rests on consent" and that "the people are sovereign." If this is correct, and modern theories of democracy could hardly countenance a contrary idea, then what is at stake in the formation of some close European or Atlantic political union is not the "sovereignty," for example, of France, or Germany, or the United States, but of the French people, the German people, or the American people. Theoretically at least, no people can "lose sovereignty" unless they choose to give all their rights and powers to a dictator. In the postwar debates, however, it was usually the states who were assumed to "lose sovereignty," that is, their autonomy or independence, if they became part of some larger whole.

[319]

The argument, in any case, has become rather academic. No European power, and no longer even the United States, is in a position today to exercise meaningful political or economic power at all times independent of others. In practical terms, regardless of the constitutional modalities, the agreement and mutual support of a rather large number of countries are necessary for the present European-Atlantic system to function well. (One must add that, because the agreement and support are often lacking, the system often does not function well.) The debate about terminology, and most especially that over sovereignty, can thus be seen to be less important than the question of the kind of arrangements and relationships that are necessary to make interdependence work in practical terms.

There are of course times when the legal question, "Who has Sovereignty?" can be extremely important, as, for example, in the U.S. debates and decisions regarding the future of the Panama Canal in 1977 and 1978.

FUNCTIONALISM

The concept of functionalism is important because it underlay much of the thinking of such European "supranationalists" as Jean Monnet. David Mitrany, who is considered the father of functionalism, hypothesized that effective international organization, if it were to overcome political division successfully, could only be achieved by means of a world state, which "would wipe out political divisions forcibly," or by "functionalism," which would

> overlay political divisions with a spreading web of international activities and agencies, in which and through which the interests and life of all the nations would be gradually integrated. That is the fundamental change to which any effective international system must aspire and contribute: to make international government co-extensive with international activities. . . . It must care as much as possible for common needs that are evident, while presuming as little as

possible upon a social unity which is still only latent and un-recognized. . . . In that way the community itself will ac-quire a living body not through a written act of faith but through active organic development. . . . That trend is to organize government along the lines of specific ends and needs, and according to the condition of their time and place, in lieu of the traditional organization on the basis of a set constitutional division of jurisdiction of rights and powers. . . . The functional approach . . . would help the growth of such positive and constructive common work, of common habits and interests, making frontier lines mean-ingless by overlaying them with a natural growth of com-mon activities and common administrative agencies.[21]

Whether following Mitrany consciously or not, much of the recent activity surrounding the institutions created within the western world (including those of the United Nations) has seemed to be a test of his theories. At the least, these theories have had widespread currency in the western world. When, for example, the way seemed blocked to a European political feder-ation, Schuman and Monnet chose a version of the path advo-cated by Professor Mitrany in their proposal of a functional union of a limited sector of European industry, the coal and steel economy of six key nations. In so doing, they went consid-erably beyond Mitrany, however, and laid more emphasis on po-litical forces and institutions, whereas Mitrany had tended to stress the economic and the nongovernmental.

Functionalism and neofunctionalism of course have their de-tractors, some of whom object that the concept does indeed erode national sovereignty. Others, more sympathetic to ideas of greater international integration, object because neofunctional-ism especially tends to put important functions under the control of remote boards and "faceless international bureaucrats," by-passing political controls by the people or their representatives. The European Communities have been open to this charge; di-rect elections of members to the European Parliament (begin-ning in 1979) constitute an important response .

Functionalism, as a process, is of course not confined to intergovernmental activity. Today, it is evident in a great variety of pervasive nongovernmental movements, institutions, and organized activities, such as the multinational enterprise or international exchanges of students, which greatly extend and deepen interstate relations.

The idea that practical cooperation can be organized to leap over national boundaries is nevertheless hopeful and intriguing. In the long run, the theory may have a certain amount of validity. But, in the 30 years since Mitrany first essayed his theories, widespread functional cooperation has failed. This failure, plus continuing regional conflicts and the obvious dangers of general war, suggest that functionalism's broader meaning remains somewhat academic. Nevertheless, within a less-than-universal context, functionalism may have a slightly greater utility, even though the experience of the European Communities suggests that the theory will still take a good deal longer to demonstrate its validity than was originally thought. Perhaps, ultimately, the concept of functionalism is working itself out on a European-Atlantic, and possibly even an Atlantic-Pacific, scale in ways which eventually will lead to effective, if still unpredictable, forms of permanent union.

INTEGRATION

The central concept of *integration* is used to refer to the processes both within a nation or smaller community, of "forming into a more complete, harmonious, or coordinated entity";[22] and among a group of nations, of "coming together . . . into a larger unit or group."[23]

Claude Ake's definition of "integration" is especially useful:

A political system is integrated to the extent that the minimal units (individual political actors) develop in the course of political interaction a pool of commonly accepted norms regarding political behavior and a commitment to the political behavior patterns legitimized by these norms.[24]

Ake has also defined the reverse situation:

> A political system is malintegrated to the extent that political exchanges are not regulated by a normative culture. In malintegrated political systems the emphasis is on effective rather than on legitimate means for pursuing political goals; in highly integrated political systems the emphasis is on legitimate rather than on effective means.[25]

According to Karl Deutsch, integration is the attainment within a territory of a "sense of community" and of institutions and practices strong enough and sufficiently widespread to assure, over a long period, "dependable expectations of peaceful change."[26] He defined "a sense of community" as the belief that common social problems must and can be resolved through peaceful change; this definition implies the resolution of social problems (normally by institutionalized procedures) without resort to large-scale physical violence.

In a systems approach, integration would be defined by the degree to which positive or negative results occurred within the system. Integration, in this sense, is "tightness of feedback."

The foregoing definitions can apply to conditions either within a given society or nation or among a group of states seeking to amalgamate. The relevance of the one situation to the other is that it would be much more difficult to "integrate" a group of nation states into some larger polity (somewhere on the scale from intergovernmental organization to federation) if each participating state were not individually "integrated" within itself. The degree of internal harmony, the coherence and appropriateness (modernity?) of the cultural pattern, the prevalence of commonly accepted political norms, the legitimacy of the national system in the eyes of its people, and the degree to which change is accomplished peacefully are all important determinants of whether or not a state can move effectively, constructively, and in a sustained way on the international stage. For this book, the second kind of integration—the process of gradually combining a number of nation states into a larger grouping (as in the Common Market or NATO), with a corresponding merger of some governmental functions—is more important. This kind of integration should be seen as a process as well as a particular condition.[27] The process is one which involves interaction not only between states, but also between individuals and nongovernmental institutions, across national borders, and particularly with the central institutions of the new intergovernmental grouping. The more the central institutions interact with individuals and nongovernmental groups, the more integrated the international polity tends to become.

International integration is distinguished from international cooperation chiefly by the actual merger of governmental functions. Thus, in the European Communities the tariffs of the member states towards nonmembers are now set by the central institutions rather than by the member nations. In the NATO defense structure, there is now an amalgamated Supreme Command and an "international general staff" that cover western Europe and take the place, at least to some extent, of the former, separate national military establishments.

COMMUNITY

Walter Lippmann is believed to be the first to have used the word *community* to describe a grouping of like-minded countries which shared a certain background and a set of concrete interests. He used this definition when he wrote of an "Atlantic Community," first in 1917 and later in 1943. When Jean Monnet was conceiving the plan for integration of the French and German coal and steel industries in 1950, Carl Friederich Ophüls, a German diplomat, allegedly proposed the title, "European Coal and Steel Community."[28] The term was used again in 1957 as part of the title for the two additional European Communities, and this usage, describing a precise, formal political creation under international law, has since overshadowed the original, looser concept of an "Atlantic Community."

The *Oxford English Dictionary* provides the generic description:

A body of people organized into a political, municipal or social unity. . .[29]

Webster's gives the definition employed by Lippmann:

A body of persons or nations united by historical consciousness or by common social, economic, and political interests. . .

and adds:

. . . participation completely willing and not forced or coerced and without loss of individuality.[30]

The *Supplement to the Oxford English Dictionary* offers the precise meaning of the capitalized word as used in the Treaties of Paris and Rome:

A body of nations acknowledging unity of purpose or common interests (Esp. in the titles of international organizations).[31]

The generic term, "community," appears to be an excellent new word for the vocabulary of international relations. The term carries with it the promise of significant integration, and yet is not as emotion-laden as, for example, is the term, "federation." For various reasons, "community" seems to be a more useful, flexible, and accurate term to describe the most currently advanced form of the integrated international institution. The word is thus likely to appear again in the future, when statesmen seek appropriate terminology for new, different, and closer groupings of nations and peoples.

A SYNTHESIS OF TERMS

The foregoing survey of terminology has sought to establish the lexicological boundaries and foundations for this book's examination of international institution building among the advanced democracies. The most significant term for this study is *intergovernmental organization* (IGO). Through the process of *international integration*, built in part around the theory of *functionalism*, a grouping of developed nation states in Europe, North America, and (more recently) the Far Pacific has engaged since World War II in the construction, to a considerable extent unconscious and unintended, of a reasonably well-functioning, new *international system*. This system, for which it is difficult to find an appropriate name, is characterized by a high degree of sophistication and political ingenuity; shows elements of *supranationality* within many of its component IGOs; and has involved a continuing debate, often irrelevant in real terms, but highly relevant in terms of domestic politics, about *sovereignty*.

Where a pooling of sovereignty (a merging of some governmental functions, the direct participation of the electorate in the affairs of the collectivity, and the conferring on central institutions of some power to enforce their decisions) takes place, a *federation* may be said to exist. However, no intergovernmental institution, within the "Atlantic-Pacific System" or elsewhere, has yet approached actual federation. Rather, these institutions have evolved a concept of *international community* to describe the loose association, or system, which has evolved among themselves.

NOTES

1. "Systems Analysis and the Study of Regions," *International Studies Quarterly*, vol. 13, no. 4 (December 1969), p. 346.

2. Arthur S. Banks, ed., *Political Handbook of the World* (New York: McGraw-Hill, 1978), p. 347.

3. "Systems Theory and the Communist System," op. cit., p. 417.

4. See, for example, James Rosenau, *International Politics and Foreign Policy: A Reader in Research and Theory* (New York: The Free Press, 1961), p. 77. See also, Morton A. Kaplan, *System and Process in International Politics* (New York: John Wiley and Sons, 1957), probably the first large-scale work on world affairs to adopt the systems approach.

5. *The Oxford English Dictionary*, Compact Edition (Oxford: Clarendon Press, 1971), pp. 3213–3214.

6. *Webster's Third New International Dictionary*, p. 2322.

7. United Nations Economic and Social Council, Resolution 288 (X), February 27, 1950.

8. Banks, op. cit., p. xiv.

9. In a few cases (e.g., the International Red Cross or the North Atlantic Assembly/NATO), nongovernmental bodies and governments are so closely bound together in a common activity that is not easy to separate "IGO" from "NGO" with surgical precision. For a guide to both IGOs and NGOs, see E.S. Tew, ed., *Yearbook of International Organizations* (Brussels: Union of International Associations, annual).

10. *Federalism and Supranational Organizations: Patterns for New Legal Structures* (Urbana: University of Illinois Press, 1966), p. 30.

11. Ibid., pp. 31–37.

12. Robertson, A.H., *European Institutions: Cooperation, Integration, Unification* (3rd ed.), (London: Stevens and Sons, Ltd., 1973), pp. 296–297.

13. Ibid., p. 129.

14. Ibid., p. 76.

15. Ibid., pp. 158–159.

16. W. Andrew Axline, *European Community Law and Organizational Development* (Dobbs Ferry, N.Y.: Oceana Publications, 1968), pp. 77–78.

17. In 1976, Belgian Premier Leo Tindemans presented, at the request of the EC Council of Ministers, a detailed report on the future of the EC. Among the many goals he proposed was an emphasis on affecting the man in the street by protecting his fundamental rights. (See *Euroforum* No. 44/76, Brussels [July 12, 1976], p. 3.) In 1978, an EC summit meeting emphasized the importance of democracy and human rights in its communique. The European Court of Justice has also moved steadily in this direction; more and more, Axline's first point is coming to characterize the EC.

18. Peter Hay, *Federalism and Supranational Organizations* (Urbana: University of Illinois Press, 1966).

19. Hay has called the Communities "limited federations" (ibid., p. 89).

20. See, e.g., *International Encyclopaedia of the Social Sciences* (New York: Macmillan, 1968), vol. 15, pp. 77–80.

21. David Mitrany, *A Working Peace System* (4th ed.), (London:

National Peace Council, 1946), pp. 14, 15, 18, 28, 34, 35. To appreciate functionalism in a contemporary context, one should see also neofunctional writings, especially, Ernst Haas, *The Uniting of Europe* (Stanford: Stanford University Press, 1958); and Ernst Haas, *Beyond the Nation-State: Functionalism and International Organization* (Stanford: Stanford University Press, 1964). For other commentaries drawing important distinctions between functionalism and neofunctionalism, see: "The Concept of Community and the European Integration Process," Journal of Common Market Studies (December 1968), pp. 83–101; Louis R. Beres and Harry R. Targ, *Reordering the Planet: Constructing Alternative World Futures* (Boston: Allyn and Bacon, 1974), pp. 101, 127–133.

22. Webster's *Third New International Dictionary*, p. 1174.

23. Ibid., p. 1174.

24. *A Theory of Political Integration* (Homewood, Illinois: Dorsey Press, 1967), p. 3.

25. Ibid., p. 4.

26. Karl W. Deutsch, et al., *Political Community and the North Atlantic Area* (Princeton, N.J.: Princeton University Press, 1957), p. 5.

27. Hay, op. cit., p. 1.

28. Merry and Serge Bromberger, *Jean Monnet and the United States of Europe* (New York: Coward-McCann, 1969) p. 96. Pierre Uri, a close advisor to Monnet at the time, recalls the event differently: "When we prepared, not the working document, but the first draft treaty, Etienne Hirsch introduced the word 'Community,' which I then had to sell to a reluctant Dutch lawyer." (Letter to the author, December 24, 1975.)

29. *Oxford English Dictionary*, vol. 1, p. 486.

30. Webster's *Third New International Dictionary*, p. 460.

31. *Supplement to the Oxford English Dictionary, 1972*, vol. 1, p. 592.

APPENDIX B

Institutional Growth of the Extended Atlantic System, 1947–1978: Charts and Historical Commentary

The six charts in this section, accompanied by commentaries, are meant to show the institutional growth of the nascent community of developed democracies during the three decades beginning in 1947. The charts can be used as a means of determining which countries belonged to which organizations at a given time; as a means of seeing the various organizations of which a given country was a member; or as a way of observing the historical change and growth of the system as a whole.

To fix the pattern of memberships at a given moment in time (usually the end of the year indicated on the chart), countries have been arranged so that the members of the most important institutions, such as NATO and the European Communities, are shown contiguous to one another. In cases of "associate" (less-than-full) membership, the appropriate "boxes" are marked with parallel slanting lines.

COMMENTARY ON CHART 1 (1947)

At the end of 1947, only three countries were bound by regional institutional arrangements in Europe.

France and the United Kingdom, under the *Treaty of Dunkirk* of March 4, 1947, had pledged that each country would "give all the military and other support and assistance in his power" to the other, in the event that it were again engaged in hostilities with Germany. The treaty reflected the bitter experience of the interwar period by also providing for common action if Germany should not fulfill her economic obligations. The treaty further declared its intention "to strengthen the economic relations between the two countries to their mutual advantage and in the interests of general prosperity." These and other clauses of the treaty were reflected later in the Brussels treaty, the Western European Union treaty, and the North Atlantic treaty.

The various *Agreements for the Occupation of Germany* dated back to World War II. They provided for an Allied Control Council, which was to exercise authority for all of Germany, and a special interallied authority for Berlin. On January 1, 1947, the British and Americans merged their zones of occupation for economic purposes and created a German Economic Council for the Bizone, which the French later joined. The year 1947 was characterized by increasing disagreements among the four wartime allies, so that by the end of the year, when the four foreign ministers again met in London, the occupation arrangements had been effectively split between the USSR (and her zone of East Germany) and the three western powers.

Various countries shown on Chart 1 were also members of the United Nations and its various subsidiary bodies. During the early part of the period represented by Chart 1, the newly established (1945) UN and its agencies were very influential in world affairs. Indeed, these universal IGOs overshadowed arrangements shown on Chart 1, in scope and activity. One UN body, the Economic Council for Europe, had to do especially with European affairs; the Council included the United States, Canada, and the USSR among its members.

There were a number of other special-purpose IGOs which are not shown on the chart, but which had either existed prior to the war (for example, the Central Commission for the Navigation of the Rhine [1815]) or had been created just after it and were considered strictly temporary (for example, the European Coal Organization and European Central Inland Transport).

INSTITUTIONAL DEVELOPMENT OF THE EXTENDED ATLANTIC SYSTEM, 1947-78
CHART 1: 1947

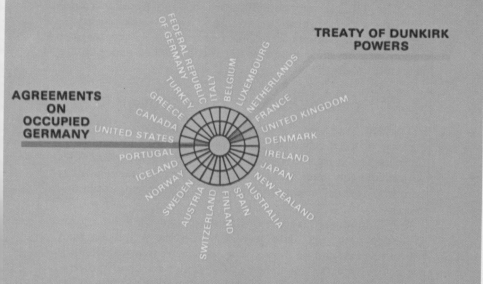

TREATY OF DUNKIRK POWERS

AGREEMENTS ON OCCUPIED GERMANY

FEDERAL REPUBLIC OF GERMANY
TURKEY
GREECE
CANADA
UNITED STATES
PORTUGAL
ICELAND
NORWAY
SWEDEN
AUSTRIA
SWITZERLAND
FINLAND
SPAIN
AUSTRALIA
NEW ZEALAND
JAPAN
IRELAND
DENMARK
UNITED KINGDOM
FRANCE
NETHERLANDS
LUXEMBOURG
BELGIUM
ITALY

Although the initiatives did not result in a new IGO, mention should also be made here of the Truman Doctrine (March 12, 1947), which announced U.S. intentions to "help free peoples resist aggression." Greece and Turkey were the immediate recipients of aid, but on June 5, 1947, Secretary of State George Marshall proposed a massive program of economic support for Europe. Subsequently known as the Marshall Plan, this program was open to the Soviet Union and the states of eastern Europe, as well as those of western Europe. However, the USSR rejected the offer and forced her satellites to follow her lead.

To avoid unnecessary complications, bilateral agreements and institutions are not shown in the charts, with a single exception. The Treaty of Dunkirk is included because of its genealogical importance for the subsequent postwar European and Atlantic defense alliances.

COMMENTARY ON CHART 2 (1949)

On New Year's Day 1948, the *Benelux Economic Union* was formed between Belgium, the Netherlands, and Luxembourg. This union was created to deal with customs and other economic affairs and continues to the present day. Benelux may, in many respects, be considered a forerunner of the European Communities (EC).

The Communist takeover in Czechoslovakia on February 25, 1948, produced great alarm in western Europe. Within less than a month, a new and much more comprehensive treaty of alliance, the Brussels treaty, was signed by five major European powers. The treaty superseded the Treaty of Dunkirk and, unlike the Treaty of Dunkirk, was no longer aimed solely at a resurgent Germany, but at possible, unnamed adversaries. The treaty's stated purposes were also to preserve democracy and to strengthen economic, cultural, and social ties among its partners.

Meanwhile, western Europe had begun to organize itself economically. With the advice and persuasion of the United States, 17 countries signed a convention to establish the *Organization for European Economic Cooperation* (April 16, 1948). OEEC's

INSTITUTIONAL DEVELOPMENT OF THE EXTENDED ATLANTIC SYSTEM, 1947-78
CHART 2: 1949

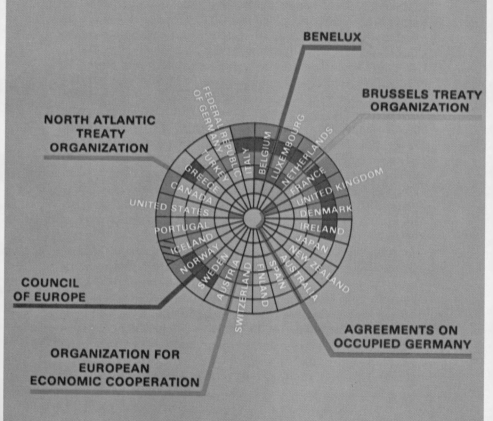

BENELUX

BRUSSELS TREATY ORGANIZATION

NORTH ATLANTIC TREATY ORGANIZATION

COUNCIL OF EUROPE

AGREEMENTS ON OCCUPIED GERMANY

ORGANIZATION FOR EUROPEAN ECONOMIC COOPERATION

FEDERAL REPUBLIC OF GERMANY • TURKEY • GREECE • CANADA • UNITED STATES • PORTUGAL • ICELAND • NORWAY • SWEDEN • AUSTRIA • SWITZERLAND • FINLAND • SPAIN • AUSTRALIA • NEW ZEALAND • JAPAN • IRELAND • DENMARK • UNITED KINGDOM • FRANCE • NETHERLANDS • LUXEMBOURG • BELGIUM • ITALY original purpose was to channel Marshall Plan aid to the European countries, but eventually it took on a far broader range of tasks connected with the integration and strengthening of the European economy.

Although the Brussels treaty powers set up a joint military command to demonstrate their resolve to defend themselves collectively, both the signatories and the United States soon came to believe that the defense of western Europe could not be organized credibly without the participation of the United States. Events in Germany, including the blockade of Berlin beginning in June 1948, underlined the seriousness and urgency of bringing the United States into the European balance. On April 4, 1949, the five Brussels treaty powers, plus the United States, Canada, and five smaller European countries signed the *North Atlantic Treaty*. This treaty eventually led to the creation of a far-flung system of joint military commands, "assigned" and "earmarked" forces, permanent logistical installations and systems known as "infrastructure," and a civilian authority (the North Atlantic Council) to coordinate military and political policies. The institutions of the Alliance became known collectively as "NATO" (North Atlantic Treaty Organization).

In August 1949, the statute of the *Council of Europe* came into force. The creation of such a council had been proposed at the Congress of The Hague in May 1948. The Council of Europe eventually concerned itself with cooperation in a broad range of fields—social, political, environmental, cultural, legal, and technical—although initially many of its supporters had believed that it would play the primary role in bringing about the political unification of Europe.

(Note: This chart shows the situation in September 1949.)

COMMENTARY ON CHART 3 (1955)

Until May 1950, efforts to create a supranational European union by means of the Council of Europe had proved unsuccessful. Britain and the Scandinavian countries had balked at giving up sovereignty; six other members, led by France, determined to

INSTITUTIONAL DEVELOPMENT OF THE EXTENDED ATLANTIC SYSTEM, 1947-78
CHART 3: 1955

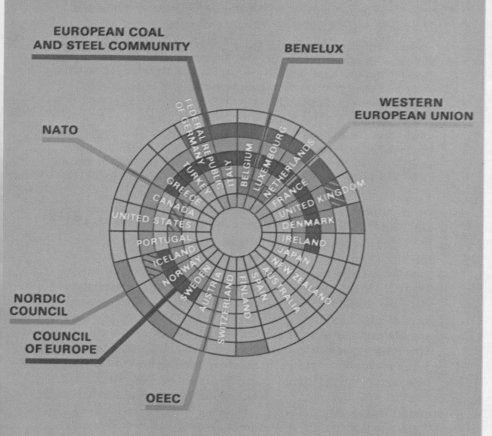

EUROPEAN COAL AND STEEL COMMUNITY

BENELUX

WESTERN EUROPEAN UNION

NATO

NORDIC COUNCIL

COUNCIL OF EUROPE

OEEC

FEDERAL REPUBLIC OF GERMANY — ITALY — BELGIUM — LUXEMBOURG — NETHERLANDS — FRANCE — UNITED KINGDOM — DENMARK — IRELAND — JAPAN — NEW ZEALAND — AUSTRALIA — SPAIN — FINLAND — SWITZERLAND — AUSTRIA — SWEDEN — NORWAY — ICELAND — PORTUGAL — UNITED STATES — CANADA — GREECE — TURKEY

⟨⟨⟨⟨ indicates Associate Membership

© Battelle Memorial Institute 1978

seek closer ties on their own. On May 9, 1950, Robert Schuman, the French foreign minister, proposed a plan for pooling the entire French and German production of coal and steel under a supranational high authority; the plan included provisions for other countries to join. Advocates of a united Europe saw this "Schuman Plan" as a first step towards political unification. The *European Coal and Steel Community* treaty was signed in 1951 by France, West Germany, Italy, and the Benelux countries and entered into force in the following year. Britain signed an association agreement with ECSC in 1954, more as an industrial and trade arrangement, than with any intention of future membership in the Community.

The political development of the ECSC coincided with heightened fears for Europe's security. The invasion of South Korea on June 25, 1950 forced the new NATO Allies to consider Soviet invasion of western Europe as much more likely than heretofore. The United States, especially strained to provide troops for the Korean War, urged that a way be found to rearm West Germany, which was still under ultimate control of the wartime allies. The French responded again by proposing the creation of a unified European Army and Defense Ministry, subject to democratic parliamentary control, within NATO. This initiative culminated in the European Defense Community treaty, signed on May 27, 1952. The statute for a European Political Community was also drafted by the six member nations in the following year. It seemed that "Little Europe" was well on the way to a comprehensive union of federal character. But as the Korean War settled down to a stalemate, the Fench National Assembly began to reconsider the implications of entering into an indissoluble union with the hereditary enemy; the French withdrew their support of EDC and EPC. The two new communities faltered and collapsed.

Despite this setback, it was generally accepted that some way would have to be found to bring Germany into the NATO defense system and to restore her full sovereignty. A series of agreements were therefore undertaken in October 1954. The principal agreement was the decision to transform the earlier Brussels Treaty Organization (see Chart 2) into a *Western European Union*. This move brought the alliance's strength up to seven member nations with the addition of Italy and the Federal Republic of Germany. WEU had broad political and cultural, as well as military, objectives but, unlike EDC, was not supranational. Further protocols brought Germany into NATO (Greece and Turkey had already joined in 1952).

In 1952, Sweden, Denmark, Iceland, and Norway established the *Nordic Council*. Each of the four national parliaments adopted a common "statute" (not a treaty because it was not signed by governments) and, in February 1953, the first session of the Council, composed of MPs from the four member states, met to begin a process of continuous cooperation and consultation. In 1955, the Finnish Riksdag also decided to join the Nordic Council.

In June 1950, Canada and the United States formalized their relationship with OEEC by becoming "associate members." The Federal Republic of Germany had also joined OEEC as a full member in late 1949.

COMMENTARY ON CHART 4 (1958)

Under constant pressure from legislators in the Coal and Steel Community's "common assembly" and fueled by the driving force of Paul-Henri Spaak, the idea of a European Community continued to grow. On March 25, 1957, two treaties were signed by the six members of the ECSC, to establish the *European Economic Community* (EEC) and *European Atomic Energy Community* (EURATOM).

The EEC treaty provided for the progressive establishment among the signatories of a common market that would eventually eliminate all customs duties and other barriers to trade; establish a common external tariff; and enable capital, goods, and labor to circulate freely among the six member nations. The EURATOM agreement envisaged the joint exploitation of nuclear energy for peaceful purposes.

The two new treaties were companions to the 1951 treaty for the Coal and Steel Community; the three organizations were to use many of the same institutions, including a European Court, an Investment Bank, and a European Parliament. In the Preamble to the Treaty of Rome, the signatories stated their intention "to lay the foundations of an ever closer union of the peoples of Europe." On January 1, 1958, the new Communities came into existence and what came to be known as the "Eurocracy" began to establish the common institutions in Brussels. This was a period of hope and enthusiasm among the partisans of a united Europe.

In 1956, Austria was able to join the Council of Europe, a state treaty having freed her from occupation by troops of the four wartime allies and restored her sovereignty.

COMMENTARY ON CHART 5 (1965)

Even before the treaties for the new European Communities entered into force, the British government proposed the creation of a "free trade area" (as defined under the 1947 General Agreement on Tariffs and Trade) that would link the new Common Market with the rest of western Europe. Negotiations along these lines were pursued in OEEC in 1957 and 1958, but were unsuccessful. With the failure of the free trade area project, a group of countries outside of the EC "Six" drew up their own agreement for a *European Free Trade Association* (EFTA), which entered into force in May 1960. The EFTA countries, sometimes known as the "Outer Seven," proceeded to abolish tariffs and other barriers to industrial trade among themselves. Each member, however, maintained its own tariffs, commercial policies, and agricultural protection systems toward countries outside EFTA. At various stages during the ensuing decade, Britain and other EFTA members (notably Denmark and Norway) alternatively used the Association, both in their efforts to join the increasingly successful European Communities and as a means of slowing the EC down. The latter efforts were distinctly unsuccessful, but the former tactics eventually resulted in EC membership for two EFTA countries plus Ireland (see Chart 6). In 1961, Finland became an associate member of EFTA. Full membership remained impossible for Finland, however, because

INSTITUTIONAL DEVELOPMENT OF THE EXTENDED ATLANTIC SYSTEM, 1947-78
CHART 4: 1958

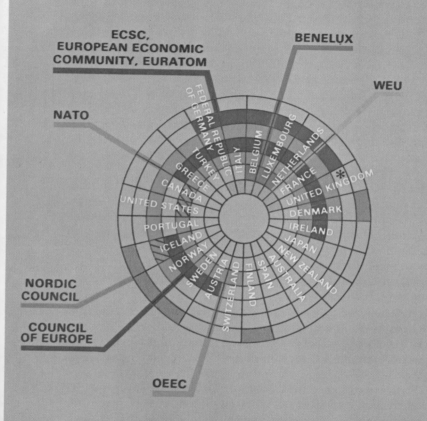

ECSC, EUROPEAN ECONOMIC COMMUNITY, EURATOM

BENELUX

WEU

NATO

FEDERAL REPUBLIC OF GERMANY
TURKEY
GREECE
CANADA
UNITED STATES
PORTUGAL
ICELAND
NORWAY
ITALY
BELGIUM
LUXEMBOURG
NETHERLANDS
FRANCE
UNITED KINGDOM ✱
DENMARK
IRELAND
JAPAN
NEW ZEALAND
AUSTRALIA
SPAIN
FINLAND
AUSTRIA
SWITZERLAND
SWEDEN

NORDIC COUNCIL

COUNCIL OF EUROPE

OEEC

✱ The United Kingdom remained an Associate of ECSC, but not of EEC or EURATOM.

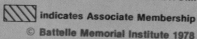 indicates Associate Membership

of her complicated and delicate political and economic relations with the Soviet Union.

By 1960, it had become clear that the advent of the three European Communities plus the development of increasingly close economic ties between Europe and North America called for a general reevaluation of the OEEC. The Organization's original task of supervising Marshall Plan aid had long been completed. OEEC had made good progress in doing away with import quotas, increasing European industrial productivity, and moving toward currency convertibility. But competition between EFTA and the EC and the new international economic problems posed by the developing countries threatened the survival of a purely European OEEC. At the same time, better means of coordination among all the Atlantic powers in monetary affairs, trade matters, and the pursuit of balanced economic growth also clearly seemed to be required. Out of all these needs and concerns, the *Organization for Economic Cooperation and Development* (OECD) was created as the successor to OEEC in 1961. For three more years, the OECD constellation remained "Atlantic" in membership, then spanned the Pacific to include Japan. By 1964, Japan's powerful economic expansion had placed her in the first rank of the world's trading and industrial nations; it was patently impossible to achieve the OECD's aims of economic coordination among the advanced countries without her, and she equally needed OECD.

In 1962, the *European Economic Community* (EEC) began to expand its membership by inviting first Greece (1962), then Turkey (1965) as Associate Members. These agreements looked toward eventual full membership, following lengthy transition periods.

Switzerland joined the *Council of Europe* in 1963. Her accession to the Council was of distinctly minor importance in the "European" or "Atlantic" scheme of things, but of considerable significance to the Swiss, who had clung to their neutral status since 1815. By becoming a full member of the Council of Europe, the Swiss indicated that they now considered themselves full and responsible partners in a European system.

INSTITUTIONAL DEVELOPMENT OF THE EXTENDED ATLANTIC SYSTEM, 1947-78
CHART 5: 1965

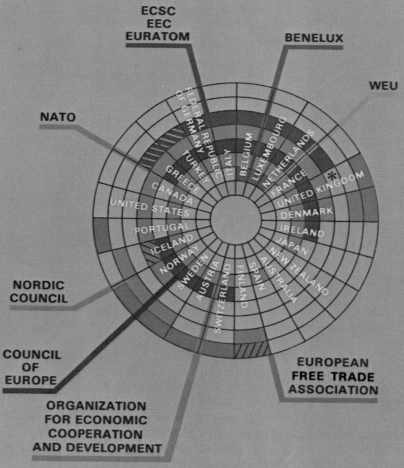

ECSC
EEC
EURATOM

BENELUX

WEU

NATO

NORDIC COUNCIL

COUNCIL OF EUROPE

ORGANIZATION FOR ECONOMIC COOPERATION AND DEVELOPMENT

EUROPEAN FREE TRADE ASSOCIATION

FEDERAL REPUBLIC OF GERMANY · ITALY · BELGIUM · LUXEMBOURG · NETHERLANDS · FRANCE · UNITED KINGDOM · DENMARK · IRELAND · JAPAN · NEW ZEALAND · AUSTRALIA · SPAIN · FINLAND · SWITZERLAND · AUSTRIA · SWEDEN · NORWAY · ICELAND · PORTUGAL · UNITED STATES · CANADA · GREECE · TURKEY

* The United Kingdom remained an Associate of ECSC, but not of EEC or EURATOM.

⧄ indicates Associate Membership

© Battelle Memorial Institute 1978

During this same period, Spain had also inched towards participation in the European-Atlantic institutional complex. She was accepted as a full member of OEEC in July 1959 and would have liked to join NATO and the European Communities, but the nature of her political regime made her unacceptable at that time to those organizations.

COMMENTARY ON CHART 6 (1975)

NATO suffered a particularly serious crisis in March 1966, when President de Gaulle made it clear that although his country would stand by the commitments of the North Atlantic Treaty, as he interpreted them, he did not view the numerous organizational engagements undertaken since 1949 to provide a joint military structure of ready forces as part of the commitments implied by the treaty. As a result, NATO military and political headquarters, as well as other NATO activities, were moved from France, to Belgium and the Netherlands. France continued to participate in the North Atlantic Council's deliberations and in various other civilian activities of the Alliance. After President de Gaulle's retirement, and particularly after the death of his successor, President Pompidou, France quietly and informally returned to the military counsels of the Alliance, although she did not resume full membership, which seemed out of the question politically. (To take account of this situation, France's membership in NATO is shown in Chart 6 as only partial.)

Following the Cyprus crisis in 1974 and the restoration of parliamentary democracy in Greece, relations between Greece and Turkey worsened. As NATO seemed unable to help the Greek cause in Cyprus effectively, Greece also announced its intention to withdraw from the Alliance's integrated military structure. Greece had resigned from the Council of Europe in 1969, after her return to a nondemocratic form of government in 1967. Upon the restoration of constitutional rule in 1974, she was welcomed back to the Council; and, in 1976, Greece joined the International Energy Agency. Portugal and Spain also joined the Council of Europe, in 1976 and 1977, respectively.

The most dramatic change in the decade between 1965 and

INSTITUTIONAL DEVELOPMENT OF THE EXTENDED ATLANTIC SYSTEM, 1947-78
CHART 6: 1978

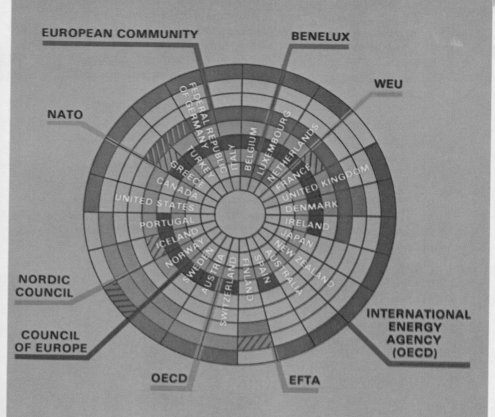

EUROPEAN COMMUNITY

BENELUX

WEU

NATO

NORDIC COUNCIL

COUNCIL OF EUROPE

OECD

EFTA

INTERNATIONAL ENERGY AGENCY (OECD)

FEDERAL REPUBLIC OF GERMANY · TURKEY · GREECE · CANADA · UNITED STATES · PORTUGAL · ICELAND · NORWAY · SWEDEN · AUSTRIA · SWITZERLAND · FINLAND · SPAIN · AUSTRALIA · NEW ZEALAND · JAPAN · IRELAND · DENMARK · UNITED KINGDOM · FRANCE · NETHERLANDS · LUXEMBOURG · BELGIUM · ITALY

1976 was the accession of the United Kingdom, Denmark, and Ireland to the three European Communities in 1973. Meanwhile, in 1967, the three original European Communities had been fused into one—the EC. The "Pacific" character of OECD was furthered when Australia and New Zealand joined in 1971 and 1973, respectively. Finland also became a full member, in 1969. EFTA meanwhile underwent a considerable change when two of its members, the United Kingdom and Denmark, left to join the EC. The seven remaining EFTA members (Iceland had joined EFTA in 1970) concluded an agreement with the European Communities providing for free trade in industrial products among the 16 members of both bodies. Israel concluded a substantially equivalent free trade agreement with the EC in 1975.

The most recent organization to be created within the System was the *International Energy Agency* (1974). Most, but not all, of the OECD members joined the IEA.

Although by 1978 no institutions had developed out of the Economic Summit, first held at Rambouillet, France, in November 1975, this "summit" might yet become a distinct organization—a kind of "steering committee" for the entire grouping of 20 or so developed democracies. (Because the Economic Summit has not developed institutions, it is not included in Chart 6.)

APPENDIX C

Major Intergovernmental and Supranational Organizations Created Between 1947 and 1978 Within the Extended Atlantic System: Basic Data

At the end of the organizational entries which follow, one or more sources are cited to indicate the location of the text of the relevant treaty or treaties. The code for these sources is:

- *Grenville* (J.A.S. Grenville, *The Major International Treaties: A History and Guide with Texts* [London: Methuen & Co., Ltd., 1974]).
- *Robertson* (A.H. Robertson, *European Institutions: Cooperation, Integration, Unification* [3rd ed.], [London: Stevens & Sons, Ltd., 1973]).
- *Lawson* (Ruth C. Lawson, *International Regional Organizations: Constitutional Foundations* [New York, Frederick A. Praeger, 1962]).

In most cases, these commentaries contain edited versions of the text; complete texts are available in the official versions of the treaties.

The membership figure at the end of each title line indicates the number of members in 1978, or at the point of transformation or dormancy of the organization. In each case, the first date shown following the title of the organization is the date when the treaty first entered into force; the second date is that of treaty— or other instrument—signature.

INSTITUTION BUILDING IN THE ATLANTIC/PACIFIC AREA: 1947–1978

1947
Agreements for the Occupation of Germany (3 members)
These various councils, committees, and authorities pursuant to the occupation of Germany were derived from the treaties and agreements that had been made by the three (and later four) wartime allies during the Second World War. By 1947, Britain, France, and the United States had broken with the USSR over the joint administration of Germany and were progressively unifying their occupation zones.

Anglo-French Treaty of Alliance and Mutual Assistance; March 4, 1947 (2 members)
In the Treaty of Dunkirk, Britain and France pledged to join together to resist any revival of German aggression and to consult regularly on matters concerning mutual economic relations, in order to promote prosperity and economic security.

Initial members: France, the United Kingdom

Text: Grenville, 398

1948
Benelux Economic Union; Benelux; January 1, 1948/Hague Protocol, March 14, 1947 (3 members)
Based on a preliminary wartime agreement (London, 1944), the Hague Protocol marked the de facto establishment of

Benelux with the creation of a customs union that possessed a common external tariff and provisions for the eventual harmonization of economic, financial, and social relations. The economic union was accorded de jure status by treaty in 1958.

Seat: Brussels

Initial Members: Belgium, Luxembourg, the Netherlands

Texts: Lawson, 173; Robertson, 454

Treaty of Economic, Social, and Cultural Collaboration and Collective Self-Defense; Brussels Treaty Organization; August 25, 1948/March 17, 1948 (5 members)
The aims of the treaty were to organize a system of automatic mutual assistance in the event of "an armed attack in Europe" and to promote economic, social, and cultural cooperation among member countries. The Brussels Treaty Organization represented an extension of the Treaty of Dunkirk to the Benelux countries, with the Soviet Union replacing Germany as the feared aggressor. In 1955, the Brussels Treaty Organization was transformed into the Western European Union (WEU).

Seat: London

Initial Members: Belgium, France, Luxembourg, the Netherlands, the United Kingdom

Text: Lawson, 149; Robertson, 332; Grenville, 399

Organization for European Economic Cooperation; OEEC; April 16, 1948/April 16, 1948 (18 full members; 3 associate or special status members)
The OEEC was established in order to facilitate the distri-

bution of Marshall Plan aid. Restoration and modernization of the war-ravaged economies of the European member countries were its initial concerns, but its goals became more general as the OEEC assumed the function of providing the chief intergovernmental framework for North Atlantic economic coordination. By the early fifties, the OEEC was aiming at increasing production, eliminating trade barriers, controlling inflation, promoting economic cooperation, and restoring balance-of-payments positions among its member countries. The OEEC developed a number of important subsidiary agencies, including the *European Payments Union* and the *European Productivity Agency*. In 1961, the OEEC was transformed into the Organization for Economic Cooperation and Development (OECD).

Seat: Paris

Initial Members: Austria, Belgium, Denmark, France, Greece, Iceland, Ireland, Italy, Luxembourg, the Netherlands, Norway, Portugal, Sweden, Switzerland, Turkey, the United Kingdom

Accessions: The Federal Republic of Germany (October 1949), Canada and the United States as associates (June 1950), Spain (July 1959)

Special status: Yugoslavia (1958)

Text: Robertson; *European Yearbook* (1st edition), Council of Europe (The Hague: Martinus Nijhoff, 1955), pp. 231–257.

1949
Council of Europe; August 3, 1949/May 5, 1949 (20 members)
The origins of the Council of Europe can be traced to the European thrust of the nongovernmental Congress of Europe held in The Hague in May 1948. The Council of Eu-

rope's democratic orientation accented the worth and dignity of the individual and has specific application in determining membership to the Council. The Council promotes cooperation among members to improve education, social services, public health, the protection of consumers, the safeguarding of the urban and natural environments, and the harmonization of law throughout Europe.

Most members of the Council also adhere to the Convention and Protocol for the Protection of Human Rights and Fundamental Freedoms. These documents provide a Commission and a Court of Human Rights that go far toward ensuring the international protection of essential political, economic, and social rights. The Court is the first international judiciary to which individuals can appeal for judgments against their own or other nation states.

Seat: Strasbourg

Initial Members: Belgium, Denmark, France, Ireland, Italy, Luxembourg, the Netherlands, Norway, Sweden, the United Kingdom

Accessions: Greece (1949), Iceland and Turkey (1950), Saar (1950), the Federal Republic of Germany (1950), Austria (1956), Switzerland (1960 as observer; 1963 as member), Cyprus (1961), Malta (1965), Portugal (1976), Spain (1977)

Deaccessions: Saar (1955, on referundum to join the Federal Republic of Germany), Greece (1969)

Reaccessions: Greece (1974)

Text: Robertson, 310; Lawson, 22; Grenville, 401

North Atlantic Treaty Organization; NATO; August 24, 1949/ April 4, 1949 (15 members)

The chief purpose of the NATO alliance is the joint collective defense and preservation of peace and security in western Europe and North America. Member countries also cooperate on political, economic, scientific, and environmental matters. NATO has an extensive common defense system, including international military headquarters that are permanently established in Europe.

Seat: Brussels (until 1967, Paris)

Initial Members: Belgium, Canada, Denmark, France, Iceland, Italy, Luxembourg, the Netherlands, Norway, Portugal, the United Kingdom, the United States

Accessions: Greece and Turkey (1952), the Federal Republic of Germany (1955)

Withdrawal from participation in the joint military institutions: France (1966), Greece (1974). (Note: Iceland has no armed forces, and it is thus in substantially the same position as France and Greece.)

Text: Grenville, 335; Robertson, 328; Lawson, 3

1952
European Coal and Steel Community; ECSC; July 25, 1952/ April 18, 1951 (6 full members; 1 associate member)
Robert Schuman proposed ECSC as the first step toward a united E rope. The treaty established a common market for coal, steel, iron ore, and scrap in the six member countries. All internal tariffs, quotas, and similar barriers to trade in these products were to be abolished. ECSC was given the power to tax industrial firms in member countries and to exercise other forms of authority new to international institutions. In 1967, ECSC was fused with the European Economic Community and EURATOM to form the European Communities (EC).

Seat: Brussels (until 1958, Luxembourg)

Initial Members: Belgium, France, the Federal Republic of Germany, Italy, Luxembourg, the Netherlands

Association: The United Kingdom (1954)

Text: Robertson, 339; Grenville, 405; Lawson, 62

Nordic Council; March 1952 (Common Statutes adopted by four parliaments)/first meeting, February 1953, treaty basis established, 1962 (5 members)
The main purpose of the Nordic Council was to provide among the legislatures and governments of member countries a forum for consultation on matters of common interest and on issues involving joint action. The Council has dealt with a wide range of economic, social, cultural, and legal activities and legislation.

Seat: Regional secretariats in each of the five members' capitals

Initial Members: Denmark, Iceland, Norway, Sweden

Accessions: Finland (1955)

Text: Lawson, 197; Robertson, 469

1955
Western European Union; WEU; May 6, 1955/October 23, 1954 (7 members)
By protocol to the Brussels treaty of 1948 (see above), the Brussels Treaty Organization (BTO) was transformed into the Western European Union (WEU) in 1955. At the same time, the Federal Republic of Germany and Italy joined the BTO powers in forming the "new" organization. The pur-

poses of the WEU remained essentially the same as those of the BTO: mutual assistance in the defense/security field and general cooperation in economic, social, and cultural matters. Originally, the treaty was also conceived as a means of "controlling" and limiting German rearmament. Between 1963, when the French first vetoed British membership in the European Economic Community, and 1973, when the United Kingdom finally joined all three European Communities, the WEU also served as the main forum for regular political consultation and exchange of views on the European economic situation between EEC countries and the United Kingdom.

Seat: London

Initial Members: Belgium, France, the Federal Republic of Germany, Italy, Luxembourg, the Netherlands, the United Kingdom

Text: Lawson, 149; Robertson, 335

1958
European Economic Community; EEC; January 1, 1958/ March 25, 1957 (6 full members; 2 associate members)
The EEC (popularly, the "Common Market") was formed with the objective of creating a general economic union among member countries by the gradual elimination of all restrictions on trade among them; the imposition of a common external tariff; the elimination of restrictions on the movement of workers, professional people, services, and capital; the formulation and implementation of common rules of competition and common policies for agriculture, transport, and external trade; and the harmonization and coordination of general economic, monetary, fiscal, and social policies. In 1967, the EEC was fused with ECSC and EURATOM to form the European Communities (EC).

Seat: Brussels

Initial Members: Belgium, France, the Federal Republic of Germany, Italy, Luxembourg, the Netherlands

Associate Members: Greece (Treaty, July 1961; in effect, November 1962), Turkey (Treaty, 1963; in effect, 1965)

Text: Grenville, 412; Robertson, 353; Lawson, 109

European Atomic Energy Community; EURATOM; January 1, 1958/March 25, 1957 (6 members)
EURATOM was formed to begin a common effort in developing nuclear power for peaceful purposes and involved cooperation in research and development, in the creation of nuclear power plants, and in other applications of nuclear energy. In 1967, EURATOM was fused with the EEC and the ECSC to form the European Communities (EC).

Seat: Brussels

Initial Members: Belgium, France, the Federal Republic of Germany, Italy, Luxembourg, the Netherlands

Text: *European Yearbook*, vol. V, 455

1960
European Free Trade Association; EFTA; May 3, 1960/ January 4, 1960 (6 full members; 1 associate member)
EFTA had two initial objectives: (1) to establish, by annual steps, free trade in industrial products among member countries and to promote trade in agricultural goods among them; and (2) to make western Europe a single market for industrial goods through agreements on such trade with the Common Market. The first goal was substantially achieved

by 1970. In 1973, EFTA entered an industrial free trade arrangement with the EC.

Seat: Geneva

Initial Members: Austria, Denmark, Norway, Portugal, Sweden, Switzerland, the United Kingdom; also extended to Liechtenstein, by virtue of its economic union with Switzerland.

Accessions: Finland (1961 as associate member), Iceland (1970)

Deaccessions: Denmark, the United Kingdom (1973, upon joining the European Communities)

Text: Robertson, 384; Grenville, 428

1961
Organization for Economic Cooperation and Development; OECD; September 30, 1961/December 14, 1960 (24 full members; 1 special status member)
In 1961, the OEEC was transformed into the OECD; Canada and the United States moved from associate to full membership status at this time. The OECD has continued to emphasize the OEEC's economic concerns and serves as the framework for the non-Communist industrial world's economic relations. The OECD promotes common policies contributing to the expansion of world trade, high economic growth, improvements in the standard of living and quality of life in member countries, and monetary stability. The organization is also concerned with assistance to less-developed countries through its Development Assistance Committee (D.A.C.). More recently, the OECD sponsored the creation of the new *International Energy Agency*.

Seat: Paris

Initial Members: Austria, Belgium, Canada, Denmark, France, Federal Republic of Germany, Greece, Iceland, Ireland, Italy, Luxembourg, the Netherlands, Norway, Portugal, Spain, Sweden, Switzerland, Turkey, the United Kingdom, the United States

Accessions: Japan (1964), Finland (1969), Australia (1971), New Zealand (1973)

Special Status: Yugoslavia

Text: Lawson, 11; Robertson, 322

1967
European Communities; EC; July 1967 (9 full members; 2 associate members)
In July 1967, the ECSC, EEC, and EURATOM were fused into a single organization, the European Communities; the EC now share the same institutional structure (Council, Commission, Parliament, Court).

Seat: Brussels (the Parliament's official seat is Strasbourg; the Court's, Luxembourg)

Initial Members: Belgium, France, the Federal Republic of Germany, Italy, Luxembourg, the Netherlands

Accessions: Denmark, Ireland, the United Kingdom (January 1973)

Associate Members: Greece and Turkey

Text: *European Yearbook*, vol. XIII, 461

1974

International Energy Agency; IEA; November 1974 (19 full members; 1 associate member)

The IEA was established by a decision of the Council of OECD in November 1974. Its aims were to develop a common level of emergency oil supplies plus common demand-restraint measures and measures for the allocation of available oil in time of emergency; to develop an information system covering the international oil market; to develop and implement long-term cooperation to reduce dependence on imported oil; and to promote cooperative relations with oil-producing countries and with other oil-consuming countries. The IEA is autonomous, but closely linked with OECD.

Seat: Paris

Initial Members: Austria, Belgium, Canada, Denmark, the Federal Republic of Germany, Ireland, Italy, Japan, Luxembourg, the Netherlands, Spain, Sweden, Switzerland, Turkey, the United Kingdom, the United States

Accessions: New Zealand (1975), Norway (1975, as associate member), Greece (1976), Australia (1979)

Text: *Legislation on the International Energy Agency*, hearing before the Subcommittees on International Resources, Food, and Energy of the Committee on International Relations, House of Representatives, 94th Congress, March 26, 1975 (Washington, D.C.: U.S. Government Printing Office, 1975), pp. 56–78.

APPENDIX D

Minor and Technical Intergovernmental Organizations Within the Extended Atlantic System*

I. ORGANIZATIONS RESTRICTED TO EUROPE

Central Commission for the Navigation of the Rhine, 1815**

Created originally by the Congress of Vienna; revised 1831, 1868, 1919, and 1963. To preserve freedom and security of navigation and equal treatment for all countries and to suppress hindrances to trade on the Rhine. Oldest IGO in the world.

Members (5): Belgium, France, the Federal Republic of Germany, the Netherlands, Switzerland

Seat: Strasbourg

International Commission on Civil Status (CIEC), 1950
Promotes treaties, does research, and acts as clearinghouse on questions of civil status and rights of individuals.

* As of 1977.
** In each case, this date is the year in which the treaty entered into force.

[357]

Members (10): Austria, Belgium, the Federal Republic of Germany, France, Greece, Italy, Luxembourg, the Netherlands, Switzerland, Turkey

Seat: The Hague

European Organization for Nuclear Research (CERN), 1954
Carries out pure research in nuclear physics in entirely nonmilitary fields. Built two cyclotrons of great power for research on high-energy particles.

Members (12): Austria, Belgium, Denmark, France, the Federal Republic of Germany, Greece, Italy, the Netherlands, Norway, Sweden, Switzerland, the United Kingdom

Observers: Poland, Turkey, Yugoslavia

Seat: Geneva

European Conference of Ministers of Transport (ECMT), 1955
Works for maximum use and the most rational development of European inland transport; coordinates activities of international organizations concerned. In 1956, created agency EUROFIMA to build standard, interchangeable freight cars. Planned a system of European trunk roads; set up European Highway Code; standardized traffic rules, road signs, signals.

Members (17): Austria, Belgium, Denmark, France, the Federal Republic of Germany, Greece, Ireland, Italy, Luxembourg, the Netherlands, Norway, Portugal, Sweden, Switzerland, Turkey, the United Kingdom, Yugoslavia

Observer: The United States

Seat: Paris

European Civil Aviation Conference (ECAC), 1955

Meets bienially to discuss operations across the North Atlantic and charter flights, airport controls, and airline schedules in Europe.

Members (18): Austria, Belgium, Denmark, France, the Federal Republic of Germany, Greece, Iceland, Ireland, Italy, Luxembourg, the Netherlands, Norway, Portugal, Spain, Sweden, Switzerland, Turkey, the United Kingdom

Observers: Canada, Egypt, Israel, Japan, Lebanon, Liberia, Mexico, the United States, Yugoslavia

Seat: Strasbourg

European Conference of Posts and Telecommunications (ECPT), 1959

Aims at harmonizing and improving the administrative and technical services of member states' postal departments. Has repeatedly arranged for issues of "European" stamps, with common design on a European theme.

Members (26): All members of the Council of Europe, plus Finland, Lichtenstein, Monaco, the Holy See, San Marino, Yugoslavia

European Company for the Chemical Processing of Irradiated Fuels (EUROCHEMIC), 1959

Carries out research on irradiated fuels; operates an international plant for processing irradiated fuel elements from nuclear reactors of member nations and recovering unused uranium.

Members (13): Austria, Belgium, Denmark, France, the Federal Republic of Germany, Italy, the Netherlands, Norway, Portugal, Spain, Sweden, Switzerland, Turkey

Seat: Mol (Belgium)

International Commission for the Protection of the Moselle River Against Pollution, 1962
Powers include fixing tolls on international section of Moselle River. Commission created following international program of canalization of the Moselle River.

Members (3): France, the Federal Republic of Germany, Luxembourg.

European Organization for the Safety of Air Navigation (EUROCONTROL), 1963
Provides air traffic control services, including training of air traffic control personnel, for upper airspace of member states; studies air navigation systems.

Members (7): Belgium, France, the Federal Republic of Germany, Ireland, Luxembourg, the Netherlands, the United Kingdom

Seat: Brussels

International Commission for the Protection of the Rhine Against Pollution, 1965
Carries out research to determine nature, quantity, and origin of pollution in the Rhine; submits proposals to members; works out details of programs.

Members (5): France, the Federal Republic of Germany, the Netherlands, Switzerland

Seat: Koblenz

European Molecular Biology Conference (EMBC), 1968
Organizes cooperation between European states for basic research in molecular biology and allied fields; provides fellowships; arranges courses; etc.

Members (14): Austria, Belgium, Denmark, France, the Federal Republic of Germany, Greece, Israel, Italy, the Netherlands, Norway, Spain, Sweden, Switzerland, the United Kingdom

Seat: Cambridge

European Space Agency (ESA), 1975
Aims at insuring effective, rational, and peaceful use of Europe's scientific, industrial, and technological resources for space research. ESA is the product of a merger of two earlier agencies, the European Launcher Development Organization (ELDO) and the European Space Research Organization (ESRO), and represents the culmination of persistent efforts by the Consultative Assembly of the Council of Europe to establish a single European space organization. ESA has agreed on a joint post-Apollo space program with the United States, to involve European construction of Spacelab.

Members (11): Belgium, Denmark, France, the Federal Republic of Germany, Ireland, Italy, the Netherlands, Spain Sweden, Switzerland, the United Kingdom

Seat: Paris

Independent European Program Group (IEPG), 1976
Agency for coordination of weapons production and procurement among European members of NATO. Goals include rationalization of the European arms industry, mitigation of European dependence on U.S. armaments, and increased sale of European weapons to the United States. Operates independently of NATO.

Members (11): Belgium, Denmark, the Federal Republic of Germany, France, Greece, Italy, Luxembourg, the Netherlands, Norway, Turkey, and the United Kingdom

Seat: Rotates (varies, depending on which country holds the annual chairmanship)

II. MINOR ATLANTIC ORGANIZATIONS

North Atlantic Assembly (NAA), 1955

The Canadian NATO Parliamentary Association, with the agreement of the Secretary General and Permanent Council of NATO, invited the presidents and speakers of parliaments in all NATO countries to send delegates to a conference of members of Parliament from the NATO countries; annual sessions have since been held. A secretariat was formed, along with substantive committees. The Secretary General of NATO gives a report to the Assembly each year; the Assembly's recommendations are passed to the Secretary General, who presents them to the North Atlantic Council; the reactions of the Council are then transmitted to the Assembly. By this means, an element of "accountability," however unofficial and informal (for NAA has no status under treaty), has been introduced. Although under Belgian law NAA has the status of an international organization, technically speaking, NAA is not an intergovernmental organization. Yet, it is undoubtedly "interparliamentary"; its funds derive, through parliaments, from governments; and it has acquired a semiofficial relationship with NATO organs established under the Treaty of Washington.

Members (15): Parliaments of Belgium, Canada, Denmark, France, the Federal Republic of Germany, Greece, Iceland, Italy, Luxembourg, the Netherlands, Norway, Portugal, Turkey, the United Kingdom, the United States

Seat: Brussels

III. MINOR ATLANTIC-PACIFIC ORGANIZATIONS

Tripartite Security Treaty (ANZUS), 1952

Mutual defense agreement of Australia, New Zealand, and

the United States. Pledges that an armed attack against any party to the treaty will be met by the other signatories "in accordance with [their] constitutional processes." The AN-ZUS Council, set up under the treaty, meets annually, chiefly for political consultation.

Seat: Rotates

Bank for International Settlements (BIS), 1930
Created after World War I to manage German reparations payments and to function as a "central bankers' central bank." Acquired importance again in the 1950s as an agent for OEEC and ECSC; later, as venue for meetings of central bank governors of major western nations and Japan. Manages currency "swap" arrangements.

Members (30): Albania, Australia, Austria, Belgium, Bulgaria, Canada, Czechoslovakia, Denmark, Finland, France, the Federal Republic of Germany, Greece, Hungary, Iceland, Ireland, Italy, Japan, the Netherlands, Norway, Poland, Portugal, Romania, South Africa, Spain, Sweden, Switzerland, Turkey, the United Kingdom, the United States (U.S. shareholders are a group of commercial banks), Yugoslavia

(Control is vested in a board composed of heads of central banks of Belgium, France, Germany, Italy, the Netherlands, Sweden, Switzerland, and the United Kingdom, plus five members nominated by certain of these.)

Seat: Basel

Group of Ten, 1962
Established as a by-product of the general Agreements to Borrow (GAB) under the International Monetary Fund. Highly informal group, but one of the main underpinnings of the Atlantic-Pacific monetary system. Approves loan re-

quests under GAB; discusses policy and structure of the international monetary system.

Members (10): Belgium, Canada, France, the Federal Republic of Germany, Italy, Japan, the Netherlands, Sweden, the United Kingdom, the United States

Seat: Paris

International North Pacific Fisheries Commission (INPFC),
1953
Aims at conservation of fisheries resources of the North Pacific Ocean; tries to insure maximum sustained productivity of the ocean's resources; conducts surveys of fishery resources.

Members (3): Canada, Japan, the United States

Seat: Vancouver, B.C., (Canada)

Nuclear Energy Agency (NEA), 1957
Aims at fostering the use of nuclear energy for peaceful purposes. Undertakes economic and technical analyses of long-term role of nuclear energy. NEA's activities in many ways parallel those of EURATOM. Invoked a special convention in 1957 to establish a European Company (EURO-CHEMIC) to process irradiated fuels. Also set up the Dragon High-Temperature Reactor Project (1959) to develop fuels for power reactors.

Members (23): Australia, Austria, Belgium, Canada, Denmark, Finland, France, the Federal Republic of Germany, Greece, Iceland, Ireland, Italy, Japan, Luxembourg, the Netherlands, Norway, Portugal, Spain, Sweden, Switzerland, Turkey, the United Kingdom, the United States

Seat: Paris

IV. BILATERAL INSTITUTIONS OF SPECIAL IMPORT

British-Portuguese Alliance, 1386
By the Treaty of Windsor, England and Portugal became permanently allied, an arrangement which has remained in force until the present day. This treaty was preceded by a commercial treaty in 1294 between the two countries.

Belgium-Luxembourg Economic Union (BLEU), 1921
Following World War I, BLEU established a customs union and tied Luxembourg's currency to the Belgian franc; continued until 1940; replaced after the Second World War by Benelux.

International Joint Commission, 1909
Created by Canada and the United States as a mixed group of both nationalities to mediate and adjudicate in disputes between the two countries. Many of the cases with which it has dealt have involved water and power rights. There is also a separate *International Boundary Commission* (1925) to attend to matters having precisely, and only, to do with the common frontiers.

U.S.-U.K. Special Relationship, 1940?–1956?
Essentially loose, but very real intergovernmental relationships growing out of World War II ties; affected diplomacy, intelligence, and the military in vital ways. The U.S.-U.K. Standardization Board (for military equipment) was a formally constituted body that developed out of this relationship (1946–1947). Although many of the links were broken or attenuated after the Suez Crisis in 1956 and the advent of the European Communities, much of the psychological essence and the practical import of the relationship remains.

U.S.-Canadian Permanent Joint Defense Board, 1940
Created During World War II, but before U.S. entry, to effect joint planning between Canadian and U.S. general

staffs for the defense of North America. Renewed in 1947, agreement has led to special joint commands, such as NORAD, for combined air defense. A precursor of NATO, and a means of reinforcement of the treaty.

Treaty of Mutual Cooperation and Security between the United States and Japan, 1960

Replaced 1951 Security Treaty; language in many respects echoes the North Atlantic Treaty (for example, pledges the parties to "strengthen their free institutions" and "seek to eliminate conflict in their international economic policies"). Renewed in 1970.

Franco-German Treaty of Cooperation, 1963

Further strengthened relations between the two countries; provided for regular consultations between the two heads of government and other ministers on questions of defense, foreign policy, and cultural policy. A massive program of exchange of persons between the two countries was set up under the treaty. In many ways a positive force, but also divisive, in that it probably rendered more difficult Britain's eventual accession to the European Communities and set up a closer relationship between France and Germany than the other EC partners enjoyed.

IV. MORIBUND OR DEFUNCT ORGANIZATIONS

European Payments Union (EPU), 1950

Not a separate organization, but a specialized organ in the general framework of OEEC; major decisions undertaken by the Council of OEEC. Instituted a general multilateral system of payments. Aided process of full convertibility of currencies. Replaced by the European Monetary Agreement (1958).

European Productivity Agency (EPA), 1953

Part of OEEC and responsible to its Council, but with its own budget and substantial financial assistance from the

United States. Phased out in 1961, EPA was an international center to stimulate and coordinate the efforts of national productivity centers. Promoted joint undertakings; operated projects to train management in modern business techniques; helped coordinate applied research on technology, effects of automation, and use of scientific manpower.

Balkan Entente, 1953–54
Agreements providing for political, social, and economic collaboration for mutual defense under Article 51 of the UN Charter. The Balkan Entente failed in part because, after 1954, Greece and Turkey were members of NATO, but Yugoslavia was not; Greek-Turkish relations were difficult because of the controversy over Cyprus; and there were conflicts in national aspirations and differences in political and social systems and ethnic backgrounds among the three member nations. Dormant in 1962.

Members: Greece, Turkey, Yugoslavia

Southeast Treaty Organization (SEATO), 1955
Regional defense alliance of western and Asian powers; initiated after the liquidation of French rule in Indochina and the partition of Vietnam (1954). Became inoperative in 1975.

Members (7): Australia, France, New Zealand, Philippines, Thailand, the United Kingdom, the United States

European Monetary Agreement, 1958
Administered by OECD, the European Monetary Agreement brought about a general system of currency convertibility; aided European nations during a transitional period; operated EPU system until that organization ceased to exist.

Washington Ambassadorial Group, 1961
In 1961 and 1962, a continuing "Berlin Crisis" revolved around the renewed efforts of the USSR to force the other

three occupying powers out of the city. France, the United Kingdom, and the United States worked intensively during this period to monitor "Berlin Crisis" developments and to plan western reactions. With the erection of the Berlin Wall in 1962, the need for this type of institutionalized coordination diminished.

European Launcher Development Organization (ELDO), 1964
Undertook development and construction of space-vehicle launchers. Consolidated into the European Space Agency in 1975 as a result of reorganization of European space programs.

European Space Research Organization (ESRO), 1964
Pure research in outer space; design of sounding rocket payloads, satellites, space probes. Grew out of British offer of "Blue Streak" rocket launcher in 1960. Along with ELDO, was consolidated in new ESA, 1975.

V. MINOR BODIES WHICH ARE ESSENTIALLY "ATLANTIC SYSTEM" IN MEMBERSHIP, BUT INCLUDE OTHER COUNTRIES

Nuclear Suppliers Conference, 1976
Organization of major exporters of nuclear technology and materials. Formed to try to curb the spread of the ability to make atomic weapons.

Members (15): Belgium, Canada, Czechoslovakia, The Federal Republic of Germany, France, the German Democratic Republic, Italy, Japan, the Netherlands, Poland, Sweden, Switzerland, the Union of Soviet Socialist Republics, the United Kingdom, and the United States

Seat: London

Intergovernmental Committee for European Migration (ICEM), 1954

Effects the movement of refugees to countries offering final resettlement; meets the specific needs of overseas countries by providing migration from Europe; promotes, through selective migration, the social and economic advancement of Latin American countries as a vital form of development aid.

Members (30): Argentina, Australia, Austria, Belgium, Bolivia, Brazil, Chile, Colombia, Costa Rica, the Dominican Republic, Ecuador, El Salvador, the Federal Republic of Germany, Greece, Honduras, Israel, Italy, Luxembourg, Malta, the Netherlands, Nicaragua, Norway, Panama, Paraguay, Peru, South Africa, Spain, Switzerland, the United States, Uruguay.

Observers (9): Cyprus, Guatemala, Holy See, Japan, the Sovereign Order of Malta, Portugal, San Marino, Turkey, Venezuela

Seat: Geneva

NOTES TO TABLE 4 (Page 370)

1. Egypt, Lebanon, Liberia, and Mexico are also observers.

2. Liechtenstein, Monaco, the Holy See, and San Marino are also members.

3. Poland is also an observer.

4. Albania, Bulgaria, Czechoslovakia, Hungary, Poland, Romania, and South Africa are also members.

5. South Africa, Argentina, Bolivia, Brazil, Chile, Colombia, Costa Rica, the Dominican Republic, Ecuador, El Salvador, Honduras, Nicaragua, Panama, Paraguay, Peru, and Uruguay are also members; Guatemala, the Holy See, San Marino, the Sovereign Order of Malta, and Venezuala are also observers.

Table 4

**Membership in minor European and other Intergovernmental
Organizations of the Extended Atlantic System**

	CIEC	NEA	EURO-CHEMIC	EURO-CONTROL	EMBC	ANZUS	ECMT	ECAC (1)	ECPT (2)	CERN (3)	ESA	BIS (4)	Rhine Commission	Group of Ten	INPFC	NAA	EPC	ICEM (5)
Austria																		
Belgium																		
Cyprus																		
Denmark																		
Finland																		
France																		
Germany																		
Greece																		
Iceland																		
Ireland																		
Italy																		
Luxembourg																		
Malta																		
Netherlands																		
Norway																		
Portugal																		
Spain																		
Sweden																		
Switzerland																		
Turkey																		
United Kingdom																		
Yugoslavia																		
Australia																		
Canada																		
Japan																		
New Zealand																		
United States																		
Israel																		

Full Membership: ▓▓▓   **Associate or Observer:** ☐

Table based on A.H. Robertson, *European Institutions*, 3rd ed. (London, New York: Stevens/Matthew Bender, 1973), p. xvii.

VII. INTERNATIONAL BODIES IN WHICH COUNTRIES OF THE ATLANTIC SYSTEM PLAY A DOMINANT ROLE

GATT (General Agreement on Tariffs and Trade), 1948

Begun as a temporary means of seeking agreement on the rules of international trade; has become virtually permanent. Original members consisted only of western nations, but others have continued to join; membership in 1977 of 83 nations. The USSR and China do not belong; four east European countries do. Principles are to assure nondiscrimination in trade, elimination of nontariff barriers, consultations to avoid damage arising from trade agreements. Six major tariff-negotiating conferences have been held since the first in Geneva in 1947. The United States, the European Communities, and other key countries of the extended Atlantic System have exercised strong leadership in GATT; probably little would have been done without their continuing initiatives.

IMF (International Monetary Fund), 1947

Based on plans agreed upon at the Bretton Wood Conference (1944) by the wartime allies (minus the Soviet Union). The Soviet Union and most other Communist countries have stayed out of IMF. The principal international coordinating body in the financial field, IMF helps members in short-term balance-of-payments difficulties, supervises the international exchange-rate system, and takes part in international development aid activities. Because of its origins and the nature of its governing and voting structures, IMF tends to be dominated by the most important industrial democracies.

World Bank (International Bank for Reconstruction and Development), 1944

Originated at Bretton Woods; dominated by the western countries and Japan. Initial emphasis directed toward restoration of war-ravaged European countries; since the 1950s, has focused mainly on economic development in the

[371]

third world. Conducts a variety of borrowing, lending, co-ordination of aid, and technical assistance activities. The vast majority of the Bank's funds for loans to less-developed countries come from the industrial democracies. Three Communist countries (Yugoslavia, Vietnam, and Rumania) take part in the activities of the Bank.

APPENDIX E

Bibliography

The following books are considered to be of special value to those who would like to delve more deeply into the evolution of the Atlantic-Pacific System and various side issues which appear to affect its development.

GENERAL REFERENCE WORKS ON INTERNATIONAL ORGANIZATIONS:

Banks, Arthur S., ed. *The Political Handbook of the World.* New York: McGraw-Hill, published annually.

This publication contains a section on intergovernmental bodies which supplies useful basic data plus updated and reasonably comprehensive accounts of principal activities and problems of the large majority of regional and universal bodies.

Yearbook of International Organizations. Brussels: Union of International Associations, published annually.

This contains entries for virtually all international intergovernmental and nongovernmental bodies. Data for each, more limited than in the *Political Handbook,* covers addresses, names of current chief executives, dates and places of founding, aims, brief data on structure and activities, publications, and current membership.

ATLANTIC COMMUNITY:

Ball, Margaret. *NATO and the European Union Movement.* London: Stevens and Sons, Ltd., 1958.

Bloom, Solomon F. *Europe and America: The Western World in Modern Times.* New York: Harcourt, Brace, and World, 1961.

Burgess, W.R., and Huntley, J.R. *Europe and America: The Next Ten Years.* New York: Walker & Co., 1970.

Davis, Forrest. *The Atlantic System: The Story of Anglo-American Control of the Seas.* New York: Reynal and Hitchcock, 1941.

Goodman, Elliot R. *The Fate of the Atlantic Community.* New York: Frederick A. Praeger, 1975.

Hovey, J. Allan, Jr. *The Superparliaments: Interparliamentary Consultation and Atlantic Cooperation.* New York: Frederick A. Praeger, 1966.

Strausz-Hupé, Robert; Dougherty, James E.; and Kintner, William R. *Building the Atlantic World.* New York: Harper and Row, 1963.

Strausz-Hupé, Robert. *The Zone of Indifference.* New York: G.P. Putnam's Sons, 1952.

Szent-Miklosy, Istvan. *The Atlantic Union Movement: Its Significance in World Politics.* New York: Fountainhead, 1965.

Uri, Pierre. *Partnership for Progress.* New York: Harper and Row, 1963.

ATLANTIC-PACIFIC RELATIONS AND TRILATERALISM:

Gasteyger, Curt, ed. *Japan and the Atlantic World.* Paris: Atlantic Institute for International Affairs, 1972.

Lawson, Ruth C. *International Regional Organizations: Constitutional Foundations.* New York: Frederick A. Praeger, 1962.

Moore, Ben J. *NATO and the Future of Europe.* New York: Harper, 1958.

Stein, Eric, and Hay, Peter. *Law and Institutions in the Atlantic Area; Readings, Cases and Problems.* Indianapolis: Bobbs-Merrill, 1967.

Keene, Donald. *The Japanese Discovery of Europe, 1720–1830.* Rev. ed. Stanford: Stanford University Press, 1969.

Reischauer, Edwin O. *Toward the 21st Century: Education for a Changing World.* New York: Random, 1974.

Sansom, G.B., *Japan and the Western World* New York: Vintage Books, Random House, 1973; first published 1950.

DEMOCRACY AND THE CIVIC CULTURE:

Almond, Gabriel A., and Verba, Sidney. *The Civic Culture: Political Attitudes and Democracy in Five Nations.* Princeton, N.J.: Princeton University Press, 1963.

Banks, Arthur S., and Textor, Robert B. *A Cross-Polity Survey.* Cambridge, Mass.: M.I.T. Press, 1963.

Crozier, Michel J.; Huntington, Samuel P.; and Watanuki, Joji. *The Crisis of Democracy: Report on the Governability of Democracies to the Trilateral Commission.* New York: New York University Press, 1975.

EAST-WEST RELATIONS:

Azrael, Jeremy R.; Löwenthal, Richard; and Nakagawa, Tohru. *An Overview of East-West Relations.* Triangle Paper no. 15. New York: The Trilateral Commission, 1978.

Halle, Louis J. *The Cold War as History.* London: Chatto and Windus, 1971.

Hosoya, Chihiro; Owen, Henry; and Shonfield, Andrew. *Collaboration with Communist Countries in Managing Global Problems: An Examination of the Options.* Triangle Paper no. 13. New York: The Trilateral Commission, 1977.

EUROPEAN INTEGRATION:

Albrecht-Carrié, René. *One Europe: The Historical Background of European Unity.* Garden City, N.Y.: Doubleday, 1965.

Axline, W. Andrew. *European Community Law and Organ-*

izational Development. Dobbs Ferry, N.Y.: Oceana Publications, Inc., 1968.

Beloff, Max. *The United States and the Unity of Europe.* Washington, D.C.: The Brookings Institution, 1963.

Bliss, Howard, ed. *The Political Development of the European Community: A Documentary Collection.* Waltham, Mass.: Blaisdell Publishing Co., 1970.

Bromberger, Merry, and Bromberger, Serge. *Jean Monnet and the United States of Europe.* Trans. by Elaine P. Halperin. New York: Coward-McCann, 1969.

Camps, Miriam. *European Unification in the Sixties.* New York: McGraw-Hill, 1966.

Coombes, David. *Politics and Bureaucracy in the European Community.* London: George Allen and Unwin, Ltd., 1970.

European Yearbook. The Hague: Martinus Nijhoff, published annually.

Feld, Werner. *The Court of the European Communities: New Dimension in International Adjudication.* The Hague: Martinus Nijhoff, 1964.

Haas, Ernst. *The Uniting of Europe.* Stanford: Stanford University Press, 1958.

Green, Andrew Wilson. *Political Integration by Jurisprudence.* Leyden: A.W. Sijthoff, 1969.

Monnet, Jean. *Les États-Unis d'Europe ont Commencé.* Paris: Robert Laffont, 1955.

Monnet, Jean, *Memoirs,* Garden City, New York: Doubleday and Co., 1978.

Northrop, F.S.C. *European Union and United States Foreign Policy.* New York: Macmillan, 1954.

Palmer, Michael, and Lambert, John. *A Handbook of European Organizations.* New York: Frederick A. Praeger, 1968.

Robertson, A.H. *The Council of Europe.* 2nd ed. New York: Frederick A. Praeger, 1961.

Robertson, A.H. *European Institutions: Cooperation, Integration, Unification.* 3rd ed. London: Stevens and Sons, Ltd., 1973.

Stein, Eric; Hay, Peter; and Waelbroeck, Michel. *European*

Community Law and Institutions in Perspective. Indianapolis: Bobbs-Merrill Co., Inc., 1976.

HISTORY OF INTERNATIONAL RELATIONS, INTERNATIONAL ORGANIZATIONS, FEDERALISM:

Freymond, Jacques. *Western Europe Since the War: A Short Political History.* New York: Frederick A. Praeger, 1964.

Hemleben, Sylvester John. *Plans for World Peace Through Six Centuries.* Chicago: University of Chicago Press, 1943.

Maine, Henry. *Ancient Law: Its Connection With the Early History of Society and Its Relation to Modern Ideas.* Boston: Beacon Press, 1963; first published, 1861.

Riker, W.H. *Federalism: Origin, Operation, Significance.* Boston: Little, 1964.

Rockefeller, Nelson A. *Unity, Freedom, and Peace.* New York: Random House, 1968.

Streit, Clarence. *Union Now,* London: Jonathan Cape, 1939.

Wendt, Frantz. *The Nordic Council and Cooperation in Scandinavia.* Copenhagen: Munksgaard, 1959.

York, Elizabeth. *Leagues of Nations: Ancient, Medieval, and Modern.* London: Swarthmore Press, 1919.

INTERDEPENDENCE, ECONOMIC:

Camps, Miriam. *The Management of Interdependence.* New York: Council on Foreign Relations, Inc., 1974.

Kaji, Motoo; Cooper, Richard N.; and Segré, Claudio. *Towards a Renovated World Monetary System.* Triangle Paper no. 1. New York: The Trilateral Commission, 1973.

Kindleberger, Charles P. *The World in Depression, 1929–39.* London: Allen Lane, 1973.

INTERDEPENDENCE, SECURITY:

Cline, Ray S. *World Power Assessment: A Calculus of Strategic Drift.* Washington, D.C.: Center for Strategic and

International Studies, 1975; 2nd ed., 1977.

Pick, Otto, and Critchley, Julian. *Collective Security*. London: Macmillan, 1974.

Rühl, Lothar. *The Nine and NATO*. The Atlantic Papers, 2/1974. Paris: Atlantic Institute for International Affairs, 1974.

INTERDEPENDENCE, SOCIETIES:

Aubrey, Henry G. *Atlantic Economic Cooperation: The Case of the OECD*. New York: Frederick A. Praeger, 1967.

Banks, Arthur S., and Jordan, Robert S., eds. *Political Handbook of the World: 1978*. New York: McGraw-Hill, 1978.

Bell, Daniel. *The Coming of Post-Industrial Society: A Venture in Social Forecasting*. New York: Basic Books, 1973.

Camps, Miriam. *"First World" Relationships: The Role of the OECD*. Atlantic Papers, 2/1975; Council Papers on International Affairs, 5. New York: The Atlantic Institute for International Affairs; Council on Foreign Relations, Inc., 1974.

Huntley, James R. *Man's Environment and the Atlantic Alliance*. Brussels: North Atlantic Treaty Organization, 1971.

Socini, Roberto. *Rapports et Conflits entre Organisations Européennes*. Leiden: A.W. Sythoff, 1960.

NORTH-SOUTH RELATIONS AND DEVELOPMENT:

Gardner, Richard N.; Okita, Saburo; and Udink, B.J. *A Turning Point in North-South Economic Relations*. Triangle Paper no. 3. New York: The Trilateral Commission, 1974.

Myrdal, Gunnar. *Asian Drama: An Inquiry into the Poverty of Nations*. Condensation by Seth S. King. New York: Random House, 1972.

OTHER REGIONAL SYSTEMS:

Brabant, Jozef M.P. van. *Essays on Planning, Trade, and Integration in Eastern Europe*. Rotterdam: Rotterdam University Press, 1974.

Hilton, Ronald, ed. *The Movement Toward Latin American*

Unity. New York: Frederick A. Praeger, 1969.

Kaser, Michael. *COMECON: Integration Problems of the Planned Economies.* London: Oxford University Press, 1967.

Kolkowicz, Roman, ed. *The Warsaw Pact.* Arlington, Va.: Institute for Defense Analysis, 1969.

The Latin American Integration Process in 1973. Washington, D.C.: Institute for Latin American Integration, Inter-American Development Bank, 1973.

Regional Politics. Vol. 2. Washington, D.C.: National Defense University, The National War College, 1977.

Schaefer, Henry Wilcox. *COMECON and the Politics of Integration.* New York: Frederick A. Praeger, 1972.

Staar, Richard F. *Communist Regions in Eastern Europe.* 3rd ed. Stanford: Hoover Institution Press, 1977.

Szawlowski, Richard. *The System of the International Organizations of the Communist Countries.* Leyden: A.W. Sijthoff, 1976.

POLITICAL INTERDEPENDENCE:

Cooper, Richard N.; Kaiser, Karl; and Kosaka, Masataka. *Towards a Renovated International System.* Triangle Paper no. 14. New York: The Trilateral Commission, 1977.

Duchene, Francois; Mushakoji, Kinhide; and Owen, Henry D. *The Crisis of International Cooperation.* Triangle Paper no. 2. New York: The Trilateral Commission, 1974.

Harmonizing Economic Policy: Summit Meetings and Collective Leadership. Policy Paper. Washington, D.C.: Atlantic Council of the United States, 1977.

Rockefeller, Nelson A. *The Future of Federalism.* New York: Athaneum, 1963.

Reves, Emery. *The Anatomy of Peace.* New York: Harper and Brothers, 1945.

THEORY:

Ake, Claude. *A Theory of Political Integration.* Homewood, Illinois: The Dorsey Press, 1967.

Deutsch, Karl W. *The Analysis of International Relations.*

Englewood Cliffs, N.J.: Prentice-Hall, 1968.

Deutsch, Karl W., et al. *Political Community and the North Atlantic Area*. Princeton, N.J.: Princeton University Press, 1957.

Guetzkow, Harold. *Multiple Loyalties: Theoretical Approach to a Problem in International Organization*. Publication no. 4. Princeton N.J.: Center for Research on World Political Institutions, 1955.

Haas, Ernst. *Beyond the Nation-State: Functionalism and International Organization*. Stanford: Stanford University Press, 1964.

Hay, Peter. *Federalism and Supranational Organizations: Patterns for New Legal Structures*. Urbana: University of Illinois Press, 1966.

Jenks, C.W. *The Common Law of Mankind*. New York: Frederick A. Praeger, 1958.

Kaiser, Karl. "Transnational Politics: Toward a Theory of Multinational Politics." *International Organization*. XXV (Fall 1971).

Kaplan, Morton A. *System and Process in International Politics*. New York: John Wiley and Sons, 1957.

Mitrany, David. *A Working Peace System*. 4th ed. London: National Peace Council, 1946.

Mosca, Gaetano. *The Ruling Class*. Trans. by Hannah D. Kahn from the original, *Elementi di Scienza Politica*. New York: McGraw-Hill, 1939.

Rivera, Joseph de. *The Psychological Dimension of Foreign Policy*. Columbus, Ohio: Charles Merrill, 1968.

Rosenau, James N., ed. *International Politics and Foreign Policy: A Reader in Research and Theory*. New York: The Free Press, 1961.

Stone, Julius. *Quest for Survival: The Role of Law and Foreign Policy*. Cambridge, Mass.: Harvard University Press, 1961.

UN SYSTEM:

Goodrich, Leland M.; Hambro, Edvard; and Simons, Anne

Patricia. *Charter of the United Nations: Commentary and Documents*. 3rd ed. New York: Columbia University Press, 1969.

Goodrich, Leland M., and Simons, Anne P. *The United Nations and the Maintenance of International Peace and Security*. Washington, D.C.: The Brookings Institution, 1955.

LEAGUE OF NATIONS:

Zimmern, Alfred. *The League of Nations and the Rule of Law*. New York: Macmillan, 1939.

INDEX

Achaean League, 1

Adams, Henry, xxiii, 4

Adenauer, Konrad, 34, 252

A.F.L.-C.I.O., 190

Ake, Claude, 322, 323

Alexander I, Czar, 2

Allied Control Council in Berlin, 13

Altruism, 255

Amin, Idi, 229

Amphictyony, 2

Andean Group, 220, 223

Anglo-French Treaty of Alliance and Mutual Assistance, 346

ANZUS (Tripartite Security Treaty, Australia, New Zealand, United States), 32, 251, 362–363

Asian Development Bank (ADB), 228, 287

Association of Southeast Asia, 224

Association of Southeast Asian Nations (ASEAN), vii, 224–228

Atlantic Alliance, xiv, 56

Atlantic Charter, xxiii; "new Atlantic Charter" (1973), 10, 263

"Atlantic Convention" resolution, 10

Atlantic Institute for International Affairs (Paris), 208

Atlantic News, 164

Atlantic-Pacific System, xv, 155; interactions and comparisons with the Soviet International System, 211–215, 232; extension of, 252; theoretical signif-

icance of, 253–255; future of, 260–274; inertia of, 260–261; national rivalries and cultural clashes within, 262–266; balance of the nations within 267–268; collective leadership for, 268–271; need for integration within, 271–275; external challenges to, 275–280; societal growth and development, 277–279, 282; negative and positive scenarios for, 288–291; structure and strategy for, 293–297

"Atlantic Partnership," 10, 86, 133, 268

Atlantic System, xiv, 15

Atlantic Union Committee (United States), 9

Argentina, 222

Aubrey, Henry, 67, 147, 160, 162, 253

Austria, 32, 197

Australia, 16, 30, 132, 184, 227, 283

Axline, W.A., 124, 317

Balkan Entente, 367

Bandung Conference, 180

Bank for International Settlements (BIS), 6, 7, 363

Banks, Arthur S., 177

Banks, Michael, 310

Balfour, Arthur, 4

Battelle Memorial Institute, i

Belgium, 103, 145

Belgium-Luxembourg Economic Union (BLEU), 365

Belgrade Conference, (1977), 150, 169

[383]

133, 134, 178–179, 180, 181, 191, 227, 245, 247, 250, 267, 268, 288, 289, 290; Arms Control Act, 33; Atomic Energy Commission, 207; United States-Canadian Permanent Joint Defense Board, 365–366; Constitutional Convention of 1787, 10; Federal Reserve banks, 6; United States-Japan Treaty of Mutual Cooperation and Security, 32, 366; United States-United Kingdom special relationship, 365

"United States of Europe," 4, 15

Universal Postal Union (1874), 3

Usenko, E.T., 234

Vandenberg Resolution in the US Senate (1949), 13

Venezuela, 50, 220, 222

Versailles Treaty, 6

Waldheim, Kurt, 182

Wallace, Helen S., 145

Warsaw Treaty Organization (WTO), 195, 196–202; Political Consultative Committee, 198–199; Unified Command, 199;

vulnerability of, 199–200; differences from NATO, 200–202

Washington Ambassadorial Group, 367–368

Watanuki, Joji, 292

Weber, Max, 253

WEU (Western European Union), 28, 56, 99–103; strengths and weaknesses, 101–103, 127, 128, 145, 251, 294, 315, 336–337, 351–352

Willkie, Wendell, 9

Wilson, Woodrow, 4, 5

World Bank (International Bank for Reconstruction and Development), 6, 371–372

World Food Conference, 193

World Food Council, 193

World Health Organization (WHO), vii, 193

Yaoundé Convention, 78

Yemen, 141

"Year of Europe," 10

Yew, Lee Kuan, 225, 227

Yugoslavia, 50, 132, 212–213

Zaire, 271